The New York Times Guide to Dining Out in New York

The New York Times
Guide to Dining Out in New York

New 1972 revised edition

Atheneum
New York
1972

Cover design: Paul Bacon

*Copyright © 1971 by The New York Times Company
All rights reserved
Library of Congress catalog card number 78-162972
Published simultaneously in Canada by
McClelland and Stewart Ltd.
Manufactured in the United States of America by
Kingsport Press, Inc., Kingsport, Tennessee
Designed by Harry Ford
First Edition*

Publisher's Note

This new edition of *The New York Times Guide to Dining Out in New York* has been brought completely up to date. It indicates new telephone numbers, new addresses, and revised prices. Over six hundred establishments are covered, many of them new and not represented in the previous edition, and there have been a number of deletions, as many restaurants have closed within the past year or so. Credit card information has also been checked and brought up to date. The publisher will welcome correspondence from anyone who finds inaccuracies, which will be checked and reflected in future printings.

A Note on Tipping

To all appearances there are many people who wonder about the mechanics of tipping (and tipping today is, unfortunately, by and large mechanical). As a general rule, 15 percent of the food bill is considered an adequate tip for waiters. If there is a captain, he is normally given 5 percent of the bill, and if there is a wine steward, he may be tipped $1 for each bottle served. If there is only a waiter who renders service, the 15 percent should prove adequate.

In theory, of course, tipping is a voluntary act, and if the table service is conspicuously bad, the gratuity should be measured according to conscience. Restaurant-goers might keep in mind that in most restaurants where there are both waiters *and* captains, the tips are not shared. That is to say, if the diner indicates a tip on the bill or leaves a sum of money as gratuity, all of it goes to the waiter even though most of the service may have been performed by the captain. Nor is the money shared with the wine steward.

Four-, Three-, Two-, and One-Star Restaurants

Four-Star Restaurants

Coach House, The
La Caravelle
La Côte Basque
La Grenouille
Peter Luger
Quo Vadis
Shun Lee Dynasty

Three-Star Restaurants

Alfredo of New York
Al Mounia
Aperitivo
Canton Village
Casa Brasil
Casey's
Charley O's Bar and Grill
Chi Mer
Christ Cella
Copenhagen
El Faro
El Parador
Forlini's
Four Seasons, The
French Shack, The
Fu Shin Restaurant
Gaiety West Restaurant and Delicatessen
Gauguin Room, The
Georges Rey, Restaurant Français
Giordano Restaurant
Hong Kong Inn
Isle of Capri
La Cocotte
La Petite Marmite
La Toque Blanche
Le Cygne
Le Manoir
Le Mistral
Leopard, The
Le Pavillon
Le Périgord Park
Little Peking Restaurant, Inc.
Lotus Eaters Park
Lüchow's
Lutèce
Mandarin House East
Mon Paris
Palm Restaurant
P. J. Clarke's
San Marco
Spanish Pavilion, The
Swiss Center Restaurants
"21"

Two-Star Restaurants

Acapulco Restaurant

Acropolis Restaurant
Adams Rib
A La Fourchette
*Al Cooper's Herald Square
    Restaurant*
*Algonquin Hotel
    Oak Room
    Rose Room*
Allen's
Allis' Restaurant
Angelo's
Antica Roma
Ararat
Arigato
Arirang House
Assembly Steak House
Au Tunnel
Ballato Restaurant
Barbetta Restaurant
Benihana of Tokyo East
Benihana of Tokyo West
Benihana Palace
Billy's
Blossom Restaurant
Bo Bo
Brasero
Brasserie
Brazilian Coffee Restaurant
Brew's
Broadway Joe Steak House
Brochetteria
Brownstone, The
Brussels Restaurant
Cabaña Carioca
Café Argenteuil
Café Brittany
Café de France

Café Nicholson
Cape Cod
Carmen's
Casa Laredo
Casa Mario
Cattleman East, The
Cattleman West, The
Cedars of Lebanon
Cheshire Cheese Restaurant
Chez Cardinale
Chez René
China Bowl, The
Christo's
Chuan Hong Restaurant
Clos Normand
Colony, The
Copter Club
Crêpes Suzette
Cuisine of Szechuan
Czechoslovak Praha
Danny's Hide-a-Way
*Dardanelles Armenian
    Restaurant*
Daruma
Deno's Place
Derby Steak House, The
Dilluvio
Dogwood Room
Doriental Restaurant
Duck Joint, The
Duff's
Du Midi
Dynasty, The
Eduardo's
Elizabeth White
El Mirador
El Rincon de España

*Empire Chinese Restaurant,
    The*
Estia
Eva Hungarian Restaurant
Filippo Restaurant
Fleur de Lis
Four Five Six
Frankie and Johnnie
French Quarter, The
Frini
Gage and Tollner
Gatti's
Gene's
Giambone
Gino's Restaurant
Giovanni
Gloucester House
Gold Coin
Goodale's
Granados Restaurant
Great Shanghai, The
Greensleeves
Grotta Azzurra
Happy Garden
Haymarket Pub
Hime of Japan
Hong Ying
Ho Shun
House of Chan
Hoy Kung
Il Bambino
*India House East
    Restaurant*
Irish Pavilion, The
Irori
Italian Pavilion
Jack's Nest
Jai-Alai
Jamaica Arms
Japanese Mie Cooking
Japanese Steak House
Jasper's
*Jimmy's Greek-American
    Restaurant*
Jimmy's La Grange
Joe's Restaurant
*Jolly Chan's Chinese
    Kitchen*
Joy Garden
Kashmir Restaurant
Keen's English Chop House
Kegon
Keneret
Kenny's Steak Pub
King Wu
Kitcho Restaurant
Kobe Steak House
Kyoto Steak House
La Bibliothèque
La Cabaña
La Crêpe Restaurants
La Croisette
Lafayette
La Fonda del Sol
La Fondo
La Fortuna
La Grillade
La Groceria
L'Aiglon
Lair, The
Lantern Light
La Petite Ferme
La Piazzetta
La Potinière du Soir

L'Armorique
La Venere West
Le Biarritz
Le Bistro
Le Chambertin
Le Champignon
Le Chanteclair
Le Cheval Blanc
Le Moal
Le Périgord
Le Pont Neuf
Le Poulailler
Le Provençal
L'Escargot
Les Pyrénées
Le Steak
Le Veau d'Or
Limerick's
Little Place, The
*Little Royal Hungarian
   Restaurant*
Long River
Lotus Eaters
Lotus Eaters East
Lotus Eaters Fifth
Lotus Eaters Royale
Lou G. Siegel
Louise Jr.
Luna's Restaurant
Mme. Romaine de Lyon
Mandarin House
Mandarin Inn
*Manganaro's and
   Manganaro's Hero-
   Boy Restaurant*
Manny Wolf's
Marchi's

Mario
Mark Twain Riverboat
Marta Restaurant
Marta's
Mary's
Maxwell's Plum
McSorley's Old Ale House
Mercurio
Mexican Village
Mikado
Mike Manuche
Minotaur, The
Mr. and Mrs. Foster
Mona Lisa
Monk's Inn
Monte's Restaurant
Mont St. Michel Restaurant
Mykonos
Nataraj
Near East Restaurant
New Port Alba
New Wah Dor
*New York Exchange
   Restaurant*
Nicola Paone
Ningpo Restaurant
Nippon
Nirvana
Nom Wah Tea Parlor
Oak Room (Algonquin)
Oak Room (Plaza)
Old Seidelburg
Omar Khayam
O'Neal's Baloon
Orsini's
Pak-India Curry House
Pamplona Restaurant

Pancho Villa's
Pantheon Restaurant
Pappas
Paradise Inn
Passy, The
Patricia Murphy's Candle-
 light Restaurant
Paul and Jimmy's Place
Peking House
Pen and Pencil, The
Peter's Backyard
Philippine Garden, The
Pierre's
Pietro's
Piraeus, My Love
P. J. O'Hara
Plaka East
Plaza Hotel
 Oak Room
Ponte's Steak House
Promenade Café
Pujol, René, Restaurant
Rajmahal
Red Coach Grill
René Pujol Restaurant
Reuben's
Romeo Salta
Rose Room (Algonquin)
Ruc Restaurant
Rugantino
Running Footman, The
Russian Tea Room
Sakura Chaya
Sam Bok
Sam Pam
San Marino
San Remo

Santa Lucia
Sardi's
Sayat Nova
Say Eng Look
Scandia
Sea-Fare of the Aegean
Shanghai Town
Sheik Restaurant, The
Sixty-Eight Restaurant
Skewer on the Table
Sloppy Louie's
Soul East
South Pacific Ports
Stage Delicatessen and
 Restaurant
Steak Casino
Steinway Brauhall
Stockholm Restaurant
Stouffer's
Sum Hey Rice Shoppe
Sun Luck Queens
Sun Luck Times Square
Sun Yah
Sweet's
Symposium
Szechuan
Tamura Restaurant
Tandur, The
Taste of Tokyo
37th Street Hideaway
Three Six Nine Restaurant
Tien Tsin
Tik Tak Hungarian
Tin Lizzie Restaurant, The
Tokyo-Bangkok Restaurant
Tom's Shangri-La
Tony's Italian Kitchen

xi

Tony's Wife
Topkapi Palace
Tower Suite
Trader Vic's
Uncle Tonoose Restaurant
Un Coin de Paris
Unicorn, The
Vasata
Vesuvio Restaurant
Via Margutta
Via Veneto
Victor's Café
Villa Pensa
Villa Vivolo
Vincent Petrosino
Wah Kee Restaurant
Wally's
Wo Ping
Xochitl Mexican Restaurant
Yano
Ye Olde Chop House
Zum Zum

One-Star Restaurants

Act I
Agra India and Pakistan Restaurant
Akasaka
Aki Dining Room
Alamo Chile House, The
Alda's
Aldo and Eddie Rapallo Restaurant
Alfie's
Amato's Italian Restaurant
Angelina's
Angelo's Italian Restaurant
Antolotti's
Artist and Writers Restaurant
Athenian Restaurant, The
Au Canari d'Or
Au Steak Pommes Frites
Balkan Armenian Restaurant
Baroque
Beirut Restaurant
Bernstein-on-Essex-Street
Black Angus
Blue Sea
Brittany du Soir
Budapest Hungarian Restaurant
Ca d'Oro
Café du Soir
Café Europa
Café Renaissance
Camelot
Canton Restaurant
Captain's Table, The
Carnegie Delicatessen and Restaurant
Casa di Pre
Castalia
Castilian, The
Ceylon India Inn
Chalet Suisse
Chandler's
Charles à la Pomme Soufflé
Charles French Restaurant

xii

Charlie Brown's
Chez Napoleon
Chez Vous
Chez Yvonne l'Escargot
China Fair
China Pavilion
Chinese Rathskeller
Chin-Ya
Chock Full O'Nuts
Coq au Vin
Daly's Dandelion
Damon's
Dawson's Ha-Penny Bar
Delsomma
Dewey Wong
Dionysos
Double Dolphin Fish House
Downing Square
Dresner's
Due Mondi
Edwardian Room (Plaza)
Elaine's
El Azteca
El Charro
Electra
El Quijote
El Radiante
Emiliana's
Esplanade, The
Esther Eng
Fedora
Fisherman's Net
500 on 8th Restaurant, The
Flower Drum Restaurant
Fonda la Paloma
Foo Chow Restaurant
Fornos

Friar Tuck
Gaetano's
Gim Beck
Girafe
Gloria's Restaurant
Golden Coach
Gold Full Restaurant
Gondola
*Grand Central Terminal
    Oyster Bar and
    Restaurant*
Grenadier
Hanover Square Restaurant
Heidelberg Restaurant
*Henry Stampler's Filet
    Mignon*
Hickory Pit Restaurants
Hide Sukiyaki
Hole in the Wall
Hong Fat Restaurant
Horn & Hardart Automats
Hyde Park Restaurant
Ile de France
Il Faro
*International Cheese Club
    Restaurant*
Italianissimo
Jade Palace
Jenedi's
Joe Allen
Joe and Rose
Joe's Pier 52
Johnnie's
John's Restaurant
Joyce's Macao
Julio Restaurant
Kabuki Restaurant

xiii

Kamehachi
Karachi
Katz's Delicatessen
King of the Sea
Kirby Allen Restaurant, The
Kleine Konditorei
Koon Shing Tea House
La Bourgogne
La Hacienda
La Locanda
Lam Kee
La Paella
La Poulard
Larré's French Restaurant
La Scala
La Strada East
La Veranda
Le Alpi
Lebanon Restaurant
Le Château Richelieu
Le Marmiton
Lenge-Saimin Restaurant
L'Entrecôte
Leone's
Les Champs
L'Etoile
Liborio
Lichee Tree, The
Lin Heong
Lino's U.N. Restaurant
Little Kitchen, The
Lord & Taylor's Soup Bar
Louise
Lucy Jung
Madison Delicatessen and Restaurant, The

Mama Laura Restaurant
Mañana
Maria Cin Cin
Maria's Patio
Mario's Villa Borghese
Mario's Villa d'Este
Marsh's Steak Place
Mary Elizabeth's
Maud Chez Elle
Max's Kansas City
Mayfair, The
Mayhew's
Mexi-Frost Specialties Company
Michael's Pub
Miller's
Minetta Tavern
Mi Tierra
Miyako
Molfetas Cafeteria
Mona Lisa East
Mona Trattoria
Mont d'Or
Moon Palace
Morgen's East
Morgen's Restaurant
Nat Simon's Penguin Room
New Hankow
New Moon Inn
Nick's Topkapi Pub
Ocean, The
O. Henry's Steak House
Old Denmark
Old Forge Steak House
Old Mexico Restaurant
Oriental Pearl
Oscar's Delmonico

Oscar's Salt of the Sea
Oviedo
Oyster Bar and Restaurant (Grand Central)
Pagano's
Paparazzi
Paprika
Parioli, Romanissimo
Parkway East
Paul Revere's Tavern and Chop House
Pearl's Chinese Restaurant
Pembles
Pergola des Artistes
Piccolo Mondo
Pine Garden Restaurant
Pink Foot, The
Pip's
Piro's
P. J. Moriarty
*Plaza Hotel
    Edwardian Room*
Port Arthur
Portofino
Press Box
Prime Burger
Rattazzi
Reidy's Restaurant
Restaurant Tokyo
Right Bank Provincial, The
Right Bank Restaurant, The
Rocco Restaurant
Roma Nova
Rosetta's Restaurant
Sam Wo
Savoia
Schaefer's
Schrafft's Restaurants
Scoop, The
Shalimar
Shanghai Café
Shanghai d'Or
Shanghai Garden
Shanghai Village
Shavey Lee
Shun Lee
Sign of the Dove
Slate Restaurant, The
Smokehouse, The
Spain
Spark's Pub South
Stage Delicatessen and Restaurant
Steak and Brew
Steak Joint, The
Steak Place, The
Suehiro Restaurant
Sun Hop Kee
Sun Luck East
Sun Luck Gourmet
Sun Luck Imperial
Sushi Ginza Restaurant
Szechuan Taste
Taco Villa
Tanpopo
Taste of India
Teacher's
Teddy's Restaurant
Temple Garden, The
Thursday's
Tomaldo's
Tonkatsu
Top of the Six's
Trefner's Restaurant

Un Rincon Argentino
Valentino's
Villa Doria
Villa Marbona
Vincent's Clam Bar
Whyte's
Wine and Apples
Wine Cellar, The
Wise Man, The
Wo Kee
Wolf's Delicatessen (at 180 Broadway)
Wolf's Delicatessen (at 799 Seventh Avenue)
Wong, Dewey
Yamashiro
Yangtze River
Yellowfinger's Butcheria
Ye Waverly Inn
Ying's
Z
Zapata Restaurant
Zoe Chase

Restaurants Listed By Area

Wall Street Area (Battery Park to Fulton Street)

Chez Yvonne l'Escargot
Chock Full O'Nuts
Fraunces Tavern
Hanover Square Restaurant
Horn & Hardart Automats
Jimmy's Greek-American Restaurant
Joyce's Macao
Kabuki Restaurant
La Crêpe Restaurant
Oriental Pearl
Oscar's Delmonico
Schrafft's
Sloppy Louie's
Sweet's
Tamura Restaurant
Vincent Petrosino
Wolf's Delicatessen
Ye Olde Chop House
Zum Zum

City Hall Area (Fulton to Canal Streets)

Chock Full O'Nuts
Horn & Hardart Automats
International Cheese Club Restaurant
Japanese Steak House
Miller's
Ponte's Steak House
Schrafft's
Teddy's Restaurant

Chinatown

Bo Bo
Canton Restaurant
Chi Mer
Chinese Rathskeller
Esther Eng
Four Five Six
Gim Beck
Gold Full Restaurant
Happy Garden
Hong Fat Restaurant
Hong Ying
Ho Shun
Joy Garden
King Wu
Koon Shing Tea House
Lam Kee
Lin Heong
Little Peking Restaurant, Inc.
Lucy Jung
Mandarin Inn
New Wah Dor
Nom Wah Tea Parlor
Pine Garden Restaurant
Port Arthur

xvii

Sam Wo
Say Eng Look
Shanghai Town
Shanghai Village
Shavey Lee
Sum Hey Rice Shoppe
Sun Hop Kee
Szechuan Taste
Temple Garden, The
Three Six Nine
Wah Kee Restaurant
Wise Man, The
Wo Kee
Wo Ping

Little Italy (Canal to Houston Streets, West of Broadway)

Angelo's
Giambone
Grotta Azzurra
Luna's Restaurant
Villa Pensa
Vincent's Clam Bar

Lower East Side (Canal to Houston Streets, East of Broadway)

Antica Roma
Bernstein-on-Essex-Street
Chock Full O'Nuts
Forlini's
Katz's Delicatessen
Parkway East

Greenwich Village (Houston to 14th Streets, West of Broadway)

Angelina's
Asti
Ballato Restaurant
Blue Mill Tavern
Captain's Table, The
Casa di Pre
Casa Laredo
Casey's
Charles French Restaurant
Chez Vous
Coach House, The
Dardanelles Armenian Restaurant
Derby Steak House, The
Duff's
El Charro
El Faro
El Rincon de España
Fedora
Filippo Restaurant
Gene's
Granados Restaurant
Hoy Kung
Il Bambino
Jai-Alai
Joe's Restaurant
Keneret
La Crêpe Restaurant
La Groceria

La Hacienda
La Petite Ferme
Lichee Tree, The
Little Place, The
Mandarin House
Mario
Marta Restaurant
Mary's
Mayhew's
Mexican Village
Mexi-Frost Specialties
   Company
Minetta Tavern
Mona Lisa
Monte's Restaurant
Nat Simon's Penguin Room
New Port Alba
Nick's Topkapi Pub
O. Henry's Steak House
Oviedo
Pappas
Patricia Murphy's Candle-
   light Restaurant
Peter's Backyard
Portofino
Rocco Restaurant
Rosetta's Restaurant
Sayat Nova
Schrafft's
Shanghai Garden
Sixty-Eight Restaurant
Smokehouse, The
Spain
Steak and Brew
Steak Casino
Steak Joint, The
Taste of India

Taste of Tokyo
Via Margutta
Villa Marbona
Wine Cellar, The
Ye Waverly Inn
Zum Zum

East Village (Houston to 14th Streets, East of Broadway)

Japanese Mie Cooking
John's Restaurant
Little Kitchen, The
McSorley's Old Ale House
Ningpo Restaurant
Rajmahal Restaurant

Chelsea (14th to 33rd Streets, West of Fifth Avenue)

Beirut Restaurant
Chock Full O'Nuts
Gallagher's
Horn & Hardart
   Automats
Lotus Eaters Fifth
Old Garden, The
Pamplona Restaurant
P. J. Moriarty
Sam Pam
San Remo
Schrafft's
Ying's

14th to 33rd Streets, East of Fifth Avenue

Allis' Restaurant
Balkan Armenian
    Restaurant
Blue Sea
Cedars of Lebanon
Chock Full O'Nuts
Cuisine of Szechuan
Daruma
Deno's Place
El Quijote
Fisherman's Net
Gloria's Restaurant
Golden Coach
Greensleeves
Horn & Hardart
    Automats
Il Faro
Italianissimo
Jack's Nest
Julio's Restaurant
La Strada East
Limerick's
Lino's U.N. Restaurant
Lotus Eaters Park
Lüchow's
Marchi's
Max's Kansas City
Mon Paris
Old Forge Steak House
Paul and Jimmy's Place
Philippine Garden, The
Roma Nova
Savoia
Schrafft's
Shalimar
Sheik Restaurant, The
Shun Lee
Spark's Pub South
Suehiro Restaurant
Yamashiro
Z

34th to 41st Streets, West of Fifth Avenue

Al Cooper's Herald Square
    Restaurant
Artist and Writers
    Restaurant
Chock Full O'Nuts
Damon's
500 on 8th Restaurant, The
Giordano Restaurant
Horn & Hardart
    Automats
Keen's English Chop House
Lord & Taylor's Soup Bar
Lou G. Siegel
Manganaro's and
    Manganaro's Hero-Boy
    Restaurant
Mark Twain Riverboat
Mikado
Morgen's Restaurant
New Hankow
Paradise Inn
Schrafft's
37th Street Hideaway
Valentino's
Zum Zum

Murray Hill (34th to 41st Streets, East of Fifth Avenue)

Akasaka
Al Mounia
Ararat
Brasero
Brew's
Chock Full O'Nuts
Due Mondi
El Parador
Empire Chinese Restaurant, The
Gatti's
India House East Restaurant
La Fortuna
Les Champs
Mary Elizabeth's
New Korea
Nicola Paone
Ocean, The
Old Seidelburg
Restaurant Tokyo
Schrafft's
Tom's Shangri-La

Times Square Area (42nd to 46th Streets, West of Fifth Avenue)

Act I
A La Fourchette
Alamo Chile House
Algonquin Hotel
  Oak Room
  Rose Room
Athenian Restaurant
Barbetta Restaurant
Benihana Palace
Brazilian Coffee Restaurant
Broadway Joe Steak House
Cabaña Carioca
Café de France
Cattle Baron, The
Chez Cardinale
China Bowl, The
Chock Full O'Nuts
Crêpes Suzette
Frankie and Johnnie
Horn & Hardart Automats
Joe Allen
Johnnie's
Kamehachi
Karachi
Kashmir Restaurant
Kitcho Restaurant
Kyoto Steak House
La Bourgogne
La Crêpe Restaurant
Le Chambertin
Long River
Mykonos
Nataraj
Oak Room (Algonquin)
Pak-India Curry House
Pantheon Restaurant
Pergola des Artistes
Rose Room (Algonquin)
Sam Bok

xxi

Sardi's
Scandia
Schrafft's
Sun Luck Times Square
Sushi Ginza Restaurant
Taco Villa
Wally's
Xochitl Mexican Restaurant

Turtle Bay (42nd to 46th Streets, East of Fifth Avenue)

Aldo and Eddie Rapallo Restaurant
Assembly Steak House
Brass Rail, The
Cattleman East, The
Charlie Brown's
Chock Full O'Nuts
Christ Cella
Copter Club
Danny's Hide-a-Way
Flower Drum Restaurant
Gondola
Grand Central Terminal Oyster Bar and Restaurant
Grenadier
Hickory Pit Restaurant
Horn & Hardart Automats
Inn of the Clock
Joe and Rose
La Bibliothèque
La Locanda
Lantern Light
Le Cheval Blanc
Mont d'Or
Oyster Bar and Restaurant (Grand Central)
Palm Restaurant
Peking House
Pen and Pencil, The
Pietro's
Press Box
Schrafft's
Scoop, The
Trattoria
Zum Zum

47th to 51st Streets, West of Fifth Avenue

Acropolis Restaurant
Amato's Italian Restaurant
Au Tunnel
Brass Rail, The
Canton Village
Cattleman West, The
Ceylon India Inn
Charley O's Bar and Grill
Cheshire Cheese Restaurant
Chez Napoleon
China Fair
Chock Full O'Nuts
Delsomma
Du Midi
Forum of the Twelve Caesars, The
Gaiety West Restaurant and Delicatessen

Haymarket Pub
Hong Kong Inn
Horn & Hardart
  Automats
Kobe Steak House
La Fonda del Sol
La Grillade
Le Alpi
Leone's
Les Pyrénées
Liborio
Maria's Patio
Marta's
Molfetas Cafeteria
Pearl's Chinese Restaurant
Pip's
Promenade Café
Rainbow Room
Red Coach Grill
René Pujol Restaurant
Schrafft's
Skewer on the Table
Smokehouse, The
South Pacific Ports
Steak and Brew
Stockholm Restaurant
Sun Luck Gourmet
Swiss Center Restaurants
  Bell Bar, The
  Fondue Pot, The
  Swiss Pavilion, The
Tin Lizzie Restaurant, The
Tower Suite
Un Rincon Argentino
Vesuvio Restaurant
Zum Zum

47th to 51st Streets, East of Fifth Avenue

Alfie's
Antolotti's
Black Angus
Brochetteria
Bull and Bear, The
  (Waldorf-Astoria)
Café Renaissance
Chalet Suisse
Chandler's
Chez Renée
Chock Full O'Nuts
Christo's
Dionysos
Downing Square
Electra
El Mirador
Fonda la Paloma
Gloucester House
Hickory Pit Restaurant
Jenedi's
Jimmy's La Grange
Kenny's Steak Pub
Lafayette
La Petite Marmite
La Piazzetta
La Toque Blanche
Le Bistro
Le Chanteclair
Le Marmiton
Leopard, The
Lutèce
Manny Wolf's
Michael's Pub
Minotaur, The

Mona Lisa East
Omar Khayam
Paparazzi
*Patricia Murphy's Candle-
    light Restaurant*
*Paul Revere's Tavern and
    Chop House*
Prime Burger
Ratazzi
Schrafft's
Shun Lee Dynasty
Tomaldo's
*Waldorf-Astoria
    Bull and Bear, The*
Wolf's, Manny

52nd to 56th Streets, West of Fifth Avenue

Angelo's Italian Restaurant
Aperitivo
Arirang House
Au Steak Pommes Frites
Benihana of Tokyo West
Brittany du Soir
Ca d'Oro
Café Brittany
*Carnegie Delicatessen and
    Restaurant*
Casa Mario
Coq au Vin
Fornos
French Quarter, The
French Shack, The
*Georges Rey, Restaurant
    Français*

Hide Sukiyaki
*Horn & Hardart
    Automats*
House of Chan
Irori
Italian Pavilion
Joe's Pier 52
La Caravelle
La Crêpe Restaurant
La Fondue
La Potinière du Soir
Larré's French Restaurant
La Scala
Le Champignon
Maud Chez Elle
Mercurio
Mike Manuche
Miyako
Orsini's
Romeo Salta
Rugantino
San Marco
Santa Lucia
Sea-Fare of the Aegean
Slate Restaurant, The
*Stage Delicatessen and
    Restaurant*
Stouffer's
Topkapi Palace
Top of the Six's
"21"
Via Veneto
Wolf's Delicatessen
Zum Zum

52nd to 56th Streets, East of Fifth Avenue

Agra India and Pakistan Restaurant
Arigato
Baroque
Benihana of Tokyo East
Billy's
Blossom Restaurant
Brasserie
Brownstone, The
Brussels Restaurant
Café Argenteuil
Café Europa
Castilian, The
Charles à la Pomme Soufflé
Chin-Ya
Chock Full O'Nuts
Clos Normand
Dawson's Ha-Penny Bar
Dilluvio
Doriental
Elizabeth White
Four Seasons, The
Friar Tuck
Giovanni
Gold Coin
Goodale's
Jade Palace
Kegon
King of the Sea
Maria Cin Cin
La Côte Basque
La Grenouillle
L'Aiglon
La Poulard
L'Armorique
La Veranda
Le Château Richelieu
Le Cygne
Le Manoir
Le Mistral
Le Périgord
Le Pont Neuf
Lotus Eaters
Lotus Eaters Royale
Louise Jr.
Mario's Villa Borghese
Mario's Villa d'Este
Mayfair, The
Morgen's East
New York Exchange Restaurant
Nippon
Pembles
Pierre's
P. J. Clarke's
P. J. Moriarty
P. J. O'Hara
Prime Burger
Reidy's Restaurant
San Marino
Schrafft's
Stage Delicatessen and Restaurant
Sun Luck East
Tanpopo
Tonkatsu
Tony's Wife
Trefner's Restaurant
Zapata Restaurant

Lincoln Center (57th to 72nd Streets, West of Fifth Avenue)

Alfredo of New York
China Pavilion
Chock Full O'Nuts
Copenhagen
Fleur de Lis
Frini
Gauguin Room, The
Ginger Man, The
Grand Tier Restaurant
    (Metropolitan Opera House)
Green Tulip, The (Plaza)
Henry Stampler's Filet Mignon
Horn & Hardart Automats
Ile de France
La Crêpe Restaurant
La Venere West
Le Biarritz
Lenge-Saimin Restaurant
Le Poulailler Restaurant
Macario's
Marsh's Steak Place
Metropolitan Opera House
    Grand Tier Restaurant
Monk's Inn
Mont St. Michel Restaurant
Oak Room (Plaza)
O'Neal's Baloon
Oyster Bar (Plaza)
Piraeus, My Love
Plaza Hotel
    The Green Tulip
    Oak Room
    Oyster Bar
Russian Tea Room
Sakura Chaya
Schrafft's
Steak and Brew
Steak Place, The
Tavern on the Green
Trader Vic's
Victor's Café
Whyte's
Wine and Apples
Yangtze River
Yano

57th to 72nd Streets, East of Fifth Avenue

Au Canari d'Or
Autopub
Blum's
Café Nicholson
Castalia
Colony, The
Daly's Dandelion
Dewey Wong
Dogwood Room
Double Dolphin Fish House
Eduardo's
El Azteca
Emiliana's Restaurant
Esplanade, The
Gaetano's

Gaiety East
Gino's Restaurant
Girafe
Hickory Pit Restaurant
Hime of Japan
Hole in the Wall
Horn & Hardart Automats
Irish Pavilion, The
Isle of Capri
Jamaica Arms
Jasper's
Jolly Chan's Chinese Kitchen
Kirby Allen Restaurant, The
La Cabaña
La Cocotte
La Croisette
Le Moal
L'Entrecôte
Le Pavillon
Le Périgord Park
Le Provençal
L'Escargot
Le Steak
L'Etoile
Le Veau d'Or
Louise
Mme. Romaine de Lyon
Mama Laura Restaurant
Mañana
Mandarin House East
Maxwell's Plum
Mayhew's
Old Denmark
Oscar's Salt of the Sea
Passy, The
Piccolo Mondo
P. J. Moriarty
Plaka East
Proof of the Pudding
Quo Vadis
Reuben's
Right Bank Provincial, The
Right Bank Restaurant, The
Ruc Restaurant
Running Footman, The
Schrafft's
Sign of the Dove
Smokehouse, The
Spanish Pavilion, The
Steak and Brew
Sun Luck Imperial
Unicorn, The
Vasata
Yellowfinger's Butcheria
Zoe Chase
Zum Zum

Upper West Side (above 73rd Street, West of Fifth Avenue)

Aki Dining Room
Chock Full O'Nuts
Chuan Hong Restaurant
Cleopatra
Great Shanghai, The
La Paella

Mi Tierra
Moon Palace
New Moon Inn
Shanghai Café
Shanghai d'Or
Symposium
Szechuan
Teacher's
Tien Tsin
Tokyo-Bangkok Restaurant
Tony's Italian Kitchen
Uncle Tonoose

Upper East Side (above 73rd Street, East of Fifth Avenue)

Acapulco Restaurant
Adams Rib
Alda's
Allen's
Brochetteria
Budapest Hungarian Restaurant
Café du Soir
Camelot
Cape Cod
Casa Brasil
Czechoslovak Praha
Dresner's
Duck Joint, The
Dynasty, The
Elaine's
Estia
Eva Hungarian Restaurant

Fu Shin Restaurant
Heidelberg Restaurant
Hickory Pit Restaurant
Horn & Hardart Automats
Hyde Park Restaurant
Kleine Konditorei
Lair, The
Little Royal Hungarian Restaurant
Lotus Eaters East
Madison Delicatessen and Restaurant, The
Mr. and Mrs. Foster
Nirvana
Pagano's
Pancho Villa's
Paprika
Parioli, Romanissimo
Pink Foot, The
Piro's
P. J. Moriarty
Schaefer's
Schrafft's
Soul East
Steak and Brew
Sun Yah
Tandur, The
Thursday's
Tik Tak Hungarian
Un Coin de Paris
Villa Doria

Brooklyn

Chock Full O'Nuts
Gage and Tollner

Lebanon Restaurant
Near East Restaurant
Old Mexico Restaurant
Peter Luger
Villa Vivolo
Zum Zum

Bronx, The

El Radiante
Mona Trattoria

Queens

Steinway Brauhall
Sun Luck Queens

Staten Island

Carmen's

Types of Restaurants

American (see also Hamburgers/Sandwiches; Seafood; Soul Food; Steak Houses)

Act I
Adams Rib
Alfie's
Algonquin Hotel
    Oak Room
    Rose Room
Allen's
Artist and Writers Restaurant
Autopub
Billy's
Blum's
Brass Rail, The
Brew's
Brochetteria
Bull and Bear, The (Waldorf-Astoria)
Café Nicholson
Camelot
Castalia
Chandler's
Charlie Brown's
Christ Cella
Coach House, The
Cookery Lafayette, The
Copter Club
Daly's Dandelion
Dogwood Room
Dresner's
Duck Joint, The
Elizabeth White
500 on 8th Restaurant, The
Forum of the Twelve Caesars, The
Four Seasons, The
Fraunces Tavern
French Quarter, The
Ginger Man, The
Green Tulip, The (Plaza)
Horn & Hardart Automats
Inn of the Clock
Joe Allen
Kirby Allen Restaurant, The
Les Champs
Lord & Taylor's Soup Bar
Mark Twain Riverboat
Mary Elizabeth's
Max's Kansas City
Maxwell's Plum
Mayfair, The
McSorley's Old Ale House
Miller's
Mr. and Mrs. Foster
Morgen's East
Morgen's Restaurant
New York Exchange Restaurant
Oak Room (Algonquin)
Oak Room (Plaza)

Old Garden, The
Pappas
Patricia Murphy's Candlelight Restaurant
Paul Revere's Tavern and Chop House
Pembles
Pip's
P. J. Clarke's
P. J. O'Hara
Plaza Hotel
    The Green Tulip
    Oak Room
Promenade Café
Proof of the Pudding
Rainbow Room
Red Coach Grill
Rose Room (Algonquin)
Running Footman, The
Schrafft's
Sign of the Dove
Skewer on the Table
Spark's Pub South
Stouffer's
Tavern on the Green
Teacher's
Tin Lizzie Restaurant, The
Top of the Six's
Tower Suite
Trefner's Restaurant
"21"
Waldorf-Astoria
    Bull and Bear, The
Wine Cellar, The
Yellowfinger's Butcheria
Ye Waverly Inn
Zoe Chase

Argentine

La Cabaña
La Hacienda
Un Rincon Argentino

Armenian

Ararat
Balkan Armenian Restaurant
Dardanelles Armenian Restaurant
Sayat Nova

Brazilian

Brazilian Coffee Restaurant
Cabaña Carioca
Casa Brasil

Caribbean

El Radiante
Jamaica Arms
Mi Tierra
Victor's Café

Cheese

International Cheese Club Restaurant
La Fondue
Monk's Inn

Chinese

Bernstein-on-Essex-
    Street
Bo Bo
Canton Restaurant
Canton Village
Chi Mer
China Bowl, The
China Fair
China Pavilion
Chinese Rathskeller
Chuan Hong Restaurant
Cuisine of Szechuan
Dewey Wong
Doriental Restaurant
Dynasty, The
Empire Chinese Restau-
    rant, The
Esther Eng
Flower Drum Restaurant
Foo Chow Restaurant
Four Five Six
Fu Shin Restaurant
Gim Beck
Gold Coin
Golden Coach
Gold Full Restaurant
Great Shanghai, The
Happy Garden
Hong Fat Restaurant
Hong Kong Inn
Hong Ying
Ho Shun
House of Chan
Hoy Kung
Jade Palace

Jolly Chan's Chinese
    Kitchen
Joyce's Macao
Joy Garden
King Wu
Koon Shing Tea House
Lam Kee
Lantern Light
Lichee Tree, The
Lin Heong
Little Peking Restaurant,
    Inc.
Long River
Lotus Eaters
Lotus Eaters East
Lotus Eaters Fifth
Lotus Eaters Park
Lotus Eaters Royale
Lucy Jung
Mandarin House
Mandarin House East
Mandarin Inn
Moon Palace
New Hankow
New Moon Inn
New Wah Dor
Ningpo Restaurant
Nom Wah Tea Parlor
Oriental Pearl
Pearl's Chinese Restaurant
Peking House
Pine Garden Restaurant
Port Arthur
Sam Pam
Sam Wo
Say Eng Look
Shanghai Café

Shanghai d'Or
Shanghai Garden
Shanghai Town
Shanghai Village
Shavey Lee
Shun Lee
Shun Lee Dynasty
Sum Hey Rice Shoppe
Sun Hop Kee
Sun Luck East
Sun Luck Gourmet
Sun Luck Imperial
Sun Luck Queens
Sun Luck Times Square
Sun Yah
Szechuan
Szechuan Taste
Temple Garden, The
Three Six Nine Restaurant
Tien Tsin
Tom's Shangri-La
Wah Kee Restaurant
Wise Man, The
Wo Kee
Wo Ping
Yangtze River
Ying's

Czechoslovak

Czechoslovak Praha
Ruc Restaurant
Vasata

Delicatessen, see Jewish

English/Irish/Scotch

Charley O's Bar and Grill
Cheshire Cheese Restaurant
Dawson's Ha-Penny Bar
Downing Square
Friar Tuck
Grenadier
Haymarket Pub
Irish Pavilion, The
Keen's English Chop House
Limerick's
Michael's Pub
Reidy's Restaurant
Ye Olde Chop House

Far Eastern, see Chinese, Indian/Pakistani, Indonesian, Iranian, Japanese, Korean, Philippine, Polynesian, Thai

French

A la Fourchette
Au Canari d'Or
Au Steak Pommes Frites
Au Tunnel
Baroque
Brasserie
Brittany Soir
Brussels Restaurant
Café Argenteuil

Café Brittany
Café de France
Café du Soir
Café Europa
Casey's
Charles à la Pomme Soufflé
Charles French Restaurant
Chez Cardinale
Chez Napoleon
Chez Renée
Chez Yvonne l'Escargot
Clos Normand
Colony, The
Coq au Vin
Crêpes Suzette
Du Midi
Esplanade, The
Fleur de Lis
French Shack, The
Georges Rey, Restaurant
    Français
Grand Tier Restaurant
    (Metropolitan Opera)
Ile de France
Il Faro
Jimmy's La Grange
La Bibliothèque
La Bourgogne
La Caravelle
La Cocotte
La Côte Basque
La Crêpe Restaurants
La Croisette
Lafayette
La Grenouille
La Grillade
L'Aiglon

Lair, The
La Petite Ferme
La Petite Marmite
La Potinière du Soir
La Poulard
L'Armorique
Larré's French Restaurant
La Toque Blanche
Le Biarritz
Le Bistro
Le Chambertin
Le Champignon
Le Chanteclair
Le Château Richelieu
Le Cheval Blanc
Le Cygne
Le Manoir
Le Mistral
Le Moal
L'Entrecôte
Leopard, The
Le Pavillon
Le Périgord
Le Périgord Park
Le Pont Neuf
Le Poulailler
Le Provençal
L'Escargot
Les Pyrénées
L'Etoile
Le Veau d'Or
Lutèce
Mme. Romaine de Lyon
Maud Chez Elle
Metropolitan Opera House
    Grand Tier Restaurant

Mon Paris
Mont d'Or
Mont St. Michel Restaurant
Passy, The
Pergola des Artistes
Pink Foot, The
Pierre's
Quo Vadis
René Pujol Restaurant
Right Bank Provincial, The
Right Bank Restaurant, The
Thursday's
Un Coin de Paris

German

Hanover Square Restaurant
Heidelberg Restaurant
Kleine Konditorei
Lüchow's
Old Seidelburg
Schaefer's
Steinway Brauhall
Zum Zum

Greek

Acropolis Restaurant
Athenian Restaurant, The
Blossom Restaurant
Castalia
Dionysos
Electra
Estia
Jimmy's Greek-American Restaurant
Minotaur, The
Molfetas Cafeteria
Mykonos
Pantheon Restaurant
Paradise Inn
Piraeus, My Love
Plaka East
Symposium
Wine and Apples
Z

Hamburgers/Sandwiches

Allen's
Brownstone, The
Chock Full O'Nuts
Hickory Pit Restaurants
O'Neal's Baloon
Prime Burger

Hungarian

Budapest Hungarian Restaurant
Eva Hungarian Restaurant
Little Royal Hungarian Restaurant
Paprika

Tik Tak Hungarian
Wine and Apples

Indian/Pakistani

Agra India and Pakistan Restaurant
Ceylon India Inn
India House East
Karachi
Kashmir Restaurant
Nataraj
Nirvana
Pak-India Curry House
Rajmahal Restaurant
Shalimar
Tandur, The
Taste of India

Indonesian

Nataraj
Omar Khayam

Iranian

Omar Khayam

Irish, see English/Irish/Scotch

Italian

Alda's
Aldo and Eddie Rapallo Restaurant
Alfredo of New York
Allis' Restaurant
Amato's Italian Restaurant
Angelina's
Angelo's
Angelo's Italian Restaurant
Antica Roma
Antolotti's
Aperitivo
Asti
Ballato Restaurant
Barbetta Restaurant
Ca d'Oro
Café Renaissance
Casa di Pre
Casa Mario
Chez Cardinale
Chez Vous
Christo's
Damon's
Delsomma
Deno's Place
Dilluvio
Due Mondi
Duff's
Eduardo's
Elaine's
Emiliana's Restaurant
Esplanade, The
Fedora
Filippo Restaurant
Forlini's
Gaetano's
Gatti's
Gene's

Giambone
Gino's Restaurant
Giordano Restaurant
Giovanni
Girafe
Gloria's Restaurant
Gondola
Greensleeves
Grotta Azzurra
Il Bambino
Il Faro
Isle of Capri
Italianissimo
Italian Pavilion
Jasper's
Jenedi's
Joe and Rose
Joe's Restaurant
Johnnie's
John's Restaurant
Julio Restaurant
La Fortuna
La Groceria
La Hacienda
La Locanda
La Piazzetta
La Scala
La Strada East
La Venere West
La Veranda
Le Alpi
Leone's
Lino's U.N. Restaurant
Little Place, The
Louise
Louise Jr.
Luna's Restaurant

Macario's
Mama Laura Restaurant
Manganaro's and Manganaro's Hero-Boy Restaurant
Marchi's
Maria Cin Cin
Mario
Mario's Villa Borghese
Mario's Villa d'Este
Marta Restaurant
Marta's
Mary's
Mercurio
Mike Manuche
Minetta Tavern
Mona Lisa
Mona Lisa East
Mona Trattoria
Monte's Restaurant
New Port Alba
Nicola Paone
Orsini's
Oscar's Delmonico
Pagano's
Paparazzi
Parioli, Romanissimo
Paul and Jimmy's Place
Piccolo Mondo
Pietro's
Piro's
Portofino
Ratazzi
Rocco Restaurant
Roma Nova
Romeo Salta
Rosetta's Restaurant

Rugantino
San Marco
San Marino
San Remo
Santa Lucia
Sardi's
Savoia
Scoop, The
Sixty-Eight Restaurant
Slate Restaurant, The
Teddy's Restaurant
37th Street Hideaway
Tomaldo's
Tony's Italian Kitchen
Tony's Wife
Trattoria
Unicorn, The
Valentino's
Vesuvio Restaurant
Via Margutta
Via Veneto
Villa Doria
Villa Marbona
Villa Pensa
Villa Vivolo
Vincent Petrosino
Vincent's Clam Bar
Wally's

Japanese

Akasaka
Aki Dining Room
Arigato
Benihana of Tokyo East
Benihana of Tokyo West

Benihana Palace
Chin-Ya
Daruma
Hide Sukiyaki
Hime of Japan
Irori
Japanese Mie Cooking
Japanese Steak House
Kabuki Restaurant
Kamehachi
Kegon
Kitcho Restaurant
Kobe Steak House
Kyoto Steak House
Lenge-Saimin Restaurant
Mikado
Miyako
Nippon
Restaurant Tokyo
Sakura Chaya
Suehiro Restaurant
Sushi Ginza Restaurant
Tamura Restaurant
Tanpopo
Taste of Tokyo
Tokyo-Bangkok Restaurant
Tonkatsu
Yamashiro
Yano

Jewish

Al Cooper's Herald Square Restaurant
Bernstein-on-Essex-Street
Carnegie Delicatessen and Restaurant

Gaiety East
*Gaiety West Restaurant
   and Delicatessen*
Hole in the Wall
Hyde Park Restaurant
Katz's Delicatessen
Lou G. Siegel
*Madison Delicatessen and
   Restaurant, The*
Parkway East
Reuben's
Smokehouse, The
*Stage Delicatessen and
   Restaurant*
*Wolf's Delicatessen (at 180
   Broadway)*
*Wolf's Delicatessen (at 799
   Seventh Avenue)*

Korean

Arirang House
New Korea
Sam Bok

Latin American (see also Argentine, Brazilian, Caribbean, Mexican)

Frini
La Fonda del Sol
Liborio

Lebanese

Beirut Restaurant
Cedars of Lebanon
Lebanon Restaurant
Uncle Tonoose Restaurant

Mexican

Acapulco Restaurant
Alamo Chile House, The
Brasero
Carmen's
Casa Laredo
El Azteca
El Charro
El Mirador
El Parador
Fonda la Paloma
Mañana
Maria's Patio
Mexican Village
*Mexi-Frost Specialties
   Company*
Mi Tierra
Old Mexico Restaurant
Pancho Villa's
Taco Villa
Xochitl Mexican Restaurant
Zapata Restaurant

Middle Eastern (see also Armenian, Greek, Lebanese, Syrian, Turkish)

Cleopatra

xxxix

Near East Restaurant
Sheik Restaurant, The

Moroccan

Al Mounia
Keneret
Mont St. Michel Restaurant

Philippine

Philippine Garden, The

Polynesian

Gauguin Room
Lenge-Saimin Restaurant
South Pacific Ports
Trader Vic's

Russian

Russian Tea Room

Scandinavian

Copenhagen
Old Denmark
Scandia
Stockholm Restaurant

Scotch, see English/Irish/Scotch

Seafood

Blue Sea
Cape Cod
Captain's Table, The
Double Dolphin Fish House
Fisherman's Net
Gage and Tollner
Gloucester House
Goodale's
Grand Central Terminal Oyster Bar and Restaurant
Joe's Pier 52
King of the Sea
Ocean, The
Oscar's Salt of the Sea
Pappas
Oyster Bar (Grand Central)
Plaza Hotel Oyster Bar
Sloppy Louie's
Sweet's
Vincent's Clam Bar
Whyte's

Soul Food

Jack's Nest
Little Kitchen, The
Soul East

Spanish

Café Renaissance
Carmen's
Castilian, The
El Faro
El Quijote
El Rincon de España
Fornos

Granados Restaurant
Jai-Alai
La Paella
Oviedo
Pamplona Restaurant
Spain
Spanish Pavilion, The

Steak Houses

Arigato
Assembly Steak House
Benihana of Tokyo East
Benihana of Tokyo West
Benihana Palace
Black Angus
Broadway Joe Steak House
Cattle Baron, The
Cattleman East, The
Cattleman West, The
Chandler's
Christ Cella
Christo's
Danny's Hide-a-Way
Derby Steak House, The
Frankie and Johnnie
Gallagher's 33
Henry Stampler's Filet Mignon
Hime of Japan
Irori
Japanese Steak House
Kenny's Steak Pub
Kobe Steak House
Kyoto Steak House
Le Steak

Manny Wolf's
Marsh's Steak Place
O. Henry's Steak House
Old Forge Steak House
Palm Restaurant
Paul's Steak Pub
Pen and Pencil, The
Peter Luger's
Peter's Backyard
P. J. Moriarty
Ponte's Steak House
Press Box
Scoop, The
Slate Restaurant, The
Steak and Brew
Steak Casino
Steak Joint, The
Steak Place, The

Swiss

Chalet Suisse
Swiss Center Restaurants
    Bell Bar, The
    Fondue Pot, The
    Swiss Pavilion, The

Syrian

Keneret

Thai

Tokyo-Bangkok Restaurant

Turkish

Nick's Topkapi Pub
Topkapi Palace

The New York Times Guide to Dining Out in New York

Credit Card Information

Many dining establishments honor various credit cards. For the convenience of patrons, reviews of these restaurants are followed by one or more of the following keys:

- **AE** *American Express*
- **BA** *BankAmericard*
- **CB** *Carte Blanche*
- **DC** *Diners Club*
- **MC** *Master Charge*

★★ ACAPULCO RESTAURANT
1555 Second Avenue (at 81st Street)   744-9229

There are several pleasant Mexican restaurants in Manhattan that serve an agreeable assortment of food. The menus have a distinct similarity and, as far as I know, there is not one with a full-fledged authentic Mexican kitchen. So be it.

Even if this one does have that déjà vu look, it is an agreeable place with handsome enough décor and good, if generally bland, cooking. A recent meal began with nachos, the appetizer made with cheese and beans and chilies baked on tortillas; fried Spanish sausages; and guacamole.

A combination platter including an enchilada, tamale, and tostada was good even if it did hedge on the flavors; and an order of chili rellenos was above par for New York. The mole (an unfortunate name when printed in English) poblano was also quite edible, although the sauce was a trifle sweet.

The piped-in music is loud, but there seem to be a few blessed 15-minute intervals when there is none.

All dishes are à la carte, with main courses in the evening from about $2.60 to $4.35. Luncheon specials are priced at about $2.25. *Cocktails, wines. Luncheon is served only on Sunday from 1:30 to 3:30 p.m. Monday through Saturday, the restaurant opens at 4:30 p.m. for dinner only.*

★★ ACROPOLIS RESTAURANT
767 Eighth Avenue (at 47th Street)   265-6035

Like that of many another Greek restaurant in Manhattan, the food of the Acropolis is substantial, abundant, and well-seasoned. The menu here is characteristic. There are only about 30 items listed, most of them made with lamb—roast lamb, baked lamb, and roast lamb head. There are also very good fish dishes; simply cooked, rewarding appetizers; and excellent soups, including the famous avgolemono, or chicken and lemon soup with rice.

It is true that both the vegetable and meat dishes are

cooked at length, and they may at times be served lukewarm, but the food is honest and the price is right. The Acropolis is a large, neat restaurant, and many of the clientele are Greek.

All dishes are à la carte, with main courses from about $1.85 for a feta cheese omelet to $3.00 for fried shrimp. *Cocktails, wines. Open 7 days a week.*

★ ACT I
Allied Chemical Tower at Times Square (15th and 16th floors)   695-1880

Act I is the best-looking restaurant in the vicinity of Times Square and, situated as it is on the 15th and 16th floors of the Allied Chemical Tower, it offers some fairly absorbing views of the city below: spires, hotels, water towers, commercial buildings, the Hudson, and glimpses of Central Park's trees by day; the gaudy, flashy necklace of lights of Broadway and Seventh Avenue by night. The food is American—fried chicken at times, stuffed green peppers, barbecued beef, steaks, things like that—and it is reasonably palatable, but, considering the cost of dining at Act I, it isn't nearly as good as it should be. A shrimp cocktail with a pedestrian chili sauce right out of the bottle; an acceptably seasoned but dry barbecued beef; a salty Roquefort salad dressing; and so on. There are complete luncheons priced from about $4.45 to $6.75; à la carte dishes at midday from about $2.75 to $5.25. Dinners (which are served from 4:30 P.M.) are priced from about $7.75 to $8.75, but desserts are an additional 95 cents. A la carte dishes in the evening are from about $5.95 to $8.50. *Cocktails, wines. Supper is served until midnight. Closed major holidays.*
AE   DC   MC

★★ ADAMS RIB
23 East 74th Street   535-2112

There are numerous restaurants in Manhattan that are far more agreeable in the evening than at noon, and this is true of Adams Rib in the Volney Hotel. After dark, when the lights are dimmed, the dining room seems handsomer and more dignified, almost vintage European.

There is a limited menu both at midday and for dinner, and the specialty of the house—unfortunately, in the evening only—is roast prime ribs of beef. It is outstanding both in texture and flavor.

At lunch and dinner, there are good, crisp salads, particularly the one with the restaurant's Caesar dressing (it does not contain anchovies or coddled egg, but it is good, nonetheless).

A chicken in wine sauce one evening was a bit overcooked and served with rice that was a bit undercooked. At the same meal, a chocolate pie was very rich and admirable, and there was also a good whipped-cream-like peach dessert listed as a Bavarian cream.

The food one noon came off far less well. The King Crab Snug Harbor had the crab buried under an indifferent cream sauce, and all of it on a biscuit. A club steak was in itself worthwhile, but it was accompanied by an undistinguished grilled tomato and a baked potato at room temperature. Adams Rib does not offer espresso coffee. But each table has a loaf of first-rate bread.

All main courses are à la carte, with main courses at noon from about $3.75 to $4.50 and in the evening from about $5.50 to $6.95. *Cocktails, wines. Open 7 days a week. Luncheon is not served on Saturday and Sunday.*
AE DC

★ AGRA INDIA AND PAKISTAN RESTAURANT
150 East 53rd Street   593-1740

There is a certain insecurity in writing about Indian and Pakistani food, particularly at this distance from Delhi. The flavors of the food with those multitudinous spices are among the most complex on earth.

There were nice contrasts in the flavors of the dishes, whether a hot chicken vindaloo or the lamb biryani (spelled biryni on the menu) or the appetizers, such as deep-fried eggplant and the crudely made but well-seasoned samosa.

The Agra is an eminently plain, nonelegant restaurant with table service to match the décor. There is no bar (a license, we were told, has been applied for), but customers bring their own wines or beer. The one thing that puts one off slightly about the Agra is the ventilation.

There is a complete luncheon priced at $1.75. Complete dinners are from about $3.75 to $7.50. *Open 7 days a week, noon to midnight.*

★ AKASAKA
715 Second Avenue (near 38th Street)   867-6410

To judge from the number of Eastern restaurants that have opened or are about to open in New York, it seems that chopsticks are about to replace the knife and fork as standard table utensils. The Akasaka lists itself as a Japanese-French restaurant, but the ambience is more Japanese-American tea room. The Akasaka is fairly large, with a sushi counter plus table service, and there is no want for customers. Perhaps that is the problem.

The food sampled there recently, such as sushi, tempura, and katsu-don (or pork cutlet on steamed rice), was competently and freshly cooked, but the service was wayward. Its haphazard character seems to stem, however, not from a lack of desire to please, but from a lack of organization. The ventilation, too, is short of perfect.

All dishes are à la carte, with main courses from about $1.50 for the katsu-don to $3.00–$4.50 for steak. *Cocktails, wines. The Akasaka opens at noon, Monday through Friday, and at 5:00 p.m. on Saturday. It is closed Sunday and major holidays.*

★ AKI DINING ROOM
420 West 119th Street   UN 4-5970

The Aki is a long-time favorite with the faculty and students of Columbia University. It is one of the best Japanese restaurants uptown and has seating in the western style. The menu is reasonably authentic, from sashimi (raw fish) to sunomono (salad), and the same menu is used for both lunch and dinner. Complete meals from $2.75 to $4.00. There is frequently a wait for tables in the evening. *Cocktails, beer, and Japanese wine. Closed Monday.*

★★ A LA FOURCHETTE
342 West 46th Street   CI 5-9744

This small, unpretentious French-style restaurant serves mostly provincial-style dishes. Daily specialties such as veal chipolata (veal balls and tiny sausages in wine sauce served with rice and vegetables), cassoulet Toulousain, and brook trout amandine are listed on a blackboard. Complete à la carte menus are also available at luncheon and dinner. Luncheon entrées from about $2.90; dinner main courses from about $3.75 to $7.50. *Cocktails, wines. Luncheon is not served Saturday. Closed Sunday, major holidays, and the month of August.*

★ ALAMO CHILE HOUSE, THE
142 West 44th Street   CI 5-4288

This is a small, crowded, noisy restaurant with a décor that is the antithesis of the "don't fence me in" school. The chili is hot, and the beer, whether domestic or Mexican, dark or light, is ice cold. For those who fancy such food, a bowl of chili without beans costs $1.50 and makes an excellent meal with a side dish of rice and a liberal sprinkling of raw onion. The most frequently ordered dish appears to be an enchilada and chili combination that costs $1.95, but it is not always as hot (from a temperature standpoint) as it might be. *Beer. Closed Sunday and major holidays.*

★★ AL COOPER'S HERALD SQUARE RESTAURANT
130 West 36th Street   CH 4-2828

This is a neat and relatively expensive restaurant

that admirably reflects the flavor of Manhattan. The service is prompt, the portions are generous, and the food is generally first-rate. There are such specialties as prime beef tongue, Romanian pastrami, and braised beef. Both luncheon and dinner are à la carte, with main luncheon courses from $3.50 to $9.75; main dinner courses from about $5.95 to $9.75. *Cocktails, wines. Luncheon is not served Saturday. Closed Sunday, major holidays, and the first 2 weeks in July.*
AE CB DC MC

★ ALDA'S
332 East 86th Street   288-6335

If there is a tremendous sameness about 99 percent of all the Italian menus in Manhattan, the fault lies to a large part with the public. Americans, by and large, comfort themselves with spaghetti and meat sauce, meat balls, or tomato sauce; veal Parmigiana; chicken cacciatore; and nothing more adventurous generally than fettuccine Alfredo.

Alda's is a small Italian restaurant which has become increasingly interesting and international. It has a menu that is like many another in town, but the chef, one suspects, has more talent than he's letting the public know about.

The assorted hot antipasto would be a standout (in New York, that is) if the same tomato sauce weren't used for each element (zucchini, mushrooms, eggplant, and so on). A dish of chicken francese, batter-fried and with lemon, was tender and delicate and good. The veal scaloppine alla Cardinale with mushrooms and pimientos was good, but the sauce was a bit too thick. A specially ordered dish of spaghetti alla matriciana with bacon and olives and a tomato sauce too similar to the antipasto sauce was on the salty side.

Complete luncheons are priced from $2.50 to $3.50 with à la carte dishes at midday from about $2.00 to $5.25. A la carte dishes in the evening are from about $2.95 to $7.25.

Cocktails, wines. Open 7 days a week.
All major credit cards.

★ ALDO AND EDDIE RAPALLO RESTAURANT
834 Second Avenue (between 44th and 45th Streets)
MU 3-1050 *and* MU 4-9856

If anyone wished to capture for a stage set the atmosphere and feeling of a small, well-received Italian restaurant, he need go no farther than the Rapallo. It has all the clichés, from minestrone and cannelloni to piped-in music and the graphic oils on the walls. The food is agreeable, however, and it is a friendly place. A la carte, with main luncheon courses from about $3.50 for spaghetti with meat sauce to $5.00 for broiled minute steak; main dinner dishes from about $5.00 for manicotti, with a prix fixe dinner at $8.00. *Cocktails, wines. On Saturday the restaurant opens at 4:00 p.m. Closed Sunday and major holidays.*
AE BA CB DC MC

★ ALFIE'S
1290 Third Avenue (at 74th Street)   628-6265

Alfie's is a popular place with a fairly steady beat from a jukebox. There is a neat décor with a birdcage and, over the bar, wooden nudes in bas-relief. The menu is international, ranging from barbecued chicken and ribs to corned beef and cabbage to veal Cordon Bleu. All dishes are à la carte, with main courses from about $3.75 to $6.95. *Cocktails, wines. The restaurant is open from 4:00 p.m. to 4:00 a.m. on weekdays, to 3:00 a.m. Saturday, and to 2:00 a.m. on Sunday. Closed Christmas Day.*
AE BA CB MC

★★★ ALFREDO OF NEW YORK
240 Central Park South (at West 59th Street)
CI 6-7050

This has long been one of the best North Italian restaurants in Manhattan. It moved some time ago to a new location on Central Park South. The décor is a bit on

the garish side (too obvious yellow draperies), but the food at its best is of a high order. The fettuccine, with its cream and grated fresh cheese (and shaved white truffles, if you can afford them), is as good as you'll find in the city. Very good veal dishes. All items are à la carte, with main courses at noon from about $3.50 to $6.50; in the evening, from about $4.00 to $8.50. *Cocktails, wines. Closed Sunday and major holidays. Luncheons are not served on Saturday.*
AE DC

ALGONQUIN HOTEL
59 West 44th Street   687-4400

The Algonquin has two of the most civilized dining rooms in the Times Square–Broadway area. They are the **★★Oak Room,** with its masculine appeal, and the **★★Rose Room,** which is more intimate. The surroundings are pleasant, the menu is well-varied, and the food, although it may not be illustrious, is nonetheless agreeable. Recommended in particular is the roast beef with Yorkshire pudding, available in the evening. Both luncheon and dinner menus are à la carte, with main courses from about $2.95 for scrambled eggs to $10.50 for planked steak Algonquin. *Cocktails, wines. Dinner is served from 5:15 p.m. and a buffet supper from 10:30 p.m. Closed Sunday and major holidays.*
AE BA DC

★★ ALLEN'S
1271 Third Avenue (at 73rd Street)   RH *4-9604*

A good-quality hamburger properly cooked is equally as interesting as a porterhouse steak and so is a bowl of chili. Hamburgers and chili, along with sirloin steak and roast beef sandwiches, are the kind of fare you will find at Allen's, a congenial, saloon-type restaurant with friendly service.

It is an honest place, with an old-fashioned, semicircular

bar, and it is a pleasant place to visit if only for a beer on draught. A blackboard menu over the small kitchen lists, in addition to various kinds of 'burgers and steak, Welsh rabbit.

There are specials each day, gazpacho and cheese-stuffed manicotti, the latter somewhat of a disappointment. The sauce for it tasted like a creole sauce rather than an Italian tomato sauce and the dish was served without grated cheese.

The cost of Allen's offerings is from about $1.35 for a hamburger to $6.25 for sirloin steak. *Cocktails, wines. Open 7 days a week.*

★★ ALLIS' RESTAURANT
48 East 29th Street   MU 4-8764

Although New York does not boast an ultimately great Italian restaurant, it does have a host of small and unpretentious places where the food is fresh and cooked to order and admirably priced. This restaurant, owned by the Allis family, is of that genre.

There is no chi-chi anywhere, from the small bar in front to the kitchen in the rear. Allis's chef makes excellent, well-seasoned, and hearty soups; an occasional unaccustomed dish such as tripe casserole; and a first-rate and robust tomato sauce. The trouble is that the same sauce seems to go into a multitude of dishes whether it is clams Posillipo, spaghetti, or pork chops pizzaiola. The clams Posillipo—cooked in the shell in that tomato sauce—are very good, by the way.

It is presumed that spaghetti and other farinaceous dishes will be cooked to order on request, but the usual spaghetti is not cooked to order and tends to be overcooked. And a dish of stuffed eggplant arrived at the table lukewarm. Allis's service is as informal as the surroundings.

The menu is à la carte, with main dishes from about $1.60 to $4.95 at lunch. Dinner entrées go from $1.95 to

$6.50. *Cocktails, wines. Closed Saturday, Sunday, major holidays, and 2 weeks in July.*
AE DC

★★★ AL MOUNIA
241 Madison Avenue (at 38th Street)   683-5860

This new restaurant in the Lancaster Hotel is an admirable branch of the famed Al Mounia restaurant in Casablanca, which some people claim to be the best restaurant in Morocco.

The food over-all is prepared creditably and well. And the décor is stunning in a Moroccan sort of way. There is a large dining room with panels ornately painted to resemble mosaics; tooled round or rectangular copper trays from which guests dine; filigree Moroccan lamps; a fountain that gurgles; and red velveteen banquettes and traditional stools.

No two people, perhaps, would agree on the 10 greatest dishes in the world, but one list would certainly include the couscous of North Africa, the principal item on the menu of Al Mounia here.

Couscous is a form of semolina, and this cereal is the basis for the dish also known as couscous. A complete North African couscous consists of meat or poultry, generally lamb or chicken, made into a stew, with the cereal steamed over the kettle.

The dishes, in addition to the couscous, include pastilla, that marvelously rich main course made with strudel-like dough filled with chicken and almonds and with sugar, of all things; kefta brochettes, which is ground meat on a skewer; good "cigars" (the only cigars that could be justifiably praised) made with tender rolled pastry and also filled with chicken; something fine called m'chermel, a stew of lamb with onions and pickled lemon quarters; a superb soup called harira, made with lamb broth and lentils and cumin-flavored, with a wedge of lemon to be added.

And so on to the desserts, which are rich and generally served with green tea. If anyone tries the couscous, please, without fail, ask for extra broth. Couscous must be bathed in sauce to reach peak excellence. The salads at the restaurant are good, too, except that they contain those vapid, tasteless California black olives.

The major fault to be found at the Al Mounia is the service. It is almost wholly without the style or finesse that a restaurant like Al Mounia needs and deserves. Service is heavy-handed at best. If the restaurant were suddenly filled, it would probably result in chaos for the management; anguish for the customers. And, oh yes, there is piped-in music. Regrettably loud.

All dishes are à la carte, with main courses midday from about $3.50 to $8.40, in the evening from about $4.40 to $9.75. *Cocktails, wines. Closed Sunday.*
MC

★ AMATO'S ITALIAN RESTAURANT
301 West 47th Street   245-9498

This is a most agreeable and inexpensive restaurant in the Broadway area. It incorporates such bad features as piped-in music, wine glasses that are too small, and a brodo that smacks of bouillon cubes. But the food, otherwise, is generally excellent, and the restaurant is as much like a sidewalk café in Italy as you're apt to find in the city. The windows open onto the street and the traffic, there are corny Venetian murals, and the place deserves more patronage than it gets. Amato's is open for dinner only. The menu is à la carte, with main courses from about $2.00 for spaghetti with tomato sauce to $5.00 for lobster fra diavolo. *Cocktails, wines. Closed Sunday and the month of July.*
DC

★ ANGELINA'S
41 Greenwich Avenue   CH 3-9650

A small, comfortable Italian restaurant with plain,

but palatable cuisine. The breaded pork chop is excellent and the tomato sauces are good. The same à la carte menu serves for both luncheon and dinner, with main courses from about $2.25 to $5.00. There is a complete prix fixe dinner with main courses from about $5.00 to $10.00. *Cocktails, wines. Closed Tuesday, Thanksgiving, and Christmas.*
AE DC

★★ ANGELO'S
146 Mulberry Street   WO 6-1277

A correspondent suggested that one should go back to Angelo's on Mulberry Street and "ask the waiter if the spaghetti chef is there. If so, indulge yourself with his wonderful clam sauce A'Mare Chiara. The chef makes the very best clam sauce except for Salvatore's in Naples."

Luigi's clam sauce did turn out to be excellent, the linguine (an imported brand, probably) cooked to perfection, and the sauce with its tiny clams in the shell made with excellent oil and redolent with garlic.

Angelo's has been around for a good many years, and the chefs do care about their food, whether it is a clam sauce, striped bass livornese in a light tomato sauce with imported black olives and capers, or an excellent sirloin steak pizzaiola with a tomato sauce and garlic. Or a simple salad.

It is a large restaurant, very Mulberry Street, with friendly yet impressively detached table service (it is no place for people in a rush) and loud recorded music.

All dishes are à la carte, with main courses from about $2.25 to $6.75. *Cocktails, wines. Closed Monday.*
All major credit cards.

★ ANGELO'S ITALIAN RESTAURANT
859 Ninth Avenue (between 55th and 56th Streets)
JU 6-0159

This is the sort of restaurant you would likely pass

by unless someone told you the food has a certain merit. It is said to be popular with certain members of the Columbia Broadcasting System's staff, and it seems to have a large following in general.

It is a small restaurant with a raffish interior and on two occasions there has been only one waitress, who quadruples in making cocktails, offering menus, clearing tables, and serving the food.

Angelo's is best known for its pizza, which is excellent, but there is a full Italian menu, the food cooked with enthusiasm and a minimum of garlic.

The portions are huge and the dishes include an above-average cold antipasto, homemade tagliatelle or egg noodles, veal scaloppine, chicken parmigiana, veal with mushrooms, and shrimp scampi. If you are overly fastidious or hurried, don't bother.

All dishes are à la carte and they are priced from about $1.50 to $5.50. *Cocktails, wines. Open 7 days a week.*

★★ ANTICA ROMA
94 Baxter Street   CA 6-9847

This is an uncommonly decent neighborhood restaurant with an Italian kitchen. There is nothing fancy about the place, but the food is prepared with care and caution and it is reasonably priced. The tomato sauces are not distinguished, but they are palatable; the osso buco is very good and so is the mixed fried seafood. The vegetables are excellent. All dishes are à la carte, with main courses at midday from about $1.50 for spaghetti marinara to $3.50 for veal magenta. In the evening, prices range from $1.75 for spaghetti to $6.50 for filet mignon. *Cocktails, wines. Closed Sunday and major holidays.*

★ ANTOLOTTI'S
337 East 49th Street   MU 8-9668 and 688-6767

A favorite and therefore frequently crowded North Italian restaurant. The menu is somewhat conventional, with its veal and pasta dishes, but all in all the foods are prepared with a good deal of finesse. The service, too, is above average. Luncheons are à la carte. Main luncheon dishes with spaghetti or salad from about $2.25 to $6.00. Dinners are both prix fixe and à la carte. Complete dinners from about $7.00 to $10.00; à la carte dishes from about $4.00 to $9.00. *Cocktails, wines. Luncheon is not served on Saturday and Sunday. Closed Christmas, New Year's Day, and Easter.*

★★★ APERITIVO
29 West 56th Street   765-5155

It is the rarest of happenings to find a restaurant in New York with considerably more than routine appeal. It's called Aperitivo, and if it doesn't have the best Italian kitchen in town, it is certainly a contender for the title.

The most impressive dish has been an excellent first course, fettuccine Alfredo. It is called that, although the dish is an original here with its blend of white and green noodles plus small tortellini tossed together with fresh cream and cheese.

But all the dishes have come off well: the small scampi in butter sauce; the tender stuffed clams; a delicious dish of gnocchi with pesto sauce; a piccatina of veal; beef pizzaiola; kidneys sautéed with mushrooms; and the oddest thing to find in an Italian restaurant, Key lime pie, perhaps the best in town.

And now to the inevitable carping. The fettuccine is splendid, but just the least bit overcooked; the lime pie is served coffee-counter style directly from the aluminum baking dishes in which the crust was made.

The décor of Aperitivo is pleasant and predictable enough, with its hanging wine bottles, obvious art, and so on, and there is piped-in music. It is a relatively small restaurant, only 25 tables. Reservations are recommended.

All dishes are à la carte, with main courses at noon from about $3.50 to $6.50; in the evening from about $4.25 to

$6.75. *Cocktails, wines. Luncheon is not served Saturday. Closed Sunday.*
BA

★★ ARARAT
4 East 36th Street   686-4622

Some of the most interesting restaurants in Manhattan are those with Middle Eastern kitchens. The owner may be Greek, Turkish, Armenian, or Syrian, but the foods are quite similar. Appetizers include stuffed vine leaves, cheese-filled strudel-like pastries, imported olives, puréed chick-peas, and puréed eggplant with sesame paste. Lamb is the basis for most of the main courses, which may include braised shanks, roast shoulder, and eggplant or other vegetables stuffed with lamb.

Probably the handsomest of the lot is Ararat. It has genuine cloth banquettes crowned with gold, a soft carpet, and hand-carved wood screens. One of the walls is hung with pleasant water-colors, and the background music is along the lines of a Chopin étude or a Dvořák symphony.

The food is good. The appetizers are prepared with care and the moussaka, or baked ground lamb with eggplant topped with an egg custard, has merit. The harpoot kufta, or ground lamb balls with pine nuts and meat filling, is interesting, if bland. Among the desserts, that ekmek kadayif (Armenian bread soaked in honey and crowned with concentrated cream) is indecently delicious. The service staff is limited and the service might be painfully slow if there is a sudden surge of business.

Complete luncheons are priced from about $3.25 to $4.25. Complete dinners cost from about $5.50 to $7.75. *Cocktails, wines. Open 7 days a week. Luncheon is not served Saturday and Sunday.*
AE   CB   DC   MC

★★ ARIGATO
142 East 53rd Street   752-5842

Some of the most interesting restaurants in New

York are the Japanese steak houses. Arigato is, in the main, a place of great appeal.

It is a large, rather stylish restaurant with the standard Japanese steak house accouterments, including the wide, rectangular tables centered with thick metal slabs that are fired from below and on which the food is cooked. All the tables are shared, so, unless you have a party of eight or 10, you will not dine privately.

There is an individual chef, a young Japanese neatly decked out in a chef's high bonnet, to cook at each table, and the bill of fare includes steak, shrimp, and chicken, each entrée or appetizer cut into bite-size pieces and cooked quickly in the center of the table. The food is excellent.

Accompanying dishes may include an oriental-style onion soup, sautéed bean sprouts with Chinese cabbage, mushrooms and onions. And most of the dishes are sprinkled with sesame seeds, which give a nutty goodness. There are two sauces, one ginger-flavored, the other sesame-flavored, for dipping. Note well that the Arigato has two faults. The ventilation is not perfect, but it is pardonable. And the piped-in-music is offensively loud.

A la carte dishes at midday are priced from about $2.95 to $3.95; complete luncheons cost $4.90. A la carte dishes in the evening cost from about $4.25 to $6.75, with complete dinners priced at $10.00. *Cocktails, wines. Closed Sunday; open only for dinner on Saturday and holidays. All major credit cards.*

★★ ARIRANG HOUSE
30 West 56th Street   LT *1-9698 and* LT *1-9699*

This is one of the most unusual and interesting restaurants in Manhattan. The food is Korean, well-seasoned and a welcome change from that found in run-of-the-mill French and Italian restaurants in the city. There is a large, split-level dining room, and the waitresses wear traditional dresses without ostentation. The menu has nu-

merous fish, poultry, pork, and beef dishes, the best known of which must be the sin sullo, in which various foods are simmered in a broth cooked over charcoal at the table. The main menu is principally à la carte, with entrées from $2.25 to $3.75. There is also a luncheon menu with complete luncheons at $2.50 and à la carte dishes from $1.50 to $2.00. Complete dinners cost from $6.50 to $7.00. *Cocktails, wines. Closed Sunday.*
AE CB DC MC

★ ARTIST AND WRITERS RESTAURANT
213 West 40th Street   LO 3-2424

This restaurant, with a comfortable, old-fashioned décor, is a favorite haunt of numerous people in the newspaper field. To many of them, the restaurant is known affectionately as Bleeck's, after the original owner, Jack Bleeck, now deceased. The same menu serves for both lunch and dinner, with main entrées from about $3.10 to $7.75. Supper is served from 10:00 P.M. to 1:00 A.M. *Cocktails, wines, draft beer. Closed Saturday, Sunday, and major holidays.*
AE CB DC UC

★★ ASSEMBLY STEAK HOUSE
207 East 43rd Street   MU 2-4120

In an area famous for its steak houses, the Assembly ranks with the best for top-quality beef and lobster generally well prepared. A relatively small and popular restaurant, it tends to be noisy at peak periods. Complete luncheons from $3.95 to $4.50; à la carte entrées from $3.45. Dinner entrées from $5.50 for swordfish to $18.50 for sirloin steak or chateaubriand for two. *Cocktails, wines. Luncheon is not served Saturday, Sunday, or holidays. Reservations are suggested.*
AE CB DC MC

ASTI
13 East 12th Street   AL 5-9773

Tourists and a host of New Yorkers seem fascinated with this opera-participation restaurant where guests join the waiters in renditions from Puccini, Verdi, and others. The menu is, of course, Italian, and the cost of a complete dinner is from about $7.75 to $9.95. Luncheon is not served. There is an entertainment tax after 7:30 P.M. *Cocktails, wines. Closed Monday and July 1 through Labor Day. AE CB DC*

★ ATHENIAN RESTAURANT, THE
709 Eighth Avenue (between 44th and 45th Streets)
581-1667 and 245-9966

This is one of several restaurants with Greek cuisine in the Broadway area. The food is moderately priced and well prepared. The à la carte lunch is from $1.75 to $6.90 for steak. The dinner menu is also à la carte, from $2.75 to $6.95. *Cocktails, wines. Open 7 days a week. AE DC MC*

★ AU CANARI D'OR
134 East 61st Street   TE 8-7987

The character of this place changes. Sometimes it seems like a tearoom for hungry shoppers; at other times it seems quite respectable. The trouble may be an exceedingly limited service staff, with only two or three people to get the food to tables on time. A recent crêpe Canari filled with chicken was good and well-gratinéed, and a serving of mussels maison was excellent. Then the food varies from an ordinary chicken Marengo to a generous portion of well-seasoned cold salmon with an admirable sour cream and cucumber sauce and green mayonnaise. There are both prix fixe and à la carte menus. At midday, à la carte items are priced from about $2.50 to $3.25; complete luncheons from about $3.75 to $5.00. In the evening, à la carte dishes are from about $4.50 to $7.50; complete dinners from about $5.25 to $8.50. *Cocktails, wines. Closed Sunday, Monday, and major holidays.*

★ AU STEAK POMMES FRITES
22 West 56th Street   CO 5-8743

This is a conventional and popular bistro with a reasonably priced menu. The luncheon menu is French and Italian, the dinner menu primarily French. The food is generally good and very much like that in a dozen other restaurants of the same genre. There are complete luncheons from about $2.00 & $2.25; complete dinners from about $3.00 to $4.75. *Cocktails, wines. Closed major holidays and 2 weeks in summer.*

AUTOPUB
767 Fifth Avenue (at 59th Street)   355-4900

This place on the beneath-the-street level of the General Motors Building must have cost a fortune. Every inch of it smacks of an expensive drawing board, from the long bar with its authentic, full-scale antique and racing cars (one of them upside down on the ceiling), to the small dining area where antique movies are shown (you watch as you dine).

It is a large restaurant with multiple dining areas; it is an overwhelming success; and it is a vast monument to all those New Yorkers who would rather be amused by their surroundings than care about dining respectably. It is an amusing place, but the whimsy doesn't soar: It is an expensive grounded kite on a windless day.

As to the food, it is best to speak first of what came off well. A thick slab of rare roast beef, tender and buttery to the taste. Impressively good hot baked potatoes with sour cream. The fresh whole loaves of bread on each table. The chopped chicken liver appetizer. The pecan pie with whipped cream. A dish of chicken was freshly broiled, but with small distinction.

And, on the other side of the coin, a most ordinary

pasty beef stew served in a bowl with noodles at room temperature; an embarrassingly indifferent brochette of scallops and shrimp served on lukewarm rice with unbuttered frozen peas that were cold. And a pervasive odor of garlic powder. An iceberg lettuce salad with a bland, blue-cheese salad dressing that was watery. A cup of vapid vichyssoise that tasted commercially made. The barbecued spareribs were not bad, though they smacked of liquid or other artificial "smoke."

The Autopub has uncommonly handsome waitresses. The waiters and busboys are decked out in garage mechanic outfits, which may be some grim commentary on some aspects of the service.

All dishes are à la carte, with main courses at midday from about $1.95 to $4.95; in the evening, about $3.95 to $6.95. *Cocktails, wines. Open 7 days a week. All major credit cards.*

★★ AU TUNNEL (formerly PIERRE AU TUNNEL)
306 West 48th Street   CO 5-9039

This is another of New York's small, unpretentious French restaurants near the theater district. It is well worth a visit whether or not you are Broadway bound, because the kitchen is generally excellent and the menu is most engagingly priced. The luncheon menu is à la carte, with main courses from about $2.30 to $5.75. The dinner menu is table d'hôte, with complete meals from about $5.00 to $6.75. There is an à la carte supper after 10:00 P.M. *Cocktails, wines. Closed Sunday and major holidays.*

★ BALKAN ARMENIAN RESTAURANT
129 East 27th Street   MU 9-7925

The best bargains among New York restaurants are those that specialize in Middle Eastern cooking. The Balkan Armenian is typical, for here one can dine on well-cooked food for less than $2. It is a relatively small, popular restaurant, and at noon there is an occasional wait for a table.

There are numerous appetizers, including excellent stuffed vine leaves and cheese pastry; delicious cold baked eggplant with tomatoes; and some ordinary stuffed mussel and white bean salad. Most of the main dishes are lamb—baked, broiled, or on skewers—but there is also roast chicken. The restaurant has the usual very sweet desserts. Main courses at midday are priced from about $2.25 to $3.75; in the evening from about $2.75 to $4.75. Seven-course dinners from $5.25 to $7.50. *Cocktails, wines. Open for dinner only on Saturday. Closed Sunday and for a summer vacation.*
AE DC MC

★★ BALLATO RESTAURANT
55 East Houston Street CA 6-9683

This is one of the best of Manhattan's small Italian restaurants. It is neat, the kitchen is above average, and the pasta dishes and tomato sauces are excellent. The same à la carte menu serves all day, with main dishes from about $2.75 to $7.25. *Beer, wines. Closed Sunday, New Year's Day, and Christmas. Reservations are recommended.*

★★ BARBETTA RESTAURANT
321 West 46th Street CI 6-9171

Barbetta, which has been in New York for several score years, may be the most elegantly decorated Italian restaurant in town. There are wall sconces, chairs with needlework upholstery, and discreetly illuminated table lamps. The food may not always ravish the palate, but it is worthwhile nonetheless, particularly the chicken, veal, and pasta dishes. The tortellini alla panna, or small meat-stuffed pasta, is good, but would be better served in a pure cream-and-cheese sauce rather than one slightly thickened with flour. Complete luncheons from about $4.50 to $7.50. Dinners are à la carte, with main courses from about $5.00

to $8.75. *Cocktails, wines. Closed Sunday, major holidays, and for a short vacation in summer.*

★★★ BAROQUE
14 East 53rd Street   EL 5-4195

When a restaurant holds claim to a luxury status, there are subtle things that are disappointing in foods—a sauce just a bit too thickened, a soup a bit too salty—and the food at the Baroque has not been, by and large, wholly up to expectations. Perhaps there has been a lapse in quality of the service—a case of mistaken orders and waiters who sport their service napkins under their armpits. The Baroque's tables are close together, but it remains one of the better New York restaurants. Luncheon entrées from about $4.00 to $5.75; dinner entrées from about $5.00 to $8.50. *Cocktails, wines. Closed Sunday, major holidays, and for 3 weeks in late summer.*
AE CB DC MC

★ BEIRUT RESTAURANT
43 West 32nd Street   OX 5-9898

The food here, as in many another Middle Eastern restaurant is very good, particularly the appetizers. These would include the baba gannouj, or eggplant salad, hummus bi tahini, which is puréed chick-peas with sesame oil, and grape leaves. The restaurant's laban, or yogurt, is excellent. The lamb dishes are somewhat standard. The décor is a bit garish, and a noisy jukebox seems to be in constant use. There is a club luncheon, minus appetizer, that costs $1.95. Complete dinners are $4.25; à la carte dishes from about $1.50 to $3.00. *Cocktails, wines. Open 7 days a week.*
AE DC MC

★★ BENIHANA OF TOKYO EAST
120 East 56th Street   593-1627 and 593-1628

Like its counterpart, Benihana of Tokyo West, this

is an interesting Japanese steak house with very good food. The menu includes clear soup with scallions, salad, chicken, and steaks. The meats are cooked on a smooth, heavy, flatiron slab in the center of each dining table. At noon à la carte dishes at the Benihana cost from about $3.00 to $4.50; special luncheons cost $4.50. In the evening, the cost of a dinner without dessert is from $5.50 to $7.25. There is also a special dinner that costs $10. *Cocktails, wines. Luncheon served from Monday to Friday only. Closed Sunday. Reservations are recommended.*
AE   CB   DC   MC

★★ BENIHANA OF TOKYO WEST
61 West 56th Street   LT *1-0930 and* LT *1-0969*

This is a most agreeable Japanese steak house, perhaps the best of its kind in the city. The steak, vegetables, and whatever are cooked at the tables, in which are solid metal slabs heated from below. The food is excellent and its appeal seems universal, inasmuch as at meal hours there are frequent and lengthy waits for tables. Service is marked by the usual Japanese politesse. Luncheons are à la carte, with main courses from $3.00 to $4.50; special luncheons cost $4.50. There are dinners without desserts from $5.50 to $7.25. There is also a special dinner that costs $10. *Cocktails, wines. Open 7 days a week. Luncheon is not served on Sunday. Reservations are recommended.*
AE   CB   DC   MC

★★ BENIHANA PALACE
15 West 44th Street   *682-7120 and 682-7121*

This is the largest and most impressive of the Benihana restaurants in New York and, according to the menu, the "massive wood beams as well as the stonework which make up a large part of the Palace are authentic, once having been integral parts of an 18th-century Japanese Palace."

The Benihana Palace is excellent on many counts and its

principal fault lies (happily for the management) in its overriding popularity. Particularly at midday, tables are hard to get. But the food, in the Benihana tradition, is excellent—well-cooked, well-seasoned, and made with first-rate ingredients.

The system is the same in all the Benihana restaurants. Guests sit around three sides of large rectangular tables, and each table is equipped with a heavy metal slab in the center. A Japanese chef stands at one side of the table and cooks the food, which consists of chicken or steak among the main courses, shrimp as an appetizer. The foods are cut into bite-size or chopstick-size pieces, seasoned and served with two sauces. Vegetables—squash, sliced onion, bean sprouts—are then cooked on the same grill and served hot.

Tables are shared at all the Benihana restaurants, and it is no place for quiet, private conversation. *Cocktails. Open 5:30 p.m. to midnight Saturday, closed Sunday.*
AE CB DC MC

★ BERNSTEIN-ON-ESSEX-STREET
135 Essex Street (at Rivington Street)   GR 3-3900

Bernstein's slogan is "Where kashruth is king and quality reigns." This is conceivably the only Jewish-Chinese restaurant in the city. There is chow mein Bernstein and lo mein Bernstein, and the food is not bad at all. There is also an elaborate Jewish menu with such specialties as stuffed cabbage, Romanian pastrami, and chopped chicken liver sandwiches. Lunch and dinner à la carte entrées run from $2.50 to $7.00. The Chinese dishes cost from about $2.75 to $7.00. *Beers and kosher wines. Closed on Jewish holidays and from 3:00 p.m. Friday to Saturday after dark.*

★★ BILLY'S
948 First Avenue (near 52nd Street)   355-8920

The same antique paneling and sentimental trap-

pings of Billy's at Sutton Place are at the present location. Gaslight fixtures, red-checked tablecloths, and turn-of-the-century bar are all there. The present establishment seems smaller, cleaner, more polished, more civilized, lower ceilinged, less personal. It is a worthwhile restaurant and tables are at a premium. At times, people stand two deep at the bar waiting their turn. The kitchen, with two exceptions, seems to maintain its standards. The exceptions are the shrimp, which seem small, and the cole slaw, which doesn't seem quite as tasty. The steaks, chops, and chicken are excellent. Other than a $1.95 lunch special, all dishes are à la carte and the cost is from $3.50 for Billy's well-known large hamburger to $7.50 for sirloin. *Cocktails, beers. Open Monday through Saturday for lunch and dinner, on Sunday for dinner only.*
AE CB DC

★ BLACK ANGUS
148 East 50th Street   PL 9-7454

Count steaks and chops among the favorite fare of New Yorkers. Here they are served in a typical, if somewhat labyrinthine, setting. Luncheons are both prix fixe and à la carte. Complete luncheons cost approximately $3.45; main courses from about $2.95 up. Dinners are à la carte, with main dishes from about $6.95 to $8.45. *Cocktails, wines. Luncheon is not served Saturday and Sunday.*
AE BA CB DC MC

★★ BLOSSOM RESTAURANT
998 Second Avenue (between 52nd and 53rd Streets)
PL 8-2290

Like Smucker's, with a name like Blossom you've got to be good. And this Blossom is doing very well, thank you. It is a friendly, pleasant place with an interesting menu and a good kitchen, and dishes that range from Greek (the real specialties of the house) to toasted bagels with cream cheese and lox.

The food is of a sort commonly referred to as "home-style," which means it is basically tasty and good without show or elegance. For example, a well-varied special appetizer called Blossom's Special is served, and it includes taramosalata, or carp roe spread; baked cheese pastries made with filo pastry; Greek meat balls; and so on. There are a simple Greek salad with anchovies and feta cheese, and good moussaka, and pastitschio, which is made with macaroni and ground meat. The menu is extensive, including such dishes as whole broiled flounder and charcoal broiled items.

But, at best, it must be said that almost all the main dishes are insufficiently seasoned, including the too bland, hot stuffed grape leaves. The egg and lemon sauce for that is woefully without taste.

All dishes are à la carte, with main dishes at lunch from $1.75 to $4.90 and at dinner, $2.25 to $6.00. *Cocktails, wines. The restaurant is open 7 days a week for lunch, dinner, and supper.*

BLUE MILL TAVERN
50 Commerce Street CH *3-7114*

The commendable things about this Greenwich Village restaurant are the neighborhood, which is colorful; the service, which is generally good; and the modest prices of the food, which is undistinguished but palatable. The restaurant is neat and is near the Cherry Lane Theater. The menu is plain and à la carte, with main courses from $1.20 for an omelet to $5.25 for filet mignon. *Cocktails, wines. On Saturday the restaurant opens at 5 p.m. Closed Sunday, major holidays, and 2 or 3 weeks in August. Reservations are accepted.*

★ BLUE SEA
135 Third Avenue (near 15th Street) SP *7-2948*

There is a dearth of good seafood restaurants be-

tween midtown Manhattan and Fulton Street, and this may be the best in that area. A point strongly in its favor is that the fish seems to be of the freshest quality. The whole flounder stuffed with crab meat is cordially recommended. On the other hand, the restaurant is overly bright and overdecorated. There are special luncheons from about $2.75 to $5.00. The à la carte menu lists dishes from about $3.95 to $7.95 for lobster. *Cocktails, wines. Only à la carte items are available on Sunday, from 11 a.m.*
AE   BA   CB   DC

BLUM'S
121 East 59th Street   755-3800

Blum's of San Francisco—in San Francisco—has always been a fairly decent place for a snack. The New York version is another matter. It is basically a sandwich and salad place with a sterile, nondescript décor that strives in a minimal way to look what is spoken of as San Franciscan.

One has several bones to pick with the local establishment, but chief among them is the crab. If they are going to list Dungeness crab—one of the glories of California—it should be fresh or in a good state of preservation. Here it seems to have been frozen (or worse, canned or pasteurized) and it is all the worse for wear—slightly mangled, too briny, and afflicted with a used texture. A dish of broiled halibut was dreadfully overcooked and dry.

There is an à la carte menu with main courses from about $1.10 for an American cheese sandwich to $3.95 for crab Louie. Complete luncheons are priced from about $1.95 to $3.50; complete dinners from about $3.25 to $5.95. *Cocktails, wines. Open 7 days a week.*
BA   MC

★★ BO BO
20½ Pell Street   WO 2-9458

The trouble with Bo Bo's, which has food made

with a fine Chinese hand, is its extreme popularity. It is a small place, notably not elegant, and at times it is next to impossible to obtain a table. However, the fare is worth waiting for. There is no written menu, and the cost of main dishes at both lunch and dinner is about $2.50 up; complete dinners are $6.50. *No alcoholic beverages, but wine or beer may be brought in. Closed for the Chinese New Year.*

★★ BRASERO
627 Second Avenue (at 34th Street)   685-8192

This is a highly agreeable Mexican restaurant with only 12 tables. It is a small enterprise run by an engaging, polite group of young men, and the dishes—more fun food than authentic Mexican—are basic and quite tasty.

There is guacamole among the appetizers (a bit too bland, we thought) and hot nachos, which are tostadas topped with ground beef, raw onions, and cheese. The combination plate includes three of a choice of taco, enchilada, burrito tamale, or empanada, and the seasonings are competently applied.

You do get the same meat filling in various dishes and the chili sauces taste the same, but there is, nonetheless, a sufficient variety of flavors. The chili sauce on each table has a commercial chili sauce base—such as Heinz—with bits of tomato and additional hot chili spices, but it is good and peppery.

The chili rellenos or stuffed chilies, one filled with the ground meat, the other with cheese, are relatively well-made and served hot. The portions are more than ample.

All dishes are à la carte, with main courses from about 85 cents to $2.95. There is a bar, but hard spirits are not presently served. Beers, both imported and domestic, are available. Guests may also dine at the bar. *The restaurant is open from 11:00 a.m. to 11:00 p.m., Monday through Saturday; 5:00 p.m. to 11:00 p.m., Sunday.*

★★ BRASSERIE
100 East 53rd Street   PL *1-4840 and* PL *1-4841*

One of New York's plainest, yet most sophisticated restaurants, the Brasserie also has one of the most interesting menus. It is international in scope, and the choucroute garnie may be the best in town. Luncheon and dinner are both prix fixe and à la carte. Complete luncheons from $3.50; complete dinners from $5.95. The Brasserie is open for sandwiches, omelets, and the like around the clock, and is frequently crowded. *Imported beers; wines by the carafe, cocktails. Reservations are accepted for dinner.*
AE   BA   CB   DC   MC

BRASS RAIL, THE
521 Fifth Avenue (at 43rd Street)   MU *7-5880*
745 Seventh Avenue (at 49th Street)   PL *7-6070*

The menu of the Fifth Avenue Brass Rail is somewhat conventional, with such dishes as spaghetti and potted meat balls, steak sandwiches, and grilled meats. The menu is both prix fixe and à la carte, with a complete dinner from $3.95; à la carte entrées from about $3.95. The Seventh Avenue Brass Rail bills its menu as "Steak House." A la carte prices go from $3.95 to $6.99, with a complete dinner for $3.95. *Cocktails, wines. Fifth Avenue is closed Sunday. Seventh Avenue is open 7 days a week.*
AE   CB   DC

★★ BRAZILIAN COFFEE RESTAURANT
45 West 46th Street   PL *7-9352*

For anyone with an interest in foreign foods, this is an uncommonly rewarding restaurant. It is a simple place, but the food is on a par with that of the best native restaurants in Rio de Janeiro. Feijoada, the national dish of Brazil, is available Wednesday and Saturday. The dish is a fascinating mélange of meats and sausage cooked with beans and served with rice, greens, and fresh orange sections. Other specialities include shrimp Bahia style with tomatoes and onions, and picadinho, the traditional savory stew served with fried eggs, rice, and beans. The same menu serves throughout the day and it is à la carte. The cost of main dishes is about $2.00 to $4.25. *Beers, wines. Closed Sunday and Christmas.*

★★ BREW'S
156 East 34th Street   684-9453

Whoever contrived Brew's restaurant zeroed in with notable accuracy on the taste of a large segment of the New York public. It is a sprawling, chummy, crowded restaurant with layers of atmosphere from the sawdust on the floor to the Tiffany lamps (what else?) that hang from the ceiling. It is all of a piece—dim lights, checked tablecloths, and noise—and not unpleasant at that.

In such a climate, the food seems almost incidental. Nevertheless, it comes off very well from freshly made vegetable soup or herring in sour cream to beef in Burgundy sauce and broiled scampi. The scampi, served on a still sizzling platter, are tender and good, although they should be served with lemon wedges. The rest of the menu is predictable—London broil, omelets, lobster tails, and so on.

All dishes are à la carte, with main courses at midday from about $1.95 to $5.50; in the evening from about $2.95 to $5.50. *Cocktails, wines. Open from 11:30 a.m. to 1:00 a.m.* After theater, supper starts at 11:00, but Brew's still serves a complete dinner until closing time. *Closed Sunday. All major credit cards.*

★ BRITTANY DU SOIR
800 Ninth Avenue (at 53rd Street)   CO 5-4820

This restaurant is bistro style and has very good French food at modest prices. All dishes are à la carte, with main luncheon courses from about $2.25 to $5.00; dinner entrées from about $3.25 to $6.50. *Cocktails, wines. Closed Sunday, major holidays, and all of August.*

★★ BROADWAY JOE STEAK HOUSE
315 West 46th Street   CI *6-6513 and* CO *5-9196*

Some of the best-known restaurants in the theater district are packed to capacity before the show, only to become mausoleums five minutes before curtain time. This isn't true of Broadway Joe. It is crowded after the overture for a very good reason: It is one of the best steak houses in Manhattan. It is a congenial, unpretentious place with wood-paneled and whitewashed walls, and the service is friendly. More important, however, the sirloin steaks are first-rate and cooked to perfection. The restaurant opens at 4:30 P.M. until midnight, and there is no menu. In addition to the steak, there is a choice of three grilled entrées—chicken, lamb chops, or chopped sirloin—served with baked potato and salad. The cost is from $4.50 to $8.50. First courses include shrimp cocktail ($3.00), marinated herring ($1.25), onion soup ($1.25), or pâté ($1.25). The large shrimp taste overcooked and bland, and the garlic in the salad dressing seems more like powdered, day-old garlic rather than freshly chopped. *Cocktails, wines. Closed Sunday and major holidays.*

★★ BROCHETTERIA
222 East 86th Street   TR *9-9240*
829 Third Avenue (between 50th and 51st Streets)
751-3750

When the first Brochetteria opened on 86th Street, it was noted that it was one of the most unusual and fascinating to open in the city in several years. The interest is still there.

The specialties are various foods on skewers, including shish kebab, beef tenderloin with mushroom, chicken liver with bacon, and the Brochetteria special, consisting of admirably seasoned meat and bacon rolls.

The foods are cooked to order over an open grill, and two things are of special interest here. The quality of the meats is good and the seasonings (each skewered assortment has been dipped in a different marinade) are subtle and skillfully blended.

It must be said that when the Third Avenue Brochetteria has been visited, it has been in the evening and under near-ideal conditions. The restaurant wasn't crowded, the food was cooked at leisure and served promptly.

This branch seems an improvement over the earlier branch, because in the original, far smaller establishment, it was necessary to share a table on occasion with strangers.

On the other hand, there is piped-in music, mostly rock, and it is loud. Among the appetizers, the Brochetteria has a very good head cheese that is best if doused with oil and vinegar and the chopped onions that accompany it. And all tables are served with an excellent large, Stygian-black loaf of bread.

All courses are à la carte, with main courses from about $1.50 for skewered lamb kidneys to $2.95 for the beef tenderloin. *Cocktails, wines. Open 7 days a week.*

★★ BROWNSTONE, THE
55 East 54th Street   421-8070

The Brownstone is a burger and sandwich restaurant with a modest menu. There are two floors decorated with neat wood paneling of Swedish aspect; it looks, in other words, like the inside of a sauna. A good hamburger, as we have often noted, is not too frequent in New York, and those at the Brownstone are good. They range from a plain hamburger on a bun (95 cents) to hamburger Stroganoff ($2.00), described as "continental saucery with buttered egg noodles, and tossed salad."

There are both counter service and table service and the former has been painfully slow for this kind of establishment. The Brownstone also has a breakfast menu and dinner service is in the planning stage. *There is no bar. Closed Saturday, Sunday, and major holidays.*

★★ BRUSSELS RESTAURANT
115 East 54th Street   PL 8-0457

In its day, the Brussels has been one of the city's most laudable restaurants. The atmosphere is still distinguished and the cuisine can be exceptionally good. The kitchen can serve ordinary dishes, however, including tough aspic on smoked trout and a mediocre preparation of sweetbreads financière, and the portions served are frequently excessive for good taste. The Brussels boasts a fine wine list and Victor, one of the city's finest wine stewards. All dishes are à la carte, with main luncheon entrées from $4.00 to $5.00; main dinner dishes from $6.00 to $8.50. *Cocktails, wines. Closed Saturday, Sunday, and almost the full month of July.*

★ BUDAPEST HUNGARIAN RESTAURANT
1481 Second Avenue (at 77th Street)   UN 1-3600

There are several small ethnic restaurants in New York offering the public excellent food that is frequently referred to as "home-style." The Budapest is one of them. The service is friendly and the portions are generous and relatively inexpensive. The specialties of the house are, of course, goulash and paprika dishes. When available, the dishes made with kolbas, or Hungarian sausage, are excellent. There are complete luncheons Monday through Friday for $2.25. Complete dinners are $4.15 to $6.00; à la carte entrées from $3.65 to $5.00. *Cocktails, wines. Dinner is served 7 days a week.*

★★ CABANA CARIOCA
123 West 45th Street   582-8510

Many of New York's most interesting restaurants—and they seem to increase at a happy pace—are those with a foreign accent. They are generally small, inexpensive, and without pretense. One of the best is the Cabaña Carioca where the food is Brazilian, authentic and good.

Here you can find an excellent pot of feijoada, the

Brazilian national dish of peasant origin made with beans, fresh and dried meats and served with fresh oranges as a garnish. The restaurant also has picadinho, a spiced ground meat specialty; salt cod dishes; and so on.

The food has an authentic flavor, and there are a number of intriguing side dishes, including manioc flour, creamed mandioca, and excellent fried potatoes. There are different Brazilian specialties on the menu each day.

All dishes are à la carte. Main dishes are priced from about $1.75 to $3.50. *Wines and beers. Closed Monday. All major credit cards.*

★ CA D'ORO
59 West 56th Street   CO 5-8518 *and* CO 5-8519

The menu at the Ca d'Oro shows more imagination than that of many of its counterparts. It lists at times an excellent frittura mista, or "mixed fry," of shrimp and squid; risotto with shrimp; pot roast with polenta; and cod in wine sauce. During the warm weather, open-air dining can be enjoyed on a sidewalk terrace. There is an à la carte menu, complete lunches are about $3.00 to $4.75, and complete dinners from $4.75 to $8.50. *Cocktails, wines. Closed Sunday, New Year's Day, Christmas, Thanksgiving, and in July.*
AE BT DC MC

★★ CAFE ARGENTEUIL
253 East 52nd Street (at Second Avenue)   PL 3-9273 *and 355-8542*

This is a French restaurant with a good deal of physical charm. If the Argenteuil maintained the excellence it sometimes achieves, it would be one of the prizes of the city. Unfortunately, the kitchen wavers at times, and the service is occasionally slipshod and slow. It is a favorite restaurant of publishing circles. There are complete luncheons from about $4.95 to $7.50. Dinners are à la carte, with main courses from about $5.95 to $8.95.

Cocktails, wines. Luncheon is not served Saturday. Closed Sunday.
All major credit cards.

★★ CAFE BRITTANY
807 Ninth Avenue (at 53rd Street)   CI 7-9566

There is an authentic French bistro-style atmosphere about the Café Brittany, and the restaurant's popularity is well-deserved. The food is plain, but excellent, whether it be an appetizer or main course. For those who fancy such, the tripe is first-rate. A la carte luncheon dishes from about $2.00 to $5.00; à la carte dinner entrées from about $3.50 to $6.00 for filet mignon. *Cocktails, wines. Luncheon is not served Saturday and Sunday. Closed major holidays.*

★★ CAFE DE FRANCE
330 West 46th Street   CO 5-8927

The Café de France is one of several relatively small, inexpensive French restaurants on New York's West Side, generally crowded—particularly at midday—with a knowledgeable clientele that enjoys bourgeois cooking. The service, mostly by French-speaking waitresses, is offhand and friendly. The food is substantially good, but there is more stress on the flavor of the sauces than on the prime quality of the kitchen's raw materials. Lunch is à la carte, with prices from $2.50 to $3.50. Dinner is table d'hôte from $5.50 to $7.00. *Cocktails, wines. Closed Sunday.*

★ CAFE DU SOIR
322 East 86th Street   289-9996

This pleasantly decorated bistro is on a street that is known but certainly not celebrated for its heavy-handed, psuedo-German cooking. By comparison with those pork-hocks-mit-sauerkraut establishments, the Café du Soir is a joy. It has dim lighting, tables with white napery, and the usual murals of French country life. The menu is predictable and the kitchen comes off creditably.

The offerings include trout amandine, fillet of sole meunière, coq au vin, and boeuf bourguignon, all the well-known standbys. There is a very good creation, a sauté of shrimp maison.

Among the regrettable things, however, list the butter that has had a refrigerator taste, the not-freshly-made-and-old-garlic-taste of the salad dressing, and the American-style coffee.

There are complete luncheons at the Café du Soir priced from about $3.50 to $5.50; à la carte dishes from about $2.50 to $4.50. Complete dinners priced from about $5.50 to $8.75; à la carte items from about $4.05 to $7.00. *Cocktails, wines. Closed Monday.*
AE DC

★ CAFE EUROPA
220 East 53rd Street   PL 5-0160

This restaurant, formerly known as Peter's Café Europa, has sleek décor and a garden open in summer. It is physically appealing with its iron grillwork and small, compartmented rooms hung with art. Some of the dishes are good, including the quiche Lorraine and mussels matinière, both of which appear frequently on the menu. The soups are generally excellent, and the duck à l'orange sampled on one occasion was creditable. The sauce for a carbonnade of beef, on the other hand, tasted pasty with flour, and the bananas au rhum were bitter and in a sauce slightly curdled. One four-course menu with a three-choice entrée serves throughout each week and the cost is $7.00 or $8.00. Pre- and after-theater suppers have entrées from $2.75 to $3.50. *Cocktails, wines. Open for dinner only. Closed Sunday.*
AE CB DC MC

★★ CAFE NICHOLSON
323 East 58th Street   EL 5-6769

This is one of New York's most fascinating restaurants. The atmosphere is rather Alice in Wonderland with such far-out furnishings as giant marble slabs in the center of the main dining room, a ceramic stove, a china dog, a Tiffany lamp, an antique clock, potted palms, ceiling fans, and decorative tiles wall to wall. With one extraordinary exception, the food is merely interesting. The meats are of first-class quality, but the lamb chops, for example, are served with an odd but edible orange marmalade sauce; the steak with a flour-based béarnaise, a sauce that the French call bâtarde. The exception is a formidably good chocolate soufflé (really a pudding) served with a chocolate sauce and whipped cream. Dining at Nicholson's is almost a theatrical entertainment, and the cost of such a four-course diversion, including a bottle of very good Spanish wine, is $16.00. The tip is included in the bill.
Cocktails, wines. The restaurant is open evenings only. Closed Sunday, major holidays, and the last 2 weeks in August.
AE CB DC

★ CAFE RENAISSANCE
338 East 49th Street   PL 1-3160

This restaurant, heavy with plush and rococo atmosphere, emphasizes Spanish and Italian food. Paella, served Monday or on request, is a specialty. Luncheons are à la carte with entrées from about $.75 to $4.50; à la carte dinner entrées from about $4.95 to $6.95. *Cocktails, wines. Luncheon is not served Saturday. Closed Sunday and major holidays. Dinner reservations are recommended.*

★ CAMELOT
1265 Third Avenue (at 73rd Street)   249-1850

This is a pseudo-elegant place that should rank high on the list of places to take out-of-towners whose visions of Manhattan's sugarplums include the Rockettes and the Roseland ballroom. The mock-opulent décor is wildly stated with tall ceilings; sprawling chandeliers; plush napery; red streamers draped as if for a jousting match; leaded, stained glass windows; and in one corner a plastic knight in armor. The works.

The waitresses come to the table and announce, "I am your waitress among others. My name is Bridgitte," or some such and before you know it Bridgitte has a salad bowl embedded in ice and spinning like a roulette wheel next to your elbow. "This is our Camelot spinning salad," she says, and you expect her to add, "Whee," as she goes about spinning and sprinkling the greens with a pink salad dressing. "There are 17 ingredients in this dressing," she says, and you can believe it once you taste it.

The menu (on rolled parchment, of course) offers only prime ribs of beef among main courses. There are no appetizers. There are a thin sliced English cut that costs $6.50; a larger Camelot cut that costs the same; and a two-inch King Arthur cut that costs $7.50. The meat itself is exceptional in quality.

The desserts are à la carte at 95 cents and a special Irish coffee is $1.95. Monday through Friday there is a buffet lunch for $2.95. Sunday brunch is $3.95. *Cocktails, wines, and tap beer. Open 7 days a week.*
AE CB DC

★ CANTON RESTAURANT
6 Mott Street   BE *3-9512*

This is one of the seemingly endless roster of small but commendable restaurants in Chinatown. The dishes on the luncheon menu are commonplace, but the à la carte menu has several admirably prepared dishes, including the steamed fish with ginger and scallions and the lo mein, or soft-noodle, dishes. There are complete luncheons from about $1.25 for chow mein to $4.50 for lobster Cantonese; à la carte dishes from about $1.25 to $4.95. *There is no bar, but beer and wine may be brought in. Only à la carte items are available Saturday and Sunday. Closed Monday.*

★★★ CANTON VILLAGE
163 West 49th Street CI 7-2076

At first glance, this restaurant is not notably different from a dozen other Chinese restaurants in the city. The surroundings are neat but prosaic, the tables are close together, and many of the customers satisfy their appetites in the usual unimaginative manner with chow mein and chop suey. But, beneath the surface, or, rather, beyond the dining room, is one of the best Chinese kitchens in Manhattan.

There is a chef with tremendous skill and imagination who will prepare exceptional crab dishes when they are in season, specially spiced chicken dishes, or any creation the guests might propose. Even the bean sprouts with pork or shrimp have a crispness that is unusual. The wor wonton—a complete meal of soup, dumplings, and various meats and seafood—is excellent.

Complete luncheons cost from about $1.40 to $4.00; complete dinners from about $2.25 to $5.00. A la carte dishes from about $2.00 for wonton to $6.50 for Chinese steak with oyster sauce. *Cocktails, wines. Open 7 days a week.*

★★ CAPE COD
1131 Lexington Avenue (near 79th Street) RE 4-9753

This is certainly not a great seafood house, but it is on a par with some of the fish eateries of far greater repute. The fish is fresh and, for the most part, cooked to order.

The Cape Cod is relatively small, with 15 or so tables, an iron grillwork room divider, and a couple of dusty artificial potted palms in the background.

The broth of the clam chowder tastes better than in most places, although the vegetables are, in the New York tradition, overcooked. There is a good combination platter with broiled half lobster, clams, sole, shrimp, scallops, and a tasty deviled crab, a specialty of the house.

The Cape Cod also offers grilled meat dishes, including a mixed grill with an interesting whole tomato baked in a thin pastry crust.

All dishes are à la carte with "special luncheons" priced from about $1.85 to $4.50; "special dinners" from about $3.45 to $7.50. The same meals with appetizer and dessert cost 90 cents more. A la carte dishes on the main menu are priced from about $3.25 to $6.95. *Cocktails, wines. Closed Saturday during July and August and major holidays.*
MC

★ CAPTAIN'S TABLE, THE
410 Avenue of the Americas (near 8th Street)
AL 4-6825

A pleasant enough fish and seafood restaurant in Greenwich Village. The bill of fare is run-of-the-mill, but the broiled fish dishes, in particular, can be good. There are complete luncheons from $1.95 to $4.00. The à la carte menu, available for both luncheon and dinner, lists entrées from about $3.50 to $9.00. *Cocktails, wines.*
AE DC

★★ CARMEN'S
750 Barclay Avenue   984-9786

This is a colorful, crude, and raffish restaurant on the southeast shore of Staten Island. The walls are hung with fringed Spanish shawls and painted gourds, and the owner, whose name the restaurant bears, hums along with the jukebox. Outside is the sound of the surf.

Meals begin with appetizers that include warm chickpeas, beet salad, and assorted greens. There is available a very good chilled gazpacho that is also crude. The finest dishes of the house are tacos that resemble empanaditas or turnovers. They are made with corn flour and fillings include lobster, shrimp, and crab meat.

The menu is both Mexican and Spanish at Carmen's, and the paella is a specialty of the house. There is nothing refined about Carmen's and the service at times is awful, but it is one of the best restaurants on Staten Island.

There are special dinners from about $4.95. A la carte dishes from about $3.95 and up. *Cocktails, wines. Closed on Tuesday. The restaurant opens at 1 p.m.*

★ CARNEGIE DELICATESSEN AND RESTAURANT
854 Seventh Avenue (near 55th Street) PL 7-2245

The Carnegie continues to be a favorite of the Broadway set, along with many others who appreciate man-sized sandwiches. One of the most popular, Max's special, is a three-decker combination of turkey, corned beef, and tongue, with cole slaw and Russian dressing, at $2.25. The menu is à la carte with sandwiches priced from about 95 cents; main entrées from about $1.95. *Beer. Open 7 days a week.*

★★★ CASA BRASIL
406 East 85th Street BU 8-5284

The intricate charm of New York, ever since the original sale of Manhattan, has involved a few surprises. Things range from the mammoth to the smallest smidgen. In the latter category is the Casa Brasil, a most agreeable restaurant. There is no written menu and the food includes such dishes as beef Wellington, roast duck, and roast veal. On Wednesday nights, there is feijoada, the national dish of Brazil, composed of black beans, roast pork, rice, sausage, tongue, orange sections, and a sprinkling of farinha de mandioca, a flour made from a tuberous South American plant. The cost of an extensive meal, first course to last, is $9.50. *There is no bar, but guests may bring their own wine. There are two dinner seatings, at 7:00 p.m. and at 9:30 p.m., and reservations are recommended. Closed Sunday.*

★ CASA DI PRE
89 Greenwich Avenue   CH 2-9255

This is a small, frequently crowded Italian restaurant in Greenwich Village. The menu is well-varied, the sauces are basic and good, and the cost of dining is relatively low. All dishes are à la carte, with main luncheon courses from about $1.70 (homemade lasagne) to $3.25 (combination seafood plate); main dinner entrées from about $3.75 (manicotti) to $5.00 (filet mignon). *Cocktails, wines. Closed Sunday.*

★★ CASA LAREDO
551 Hudson Street (at Perry Street)   989-8520

This place is a bit on the fey side, but it's fun. And it has Tex-Mex food—that highly seasoned and imaginative Texas version of Mexican cooking—of a very high order. The neat décor includes exposed brick, a whitewashed wall, a carefully hung sombrero, and what looks like a campy version of the ruins of the Alamo. The small tables are as close together as they could possibly be and not be contiguous.

The food is good and, for that genre of cuisine, inspired. The fried tortillas or tostadas are crisp enough almost to be melting; the tamallitos or "small" tamales are nicely textured and well-flavored from the meat filling to the tomato sauce on top, and so on through the meat- or cheese-filled chilies rellenos, the tacos with chili-flavored beef and bits of cheese, enchiladas, and refried beans. Happily, the chef does not compromise in his use of spices; the peppery chilies are as they should be.

The Mexi-flag enchiladas—in the colors of the Mexican ensign—are interesting: chicken enchiladas covered with green chili sauce, white sour cream sauce, and a red tomato and chili sauce. Among the desserts, the Osgood pie crowned with whipped cream tastes like a fruitcake baked in a pastry shell.

Most of the dishes at the Casa Laredo are à la carte, with main courses from about $1.00 for a bowl of chili to $3.95 for sirloin steak. Combination plates are priced from about $3.00 to $4.00. The margaritas seem to be made with bottled, rather than fresh, lime juice. *Cocktails, beers. The restaurant is open for dinner only Monday through Friday. It opens at 2:00 p.m. on Saturday and Sunday.*
AE DC MC

★★ CASA MARIO
136 West 55th Street   CI 6-6262

This is a notably agreeable restaurant. The dishes on the menu are prepared with care and the management pays attention to the detail in the dining room. The fettuccine Alfredo is excellent. There are complete luncheons from about $3.25 to $4.50. The dinner is à la carte, with entrées from about $3.00 to $7.00. *Cocktails, wines. Luncheon is not served Saturday. Closed Sunday and major holidays.*
AE CB DC

★★★ CASEY'S
142 West 10th Street   989-8925

There is something reminiscent of Paris's Left Bank in the décor and clientele of Casey's, a long-time favorite of the high-style residents of Greenwich Village. It is one of Manhattan's handsomest, most relaxed restaurants—happily "un-arty"—although it has distressed brick walls, modern art, potted plants, and antique iron chandeliers. The customers' garb has an unstudied, sophisticated nonchalance.

The many good things to say about Casey's kitchen almost make the restaurant's awkward things seem worthwhile. The good things include the coarse duck terrine, wildly scented on two occasions with fresh garlic (yum-yum); an unbelievably fresh fillet of red snapper, beautifully, simply broiled; a very good coquille of scallops with a soupçon too much tomato; and an extravagantly good dish of veal scallops with mushrooms in cream sauce with noodles.

The dinner menu is à la carte, with main dishes from about $4.75 for striped bass with butter sauce to $8.75 for sirloin steak with marchand de vin sauce. Lunch, also à la carte, ranges from $2.50 for moules marinière to $4.50 for minute steak. *Cocktails, wines. Open 7 days a week. Luncheon is not served Saturday and Sunday.*
AE DC

★ CASTALIA
712 Madison Avenue (near 63rd Street) 688-2440 and 688-5279

If this restaurant would settle down and concentrate on Greek cooking, it might turn out to be spectacular. The few Greek dishes sampled there have all had a good deal going for them—the crisp Greek salad with anchovies, cucumber, feta cheese, stuffed vine leaves, oil and vinegar; the traditional taramosalata or carp roe hors d'oeuvre; the exotheco, an interesting dish of lamb crowned with tomatoes, green pepper, and feta cheese, all baked in parchment; and the moussaka or ground lamb dish with a custardlike topping.

But whereas the restaurant is Greek-oriented, the menu is really a mixed bag, reminiscent of les Drug Stores of Paris, but not nearly so sophisticated. The kitchen will provide anything from a hamburger or chopped chicken liver to ravioli parmigiana or Southern-fried chicken and malted milk.

Regrettably, some of the cold dishes, such as the Greek salads, were on one occasion served on hot dinner plates. Lunch prices go from 80 cents for a grilled cheese sandwich to $3.00 for a fisherman's platter; very few Greek

dishes are listed. The dinner menu offers a wider sampling of Greek food: à la carte entées are $2.25 to $3.95. *Cocktails, wines. Closed Sunday, New Year's Day, Labor Day, and Christmas.*
AE DC MC

★ CASTILIAN, THE
303 East 56th Street   688-6435

This is another of those restaurants where it seems there may be more talent in the kitchen than is always evidenced in the dining room. If only, one feels, the broth for the caldo gallego had been a little richer, the shrimp in the mariscado and in the creole dish a little more tender, the gazpacho a bit less oily.

Neat as a new Spanish tile, with a pleasant décor, The Castilian is situated near Sutton Place. There are rough plaster walls, arches here and there, a long bar, and two dining areas. And it must be said that the menu is, in a relative sense, inexpensive. And the portions are generous.

All the dishes are à la carte and priced at noon from about $1.75 for arroz con pollo to $2.95 for lobster in green sauce. The same dishes in the evening are priced from $3.00 to $5.00. *Cocktails, wines. Open 7 days a week. The restaurant opens at 1 p.m. on Sunday.*
AE DC

CATTLE BARON, THE
221 West 46th Street   265-0480

This restaurant in the Times Square area has a choice of two prix fixe dinners for $6.95. One may have a boneless sirloin steak or roast prime ribs of beef with baked potato, salad, and dessert, with all drinks included in the price.

Open 7 days a week for lunch and dinner—dinner service starts at 4:30 p.m.
All major credit cards.

★★ CATTLEMAN EAST, THE
5 East 45th Street　　MO 1-1200

The average New Yorker is a pushover for showmanship, and, among the town's restaurants, it is nowhere better evidenced than at this many-roomed, gas-lit, and unabashedly contrived dining establishment. Customers flock here for such dishes as steaks, baked potatoes, and delicatessen sandwiches. The steaks and prime ribs of beef are excellent. The menu offers all à la carte dishes. The cost of main courses at midday is from about $1.95 for a sandwich to $8.25 for steak; in the evening from $5.25 to $9.95; at supper (11:00 P.M. to 2:00 A.M. except Sunday) from $4.50 for pot roast to $8.50 for steak. Brunch is served Sunday from 12:00 noon to 3:00 P.M., with entrées from $2.25. *Cocktails, wines.*
All major credit cards.

★★ CATTLEMAN WEST, THE
154 West 51st Street　　265-1737

The Cattleman—a branch of it, anyway—is on Broadway, and, in the opinion of some, that's where it belonged all along. Dining out is frequently a theatrical experience in more ways than one in Manhattan, and nowhere in the city is it more wildly evident than in this addition. And, for what it is—the décor, that is—it is posh and laudable, even more than in The Cattleman at 5 East 45th Street.

There are Victorian chairs, an antique pipe organ (the pipes at least), simulated gas lamps, beveled glass panes, even semiprivate parlors, and the whole thing done in shades of red and gold. But if you suffer from claustrophobia or demophobia, watch out. There is a network, a veritable maze of rooms, with tables close together.

The food isn't bad, and the roast rib of beef, in particular, was impressively good and properly rare. It takes more talent to make a good meat loaf than to grill a good steak, and a meat loaf at The Cattleman was of good texture and well-seasoned with coriander.

What is atrocious at The Cattleman is the table service. The table arrangements being what they are, it is scarcely surprising that waiters bump, not only into each other, but also into the customers.

The menu is à la carte, with main dishes at midday priced from about $2.35 to $7.75; in the evening, from about $4.25 to $7.75. There are special menus with "junior portions" for "junior outlaws" under 12. *Cocktails, wines, and excellent draft beer. Open 7 days a week, closed for lunch on Sunday.*

★★ CEDARS OF LEBANON
39 East 30th Street   MU 6-9634 and 679-6755

This is a Middle Eastern restaurant with a strictly utilitarian aspect. It should appeal to people with a taste for interesting lamb dishes, excellent appetizers flavored with sesame oil, and budget prices. The appetizers, such as the mashed chick-peas with sesame oil (50 cents) and a similar eggplant mixture (50 cents), are particularly outstanding. Main courses include a generally good shish kebab ($1.90) and kafta kebab, or chopped lamb on a skewer ($1.30). A complete luncheon (entrée, dessert, and coffee) costs $1.50; complete dinners, including a sampling of four appetizers from $2.95 to $3.25. A la carte dishes from about $1.30 to $2.20. *Cocktails, wines. Closed major holidays and Sunday in July and August.*
All major credit cards.

★ CEYLON INDIA INN
148 West 49th Street   CO 5-9822

This is reputedly the oldest Indian restaurant in the United States, and the atmosphere is exotic. The dishes are interesting, but the ventilation could be improved. At noon, the menu is à la carte, with entrées from about $2.95 to $4.50. There is a businessmen's lunch for $1.50 to $2.00 served Monday through Friday from 12:00 noon to

2:30 P.M. Luncheon is à la carte on weekends. There are complete dinners from $3.75 to $10.00. *Cocktails, wines.*
AE DC

★ CHALET SUISSE
6 East 48th Street   *355-0855*

This is conceivably the best of the Swiss restaurants in New York and it should be a good deal better than it is. There are some admirable dishes, including the Bündnerfleisch, a dried beef, thinly sliced, from the Grisons; the Swiss potatoes; the museau de boeuf, or oxsnout salad; and a veal à la Suisse, which is cooked in cream. But the veal Cordon Bleu was a disappointment: the cheese was not properly sealed in the thin slice of veal before cooking. However, the really regrettable thing about the Chalet Suisse is the ventilation. One of the restaurant's specialties is the fondue bourguignonne, in which meats are cooked in oil at the table, and, as a consequence, the smell of cooking fat permeates the dining room. One meal was accompanied, incidentally, by a very good and interesting bottle of Dole de Sion, one of the best and best-known Swiss wines. It travels very well. There are complete luncheons from about $4.75 to $5.00; complete dinners at $8.25, with à la carte dishes from about $4.25 for fondue Neuchâteloise to $9.00 for entricote. *Cocktails, wines. Luncheon is not served on Saturday. Closed Sunday, major holidays, and 3 weeks in August.*
AE CB DC

★ CHANDLER'S
49 East 49th Street   PL *1-1960*

A large, popular, and somewhat flashy restaurant that is best known for its steaks and generous portions. There are fish dishes, too, and such specialties as chicken in the pot and boiled beef in the pot. All dishes are à la carte, with main courses at midday from about $3.40 for a Western omelet to $9.25 for sirloin steak. In the eve-

ning, the prices range from about $5.75 for broiled chicken to $9.00 for filet mignon. *Cocktails, wines. On Saturday the restaurant opens at 4:00 p.m., on Sunday at 3:00 p.m.*
AE BA DC

★ CHARLES A LA POMME SOUFFLE
157 East 55th Street   EL 5-8280

This is a small and popular French restaurant where, on at least one occasion, one has seen members of the Kennedy family with young children in tow. There is no menu, but the names of the available dishes are recited by the maître d'hôtel or owner. They do not seem to change appreciably throughout the year. Among the appetizers, the batter-dipped and fried shrimp are good. The stuffed clams are too breaded and lacking in flavor. One order of roast lamb was generous, pink, and tender. A quiche was too salty, but the custard was delicate. There are, of course, souffléed, or puffed, potatoes. And canned peas. The cost of a complete luncheon is $4.50. Dinners cost from $8.00 to $8.50. *Cocktails, wines. Open 7 days a week. Luncheon is not served on Sunday. Closed New Year's Day, Thanksgiving, and Christmas.*
AE BA CB DC

★ CHARLES FRENCH RESTAURANT
452 Avenue of the Americas (between 10th and 11th Streets)   GR 7-3300

Charles is a long-established restaurant in the Greenwich Village area, one of the few with pretensions to a French and international cuisine, and there is always the feeling that the kitchen should be a good deal better than it is. The smoked salmon is served with a large and unsightly leaf of iceberg lettuce, and the cheese assortment is a disaster. A waiter explains that very few people here order cheese and there is small wonder. One of the specialties of the house is the boiled beef, which is ac-

ceptable. The flavor of the double lamb chop on one occasion was excellent, although it was accompanied by oil-soaked deep-fried potatoes. The décor of Charles is theatrical, but pleasant. Luncheons are à la carte, with main dishes from about $2.50 to $6.25. There are complete dinners for $9.25. A la carte items range from about $4.75 to $8.00. *Cocktails, wines. On Saturday and Sunday the restaurant opens at 4:00 p.m.*
AE BA CB DC

★★★ CHARLEY O'S BAR AND GRILL
Rockefeller Center, 33 West 48th Street   582-7141

This is one of the most joyous, colorful, and smartly contrived restaurants ever to open in New York. At noon, the restaurant has an elbow-to-elbow ambience, pretends to be an Irish saloon (which it isn't) and has the best shrimp on ice, herring in cream, corned beef sandwiches, and foaming, old, delicious draft beer. Charley O's is a largish restaurant with a long, handsome, and sturdy bar for beer and spirits and another equally sturdy bar where the sandwiches, including tartar steak, shrimp, and so forth, are dispensed. Guests help themselves to forks, knives, and napery. The food in the main dining room is less festive, but at its best it is excellent. There is such interesting fare as pigs' knuckles with a vinaigrette sauce, soused shrimp, and such main dishes (they vary every day) as boiled ham and cabbage, braised brisket of beef with egg barley, and roast ribs of beef with boxty pudding, made with potatoes. It must be noted that the pudding has been tough, but the roast beef has been first-rank. All dishes on the menu are à la carte, with main courses from about $3.75 to $8.25. The sandwiches at the bar cost from about $1.50. In addition to sandwiches at the bar, there are also soup and one main course each day. Supper is served from 11:00 P.M. to 1:00 A.M. Brunch, which runs from $3.95 to $7.25, is served on Sunday from noon to 4:00 P.M. *Cocktails, wines. Open 7 days a week. All major credit cards.*

★ CHARLIE BROWN'S
Main floor of Pan Am Building, 200 Park Avenue (at East 45th Street) MO 1-2520

An extremely popular and handsome place. At midday, there is almost always a line of people waiting for tables, and the noise level is high. The service is confused. Two waiters at times seem to share responsibility for a table, with one not knowing what the other is up to. Seafood dishes, chops, steaks, curries, and stews are predominant on the menu. The menus are à la carte, with main courses at midday from about $2.95 to $7.95. In the evening, main courses cost from about $4.50 to $8.25. *Cocktails, wines. Closed Sunday and major holidays. All major credit cards.*

★★ CHESHIRE CHEESE RESTAURANT
319 West 51st Street 765-0610

Of the spate of so-called English restaurants and pubs in New York, the Cheshire Cheese may well be the most impressive. It is an agreeable place on the West Side, fairly close to Broadway theaters, and both the food and service are above average. The menu is along the lines of steak and kidney pie, steak and mushroom pie, and sausages and chips. There are very good homemade soups. All dishes are à la carte, with main courses at noon from about $2.25 to $5.95; in the evening, from about $4.95 to $9.00. *Cocktails, wines. On Saturday, the restaurant opens at 5:00 p.m. Closed Sunday and Monday and July and August.*
AE

★★ CHEZ CARDINALE
347 West 46th Street CI 5-9732

This is a most agreeable restaurant in the Broadway area with a French and Italian menu. From the antipasto Italienne to the mousse au chocolat, the menu doesn't offer many surprises, but the food is well-prepared. There is a pre-theater dinner that has an appetizing assortment

of hors d'oeuvres, including shrimp with mayonnaise cocktail sauce, pâté maison, and eggs à la russe. The cost of the pre-theater dinner ranges from $4.25 to $6.95. Dinners are otherwise à la carte, with main dishes from $3.95 to $7.00. Complete luncheons are about $3.75, with à la carte entrées from $2.50 to $4.75. *Cocktails, wines. Closed Sunday.*
AE CB DC MC

★ CHEZ NAPOLEON
365 West 50th Street   CO 5-6980

This small French bistro might not be to the emperor's taste, but it is a pleasant place to dine before the theater. The lamb is particularly good; the boeuf bourguignon, made solidly of meat, is a little heavy-going. There is the usual list of appetizers and desserts, and prices are reasonable. Complete luncheons cost from $3.50 to $5.50; à la carte main courses from $1.75 to $4.00. Dinner is à la carte, with entrées from about $3.25 to $6.00. *Cocktails, wines. On Saturday the restaurant opens at 5:00 p.m. Closed Sunday, major holidays, and for several weeks in August.*

★★ CHEZ RENEE
248 East 49th Street   EL 5-1810

This is a fairly engaging restaurant, and if all the bistros in town had equal charm and food of equal merit, New York might be a pleasanter place to live in. During the summer months, a garden is open where guests may sit under an ailanthus tree and dine on coq au Riesling or trout grenobloise. Dishes remembered from summer or winter at the restaurant include a fine-grained pâté maison, a soupe MacIlwane (vaguely resembling a cold vichyssoise, but containing bits of tomato and chopped scallion) and a fillet of sole Orly (batter-fried). At one meal, the establishment's sweetbreads came off poorly and seemed a bit spongy. The kitchen at Chez Renée is small, and, when the

dining room is crowded, the service may tend to be maddeningly slow. Complete luncheons range from about $4.00 for an omelet to $7.00 for mignonettes of beef bordelaise; complete dinners from about $7.50 for sole meunière to $9.75 for steak au poivre. *Cocktails, wines.* **Luncheon is not served Saturday.** *Closed Sunday.*
AE

★ CHEZ VOUS
78 Carmine Street   CH 2-2676

Despite the name, this impeccably neat restaurant in Greenwich Village offers South Italian cuisine. Luncheon and dinner are à la carte, with main courses at midday for about $2.75 to $6.00 for steak and in the evening from about $3.25 to $7.50. *Cocktails, wines. Luncheon is not served Saturday. Closed Sunday (except in summer) and major holidays.*

★ CHEZ YVONNE L'ESCARGOT
54 Stone Street   944-9887

This rather large bistro in the city's financial district boasts a very plain menu with well-prepared French cuisine. Those who fancy rare lamb will find it here on request, and the snails, stuffed with shallot butter, are notable. The menu, which is à la carte, is the same for luncheon and dinner. Main courses range from about $3.50 for an omelet to $5.50 for steak with maître d'hôtel butter. The snails, served as an appetizer, are somewhat expensive, but worth the price at $2.50 a half dozen. Like many restaurants in the neighborhood, Chez Yvonne is open from 11:30 A.M. to 7:00 P.M. *Cocktails, wines. Closed Sunday, and all major holidays.*

★★★ CHI MER
12 Chatham Square   267-4565

This is one of the best Chinese restaurants to open in Chinatown in recent memory.

But *nota bene*, if anyone is disappointed during a visit here, it may be because of the service.

The menu of the Chi Mer is lengthy and well-varied, and the kitchen is admirable. The chef turns out commendable fried dumplings (they should be eaten with a sauce made of a little white vinegar, a touch of hot oil, and soy sauce to taste). The baked carp is first-rate and so is the chicken in hot sauce.

The Chi Mer is one source for the Chinese hot pot (oriental fondue) and it is available two ways. It is a dish for several people served in a special brass container with foods such as shrimp balls, shrimp, lobster, liver, and pork balls in a simmering broth. Whether or not they will serve this dish when the restaurant is crowded, except on special request, is questionable.

There are some interesting fried noodle dishes and the only fault found on one occasion was with the shrimp in brown sauce (the shrimp were too salty) and the hot and sour soup, which was neither this nor that.

The printed luncheon menu was not offered on a couple of noonday visits, but there was one on the counter and it lists à la carte dishes from about $1.30 to $2.25. The principal menu has à la carte dishes from about $2.40 to $4.50. *Cocktails, wines. Open 7 days a week.*

★★ CHINA BOWL, THE
152 West 44th Street   JU 2-3358

If there was ever a restaurant whose reputation seemed solidly based on such dishes as chop suey, chow mein, egg roll, and fried rice, The China Bowl is it. It certainly has no want for customers and, although one visitor cannot vouch for those plates piled high with chop suey et al., the food otherwise is quite palatable.

The wonton soup seems freshly made and the shrimp with bean sprouts are tasty. Let it be said that this is one restaurant where the dishes on the luncheon menu seem as good as those on the larger, higher-priced à la carte menu.

Complete luncheons cost from about $1.30 to $3.50; a complete family dinner for two costs $6.20. A la carte dishes are priced from about $2 to $5.20. *Cocktails, wines. Luncheon is not served Sunday. Open 7 days a week.*

★ CHINA FAIR
136 West 50th Street   CI 7-4587

The menu of the China Fair may look conventional, but the food is not at all bad. It is a large, neat restaurant and popular with businessmen of the area. It is only a step or so from Radio City Music Hall and would be a good place for a family meal or for couples, for that matter.

A winter melon soup turned out to be agreeable, although the broth for a bowl of wonton tasted as if it had come from the hot water tap. A braised duck dish was good and so was a simple combination of roast pork with bean sprouts.

Complete luncheons cost from $1.60 to $3.95; complete dinners cost from $2.30 to $5.25. A la carte dishes from about $2.20 to $3.60. *Cocktails, wines. Open 7 days a week.*

★ CHINA PAVILION
200 West 57th Street   765-4340

There was a time many years ago when some of the most celebrated of New York's Chinese restaurants served substantial, conservative, competently prepared dishes made without question from quality ingredients. Since that time, Chinese food available in numerous restaurants has become far more adventurous and, therefore, exciting to the palate. The China Pavilion fits the original pattern. The food is acceptably good, but not in the least daring.

All the dishes sampled there could benefit from scallions or ginger or coriander leaves or a smidgen of garlic. And this would include the teriyaki-like beef served as an appetizer, chicken in foil, boneless chicken Cantonese, and Mandarin shrimp. An exception was the squabs Cantonese, which were simply prepared but excellent. The restaurant is large, neat, and close to Carnegie Hall.

Complete luncheons cost from about $2.30 up, with à la carte dishes from about $2.40 to $18.00 for Pekin duck; $6.50 per person for a complete dinner. *Cocktails, wines. Open 7 days a week. Luncheon is not served Sunday.*
AE DC

★ CHINESE RATHSKELLER
45 Mott Street   962-8943

This downstairs establishment on a main street in Chinatown is a favorite with tourists and many Chinese. The quality and the flavor of the food varies, and it is best to order from the à la carte menu. The lobster with chicken livers is an unusual combination and can be delicious. Complete luncheons from about $1.70 to $5.00. A la carte dishes are available at all times, with main courses from about $1.75 to $6.25. Complete dinners are priced from $2.35 to $5.00. *Cocktails, wines. Luncheon is not served Sunday.*
AE CB DC MC

★ CHIN-YA
210 West 55th Street   586-0160

This is not the most polished Japanese restaurant in New York, but the chef is conscientious and the kitchen has its merits. The entrance is via a long, American-style bar where customers have hamburgers at noon with their martinis. In the dining room, greeting by waitresses in obis and kimonos is sincere but diffident. There are three small dining areas: a sushi bar, a six-table area with chairs, and a tatemi room with seating on the floor.

The soups, whether clear or bean, are good; the sushi or raw fish on vinegared rice is excellent. A recent order of shioyaki or salt-broiled fish, in this case porgy, was hot, fresh, and well-seasoned; an order of beef teriyaki was well worth recommending.

Luncheon prices are around $3.75; complete dinners are around $5.00. *Cocktails, imported beers. Open 7 days a week. Luncheon is not served Saturday and Sunday.*

★ CHOCK FULL O'NUTS

There are about 80 of these first-class establishments in the metropolitan New York area. They are clean as a whistle, and the sandwiches and pastries are of a high order. The doughnuts and coffee cake are particularly good. Counter service only. Freshly squeezed orange juice, available in the morning, costs 20 cents. Sandwiches, whether lobster salad or egg salad, cost 50 cents. *No alcoholic beverages. Closing hours at the various locations differ. Most of the restaurants are closed Sunday.*

★★★ CHRIST CELLA
160 East 46th Street   OX 7-2479

Although by most standards it is relatively obscure, this small, immaculate establishment has an international reputation. As to the cost, it is on a par with many of the city's most expensive restaurants. The steaks and lobsters are superb, and some of the less lordly dishes are good, too. There is no menu. A la carte prices are from $5.00 to $9.75 at lunch and from $6.00 to $9.75 at dinner. *Cocktails, wines. Luncheon is not served Saturday. Closed Sunday and, during July and August, Saturday also. Closed major holidays. Reservations are recommended.*
AE   DC   MC

★★ CHRISTO'S
143 East 49th Street   EL 5-6531

This is a pleasant, comfortable, neat, and frequently crowded steak house, and, what's more, the food is good. Although the emphasis is on steaks and chops, the evening menu has Italian entrées; at luncheon there are several American dishes, such as shirred eggs with country sausage. Both menus are à la carte, with main courses at midday from about $3.25 for a Western omelet to $8.50 for a small prime sirloin steak. In the evening, the prices range from about $5.25 for chicken in the pot to $8.50 for filet mignon. *Cocktails, wines. On Saturday and Sunday, the restaurant opens at about 4:30 p.m. Most major credit cards.*

★★ CHUAN HONG RESTAURANT
2748 Broadway (between 105th and 106th Streets)
866-5920

Upper Broadway is a center for out-of-the-ordinary Chinese restaurants, and this is one of the latest on the roster. The food is prepared with great skill and variety whether it is sautéed shredded chicken, sweet and sour fish, a dumpling, or various Szechuan dishes, which are uncommonly good for those who relish highly spiced foods. The Chuan Hong is a small, inexpensive restaurant, with, apparently, only one waiter. As always, it is best to order from the à la carte menu. There are complete luncheons from about 95 cents to $2; complete dinners from about $1.75 to $3.50. A la carte dishes from about $1.50 to $3.25. *There is no bar, but customers may bring their own wine or beer. Open 7 days a week.*

★★ CLEOPATRA
2527 Broadway (near 94th Street)   *865-3000*

This is an interesting Middle Eastern restaurant that enjoys a well-deserved success.

It has a colorful, angular, freshly-painted décor, a limited number of seats, and a small kitchen that turns out such appetizers as eggplant and sesame spreads, chickpea and sesame spreads, interesting and fiery hot pickles of turnip, carrot, hot pepper.

The soups are freshly made and excellent, and the main courses are cooked with conscience. The latter include various stuffed vegetables, among them green peppers, squash, and eggplant, plus grilled dishes such as the ubiquitous shish kebab and kofta or ground lamb on a skewer.

One menu serves throughout the day and the dishes are à la carte, with main course prices which include soup and salad from about $2.00 to $5.50. *There is no bar, and patrons are encouraged to bring their own liquor. Open 7 days a week.*

★★ CLOS NORMAND
42 East 52nd Street   753-3348 and 753-3349

This is physically a most agreeable French restaurant. There are original tiles by Jean Pagès and the overall atmosphere has the warmth of a Normandy village. Many of the dishes come off very well. Remembered in particular are a cream of lettuce soup and a cream of mussel soup. One also recalls with special favor a tender, admirably cooked dish of thin white slices of veal with a tarragon cream sauce. The quiche, made with Alaska king crab meat and other seafood, is very good and far superior to an all but inedible dish of braised sweetbreads that were undercooked and spongy. The luncheon menu is à la carte, with main courses from about $3.00 to $5.00. The dinner menu is prix fixe. The cost of a complete meal in the evening is $7.95. *Cocktails, wines. Closed Sunday and major holidays.*
AE DC

★★★★ COACH HOUSE, THE
110 Waverly Place   sp 7-0303

The Coach House is the finest restaurant in the Greenwich Village area and one of the best in the city. It is a handsome, conservatively styled place with a management that has a dedicated interest in its profession. The kitchen is largely American, and specialties of the

house include black bean soup, excellent steaks, charcoal-grilled giant lamb chops, and pecan pie. When available there is also an extraordinarily good French dessert called dacquoise. There are complete luncheons from about $4.00 to $6.00 and à la carte entrées at midday from about $2.50 to $4.50. There are complete dinners from about $10.00 to $13.25. and à la carte main courses in the evening from about $4.50 to $9.75. *Cocktails, wines. Closed Monday. Lunch served Tuesday through Friday only. Reservations are recommended.*
Most major credit cards.

★★ COLONY, THE
30 East 61st Street   TE *8-6745*

When most luxury restaurants decline in one way or another, it is generally because of a change in quality or talent in the kitchen. In the case of The Colony, the change has been in the dining room. The menu, once written by hand, is now composed by machine; the long-stemmed red roses that once abounded in the main dining room are now artificial; and the flowers on the table are commonplace. The handsome rolling silver "wagon," where roasts and other specialties of the day were carved, has been dispensed with. On the other hand, the food is for the most part admirable. There are a commendable canapé Colony with crab meat, smoked trout with horseradish, and first-rate main dishes. And it is still a haven for the wealthy and famous. All dishes are à la carte, with main courses at midday from about $4.95 to $5.50; in the evening, from about $6.25 to $9.25. *Cocktails, wines. Closed Sunday, Monday, major holidays, and certain weeks during the summer.*
AE DC

★★★ COPENHAGEN
68 West 58th Street   MU *8-3690 and* MU *8-3691*

For a herring fancier, there should be nothing but

unreserved enthusiasm for the Copenhagen's remarkable assortment. There are herring with mustard, herring with curry, herring with horseradish, plus six or seven more, and all of them are a joy. The remainder of the Copenhagen's food is not on a par with the best that Denmark has to offer, but it is palatable nonetheless and will cosset the appetite. Both the luncheon and dinner menus are à la carte. The cost of the abundant Danish cold table at midday is $4.75; in the evening, $7.75. Main course dishes at midday cost from $3.50 to $4.50; in the evening, from about $4.00 to $6.75. Also, Danish open-faced sandwiches, ranging in price from $1.10 to $3.75, are served all day. *Cocktails, wines. Closed Sunday, New Year's Day, July 4, Thanksgiving, and Christmas.*
AE CB DC

★★ COPTER CLUB
Pan Am Building, 200 Park Avenue   973-2100

From a certain height, the views of Manhattan on a clear day or cloudless night are breath-taking. Considering that, it is astonishing how few restaurants in town celebrate the fact. One of the best is the Copter Club. The view from the windows on the fifty-eighth floor is, of course, spectacular. It should also be mentioned that the interior of the Club is handsome. What is equally interesting is the menu. For the fixed price of $5.00, a guest may dine on roast beef or a blend of seafood in wine sauce, with salad, dessert, and coffee. That is the menu Q.E.D. and it is a refreshing change from those windblown, pompous, and overly ambitious bills of fare that have been with us late and soon for several years. There is fault to be found with the salad, which contains iceberg lettuce, the least distinguished of salad greens. *Cocktails, wines; with or without dining, the lounge is open to the public. Luncheon is served from 12:15 p.m. to 2:15 p.m. Monday through Friday. Reservations are essential. Dinner is not served.*
AE

★ COQ AU VIN
939 Eighth Avenue (near 56th Street)   CI 5-9557

A small French bistro-type café with a conventional menu and bourgeois cooking. All dishes at lunch are à la carte, with main luncheon dishes from about $2.25 to $5; dinner main courses from about $2.75 to $6.00. Table d'hôte, $4.75 to $7.75. *Cocktails, wines. Luncheon is not served on Saturday and Sunday.*

★★ CREPES SUZETTE
313 West 46th Street   265-9510 and 581-9717

This is a very good, small, and inexpensive restaurant in the Broadway–Times Square area. There is nothing pretentious about the surroundings or the neighborhood, but it is a pleasant place to dine with a modest purse. All the dishes are à la carte, with main courses at midday from about $2.25 to $3.25 and in the evening from about $2.50 to $6.00. *Cocktails, wines. Luncheon is not served Saturday. Closed Sunday and major holidays.*

★★ CUISINE OF SZECHUAN
33 Irving Place   982-5678

If there seems to be, as has been alleged, a preponderance of Chinese restaurants in these pages, it is not necessarily the fault of the management.

It is simply a fact of life that infinitely more Chinese restaurants have opened in New York within the last few years than have French or Italian or any other. It is also a fact of life that Szechuan cookery—characterized by spices, often fiery hot spices—figures large in many of these restaurants' menus.

One of the latest to open offers only Szechuan cooking and it is called Cuisine of Szechuan. The best thought is that this restaurant offers some of the best and, we will wager, most authentic Szechuan cooking in town. Please note that the food will not be for all palates. It is not only spicy, but a good deal of oil is used in the cooking.

As devotees, however, we have recently reveled in the cold aromatic sliced beef as an appetizer; camphor duck (the duck smoked over camphor wood) and served with a spiced salt or hoisin sauce with scallions; an excellent, brothy soup of pork shreds and pickled Szechuan cabbage; hot bean curd Szechuan-style, with ground pork, red pepper seasoning, and scallions; hot spiced ginger shrimp in ginger sauce; chunked chicken with hot sauce; and so on.

The décor of Cuisine of Szechuan is as plain as the paper placemats or the plastic tables from which one dines. Invariably, of course, the food is better on the à la carte menu than that of the fixed-price menu.

On the small menu, prices range from about $1.30 for combination dishes to $3.95 for lobster Cantonese. A la carte dishes from about $1.25 to $12 for Pekin duck, which serves several. *There is no bar, but customers may bring their own wine and beer. Open 7 days a week.*

★★ CZECHOSLOVAK PRAHA
1358 First Avenue (at 73rd Street)   YU 8-3505

At midday, in particular, the food of the Czechoslovak Praha is one of the best bargains in Manhattan. One can dine reasonably well on main courses that cost from $1.75, for Czechoslovak sausages with potato and sauerkraut. The sliced dumplings are light and outstanding. There are complete dinners that range in cost from $4.95 for a goulash to $7.25 for filet mignon. The décor of the restaurant is simple and there is noise at times from an all too persistent jukebox. *Cocktails, wines. Dinner is served from noon on Sunday.*

★ DALY'S DANDELION
1029 Third Avenue (at 61st Street)   838-0780

One of the oldest saloons in Manhattan, formerly called Daly's. Its surroundings are very pleasant, and its service friendly and polite. The walls are neatly papered with a dandelion pattern, but its old-fashioned bar, white tile floor, and stained glass have been retained. Best of all, the hamburgers are excellent and the brews on draft are cold and good. A thin, chilled vichyssoise is also good. The restaurant's mint-flavored gazpacho leaves much to be desired: it is a crude version of the Spanish soup, a far too thick dish of coarsely puréed or chopped vegetables. The cumin-flavored chili con carne is also amateurish. The menu, on a cedar shingle, lists prices from about $2.00 for hamburgers to $6.75 for shell steak. *Cocktails, beers, and ale. Open 7 days a week until 3:00 a.m.*

★ DAMON'S
153 West 36th Street   LO 4-3636

The kitchen at Damon's is much like that of several other reasonably good Italian restaurants in New York. This restaurant is in the garment district and is, particularly at midday, a crowded rendezvous for members of the dress industry. Among the best dishes are breast of chicken parmigiana with cheese and tomato and chicken Gismonde with spinach. The portions, of whatever category, are mammoth. All dishes at Damon's are à la carte, but include pasta or salad. At midday, they run from $4.95 to $5.95 and in the evening from $4.95 to $12.95. *Cocktails, wines. Open for lunch and dinner Monday through Friday, lunch only on Saturday. Closed Sunday and all major holidays.*
All major credit cards.

★★ DANNY'S HIDE-A-WAY
151 East 45th Street   YU 6-5350

Danny's is one of New York's best-known steak houses, and it certainly fits the town's classic pattern for such establishments. It is a large restaurant, and food is served on several levels. As to décor, there is a somewhat circus-like mélange of wall hangings, cartoons, photographs, paintings, Western saddles, hammered brass

plaques, plaster masks, and swords. The steaks and chops are excellent at Danny's, and the kitchen standards are reasonably high in other areas as well. All dishes are à la carte, with main courses at midday from about $2.90 for ravioli to $6.00 for seafood salad. There is no printed menu in the evening, and the food is expensive. The cost of a cup of minestrone, for example, is $1.00. Grilled lamb chops cost $6.75; grilled sirloin steak, $7.50. Danny's Hide-A-Way has on each table some of the most uninteresting-looking bread in town. *Cocktails, wines. Lunch is served Monday through Friday only. On Sunday, the restaurant opens at 4:00 p.m. Closed major holidays.*
AE BA CB DC MC

★★ DARDANELLES ARMENIAN RESTAURANT
86 University Place CH 2-8990

This is probably the most elegant of New York's Middle Eastern restaurants, and the food, particularly such appetizers as chick-pea spread and cheese buerek, are both interesting and good. There are complete luncheons from about $3.10 to $3.60; complete dinners from about $5.75 to $8.50. A la carte dishes cost from $3.75 to $6.50 in the evening. *Cocktails, wines. Luncheon is not served Saturday. Closed Sunday and major holidays.*
AE CB DC MC

★★ DARUMA
310 Third Avenue (between 23rd and 24th Streets)
228-3939

This is a vast Japanese restaurant in a location that was, someone said, once a pool hall. The Daruma has some qualities so awful and in such depth as to be almost endearing. The gaudy décor with its low-hanging, multicolored lamps; the haphazard service, on one occasion maddeningly slow; plastic bamboo plantings; and a fitfully spurting multicolored fountain. In the evening, there is rather loud Western-style piano music.

On the other hand, if you have the patience and a sense of humor, the Daruma is cordially recommended, for the food at its best is excellent. For example, the sashimi is as fresh as you'll find anywhere in the city and the broiled eel is excellent. So is the teriyaki. Even the sukiyaki, which is not cooked at the table as it should be, is above average in its seasonings, and there is an interesting dish called buta tofu made with pork and bean curd. There is a sushi bar.

Please take note that the best meal sampled at the Daruma was enjoyed under ideal conditions. There were fewer than 10 people in the dining room, permitting one waiter to concentrate on our table. The restaurant's ventilation is less than perfect.

Complete luncheons—without dessert—at Daruma are priced at $2.95, with a cup of Japanese wine. Complete dinners including dessert cost from about $4.95 to $6.95. *Cocktails, wines. Open 7 days a week. Luncheon is not served on Sunday.*
All major credit cards.

★ DAWSON'S HA-PENNY BAR
159 East 53rd Street   PL 2-1387

This is a fascinating and frequently crowded restaurant offering what may be the most copious hot and cold luncheon buffet in town. It has such items as deviled beef bones, pickled eggs, Scotch eggs, cold meats, and salads. The food is good, but not consistently special. There is a large variety of main courses available for both luncheon and dinner. The free-wheeling "pub" lunch costs $3.25. In the evening, the main courses cost from about $4.95 to $5.95. *Cocktails, wines. On Sunday, the restaurant opens at 5:00 p.m.*
AE   CB   DC

★ DELSOMMA
266 West 47th Street   CO 5-9294, PL 7-9079, *and* PL 7-9234

The Delsomma is an Italian restaurant with a kitchen that is notably like that of a dozen other just-satisfactory Italian restaurants in the theater district. The menu, with its eggplant parmigiana, baked ziti Sicilian-style, and linguine with white or red clam sauce, is thoroughly familiar. The food is good and, its most commendable aspect, inexpensive. There are complete three-course luncheons priced from about $2.75 to $3.55. The evening menu is à la carte with entrées from about $2.70 for spaghetti with tomato sauce to $7.75 for sirloin steak pizzaiola. *Cocktails, wines. Dinner is served Saturday from noon. Closed Sunday and Christmas.*
AE CB DC MC

★★ DENO'S PLACE
155 East 26th Street

One of the nicest attributes you can ascribe to a kitchen or a dish is to say it is basically honest, and the food at Deno's Place is basically honest.

It is a colorful, offbeat restaurant with a close atmosphere, low ceiling, walls papered in bordello red, Chianti bottles cum candlesticks with wax down the sides, antique posters, and piped-in music. And it has no want of customers, for tables at times are hard to come by, and part of the popularity must derive from the prices, which are reasonable.

On one evening, there were only two waiters doing some of the fastest footwork one could ask for, but even with their enthusiasm there were delays between courses. Interestingly enough, one of the best dishes sampled at Deno's was the antipasto. Not elaborate, just greens, anchovies, cracked olives, pickled pimiento strips, and Greek cheeses on greens, but uncommonly well-seasoned with oil, vinegar, and herbs.

The tomato sauces are well- and freshly-made and the pasta seems freshly cooked, although for some tastes, including mine, a trifle overcooked. If you order the shrimp diavalo with linguine, ask them to cut down on the pepper flakes. They can be exaggerated.

Dishes are à la carte, with main courses from about $1.50 for a hamburger to $6.25 for a filet mignon. *There is no bar, but beers and wines are available. Closed Monday and major holidays.*

** DERBY STEAK HOUSE, THE
109 Macdougal Street   GR 5-0520

Although Macdougal Street in Greenwich Village is noted for its seedy aspects and colorful nature, it also has one of the best steak houses south of Steak Row. This is a friendly, respectable place with an atmosphere vaguely reminiscent of the 1920s. There are brick walls, a mosaic tile floor, and waiters in straw boaters.

The steaks, chops, and so on are grilled in the dining room over fiery coals behind a plastic shield, and the foods are cooked to a turn. Among the appetizers, the barbecued shrimp are excellent. Among the side dishes, the lettuce salad and the sliced tomatoes are good. The apple pie for dessert is first-rate.

On the dissenting side, the grilled chicken tasted as if it had been seasoned with garlic powder rather than fresh garlic, and all the grilled dishes should be brushed with melted hot butter before serving.

All dishes are à la carte, with main courses from about $2.95 to $5.75. *Cocktails, beers. Open for dinner only, 7 days a week, except Thanksgiving and Christmas.*
AE DC MC

* DEWEY WONG
206 East 58th Street   758-6881

The owners of this Chinese restaurant seem to be

people of genuine goodwill and enthusiasm. The surroundings are pleasant enough, from the Chinese scrolls and mirrors to the smiling personnel throughout. Some of the chef's dishes come off very well, including the chicken à la Wong's made with breast of chicken stuffed with Chinese sausage, breaded and deep fried; the whole leaf spinach cooked quickly in oil; very good chicken and corn soup; and lobster and chicken kew with black mushrooms, water chestnuts, and assorted Chinese vegetables (although this last seemed heavy with monosodium glutamate). Among the appetizers, the batter-fried chicken wings are interesting.

For the most part, however, Dewey Wong's menu is stereotyped and has too few innovations. It seems dated. This is the kind of Chinese food one could have expected 10 years or more ago, and there's been a lot more imagination introduced into Manhattan's Chinese kitchens since then.

The food at Wong's is for the most part palatable, but two dishes that did not come off on two separate occasions were the lobster roll, with bits of chewy lobster meat (one could swear it had been made from frozen rock lobster tails), and the tough lobster in the lobster soong.

Main luncheon courses at Dewey Wong's are priced from about $2.25 to $5.25. A la carte dishes from about $3.25 for roast pork egg foo young to $7.50 for steak with snow pea pods, mushrooms, and Chinese cabbage. *Cocktails, wines. Open 7 days a week. Only dinner is served on Sunday.*
AE DC MC

★★ DILLUVIO
957 First Avenue (between 52nd and 53rd Streets)
752-9429

If there are no great Italian restaurants in Manhattan to match the best of Florence or Rome, there are dozens of agreeable, small *ristoranti* that make for a pleasant evening. The Dilluvio is a case in point.

A "neighborhood" restaurant, it has an uncomplicated menu (Manhattan basic) with pasta dishes in various guises (spaghetti meat sauce, ziti clam sauce, noodles alla marinara, and so on), veal in the usual fashion, and eight or so fish or seafood dishes.

The food is neatly cooked, and we recall with some pleasure the spaghetti with a simple and proper marinara sauce; excellent batter-fried veal, à la francese or "French style," with lemon; shrimp areganato, a bit on the dry side, but acceptable; and very good, if not to say outstanding, zucchini with tomato sauce. This, with a bottle of Valpolicella, is proper in all respects.

The antipasto at the Dilluvio is as uninspired as it is anywhere else, and the flowers on the table have seemed to have been reposing for quite a spell. If anyone wants to find a genuine drawback in the Dilluvio, however, it is in the placement of the tables. They are red-tablecloth-to-red-tablecloth, in some cases too close for comfort, and if the place were ever filled, it could be awfully unpleasant.

The food is à la carte, with main dishes from about $2.25 for spaghetti meat sauce to $6.75 for filet mignon. *Cocktails, wines. The restaurant is open from noon until 2:00 a.m. 7 days a week.*

★ DIONYSOS
304 East 48th Street   758-8240

This is a large, colorful, and multi-tiered Greek restaurant that has become a rollicking Manhattan success, particularly in the evening. It has an interesting clientele; very good service, all things considered; and a kitchen that is notably routine.

The food is by no means unpalatable and much of it is well-seasoned, but some of the dishes are overcooked (the macaroni in the pastitsio; the vegetables, carrots, beans, and peas, which, if sampled in a blindfold test, would be indistinguishable) and they are served lukewarm.

The spinach pie is decent and the vine leaves with ground meat quite good. The taramosalata or roe paste has the texture of mashed potatoes. In any event, Dionysos, with its white walls and vibrant wall hangings, is very much alive with music and dancing in the evening.

Complete four-course luncheons are priced from about $4.25 to $5.25. Dinners are à la carte, with main courses from about $5.00 to $8.50. *Cocktails, wines. The restaurant opens at 6:00 p.m. on Saturday. Closed Sunday.*
AE DC

★★ DOGWOOD ROOM
50 East 58th Street   PL 9-1710

A woman from Niagara who dined recently at Lottie's Dogwood Room said, "Whenever I go to New York, I want to go to a place where there's a piano, and this is lovely." From the baby grand came Gershwin and Porter and Berlin, and the restaurant couldn't have been a more fortuitous choice. It's an interesting place and one of the few where the fried chicken seems worth recommending. It was served with typically Southern, which is to say, very sweet candied yams; black-eyed peas; and well-made corn bread and freshly cooked biscuits.

Such Southern dishes are specialties of the house at the Dogwood Room, but they by no means dominate the menu, which is typically American. The restaurant also has beef pot pie, chicken à la king, and so on, and, for the most part, the kitchen seems more than competent. However, it has occasional flaws, such as overcooking.

The Dogwood's cheesecake, a Yankee dish if there ever was one, was both watery and crumbly. If you're in the market for Southern food, American food, plus a pleasant piano, the Dogwood Room will probably prove agreeable.

Luncheons are à la carte, with main courses from about $2.25 to $3.95. Complete dinners cost from about $4.95 to $6.95. *Cocktails, wines. Closed Sunday and major holidays.*
All major credit cards.

★★ DORIENTAL RESTAURANT
128 East 56th Street   688-8070

It may seem like damning with faint praise to give a certain rank to a restaurant and then to say it is quite ordinary. But that's the way it is with the Doriental. Dining there is pleasant enough. The ingredients are fresh, the fat used for deep-fried dishes is sprightly enough for good digestion, and the seasonings, such as they are, are guaranteed not to offend even the most guarded palate. There's the rub.

There is such a lack of imagination and daring in the use of ginger, scallions, garlic, and the like that the kitchen is too reminiscent of other "good," wholly successful, and notably unadventurous Chinese kitchens in Manhattan. And don't argue with success. There are, at times, people standing in line to get a table here.

At midday, main courses with desserts are priced from about $1.70 to $3.00. All dishes on the principal menu are à la carte, with main courses from about $2.75 to $7.75. *Cocktails, wines. Open 7 days a week. Lunch is served Monday through Friday only.*
All major credit cards.

★ DOUBLE DOLPHIN FISH HOUSE
1033 First Avenue (near 57th Street)   PL 9-4176

The décor here is neat nautical blue, and the service is happily friendly and generally efficient.

At its best, some of the seafood dishes are excellent, and this would include the bouillabaisse, well-seasoned, saffron-flavored, and nicely gelatinous as it should be, and the shrimp or seafood creole.

One order of scrod was on its way to becoming fullblown cod—tasteless and chewy and desperately in need of melted butter. A certain salad consisted of overly chopped pieces of lettuce on a too small plate. And for cheese, a dark wedge of ammonia-flavored Camembert that had achieved its prime at least two weeks earlier.

Complete luncheons are priced from $2.50 to $4.95. Dinner entrées are à la carte, with main dishes from about $3.95 for mackerel and $7.50 to $9.25 for lobster. *Cocktails, wines. Open 7 days a week. Brunch is served from noon to 3:00 p.m.*
AE CB DC MC

★ DOWNING SQUARE
500 Lexington Avenue (near 48th Street)   826-9730

If you are in a convivial mood, aren't allergic to cigar smoke, enjoy food served in a motherly abundance, and aren't distracted by the babble of voices that drown out piped-in music, you may find much to admire at Downing Square.

The menu is not altogether British, although the mutton chop, properly cooked, tasted properly muttony. The quality of the foods in an "English mixed grill" was impressive, although the meats seemed to have been dipped into a sweetish marinade before grilling. The menu embraces such items as veal cordon bleu, chicken parmigiana, and chicken soup with matzoh balls.

All dishes are à la carte. At midday, main courses cost from about $2.95 to $7.95; in the evening from about $5.75 to $10.00. *Cocktails, wines. Open 7 days a week. Luncheon is not served Saturday and Sunday.*
AE CB DC MC

★ DRESNER'S
1479 York Avenue (near 78th Street)   RE 4-9344 *and* 722-9477

The first thing to consider about Dresner's is the

cost of dining here. It may not have the most distinguished kitchen in town, but the menu is well-varied and the food is agreeably prepared. The menu runs along the lines of broiled chicken livers, broiled shrimp, broiled chicken and chops, and all dishes are à la carte. At midday, the cost is from about $1.00 for sandwiches to $1.95 for most main courses. Entrées in the evening cost from about $1.95 for veal parmigiana to $2.35 for broiled tenderloin or London broil. *Cocktails, wines.*

★★ DUCK JOINT, THE
1382 First Avenue (near 74th Street)   861-1102

This restaurant is built on a fascinating idea—a menu whose main dishes and several appetizers are based on duck or goose.

It is a pleasant place, with the duck idea repeated in ceramic pieces, in tile, in ashtrays, and with a few decoys placed here and there. There are an open kitchen to the rear where the chef stands in his toque blanche, and a cold corner near the entrance with a handsome display of pâtés and terrines and hanging sausages.

There are several good things about the food. There is a splendid appetizer, the melon with ginger and fresh lime. The roast duck is excellent and so is the sage dressing. The pâtés and terrines are well-seasoned and have a nice texture. The menu does include lamb, braised beef, and Wienerschnitzel.

There is a very good accompaniment for one of the dishes, freshly cooked cabbage with caraway seeds, seasoned delicately with onion and vinegar. The braised duck with green grapes is reasonably good, although the sauce will seem far too sweet for some palates.

An order of roast goose tasted as though it had been cooked the day before and reheated. And while those pâtés and terrines at the entrance are inviting to the eye, the appetizers themselves are sliced and served from the kitchen. A disappointment.

And a final woe, there is piped-in music.

All dishes are à la carte with main courses from about $4.75 to $5.75. *Cocktails, wines. The restaurant opens at 5:30 p.m. every day except Monday, when it is closed.*

★ DUE MONDI
120 East 40th Street　　YU 6-6434

The Due Mondi has a thoroughly competent kitchen and produces food that is, if not distinguished, very well-seasoned. There is an excellent hot mushroom appetizer, and main dishes include the usual veal and chicken dishes parmigiana, ravioli, cannelloni, and manicotti. A slice of rum cake sampled on one occasion had the flavor of the refrigerator. The Due Mondi is a large restaurant and is crowded at noon. All dishes are à la carte, with main courses from $4.25 to $7.95. *Cocktails, wines. On Saturday, the restaurant opens at 5:00 p.m. Closed Sunday.*
Most major credit cards.

★★ DUFF'S
115 Christopher Street　　AL 5-1660

An Italian restaurant? Named Duff's? Well, that's what it is, and it's generally a good one.

Any Italian restaurant in Manhattan that veers away from the neo-Neapolitan concept of a tomato sauce used to bathe all the dishes on a menu deserves some sort of accolade, and Duff's has several unaccustomed sauces for their pasta.

Here they offer spaghettini puttanese (a humorous if somewhat indecent name), in which the pasta is sauced with melted anchovies and black olives; spaghettini primavera, with its sauce of fresh tomatoes and basil; spaghettini carbonara, this one with chopped bacon and onions; and so on.

As to a dish of chicken alla Valdostana, the breast of chicken covered with mushrooms and melted cheese was as moist as you could hope for. A dish of veal scaloppine alla Mario with prosciutto and cheese was very good, although a bit on the salty side, perhaps because of the ham.

Duff's has a pleasant interior. There are a long bar, theater posters on the white brick walls, and accommodating table service. The dining tables are of freshly scrubbed wood and over each is a hanging lamp à la gaming table.

Some of the dishes at Duff's come off less well than those described: The meat on a knuckle of veal (osso buco) was tasty, but a bit chewy; and the assorted hot antipasto was acceptable; but the fillings for the vegetables were too similar and the taste level was too unvaried over-all.

All dishes are à la carte, with main courses from about $2.95 to $6.95. *Cocktails, wines. The restaurant opens at 5:00 p.m. every day except Sunday, when it is closed.*
AE DC MC

★★ DU MIDI
311 West 48th Street   CO 5-9395 *and* 582-6689

Among the many small bistros of Manhattan, East Side or West Side, Du Midi is one of the best. The dishes are French provincial, prepared with admirable care and reasonably priced. Luncheons are à la carte with main courses from about $2.00 to $4.25. Dinner entrées are from $4.95 to $6.50. Du Midi is close to many Broadway theaters, and dinner is served from 5:00 P.M. until midnight. *Cocktails, wines. Dinner is served from noon on Saturday and from 1:00 p.m. on Sunday.*

★★ DYNASTY, THE
200 East End Avenue (between 89th and 90th Streets)
369-4986

It does at times seem too good to be true that so many worthwhile Chinese restaurants have opened in New York. This one is well above average.

Like several other Chinese restaurants in Manhattan, there is a certain emphasis here on Szechuan cooking, which is to say that such dishes are more "spicy hot" than others. Some of the outstanding dishes have included the beef in hoisin sauce and the chicken with peanuts.

The Dynasty has excellent fried dumplings and a generally excellent assortment of hors d'oeuvres, including chicken in parchment, baby spareribs, and spring rolls. The spring roll dough has twice been crisp outside, but a bit soggy underneath. The Szechuan beef was good, but on the dry side.

This is a large, comfortable restaurant with handsome surroundings that would be improved if they would get rid of a few plastic plants. And the music is, at times, too loud.

There is one menu at present with all dishes priced from about $3.75 to $5.50 ($16 for Pekin duck, which may be ordered in advance). A captain stated that there will soon be a luncheon menu with complete meals from about $2.75 to $3.25. *Cocktails, wines. Open 7 days a week.*

** EDUARDO'S
1140 Second Avenue (at 60th Street)   MU 8-7390

This is a happy and festive place that is alive with young people who come here precisely for pizza. The menu is fairly extensive, however, and the food is good and moderately priced. The à la carte menu, available both day and night, has dishes from about $2.00 for spaghetti with garlic and oil to $6.00 for sirloin. *Cocktails, wines. Open 11:00 a.m. to 2:00 a.m. Tuesday through Saturday, Sunday from 3:00 p.m. to 2:00 a.m. Closed Monday, Thanksgiving, and Christmas.*

* ELAINE'S
1703 Second Avenue (near 88th Street)   831-9566

An arty restaurant with rock 'n' roll on the jukebox and an up, up, and away ambience in general. One source states that Elaine's is a "sanctuary to actors, writers, photographers, playwrights, Europeans, and any number of unbelievably pretty girls." It is a place of smiling customers, and the cuisine is Italian.

The food at its best is excellent, and this would include a special seafood salad containing shrimp, squid, olives, capers, mussels, parsley, sweet peppers, oil, and lemon. It was not on the menu. The pasta dishes are especially well-cooked, and some of the main dishes—veal with prosciutto and cheese—are excellent.

A dish of steamed mussels as an appetizer seemed to have been cooked in an excess amount of pure dry white wine, and the broth was on the acid side. As to an order of chicken breast on a bed of spinach, it would be difficult to say if the chicken had been sautéed or steamed. The waiters have that very bad New York habit of emptying dirty ash trays into dinner plates when they are removed.

All dishes are à la carte at Elaine's, and the price is from about $3.00 for pasta to $7.00 for steak. *Cocktails, wines. Only dinner is served, starting at 7:00 p.m. Closed Monday.*

★ EL AZTECA
370 East 69th Street   734-9843

Some of the Mexican cooking in this new restaurant is quite good, and some of the foods best remembered are the tender, thin tostadas and tortillas; the seviche of cold marinated fresh mackerel; a very good chicken mole poblano with its dark nutty sauce; and an exceedingly tender flan dessert with its burnt sugar sauce.

One combination platter included a cheese-stuffed green pepper; a slice of hip steak with an interesting aged flavor, which must have come from a marinade; and a cheese enchilada. A platter of chicken enchiladas with sour cream green sauce became rather monotonous after a few bites and the cheese was stringy.

The foods here, generally, seem to have a similar taste level—not enough flavors from one to the other—and the restaurant's ventilation leaves something to be desired. There is the odor of frying foods on entering, and although one becomes accustomed to it after a while, it does remain lightly in the clothes.

All dishes are à la carte, with main courses at midday from about $3.00 to $5.50; in the evening, from about $3.25 to $6.00. *There is no bar, although a waiter stated that a license had been applied for. Lunch is served from noon to 3:00 p.m.; dinner, from 5:00 to 11:00 p.m. Closed Sunday.*
Most major credit cards.

★ EL CHARRO
4 Charles Street (near Greenwich Avenue)   CH 2-9547

El Charro bills itself as "A Bit of Mexico in Greenwich Village," and it is a worthwhile place for those with a palate for well-spiced foods. It is a small restaurant with a lusty but neat décor, and the service is excellent. There are very good combination plates with tostadas, tacos, and enchiladas. A specialty of the house is a fiery, but appetizing chicken Mexican style. The menu is à la carte, with main courses from about $3.25 to $5.00. *Cocktails, wines. Open for dinner only. Closed Sunday and major holidays.*

★ ELECTRA
949 Second Avenue (between 50th and 51st Street)
421-8425

If the sum of this restaurant were equal to some of its parts, it would be most agreeable indeed. The entrées, including the moussaka, the pastitsio (a blend of cinnamon-scented ground lamb, macaroni, and custard), and the baked lamb, are excellent. The plate of assorted

Greek appetizers lacks the style and imagination found in several of the city's restaurants of similar genre. The décor is nondescript modern. The menu lists à la carte entrées from about $1.55 to $2.95. *Cocktails, wines. Open 24 hours a day 7 days a week.*

★★★ EL FARO
823 Greenwich Street (corner Horatio Street)
WA 9-8210

This is an extraordinary restaurant with an excellent Spanish kitchen and a décor that has as much the feel of a small European restaurant as any restaurant in Manhattan. The menu encompasses such dishes as three kinds of paella and lobster with green sauce, and the preparation of all of them is admirable. El Faro has its crude aspects, including bare, Formica tables, but it enjoys a well-deserved popularity and reservations are recommended. All dishes are à la carte with main luncheon dishes from about $1.50 to $4.00 and main dinner entrées from about $3.00 to $4.00. *Cocktails, wines. Open 7 days a week.*

★★ ELIZABETH WHITE
987 First Avenue (near 54th Street)   759-7850

Elizabeth White has long been a citadel of low-cost American-style dining in New York. It has moved to a new location, and, although the prices are considerably elevated above what they were, say, 20 years ago, they compare favorably with those of many another restaurant in town.

Elizabeth White's kitchen turns out what is generally spoken of as home cooking—sautéed pork chops with apple sauce; roast turkey with dressing; grilled country sausages with apple sauce; peach shortcake; and so on. There are steaks and chops and broiled fish, and the food, all in all, is competently cooked.

A la carte prices range at noon from about $1.35 to

$1.95, with complete meals from about $2.35 to $2.95. A la carte prices go in the evening from about $2.65 to $5.50, with complete meals from about $4.20 to $6.75.

Elizabeth White has a no-nonsense décor with about 25 tables and a faithful clientele, some of whom are not as spry as they used to be. *Cocktails, wines. Open 7 days a week. Luncheon is not served Saturday and Sunday.*

★★ EL MIRADOR
899 First Avenue (between 50th and 51st Streets)
PL 5-5536

This is a simple, modest, and agreeable Mexican restaurant in the Beekman-Sutton Place area. The food is prepared with care and imagination, and, if it seems a bit bland, there is an excellent hot sauce on the side.

The tostadas at El Mirador are feather-light; the guacamole is well-seasoned; and the tostaditas nachos, another appetizer made with melted cheese and tomato sauce, are appealing.

The restaurant is a good source for mole verde, chicken in a green mole sauce made with Mexican green tomatoes and seasoned delicately with fresh coriander sauce. Plus, of course, the usual assortment of enchiladas and tacos.

The chilies rellenos or stuffed green chilies taste good, but they are not as puffed and gossamer as they should be. There are only 12 tables at El Mirador, and they are situated close together.

All the dishes are à la carte, with main courses from about $3.25 to $4.00. *There is no bar, but Mexican beers are available. Closed Sunday and major holidays. Lunch is served Monday through Friday only.*

★★★ EL PARADOR
325 East 34th Street   679-6812

The hottest thing in New York is a seat of any sort at El Parador. As several thousand patrons know, El

Parador has been eminently successful from the very beginning, but, whereas the customers once lined up three-deep at the bar while waiting for a table, they now line up five- or six-deep. And a delay in seating up to an hour and a half is not uncommon, though they say that if you arrive by 6:00 P.M., you may find immediate seating.

El Parador's success is by no means undeserved, for Carlos Jacott, the owner, has the soul of a good host. And his kitchen, to my taste, continues to offer the best Mexican cooking in Manhattan and perhaps the United States. There are purists, of course, who say it is not authentic, and this may be true to one degree or another. But El Parador's food—dishes such as cheese enchiladas, beef enchiladas, tacos with guacamole, chilies rellenos, and so on—offers the subtlest and most admirable variations of flavors. It is cooked with care and conscience.

There is no pretense in the décor of El Parador. It is simply decorated with exposed brick walls, a few Mexican plates here and there, and a carpet on the upstairs floor.

All dishes at El Parador are à la carte, with main courses from about $4.50 to $6.00. As almost anyone who has visited El Parador knows, the bar makes some of the best margaritas in town. *Cocktails, domestic and Mexican beers, and Spanish wines are available. Dinner only. Closed Sunday and major holidays. Reservations are not accepted.*

★ EL QUIJOTE
226 West 23rd Street   WA 9-1855

There is a certain tawdry appeal about this well-known Spanish restaurant in the Chelsea Hotel. A large mural depicts the adventures of Don Quixote, and the other walls are hung with a grab bag of paintings in garish colors. The atmosphere is casual in both the dining room and the kitchen. But many dishes are well-prepared, including the paellas: the Valenciana with chicken, sea-

food and sausages; and the mariscada with only seafood. The luncheons in particular at El Quijote are a bargain, with à la carte main dishes priced from about $1.50 for the ground meat specialty called picadillo à la creole to $2.25 for a generous portion of paella Valenciana. A la carte dishes on the dinner menu cost from $3.95 to $5.50. There is an elaborate prix-fixe Sunday dinner for $4.50. *Cocktails, wines. Luncheon is not served Saturday and Sunday.*
AE CB DC MC

★ EL RADIANTE
640 Prospect Avenue (near Kelly Street), the Bronx
MO *9-8055 and* MO *9-8163*

In spite of the numerous Puerto Ricans in New York, there are relatively few Puerto Rican restaurants of stature; this is probably the best. The food is hearty, and some of the dishes include combinations of rice, pigeon-peas, pork, and chicken. There are robust meat and vegetable soups, some flavored with coriander. All dishes are à la carte and range from $2.80 for rice and pigeon-peas to $5.00 for paella Valenciana. *Cocktails, wines. Open around the clock except for cleaning periods from about 5:00 a.m. to 6:00 a.m.*

★★ EL RINCON DE ESPANA
226 Thompson Street   475-9891

This Spanish restaurant is a genuine find, a fact that is reported reluctantly because it is geared to a petty pace and a host of new customers might wreak who-could-predict-what havoc. With that apologia and warning, let it be said that El Rincon has one of the best Spanish kitchens in the city. As to the small dining room, there is at times loud Spanish music from a jukebox and flamenco music in the evening.

An engaging enthusiasm and dedication pervade that are thoroughly evident in the food. The most famous specialty is, predictably, paella, and it is very good. But the seafood dishes, the mariscadas and zarzuelas, are exceptional.

One of them in a light, delicate, rich, and creamy tomato sauce can be rather peppery, with a Spanish version of paprika. But the chef will modify the spice on request. The seafood dishes in a gossamer egg sauce or in a green sauce are delectable. Note, however, that the chef is Galician and not in the least averse to fresh garlic. His caldo Gallego, the Galician soup made with white beans and mustard greens, is excellent. The restaurant's gazpacho is perhaps a bit too heavy with garlic and pepper and could do with a bit more oil and vinegar.

Among the appetizers, the Spanish mountain ham is recommended, although the slices may be too thick for the most critical preferences. The owner-waiter recently recommended a white wine of Bilbainas that was too sweet for one palate; a rioja fino ordered subsequently was far more suitable.

All dishes are à la carte, with main courses at midday from about $1.40 to $3.00; in the evening, from about $3.25 to $4.50. *Cocktails, wines. Closed Monday and major holidays.*
AE BA CB DC MC

★ EMILIANA'S RESTAURANT
1111 First Avenue (at 61st Street)   838-9726

This is a rather large, friendly Italian restaurant close to the Sutton Place area that looks like a dimly lighted saloon. There is a bar in front with banquettes and a dining room with a creaky floor to the rear. There are some interesting aspects to dining here.

On one occasion, for example, there was genuine, handmade spinach ravioli, a novelty in that the vast majority of all ravioli served in New York is stamped out by machine. There was also a dish called chicken francese, or chicken French-style, with lemon, and it would have been good except it was overly salted. A dish of osso buco, or veal knuckle, was better.

The chief fault to be found with Emiliana's is that the chef seems to overcook some of his dishes, including an order of gnocchi and broccoli.

On the other hand, the dishes at Emiliana's are modestly priced, with main courses from about $1.60 to $4.00. *Cocktails, wines. There is dancing Friday and Saturday evenings. Open 7 days a week except Thanksgiving and Christmas.*

★★ EMPIRE CHINESE RESTAURANT, THE
191 Madison Avenue (between 34th and 35th Streets)
683-3465

This is a Chinese restaurant with screens and scrolls and mirrored columns. The boast of the place is that it can, unlike most of its competitors, produce Pekin duck on one hour's notice. And the duck is good, if unauthentic. In lieu of the traditional water-flour-sesame-seed doilies, The Empire serves slices of yeast rolls with the crisp duck skin. The kitchen may tamper with tradition, but the food is generally very good. Luncheons cost from about $1.85 for chow mein to $3.95 for chicken and triple delight. The à la carte menu has main courses from about $3.25 for moo goo gai pan to $12.00 for the duck, which is two courses for two. *Cocktails, wines. Only à la carte items are available on Sunday, from 1:30 p.m. Closed Thanksgiving.*
DC AC

★ ESPLANADE, THE
969 Lexington Avenue (near 70th Street)   UN 1-2015

The management of this small neighborhood restaurant is Swiss and the menu is French and Italian. The cuisine is moderately expensive, but very good. Many of the dishes, such as the bay scallops sautéed and kidneys Esplanade, are prepared to order. Luncheons are à la

carte with main courses from about $2.50 to $3.50. There are complete dinners from about $5.00 to $6.00 and à la carte entrées in the evening from about $3.50 to $6.00. There is a 50-cent cover charge on a meal when no alcoholic beverage is bought to accompany it. *Cocktails, wines. On Saturday the restaurant opens at 5:30 p.m. Closed Sunday.*
AE DC

★ ESTHER ENG
18 Pell Street   732-0175

Legend has it that the late Esther Eng and her associates, most of whom were of the Chinese theater, were stranded in New York and opened one of the best of the town's Chinese restaurants, Bo Bo, at 20½ Pell Street. Miss Eng eventually opened her own establishment at 18 Pell Street, and the food is good, although not up to the nearby Bo Bo's. The décor of Esther Eng is conventional, the reception is warm, and the service, on one occasion at least, excellent. There is a complete luncheon from about $1.40 to $2.00. A la carte entrées, available at all times, cost from about $3.25 to $5.75. *Cocktails, wines. Dinner is served Sunday from 11:30 a.m.*
AE CB DC MC

★★ ESTIA
308 East 86th Street   628-9100

Never underestimate the enthusiasm of the grecophiles in New York. This pleasant Greek restaurant is frequently patronized to capacity. And it isn't all that small.

There is a long room on two levels with décor that includes birdcages, brick walls, and Greek tapestries. The kitchen may be as competent as you'll find in any Hellenic restaurant in the city. There are very good appetizers—eggplant purée with sesame oil; stuffed vine leaves (which may also be had as a main course); cucumbers with anchovies; and, of course, taramosalata, that excellent paste made with fish roe and lemon.

The Estia's taramosalata is a little too smooth (it should have a somewhat grainy texture), but it is well-seasoned and served with hard-cooked eggs. The lamb peasant-style with tomatoes is a very good main course, and the moussaka lightly seasoned with cinnamon is plain, but appetizing. The striped bass spetsiota was recently overcooked and perhaps cooked too far in advance. The restaurant on certain days offers baby lamb and suckling pig on a spit.

The menu is à la carte, with main courses from about $4.00 to $5.50. *Cocktails, wines. The restaurant opens at 5:00 p.m. every day.*
AE DC MC

★★ EVA HUNGARIAN RESTAURANT
1556 Second Avenue (between 80th and 81st Streets)
861-1096

If you have a hankering for what is frequently called "home-style" cooking, you will find much to admire at the Eva Hungarian. It is a cafeteria-style, self-service restaurant, but the food—although served from a steam table—seems cooked with uncommon care.

There are things like a rich goulash soup, a meal in itself; good chicken paprikás; Szekely stuffed cabbage; braised veal shanks; and so on. Considering the quality of the ingredients, the price is right.

One dish that was not the equal of the others was the palacsinta, a rolled, filled pancake dessert. It had been made too far in advance and tasted it.

The cost of a business lunch is $1.60, and à la carte dishes are priced from about $1.60 to $2.50. *Wines, beers. Closed Monday.*

★ FEDORA
239 West Fourth Street   CH 2-9691

    This is an odd, inelegant, pleasant little restaurant in Greenwich Village, with attentive service, even if it is unprofessional (it seems polished by comparison with that in some of its more ambitious counterparts uptown). The food is honest and, although you may not dine on champagne and lark's tongues, you can have a decent and extensive dinner for $2.75 to $6.50. Some of the customers are Village characters (ladies wearing beehive hats and sipping extra dry martinis) and the waiters when not in motion stand at the rear of the restaurant smoking cigarettes.

The food is largely of Italian inspiration—perhaps mock-Italian—and the pasta is generally overcooked. The greens in the salads are crisp and excellent with Romaine and Boston lettuce and not a trace of iceberg.

In addition to the complete dinner, there are à la carte dishes priced from about $2.50 up. *Cocktails, wines. The restaurant is open for dinner only. Closed Tuesday and Christmas.*

★★ FILIPPO RESTAURANT
146 West Houston Street   228-3090

    This is an agreeable, wholly unpretentious Italian restaurant in Greenwich Village, with a small kitchen in the dining room and only a dozen or so tables. The chef is young and enthusiastic and seems to know what he's about. Happiness would have been to sample the spaghetti with fresh sardine sauce he'd cooked for himself (we were already in the middle of sausages with peppers, shrimp marinara, and spaghetti when it was spotted). If you're not in the mood for Italian dishes, try the fish.

Filippo's spaghetti is cooked to order. There is only one menu for lunch and dinner. The price of a main course includes pasta or salad or vegetable from $1.75 to $3.75.

Wines, beers. Closed Monday, major holidays, and 2 weeks in July.
MC

★ FISHERMAN'S NET
493 Third Avenue (near 33rd Street)   LE 2-1683

There is one thing about the vast majority of New York restaurants—their menus are nothing if not predictable. Most of the Italian restaurants are alike, and so are the small French bistros. The menu at the Fisherman's Net resembles a dozen or so others, but the fish is fresh and the service amiable. There are complete luncheons ranging in price from about $2.50 for broiled swordfish to $3.60 for a shrimp platter. The à la carte menu available at all meals has entrées from about $2.75 for broiled sea trout to $8.85 for a large broiled lobster. *Cocktails, wines. Open 7 days a week, except Thanksgiving and Christmas. Luncheon is not served on Sunday. All major credit cards.*

★ 500 ON 8TH RESTAURANT, THE
500 Eighth Avenue (at 35th Street)   736-6171

This is a large restaurant with gauche-modern décor in the garment district. It has one of those thoroughly familiar menus with the usual listings of broiled sole, deep-fried sea scallops, old-fashioned beef stew, and on and on, but the restaurant also has an excellent chicken soup with matzoh balls and very good sandwiches. A special luncheon is $3.95; complete dinners are about $4.95. A la carte entrées at lunch are from $3.25 to $7.65; in the evening, they are $4.25 to $8.50. *Cocktails, wines. Closed Sunday, and Saturday and Sunday in the summer.*

★★ FLEUR DE LIS
141 West 69th Street   874-9060

An uncluttered, provincial-style French restaurant with an extensive menu. The food is hearty in concept

and appointment; service is friendly and willing. The pâté is robust and garlicky; the coq au vin and tripe à la mode de Caen are good, and the restaurant's version of cassoulet delighted one palate. The menu is à la carte with luncheon entrées from $2.50 to $4.75 and dinner entrées from about $3.50 to $9.00. *Cocktails, wines. Dinner is served from noon on Sunday.*
Most major credit cards.

★ FLOWER DRUM RESTAURANT
856 Second Avenue (near 45th Street)   OX 7-4280

This is a rather spacious and colorful Chinese restaurant whose menu boasts four schools of Chinese cooking and seasonal menus. The luncheon menu is prix fixe and somewhat routine, with entrées, such as chow mein and shrimp in lobster sauce, from $1.95 to $3.95. The dinner menu, also available at midday, is à la carte and more inspired. The cost of main courses is from about $2.50 to $8.00. *Cocktails, wines. Only à la carte items are available Saturday and Sunday.*
AE CB DC MC

★ FONDA LA PALOMA
156 East 49th Street   *421-5495*

With a little imagination this could develop into one of the pleasantest Mexican restaurants in town. The food at Fonda La Paloma is very good, whether it is enchilada, taco, or stuffed chilies, and a better guacamole would be hard to find. The fault lies in the tables, a bit rickety and too close together, and the service, friendly but slow. One menu at the restaurant serves throughout the day. It is à la carte with entrées from about $4.25 for chicken tacos to $5.50 for steak. *Cocktails, wines. On Saturday, the restaurant opens at 5:00 p.m. Closed Sunday.*
AE CB DC

★ FOO CHOW RESTAURANT
1278 Third Avenue (between 72nd and 73rd Streets)
861-4350

The menu of the Foo Chow seems more interesting than that of many other Chinese restaurants in town, particularly those outside Chinatown. The quality of the ingredients here seems first-class, but some of the dishes seem to lack sufficient seasoning, and one always suspects that this is done as some sort of compromise. A dish of crab and bean curd, for example, seemed far too bland. A dish of chicken with bamboo shoots had more character, but there did seem to be the taste of garlic powder, which is a negative substitute for freshly chopped garlic.

One outstanding dish was a platter of fried dumplings, expertly filled with a pork and ginger mixture and eaten with a table-made sauce of soy, white vinegar, and oil.

A la carte dishes are priced from about $2.75 to $7.00. Uninspired lunch combinations go from $1.50 to $2.50. *Cocktails, wines. Open 7 days a week. Luncheon is not served Saturday and Sunday.*
AE DC MC

★★★ FORLINI'S
93 Baxter Street   349-6779

If Forlini's is feverishly crowded at times, it is for the best of reasons. It has within the last few years become one of the best Italian restaurants in Manhattan.

It is a rather large friendly restaurant in Little Italy with two dining rooms and a long bar. Forlini's menu looks generally like that of a hundred more Italian restaurants in town, but the food is cooked with exceptional care. For example, the grilled fish is actually grilled, rather than placed under the broiler.

Among dishes sampled recently, the small pasta in an eggdrop soup was especially good and so was the escarole in broth. Among the main courses, the osso buco was expertly prepared and served with an excellent risotto with mushrooms and chicken livers. An order of boneless chicken parmigiana was commendable.

One of the reasons for the excellence of the food at Forlini's is the turnover in clientele and, at times, particularly in the evening, some of the special dishes may not be available. The menu is generally à la carte, with main courses from about $1.75 to $7.50, although complete meals may be ordered by adding $2.50 to any à la carte dish. *Cocktails, wines. Open 7 days a week, except Christmas and the first 2 weeks in August.*
AE MC UC

★ FORNOS
236 West 52nd Street   CI 7-9420

There are Latin-Americans and others in town who think of this as one of the best Spanish restaurants in the city. The menus are à la carte, with main courses from about $4.00 to $7.00. To be sure of good food, it is best to order several hours or a day in advance. *Cocktails, wines. Luncheon is served Monday through Friday; dinner, Monday through Saturday. Closed Sunday and the last 2 weeks in August.*

FORUM OF THE TWELVE CAESARS, THE
57 West 48th Street   PL 7-3450

In New York, it is possible to be almost constantly appalled at restaurants with a superficial grandeur and elevated prices that dare in sum to be brazenly pedestrian. The Forum of the Twelve Caesars fits the pattern. There is gloriously starched napery, handsome silver, service plates in bas-relief, and, in the midst of it all, too often to be called chance, food that is mediocre beyond redemption. The menu is as broad as the gestures of the waiters and, like the waiters, it is mostly show without substance. There are some good dishes all right, including the gazpacho in summer, the leek and sausage pie, and the live trout, although that, too, is sometimes over-

cooked. But the mixed grill! Such a difficult dish to spoil, with the least care. You ask for a lamb chop rare, and it is duly recorded by the waiter. The chop and other meats arrive overcooked and drenched in a heavy sauce, strongly spiced. All dishes are à la carte with luncheon entrées from about $3.25 for egg dishes to $10.75; those at dinner are from about $5.75 to $8.50. There is an excellent and, for this genre of restaurant, reasonably priced wine list. *Cocktails, wines. Luncheon is not served on Saturday. Closed Sunday during the summer.*
AE BA CB DC

★★ FOUR FIVE SIX
2 Bowery   964-5853

The many people in Manhattan who claim the old Four Five Six restaurant (the Say Eng Look) across the way from this establishment as one of the best Chinese restaurants in Chinatown should also be pleased with this branch. The name, incidentally, has to do with a grouping of tiles in Mah-Jongg.

All the dishes sampled here have ranged from very good to outstanding, from the double fried pork and shrimp with Formosa mushrooms and snow peas to an incredibly good dish (not on the menu) called dai cheng chicken. The chicken is in a dark, quite spicy sauce, with black mushrooms, bamboo shoots, and red peppers. The fried fish with seaweed is a standout.

The luncheon menu has a lot of the stereotyped dishes, including chow mein and pepper steak, but there is also phoenix tail fish, chicken with brown sauce, and shredded pork with salted cabbage.

By most standards, the décor of the Four Five Six is on the sophisticated side. The restaurant occupies two floors. There is the feeling here that the food will be at its ultimate if you visit the restaurant with a Chinese friend.

There are complete luncheons priced from about $1.15 to $1.85. All dishes on the principal menu are à la carte with main courses from about $1.95 to $3.25. *There is no bar. Open 7 days a week.*

★★★ FOUR SEASONS, THE
99 East 52nd Street   PL *1-4300*

The Four Seasons, like cheese and wine, improves with age. It has always been one of the most inventive restaurants in the city, and it is essentially how a New York restaurant should look. It has an opulence that is rare to behold and boasts works of art by Picasso and Miró and a stunning floating sculpture by Richard Lippold. The presentation of the foods, whether a ring of littleneck clams on ice or an exceptionally good seviche in a silver shell, is admirable. One recalls, among others, a notable dish of poached chicken with thin noodles and a rich broth and a well-made omelet with morels, or woodland mushrooms. All dishes are à la carte, with main luncheon courses from about $4.25 for eggs Benedict to about $11.00 for tournedos; main dinner entrées are from about $6.50 for flounder to $11.00 for filet mignon. There is a $1.25 cover charge at lunch, $1.50 at dinner. *Cocktails, wines. Luncheon is not served Saturday during the summer. Closed Sunday.*
AE BA CB DC MC

★★ FRANKIE AND JOHNNIE
269 West 45th Street   CI *5-9717*

There is a dearth of good eating establishments in the Broadway area, and Frankie and Johnnie, which bills itself as "Simpson's in the Strand," is one of the best. It is an excellent steak house and therefore immensely popular. It is small, crowded at the dinner hour, and a trifle noisy. The steaks are first-rate and the service enthusiastic. In addition to grilled dishes, the menu lists such items as chicken in the pot with matzoh balls, shrimp creole, and creamed chicken au gratin. The menu is à la carte with main courses from about $5.50 for chicken à la king to

$8.25 for filet mignon. The restaurant, which serves dinner only, opens at 4:30 P.M. *Cocktails, wines. Closed Sunday and major holidays.*
AE DC

FRAUNCES TAVERN
54 Pearl Street (at Broad Street) BO *9-0144*

The history is here no doubt. This is, as the literature says, "one of America's oldest buildings." It was built in 1719 and was acquired in 1762 "by Samuel Fraunces as the Queen's Head Tavern, scene of Washington's farewell to his officers on December 4, 1783." There is also musty décor, but the "olde worlde" ambience is considerably done in by the loud piped-in music. The menu is limited, good at times, but dull. The seafood is fair to middling. The roast beef was of obviously good quality. No particular care was taken with the vegetables or the tearoom-variety salads. And on and on. There is one menu for lunch and dinner. Main courses cost from about $2.75 to $7.95 for steak. *Cocktails, wines. Closed weekends.*
Most major credit cards.

★★ FRENCH QUARTER, THE
The Americana Hotel, Seventh Avenue and 52nd Street
581-1000

It goes by many names—smorgasbord, cold table, hot and cold buffet, etc.—but it has, in the last few decades, become an American institution.

The hot and cold buffet served at noon at The French Quarter has much to recommend it, keeping in mind, of course, that the cost is only $2.75 for all you can eat. There are not many restaurants in town with a comparable offering of food in relation to price.

There are many items on the buffet and the cold dishes, in particular, come off very well. There are generally shrimp with rémoulade sauce (which, along with fried chicken, are about the only New Orleans-related things on the menu, despite the name); cold fried chicken; pickles, including watermelon rind and pickled corn; salads, including cole slaw, potato salad, and cold beets; and so on. The rémoulade sauce was surprisingly like that found in New Orleans.

Among the hot dishes are roast beef, brisket of beef, and either shrimp or chicken creole. The roast beef was a bit tough; the creole dishes tasted mass-produced.

There is no buffet in the evening, but they do serve assorted "creole" hors d'oeuvres with cocktails—fried shrimp; barbecued ribs; and small, well-seasoned meat patties—that cost $1.

The setting is comfortable, a bit corny but pleasant—a large square bar in the center with mock French Quarter décor and beautiful waitresses in net stockings and with sequins on their black shoulder straps.

The bar's martinis are not 10-to-1 (more like 3-to-1) as noted on the place mats, but the draught beer is thoroughly iced and excellent. *Cocktails. Open 7 days a week. Luncheon is not served Saturday and Sunday.*
AE CB DC

★★★ FRENCH SHACK, THE
65 West 55th Street   CI 6-5126

The French Shack ranks with the best medium-priced French restaurants in New York. The kitchen is far more than merely competent. Some of the specialties of the house, which do not, incidentally, invariably appear on the menu, are well above average and include cassoulet and veal with fines herbes. There are two faults to be found with the restaurant: it is generally crowded, and a few of the tables are too close for comfort. The service staff is few in number and, although the service is industrious, it sometimes seems annoyingly slow. The cost of a complete luncheon is from about $4.50 to $6.50. Dinner is à la carte, with main courses from about $4.00 to

$8.50. *Cocktails, wines. On Sunday the restaurant opens at 5:00 p.m. Closed major holidays and the month of July.*
AE DC

★ FRIAR TUCK
914 Third Avenue (near 55th Street)   688-4725

The Friar Tuck, another in a long list of would-be English pubs in Manhattan, has become one of the busiest restaurants in the city. The piped-in music can scarcely be heard above the din of voices. There are cobblestone walls, beams, red tablecloths, and candlelight, and the restaurant is on two levels. The lower one resembles a dungeon. There is sidewalk dining from April through October. Two dishes were eaten with pleasure at the Friar Tuck. A mutton chop with kidney came off exceptionally well and so did the roast prime ribs of beef. Some of the dishes, such as the shepherd's pie, seem ordinary, and the sauces for other meat dishes have a pasty look. A word should be said for the waitresses: all of them seem models of enthusiasm and efficiency. Complete luncheons are priced from $2.85 to $3.35. A la carte dishes from $1.35 for a hamburger to $7.95 for sirloin steak. *Cocktails, wines.*
AE BA DC MC

★★ FRINI
271 Amsterdam Avenue (near 72nd Street)   TR 4-8950

Anyone with a penchant for excellently prepared Latin-American food in a restaurant that may be short on décor will probably find Frini to his liking. The food is good, whether it is a combination Mexican plate with tamale, tacos, rice, and beans ($2.95) or the spiced chopped meat stew known as picadillo à la española ($3.25). The Venezuelan hallacas ($3.25), with its meat and olives in a steamed cornmeal coating with cheese, is also especially good. Frini's is small, and at peak dining

hours there may very well be a wait for a table. *Beers, wines. Only à la carte items are available Saturday and Sunday, from noon. Closed Monday.*
MC

★★★ FU SHIN RESTAURANT
318 East 86th Street   535-3401

There was a time when 86th Street concerned itself mainly—and to no great distinction—with the pig's feet and sauerkraut school of cookery. And wurst. Within recent memory, however, several restaurants have opened there, international in scope, and more than a little worthwhile.

One of the most welcome is the Fu Shin, which is Chinese and one of the best this side of Chinatown. It is a conventional-looking place, but the menu isn't. Oh, for sure, you can get chow mein and things foo young, and, if you order things of that ilk, you get what you deserve.

On the other hand, the menu offers a very good moo shee pork, the shredded pork dish with tree ears and day lily stamens; first-rate fried dumplings; very good shredded chicken with shredded snow peas; excellent cubed chicken with hot pepper. But for these dishes you must specify whether you really like it authentic or watered down for the Western palate.

The Fu Shin has established itself as a place of some importance, and reservations are recommended. At noon there are combination platters with dessert priced from $1.75 to $2.75, with à la carte dishes from about $1.85 to $3.95. The principal menu lists dishes from about $1.95 to $10.00 for Szechuan duck. *Cocktails, wines. Open 7 days a week. Luncheon is served on Wednesday, Thursday, and Friday.*
AE   DC

★ GAETANO'S
242 East 58th Street   PL 9-4660

Gaetano's, which has been around for several years and is now in a new location, offers a fixed price menu with a limited choice of entrées, and the idea, although not original, is a good one.

There is no written menu. It is outlined by a waiter, and there are five courses each evening. The cost of a complete and abundant meal is $8.00. A recent dinner included a first course of stuffed clams; minestrone; linguine all'Alfredo; a choice of three main dishes, which were veal scaloppine, contrefilet of beef, or scampi; salad; a dessert of cannoli and grapes; and coffee.

The clams were excellent; the minestrone was a decent vegetable soup; the sauce on the linguine was too "loose" and needed both butter and cheese; the breaded veal was of good quality, but the crumbs didn't adhere properly to the meat; the beef was tasty; and the cannoli were of good flavor, but the pastry was not as crisp as it should have been. Salads are served in cereal bowls.

Gaetano's is a pleasant place with its low ceiling, hanging plastic plants, and rough-textured plaster walls the color of pink cake frosting. *Cocktails, wines. The restaurant opens every day at 6:00 p.m. except Sunday and Monday, when it is closed, as it is on major holidays.*

★★ GAGE AND TOLLNER
372 Fulton Street, Brooklyn (near Borough Hall)
TR 5-5181

This establishment, founded in 1879, is four years older than the Brooklyn Bridge and just about equally revered. The most notable entrées on an extensive menu are the steaks, fish, and seafood. There are about 50 ways of preparing oysters and clams listed on the menu. The turn-of-the-century décor with arched mirrors is admirable. The à la carte menu, available all day, ranges in price from about $2.75 for sausages to $8.00 for sirloin steak. Special lunches, served Monday through Friday, cost about $3.50 to $4.50. The restaurant closes at approximately 9:00 P.M. *Cocktails, wines. Closed Sunday and major holidays.*

★★★ GAIETY WEST RESTAURANT AND DELICATESSEN
224 West 47th Street   765-1240
GAIETY EAST
684 Lexington Avenue (between 56th and 57th Streets)
PL *9-3455*

The original Gaiety Restaurant was a cubicle-size establishment in the theater district, and it was called the biggest little restaurant in New York. But there are now two Gaietys—East and West. The chronicles say that John Barrymore used to go there after the bars closed, and the management once filled an order for pickles and salami dispatched by air to Zero Mostel, who was making a film in Spain. The original Gaiety closed.

The new Gaiety West has its faults, but it also has the best sandwiches (along with its competitor, the Stage Delicatessen). The seating capacity has been vastly increased, but the quality of its sandwiches is undiminished. The hot corned beef, the fresh brisket of beef, the pastrami, chopped chicken liver and so on are overstuffed into some of the freshest rye bread in Manhattan. On each day's menu (at least on three recent visits) there has been a "Today's Special" of boiled beef in pot with matzoh ball, and the meat, short ribs of beef, is excellent, although the peas in the broth are canned.

There are up- and downstairs dining rooms, counter service, take-out service, and a bar at the Gaiety West. The décor—reported to cost six figures—is just plain modern. In a pure sense one could carp about much minutiae including the piped-in music, the maraschino cherries in the grapefruit halves, and the slow bar service, but with those sandwiches one is able to forgive all. And be thankful for an available seat.

The cost of sandwiches is from 80 cents for a frankfurter to $3.25 for sturgeon and cream cheese on a bagel. The most expensive item on the menu is the tenderloin steak at $3.50.

Like its predecessor, the Gaiety West is open night and day. It is closed from 4 A.M. to 7 A.M. for cleaning. Orders are delivered any place in town. *Beer at both, cocktails West only.*

GALLAGHER'S 33
133 West 33rd Street   736-3373

If all or most of the food at the new Gallagher's 33 was up to two desserts sampled recently, it would be something to praise with small reservation. One was a sinfully rich and creamy cheesecake, the other a melting and seductive chocolate layer cake. The décor is pleasant enough; it takes its theme from Madison Square Garden a half block away.

As to the main courses, there seems to be a tendency to either overgrill or underbroil the meats. The overcooked ones recently included a thick dry slice of liver and double lamb chops. A somewhat chewy sirloin steak was returned to the kitchen for reheating. An order of creamed spinach, brought to the table halfway through a meal, was watery. The salad dressing, including the Russian and Roquefort, are commonplace. The mustard sauce is good.

All dishes are à la carte, with main dishes at midday from about $3.25 to $6.85; in the evening from about $5.75 to $7.50. *Cocktails, wines. Closed Saturday and Sunday.*
Most major credit cards.

★★ GATTI'S
246 East 40th Street   MU 6-7670

Casual elegance is the atmosphere engendered by

the brick walls lined with wine racks, stately archways, rolling service carts, strolling musicians, and waiters in peasant-style striped shirts and cummerbunds at the Trattoria Gatti. A fairly large and popular restaurant on three floors, it is divided into small rooms to give an intimate setting. The extensive à la carte menu offers a wide variety of Italian dishes, generally well-prepared, as well as a selection of steaks and chops. There is a supplementary kitchen to prepare the pasta products and ice cream specialties served. Scaloppine alla Gatti and misto di pesce livornese (Italian-style fish stew) are recommended specialties of the house. All dishes are à la carte, with main luncheon courses from about $3.00 to $6.50; main dinner courses from about $3.95 to $6.95. *Cocktails, wines. On Saturday, the restaurant opens at 5:30 p.m. Closed Sunday and major holidays.*
AE CB DC

★★★ GAUGIN ROOM, THE
2 Columbus Circle　　LT *1-2311 and* LT *1-2721*

Visitors to afternoon or evening performances at Lincoln Center should not overlook The Gauguin Room on the ninth floor of The Gallery of Modern Art. This is one of the pleasantest dining rooms in New York. The Polynesian food, although specialized, is delicious, and it is prepared with admirable care. There is an excellent assortment of appetizers including crab-meat puffs, tempura shrimp, and barbecued pork with pineapple. The curries, whether of shrimp, chicken, or filet mignon, are well-spiced, and the steak teriyaki is first-rate. There is no handsomer cocktail lounge in all the city, and the drinks are served in generous portions. It is true that there is a $1.00 admission fee to enter the gallery in order to gain access to the restaurant, but the food is worth it. The menus are à la carte, with main courses at noon from $2.95 to $7.25; in the evening from $3.50 to $7.75. *Cocktails. Wines are available, but beer is recommended.*

Closed Monday. Tuesday through Saturday, lunch from 12:00 noon to 2:30 p.m. and dinner from 5:00 p.m. to 8:00 p.m. On Saturday and Sunday, the restaurant is open from noon to 6:00 p.m., and the last seating is 5:00 p.m.

★★ GENE'S
73 West 11th Street   OR 5-2048

This is an enormously agreeable Italian restaurant with a kitchen that is superior to most of its kind in the city. And the management seems to be painstaking in caring for customers. There is an interesting appetizer and main course called shrimps Robert; the pasta dishes are good, particularly the fettuccine Alfredo with prosciutto; and the breast of capon Gismonda is excellent. The veal at Gene's is of only average quality, but its preparation is admirable. Complete luncheons cost from $3.00 to $5.00; à la carte dishes at midday from $1.25 to $3.25. Complete dinners cost from $5.00 to $7.50; à la carte dishes in the evening from $4.00 to $7.50. *Cocktails, wines. On Sunday, dinner is served from 1:00 p.m.*
AE   DC

★★★ GEORGES REY, RESTAURANT FRANCAIS
60 West 55th Street   CI 5-6764

Georges Rey has a highly satisfactory French kitchen. This is a large restaurant and the service is competent. It is one of the most congenial restaurants in Manhattan, and by most local standards reasonably priced. Prix-fixe meals cost from $3.75 to $6.50 for luncheon, $6.75 to $9.50 for dinner. A la carte prices are from $2.75 at midday and from $4.75 in the evening. A la carte prices at supper start at $1.50. *Cocktails, wines. On Sundays and holidays the restaurant opens at 4:30 p.m.*
AE   MC

★★ GIAMBONE
42 Mulberry Street   WO 2-8187

If New York does not have a great Italian restaurant to compare with the best of Florence or Rome, it has a fair number where you can find very good bourgeois Neapolitan cooking, and Giambone is one of them. It is in Little Italy, and the food is cooked to order, which in itself is a bonus.

Here you can find an excellent, if a bit robust, marinara sauce, a highly palatable saltimbocca or veal with prosciutto, admirable veal French-style, pork chops pizzaiola, and creditable unaccustomed dishes such as stuffed squid.

The bothersome thing is that so many dishes are not available. Recently there was neither cappelletti in chicken broth nor chicken rollatine, although both are listed on the menu. And equally bothersome is the service. The waiters are friendly enough (there was only one at a recent dinner and only one at a recent lunch) and they travel fast, but the service over-all leaves much to be desired.

The décor of Giambone's is far from fancy—except for the bar, it might be a luncheonette. But the chef knows what he is doing, and you'll have to ignore the rest.

One menu serves throughout the day. The cost of main dishes is from about $2.25 to $7.50. *Cocktails, wines. Open 7 days a week.*

★ GIM BECK
70 Mott Street   226-8778 and 925-0540

This is one of a series of noodle and wonton shops in Chinatown, most of which are distinguished by their small size, wall menus printed in Chinese calligraphy, and smiling or non-smiling waiters who have some difficulty in communicating with non-Chinese speaking customers.

In any event, the food, even when ordered in such hit and miss fashion, can prove exceptionally tasty—rich wheat noodle dishes with bean sprouts, Chinese cabbage, scallions and fresh coriander leaves and a choice of pork, chicken, or beef; rich gluten noodles with the same meats; excellent wonton; and so on. These dishes also represent some of the best food bargains in the city.

Most of the dishes cost around $1.50 and the portions are copious. There are only about 8 tables at the Gim Beck, and these may be shared with strangers. The hot tea is served in tumblers. *There is no bar. The restaurant is open 7 days a week.*

GINGER MAN, THE
51 West 64th Street   SC *4-7272 and* SC *4-7158*

The only thing that seems to have remained constant since the Ginger Man opened is the décor. The food is certainly not the same. However, the entrance area was full at 12:45 on a Monday afternoon (filled with guileless tourists, it would appear). In a back room there is an unpleasant, musty odor and piped-in music. An omelet Grandmère lacked a fresh herb flavor and was devoid of salt and pepper. An order of shashlik was overcooked, dry, tough, and gristly. The rice was reheated. A roulade Leontine—a chocolate roll—was still frozen in the middle. A mousse of chocolate was ordinary. All dishes à la carte, with main courses at midday from about $2.00 for a cheese omelet to $4.65 for sirloin; in the evening, from about $4.85 to $7.15. The supper dishes go from $1.25 to $5.85. *Cocktails, wines. Open 7 days a week. Closed major holidays.*
AE   CB   DC   MC

★★ GINO'S RESTAURANT
780 Lexington Avenue (near 61st Street)   TE *8-9827*

In any list of New York restaurants with Italian cuisine, Gino's should be ranked among the best. The food is not altogether subtle, but its character is laudably good South Italian. There is a faithful, knowing clientele and the restaurant is generally crowded. The menu is extensive and both lunch and dinner are à la carte. Main luncheon courses from about $2.65; dinner courses from about $3.75. *Cocktails, wines. Open 7 days a week, except for New Year's Day, Thanksgiving, and Christmas. Reservations are not accepted.*

★★★ GIORDANO RESTAURANT
409 West 39th Street   WI 7-9811

This is a raffish, excellent Italian restaurant in an unlikely neighborhood near the entrance to the Lincoln Tunnel. It is the sort of place about which people say, "Don't praise it too highly, you may spoil it." There are brick walls and posters and a relaxed clientele. The veal and fish dishes are recommended in particular. There is no menu, and the cost of main dishes at lunch is $3.75 to $6.25; dinner ranges from about $4.50 to $7.50. There is a garden for outdoor dining during the summer months. *Cocktails, wines. On Saturday and Sunday the restaurant opens at 5:00 p.m. Closed New Year's Day, Thanksgiving, and Christmas.*
AE   BA   CB   DC   MC

★★ GIOVANNI
66 East 55th Street   PL 3-1230

The kitchen at Giovanni's is, for the most part, excellent, and the restaurant's appetizers are among the most creditable in town. The cold clams aspic, celery root rémoulade, herring, stuffed eggs, and head cheese vinaigrette are all of high order. The trouble with the restaurant is the seating. The tables are too close together, and listening to a stranger's conversation is often unavoidable. Both luncheon and dinner are prix fixe; complete meals at midday from $7.00, and in the evening from $9.75. The menu is French and Italian. *Cocktails, wines. Closed Sunday, Saturday and Sunday in summer, and most major holidays.*

★ GIRAFE
208 East 58th Street   PL 2-3054

Understated elegance is the atmosphere at Girafe, with its red carpet, potted palms, fine crystal, armoire of ceramic beasts, and photomurals of the African veldt. The menu is international: a preponderance of Italian dishes at noon and the predictable steak, lobster, and duck at night. The service is highly professional and attentive.

Judging from an excellent fettuccine Alfredo with homemade noodles, the chef is Italian. It was not prepared tableside. An antipasto appetizer was uninspired, but the spiced mushrooms Sardinia were good. The French onion soup came off well, but a Scotch barley soup turned out to be creamed and a disappointment.

The scampi Mediterraneo, with a light garlic flavor, could not be improved upon. At one luncheon, the chicken and veal patty, Russian-style, had good texture and seasoning, but was marred by a starchy cream sauce. The Brie cheese served looked suitably ripe from a distance, but proved to be cold and lacking in flavor.

The house special dessert, frozen mocaccino, layers of orange sherbet, chocolate, and mountains of whipped cream, was a letdown.

A spiral staircase leads to a second-floor room that is available for private parties. Menus are à la carte, with main entrées at lunch from $3.75 for an omelet fines herbes to $6.50 for minute steak. Dinner entrées go from $4.75 for pasta to $22 for Chateaubriand to serve two. Women's menus have no prices. *Cocktails, wines. Open for lunch, dinner, and late supper snacks, Monday through Saturday. Closed Sunday.*
Most major credit cards.

★ GLORIA'S RESTAURANT
134 East 26th Street   MU 4-8875

A tiny, tiny, darkly illuminated restaurant with one of the most unobtrusive entrances in Manhattan. It is, nonetheless, a well-known pocket of eating, and reservations are almost invariably essential. It is a nice, friendly, warm place with paintings hung askew, candlelight, and plastic poinsettias on the walls. There are less than a dozen tables and, on one occasion, only one waiter, who was busier than a whirling dervish. The trouble is that no one man could whirl fast enough to properly accommodate the crowd.

The menu at Gloria's is, by and large, conventional, with the usual parmigiana listings, spaghetti and other pastas with various sauces, scampi, veal and peppers, and so on. Gloria's huge success seems due to three things: It is a "fun" place to visit, it is inexpensive, and the food is cooked with reasonable care, although the large antipasto is an edible cliché.

All dishes are à la carte, with main courses from about $1.55 to $3.95. The restaurant is open evenings only, starting at 6:00 P.M. *There is no bar, but wines may be brought. Closed Sunday, major holidays, and the first 2 weeks in July.*

★★ GLOUCESTER HOUSE
37 East 50th Street   PL 5-7394

Manhattan does not boast an altogether great fish and seafood house with extraordinary gustatory creations. However, if there were a sweepstakes for Manhattan's most outstanding one, the Gloucester House might come off best. The décor is plain, polished, and atmospheric, without seeming coy. The food is plain and good, with most dishes in the broiled and steamed category. Best of all, the fish is fresh. All dishes are à la carte and the same menu serves for both lunch and dinner. The cost of main courses is from about $4.25 (parsley omelet) to $12.50 ("jumbo" lobster) with potatoes and salad. *Cocktails, wines. On Sunday, the restaurant opens at 1:00 p.m. Closed Thanksgiving and Christmas.*

★★ GOLD COIN
994 Second Avenue (between 52nd and 53rd Streets)
PL *8-1251*

This is one of the best of the city's "bourgeois" Chinese dining spots. The food may be somewhat Westernized, but it is first-class, nonetheless. Complete luncheons from about $2.25 to $3.00; dinners à la carte with main dishes from about $4.50 to $7.75. *Cocktails, wines. On Saturday and Sunday the restaurant opens at 3:00 p.m. Closed major holidays and the first 2 weeks in August.*
AE CB DC MC

★ GOLDEN COACH
578 Second Avenue (near 32nd Street)   OR *9-4669 and* OR *9-4670*

This Chinese restaurant in the Kips Bay Shopping Center has a pleasant atmosphere and the waiters are agreeable. The special luncheon is ordinary and the à la carte dishes, available at all meals, range from so-so spareribs to a most palatable combination of chicken and lobster. Complete luncheons from $1.40 to $3.00; à la carte dishes from about $2.50 to $7.00. *Cocktails, wines. On Sunday, dinner is served from 2 p.m.*
AE CB DC MC

★ GOLD FULL RESTAURANT
198 Canal Street   *964-0083*

Don't be put off by the cafeteria-and-steam-table atmosphere of this rather seedy-looking Chinese restaurant on the border of Chinatown. The food that comes from the kitchen, the roast duck in particular, can be exceptional. The steamed sea bass with ginger and the shrimp in the shell with black bean sauce, not listed on the menu, by the way, have merit. A casual visitor discovered them at a late luncheon hour when the staff sat down to dine.

A spokesman for the restaurant explained that the various foods on the steam table were mostly for the "working people" in the neighborhood to take out. The duck may also be taken out. It is subtly seasoned with Chinese flavors.

The cost of a special steam-table lunch at Gold Full is $1.50. Complete dinners are priced from $5.50 for two to $13.75 for five. A la carte dishes are priced from about $1.25 for roast pork lo mein (noodles) to $4.50 for steak kew. *Beer is served. Closed Tuesday.*

★ GONDOLA
729 Third Avenue (between 45th and 46th Streets)
MU 2-9658

The décor of the Gondola restaurant, with its red-carpeted wall behind the bar and red pinpointed lighting, is real fancy. Some of the dishes, particularly those made with fish and seafood, are excellent, and some, including the meat sauces for spaghetti, are ordinary. The risotto is made with genuine Italian rice. The most admirable thing about this establishment, perhaps, is the service, about as agreeable as you are likely to find in New York. Luncheon and dinner prices are à la carte with main courses from about $3.50 to $4.50. *Cocktails, wines. Closed Sunday and all holidays.*
Most major credit cards.

★★ GOODALE'S
986 Second Avenue (near 52nd Street)   755-7317

There are several things to admire about this very small seafood restaurant on the East Side, but chief among them is its departure from the commonplace fish houses of Manhattan.

The menu is limited, but it shows imagination, and the food is cooked with care. With cocktails, for example, guests are offered excellent meat balls seasoned with curry and bourbon. Among the first courses, there is available a cold, silken avocado soup, lightly flavored with rum; and exceptionally well-seasoned baked clams with crusty crumbs and bacon: a happy cry from the customary offerings about town, baked clams that are at once tough, lukewarm, and overly seasoned with orégano.

Among the main dishes at Goodale's, the broiled Mediterranean shrimp with melted butter and the broiled swordfish with lobster butter sauce are commendable.

Goodale's pumpkin pie, by the way, is overly spiced and heavy.

The proprietor is an affable New Englander. The décor is pleasant, with boat pennants here and there on walls of wood and brick.

The menu at both lunch and dinner is à la carte and the cost of main courses is from about $3.10 to $7.00. *Cocktails, wines. Closed Saturday and Sunday, major holidays, and 2 weeks in the summer.*
AE   BA   CB   DC

★★ GRANADOS RESTAURANT
125 Macdougal Street   OR 3-5576

This is one of the most notable of New York's Spanish restaurants. The cooking is not grand luxe, but is more on the order of what may be found in a well-run casa de huespedes, or boarding house, in Spain. There is an excellent dish made with shrimp lightly seasoned with garlic, scallions, tomatoes, and a sauce listed as salsa de la casa. In midsummer, there is an interesting gazpacho containing sour cream and seedless grapes. Some of the dishes, such as pork with pine nuts, have a commendable flavor, but the meat is of medium quality. The restaurant's flan, at times, is overcooked. The restaurant, located in Greenwich Village, has tables close together, and at peak dining hours they are generally filled. The à la carte main courses are from about $3.00 for eggs à la malagueña to $6.50 for a steak with wine sauce. The range for complete dinners is from $4.00 to $7.50. *Cocktails, wines. The restaurant opens at 5 p.m. There is a sidewalk café for outdoor dining May through September. Closed Thanksgiving.*
AE   CB   DC

GRAND CENTRAL TERMINAL
★Oyster Bar and Restaurant (MU 9-0776). The chefs here have the blithe and wonderful notion that calories were never invented. The fame of this institution is worldwide and is based primarily on rich and buttery seafood stews and pan roasts. Unfortunately, the deep-fried dishes do not come off as well. Seafood stews start at $2.65. *Cocktails, wines. Closed Sunday.*
AE CB DC

★★ GREAT SHANGHAI, THE
2689 Broadway (near 102nd Street)   UN 4-5906

Almost anyone with a penchant for reasonably priced, well-prepared Chinese food should find much to reward him on the menu of The Great Shanghai. The restaurant, near Columbia University, is spacious, and, despite the mass production, the kitchen is competent. There are Chinese egg rolls and wonton soup on the menu, but, happily, more adventurous dishes are listed as well. There are complete luncheons from about $1.35 to $3.50; complete dinners from about $1.75 to $3.95. The à la carte menu lists main courses from about $1.50 to $9.50. *Cocktails, wines. Dinner is served Sunday and holidays from noon.*
CB DC MC

★★ GREENSLEEVES
543 Second Avenue (at 30th Street)   684-9886 *and* PL 3-1293

The name of this pleasant little pub sounds Irish, but the only thing that really smacks of the old sod is some of the piped-in music and the Irish coffee. The menu seems basically Italian, with a few broiled dishes and a hot turkey platter with french fries.

There are nice surroundings—a wall clock, indoor shingling, small tables, and Tiffany lamps. Best of all, the restaurant is staffed by seemingly honest, earnest young people, and the food at its best is commendable.

The veal dishes seem to be a forte of the place, including the veal with marsala and mushrooms and the veal French-style with lemon and parsley. Both came off very well at lunch and so did a steak sandwich with meat of good quality and flavor. One evening there was a very good, tender shish kebab made with fillet, mushrooms, and onions, although it was served on a bed of overcooked rice. A side order of spaghetti seemed to have been cooked in advance, reheated, and not properly drained before serving.

Most dishes at midday are à la carte and cost from 95 cents for a hamburger to $3.95 for steak kebab. Special lunches are $1.75. Dinner entrées go from about $3.00 to $6.50. *Cocktails, wines. Open 7 days a week. Brunch is served on Sunday. Closed major holidays.*

★ GRENADIER
863 First Avenue (at United Nations Plaza)   PL *3-2960*

Of the numerous Irish-Scotch-English pubs in New York, the Grenadier seems to come off with as much of a flourish as any. There is a fusty smell about the premises, particularly noticeable on entering, as well as various portraits of the Royal Family, including Victoria and David Edward as the young Prince of Wales. The enterprise is under the surveillance of several dapper young men whose clothes have an English cut.

The food isn't bad. There are some interesting appetizer and buffet items, including Scotch eggs, meat balls, and stuffed clams with tomato sauce. Each of them could do with more seasoning. There is steak and kidney pie, of course, as well as English mixed grill and London broil.

The roast prime ribs of beef came off extremely well, although the accompanying Yorkshire pudding was on the tough side. The service is so-so, and the size of the portions is overpowering.

All dishes are à la carte. At lunch, the price range is from $2.60 to $5.25. Entrées in the evening cost from about $4.95 to $8.00. *Cocktails, wines. Luncheon is not served*

Saturday. Closed Sunday and major holidays.
AE DC

★★ GROTTA AZZURRA
387 Broome Street   CA 6-9283

Longtime patrons of the Grotta Azzurra are some of the most avid restaurant-goers in town. The food is always of first quality and generally prepared with admirable care. The trouble is that the management and the waiters seem generally preoccupied with old customers and consequently the casual visitor may get off-the-cuff treatment. But those who wait their turn should find much to their liking, whether it is fish, fowl, or pasta. The menu is à la carte, with entrées priced from about $2.50 to $11.50. *Wines, beers. Closed Monday and 2 weeks in July.*

★ HANOVER SQUARE RESTAURANT
1 Hanover Square   WH 4-9251

This is a colorful restaurant with a turn-of-the-century atmosphere and an interesting menu that lists such German dishes as schnitzel à la Holstein and hasenpfeffer. The dish called chicken in the pot is served with some of the best marrow dumplings in all the city. Many of the restaurant's customers toil on Wall Street. Lunch and dinner prices are about $3.30 to $7.50. Dinners are served only until 7:30 P.M. *Cocktails, wines. Closed Saturday, Sunday, and major holidays.*
AE CB DC

★★ HAPPY GARDEN
12 Bowery   349-9677 and 349-4706

This restaurant in or near Chinatown has been warmly endorsed by several members of the Chinese community, and it is encouraging that most of the customers are often Chinese.

In late spring, when fresh crab is in season, the crab Chinese-style at the Happy Garden is excellent, with its egg and meat sauce lightly spiced with ginger and scallions. The deep-fried duck or wor shu opp is very good, crisp, golden brown, and meaty. There are three kinds of wonton—beef, pork, and chicken—and these had been cordially recommended by friends. The filling was good and the chicken for one dish as fresh and tender as one could hope for, but it was served lukewarm. And try to get a pair of chopsticks. It takes a good deal of handwaving and patience. The décor is standard New York Chinatown with plastic-top tables, walls with Chinese calligraphy, and paper napkins.

The menu is à la carte, with main courses from about $1.50 to $3.75. *There is no bar. Open 7 days a week.*

★★ HAYMARKET PUB
772 Eighth Avenue (between 47th and 48th Streets)
586-9360

Although the Haymarket is in a somewhat raffish neighborhood in the Broadway area, the pub itself has a certain charm. There is a long brass bar with mirror where sandwiches are served, a small counter area with grill, and a large dining room to the rear with a mosaic pattern skylight overhead.

One of the best bargains in the house (and the menu over-all is moderately priced) is the beef kebab with cubed sirloin, green peppers, onions, and tomatoes on a skewer. The marinade in which the meat soaked has a nice flavor. It costs $3.15. The house steak is good, too.

All dishes are à la carte from 95 cents for chili con carne to $3.95 for the steak. *Cocktails. Open 7 days a week, except Christmas.*

★ HEIDELBERG RESTAURANT
1648 Second Avenue (between 85th and 86th Streets)
RE 4-9531

There are so many awful mock-German restaurants in Yorkville that a decent kitchen there would stand out like a beacon in the River Rhine. The Heidelberg is really a neighborhood restaurant and bar, very plain, with plastic flowers in bud vases, fading murals, and indifferent table service by waitresses. But the food is well above average, including the rich, paprika-colored goulash soup with beef and the ochsenmaul salad—thin sliced beef appetizer with onions and vinaigrette sauce.

The Heidelberg's roast duck is crisp-skinned, tender, and very good and the pigs' knuckles with sauerkraut are cooked with care. The dumplings are gossamer compared with what one is accustomed to in New York, and desserts are well-made.

One menu serves throughout the day and all dishes are à la carte. The cost of main courses is from about $3.50 to $5.50. *Cocktails, wines, and numerous German beers. Open 7 days a week.*

★ HENRY STAMPLER'S FILET MIGNON
Central Park West at 61st Street   PL 7-3165

This is a conventional steak house with grilled meats, salads, and casseroles. Luncheons are prix fixe from $3.25 to $5.00. Dinners are à la carte, with main courses from about $4.00 to $8.50. *Cocktails, wines. Dinner served 7 days a week; lunch, Monday through Saturday.*
AE   CB   DC   MC

★ HICKORY PIT RESTAURANTS
784 Lexington Avenue (at 61st Street)	PL 2-9599
863 Second Avenue (at 46th Street)	PL 2-5969
1266 Third Avenue (at 73rd Street)	UN 1-9540
168 East 86th Street 831-1010	
924 Second Avenue (at 49th Street)	593-2077

There are several of these restaurants in Manhattan and their specialty is charcoal broiled hamburgers.

If everything came off as well as the 'burgers, the establishments would be commendable, indeed. The meat is of good quality, freshly ground, and cooked directly over hot coals. Thus, it acquires the smoky taste normally associated with charcoal grilling. The hamburgers are served with excellent garlic pickles and even the french-fried potatoes are crisp and seem cooked in fresh oil.

The Hickory Pits offer a mixture of salad greens and a choice of two salad dressings, one French, the other Russian. The French is yellow and homogenized and looks like lubricating oil. The Russian has a mayonnaise base and one communal serving dish filled with it had a tired film on top. The hot apple pie tastes commercial.

Hamburgers cost 95 cents; cheeseburgers, $1.10. *There is no bar. There is a variance in the hours during which the Hickory Pit restaurants are open. On weekends and for late evening dining, it is best to telephone.*

★ HIDE SUKIYAKI
304 West 56th Street   JU 2-0030

A small, upstairs restaurant with a friendly atmosphere and a very good Japanese kitchen. The menu is unpretentious and so is the food, which runs along the lines of sukiyaki, teriyaki, and grilled dishes. The Hide is convenient to the upper-Broadway theaters. The same menu serves for both luncheon and dinner. A la carte dishes range from $1.00 to $3.75; complete dinners are $3.90 to $4.90. *Sake, beers. Closed Sunday and during a few weeks in the summer.*

★★ HIME OF JAPAN
1185 Second Avenue (at 63rd Street)   355-4065

There is a strongly mixed feeling about this Japanese steak house on the East Side. It is a small place with a tempura bar and the usual assortment of large, rectangular tables rimmed with wood and each with a heavy metal slab in the center. The slabs are where steaks and other dishes are cooked by young Japanese chefs as the customers watch.

The steaks are uncommonly good and so are the sauces

and vegetables that accompany them. The latter include zucchini and onions, bean sprouts and slivered carrots. The restaurant's teriyaki of chicken—exceptionally tender and succulent—is excellent. But the service.

On one visit, an order of steak was cooked and served for a guest nearly half an hour before the host's chicken appeared. But the food at the Hime is of such quality it is possible to indulge in a bit of charity here and there. Soups and pickles are served with all main dishes.

Luncheons are à la carte, with main courses at midday from about $2.50 to $3.70. Complete dinners are priced from about $4.50 to $6.50. *Cocktails, beers. Lunch is served Monday through Friday. Open 7 days a week for dinner.* AE DC MC

★ HOLE IN THE WALL
1055 First Avenue (between 57th and 58th Streets)
PL 2-0540

Sandwiches of considerable quality and imagination are available in New York's numerous delicatessens. The Hole in the Wall is, as the name implies, a small establishment with a seating capacity of about 20 persons (also "take-out" orders). The sandwich list is fairly typical: pastrami, corned beef, Nova Scotia lox, liverwurst, turkey, and so on, with new pickles on the side. They are good, although the filling for one sandwich with chicken livers tasted vaguely sweet.

There are other dishes, such as beef goulash with noodles. One order of chicken in the pot wasn't bad at all, though the broth wasn't exactly what mama used to make. It tasted as if the chef had fudged a little with a broth powder or cube.

All dishes are à la carte. Sandwiches from about 85 cents to $3.00. Main dishes from $2.50 to $3.50. *There is no bar, but beers are available. Open 7 days a week.*

★ HONG FAT RESTAURANT
63 Mott Street   WO 2-9588

This is a very small and decidedly offbeat restaurant in Chinatown. Soft-noodle dishes are the specialty of the house, but almost all the foods are interesting and excellent, whether fried squab or Chinese-style crab. The service is imperiously indifferent, and for an ultimate meal it is best to speak Chinese or be accompanied by someone who does. Portions are copious and all dishes are à la carte from about 80 cents to $4.00. *No alcoholic beverages. Open 24 hours a day, 7 days a week.*

★★★ HONG KONG INN
33 West 47th Street   489-9897

This is a rather special Chinese restaurant. The food sampled here has been of an almost consistently high caliber, some of it inspired.

There is an excellent whole steamed flounder with pork shreds, water chestnuts and scallions, and a ginger-flavored sauce; a superior hot and sour soup; two excellent bean curd dishes—one with pork and another with beef, both lightly spiced and seasoned with coriander.

Both the spring rolls and fried dumplings are good. A dish of beef Saichow was a bit chewy, but with first-rate spinach as an accompaniment.

The shredded meat dishes are not as finely cut as they might be, and the chef may be tempering his spices a bit too much, for some of the dishes seem bland.

Upstairs, at least, the Hong Kong Inn is one of the handsomest Chinese restaurants in town with stylish Chinese wallpaper and splendid carved ceilings that probably date to the turn of the century.

At noon, combination platters (please order by number, the menu says) are priced from about $1.85 to $2.95, dessert included. A la carte dishes on the luncheon menu are priced from about $1.75 to $4.50. Complete dinners in the evening cost from about $4.95 to $7.25. A la carte dishes

on the principal menu, available throughout the day, are priced from about $2.50 to $4.95. *Cocktails, beers. Open 7 days a week.*
Most major credit cards.

★★ HONG YING
11 Mott Street   WO 2-9821

An uncommonly good Chinese meal can be had at this rice shoppe, as it calls itself, and it might include an excellent steak with an emerald green vegetable, shrimp in the shell, fried squab, and stuffed, boneless fish. The décor of the Hong Ying is standard New York Chinatown, and the people are friendly. The Hong Ying's business card says that the "prices are strictly moderate" and they are that.

The luncheon menu is à la carte and the prices range from about 80 cents to $1.95. The finest food will be found on the principal menu, however, and these prices à la carte are from about 80 cents to $3.75. There are family dinners that begin at $5.20 for two persons. *There is no bar. Open 7 days a week.*

★ HORN & HARDART AUTOMATS

This is the wonderful world of the nickel-in-the-slot, although steam tables are replacing the coin-operated compartments at most locations. The restaurants—there are about 50 around Manhattan and Brooklyn—have long been a favorite of children and many of their elders. The offering of foods is extensive, and baked beans is the best-known dish. *The restaurants are open at varying hours and some are closed on Sunday.*

★★ HO SHUN
87 Mulberry Street   233-3450

This is another of the casual restaurants in Chinatown where guests are greeted and treated with considerable indifference; where you might be served soup before or after the main course, depending on the waiter's mood; and the atmosphere is nothing to brag about. There are only 12 tables in an overly bright room. But the food at its best is excellent.

The fried dumplings (to be eaten, by the way, with a drop or two of hot oil and a splash of white vinegar, which are on each table) are excellent; so are the noodle and soup dishes; and recommended in particular is the chicken à la shantung ($3.80, and the most expensive item on the menu, but it easily serves four). The chicken is braised with a touch of garlic and star anise and served garnished with fresh coriander leaves. The chicken with green or red peppers is good, too.

A dish of moo shu pork (a quick sauté with shredded bamboo shoots) with pancakes was all right, but had too much padding with vegetables rather than meat. The hot and sour soup had little character.

There is only one menu and it is à la carte, with main courses from about $1.90 to $3.80. *Open 7 days a week.*

★★ HOUSE OF CHAN
Seventh Avenue at 52nd Street   PL 7-4470

This is a large, efficient, and popular Chinese restaurant near Times Square. The ingredients in the kitchen are of undisputed quality, but, where seasonings are concerned, the chef is far from adventurous. Most dishes seem toned down for the tourist trade. One of the nice things about the House of Chan is that it is open for supper until 1:30 A.M. There are complete luncheons that cost from about $1.75 for shrimp fried rice to $3.15 for lobster with vegetables. The à la carte menu is priced from about $1.85 to $18.00 for Pekin duck. *Cocktails, wines. Only à la carte items are available on Sunday, from 2:00 p.m.*
AE   DC

★★ HOY KUNG
21 East Eighth Street (near University Place) 982-7280

There seems to be a chef at the Hoy Kung who knows what he's about in the kitchen, whether making such appetizers as chicken in parchment or such main dishes as Manchurian spiced beef; moo-shu-yoke with pancakes; crab with chicken livers; or the ubiquitous butterfly shrimp with bacon.

The one criticism that could be leveled at the Hoy Kung kitchen is that the chef is too timid in his seasoning. With the exception of the spiced beef, the dishes seem a bit bland—not for want of hot pepper, but he could be more generous with the ginger, garlic, scallions, and the like. In any event, this is immaculate and polished and in one of the most civilized precincts of Greenwich Village.

There are complete luncheons priced from about $1.85 to $4.35; complete dinners from about $2.95 to $6.25. A la carte dishes are priced from about $2.00 to $6.25. *Cocktails, wines. Open 7 days a week.*
AE DC MC

★ HYDE PARK RESTAURANT
998 Madison Avenue (at 77th Street) RE 4-0196

The Hyde Park offers an extensive potpourri of international dishes, but the menu is primarily Jewish and American. The food is well-prepared and there are daily specialties, such as sauerbraten, boiled beef in sauerkraut soup, and stuffed cabbage. There are complete luncheons from about $3.40 to $4.95 and à la carte dishes from about $1.90 to $7.95. In the evening, there are special dinners from about $4.85 to $6.95 and à la carte items from about $3.65 to $7.95. Sunday brunch, served from noon to 3:00 P.M., costs from $3.75 to $4.90. For children under 12, brunch is $1.00 less. *Cocktails, wines. Supper is served from 10:00 p.m. to 1:00 a.m.*
AE BA CB DC MC

★★ IL BAMBINO
94 University Place (at 12th Street) OR *5-9844 and 989-7680*

This restaurant is inexpensive and has a satisfactory Italian menu. When weather is favorable, there is outdoor dining. The kitchen's scaloppine is commendable. Luncheon and dinner are both table d'hôte and à la carte. Complete luncheons from about $2.25 to $3.50; à la carte dishes from about $1.75 to $3.00. Complete dinners from $3.50 to $6.00; à la carte main dishes from about $2.50 to $4.75. *Cocktails, wines. Luncheon is not served on Saturday. Closed Sunday, New Year's Day, and Christmas.*

★ ILE DE FRANCE
20 West 72nd Street *799-2254*

Dining well in the vicinity of Lincoln Center at reasonable (or any) cost poses something of a problem. One of the few good restaurants in the area is the Ile de France in the Franconia Hotel. The décor is nondescript, the menu will look all too familiar to those who know the town's French-bistro-style restaurants, but the kitchen has merit and the food is reasonably priced. And, unlike restaurants at closer proximity to Lincoln Center, it is almost always possible to get a table here. Complete dinners from about $4.75 to $7.50; à la carte entrées from about $3.75 for coq au vin to $7.00 for chateaubriand. *Cocktails, wines. Open for dinner only. Closed Monday.*

★ IL FARO
325 East 14th Street GR *7-9628*

Although it has moved from its original basement location, Il Faro has the look of a landmark. One couple with three children reminisced recently that this is the place they did their courting in back in impoverished student days. It is still a bargain, and the food is good, starting with a well-assorted antipasto, whose various components include sweet red peppers, salami, tomatoes, lettuce, and beets. The parts look familiar, but here they have character.

The pasta is excellent and the ziti with eggplant is recommended in particular.

The menu is both Italian and French, and the restaurant's décor resembles that of many of the small French restaurants on the West Side in the Broadway area. A garden is open in summer. The French entrées include veal scallops viennoise, crab in béchamel sauce, and sweetbreads à la créme. The latter, with many mushrooms, seems to have been made with chicken base rather than a good homemade chicken stock, and that is a disappointment, but otherwise a recent dinner was hard to fault.

All dishes are à la carte, with main dishes from about $1.25 to $2.75. *Cocktails, wines. Open for dinner only. Closed Sunday and major holidays.*
AE CB DC

★★ INDIA HOUSE EAST RESTAURANT
201 East 34th Street   MU 4-9367

A true curry bears only a vague resemblance to most of the homemade dishes in this country made with curry powder. All the dishes at the India House have their own spices and flavors, and they are very good. Several foods, the shrimp for example, may seem overcooked to some local palates, but they are long-cooked in the traditional manner. The restaurant has, by the way, an excellent pungently condimented soup called mulligatawny. In addition to curries, the India House has skewered dishes: keema, which is a spiced chopped-meat dish, and chicken breast stuffed with cheese, which sounds un-Indian. The India House East is brightly garish and the service is friendly. Special three-course luncheons cost from $1.50 to $2.50. Complete dinners from about $3.95 to $5.40; à la carte entrées from about $2.50 to $3.95. *On Saturday and Sunday, the restaurant opens at 5:00 p.m.*
AE CB DC MC

INN OF THE CLOCK
United Nations Plaza Building, 866 United Nations Plaza (at 48th Street)   752-0424

If you lived in the impressive United Nations Plaza Building and if it were raining and taxis were hard to come by, it might offer a good excuse to have lunch or dinner at the Inn of the Clock on the first floor. The décor is pleasant and resembles a stage set of an inn with clocks, oak, and antique-like lighting fixtures. The food is adequate, but nothing to revel in; the service polite, but imprecise. Among pleasant dishes remembered was a first course of crab with avocado, and the chicken in a dish called chicken in pot. An order of rare roast beef was of good quality, but served lukewarm. One also recalls an overly aged Liederkranz and an overly cornstarched rhubarb pie. If you drop in on a rainy night, order the single lamb chop with watercress and baked potato. The à la carte entrées at noon are about $3.25 to $5.25 with a businessmen's lunch at $3.95. In the evening, there is a dinner for $6.95; à la carte entrées from $3.95 to $7.35.
AE CB DC

★ INTERNATIONAL CHEESE CLUB RESTAURANT
153 Chambers Street (between Hudson and Greenwich Streets)   964-0024

This restaurant may be worth a visit simply because it is one of a kind in the city. It is on the second floor of a well-known cheese store, Cheese of All Nations, and the fare includes samplings of various cheeses, plus dishes made with cheese, such as soupe à l'oignon, hot grilled cheese, hot scraped cheese, quiches, and Welsh rarebit. The food is so-so. The menus are à la carte with main dishes at midday priced from $2.50. *Various wines; no cocktails. Open for lunch only. Closed Sunday.*
AE MC DC

★★ IRISH PAVILION, THE
130 East 57th Street   759-9040 and 759-9041

This pavilion, reminiscent to one customer of a small pavilion at some World's Fair, is a neat idea. It melds a commercial display of Irish products—woolens, cookware, rugs, ceramics, and so on—with food that is typically Irish (genuine Irish smoked salmon) and some that is not so typically Irish (corned beef sandwiches, cheesecake, and Jell-O).

To make up the décor, there is a long copper bar, one whitewashed brick wall hung with modern art, pin-point lighting, plus the fairly colorful merchandise. The tables are small and close together and the waitresses are garbed in green mini-smocks.

The menu is limited and à la carte and one of the best items on it is the smoked salmon, thinly sliced and served in a generous portion on iceberg lettuce leaves with capers, and oil and vinegar on the side. A pepper mill would be welcome. The Irish Pavilion gets air shipments of Dublin Bay prawns, a nice addition.

The rest of the menu is conventional, including the chef's salad with julienne ham and cheese, pot pie, and roast prime ribs of beef. The corned beef in the sandwiches is lean and of good quality, the ham in the sandwiches of no particular distinction.

The cost of the entrées is from about $1.75 for a ham sandwich to $3.95 for Killybegs crab and Dublin prawns. The plate of imported smoked salmon is a luxury. It costs $3.50 per serving. *Cocktails, wines, Irish beers, and Irish coffee. Closed Sunday.*

★★ IRORI
60 West 56th Street   247-3349

This is the kind of restaurant of such special virtues that one might like to keep it quietly to himself. If the crowds come and it catches on, it may very well be spoiled. It is a small Japanese steak house with very few tables and part of the present pleasure is the unhurried ministrations of the young chefs who cook at each table.

There are very good clear soups and the main courses —steak, seafood, or chicken breasts—are cooked on a hot metal slab in the center of each table. The chefs cook to order green peppers, whole mushrooms, and zucchini strips, then the main course followed by a heaping dish of fresh bean sprouts.

The foods are expertly seasoned and served with two soy sauces, one seasoned with fresh ginger and lemon, the other with sesame seeds.

A la carte lunch entrées are about $3.50 to $5.25. A la carte dishes are priced from about $5.50 to $6.80 at dinner. The tables at the Irori accommodate 6 customers each, and, when the occasion demands they are shared. *Cocktails, wines. Open 7 days a week.*

★★★ ISLE OF CAPRI
1028 Third Avenue (at 61st Street)   752-9410

This is almost without question the best small Italian restaurant in New York. The word "small" is used advisedly to indicate a restaurant of the trattoria style, rather than one of those over-blown establishments where there is more attention to décor than to the kitchen.

There is something quite personal and special about the food at the Isle of Capri. It is cooked by or under the direction of Signora Maria Lamanna, and there is lots of embracing and kissing when long-time customers greet the signora. She deserves it.

The food is good, be it a bracciole of chicken or beef, any of numerous veal dishes, the bread, or the house salad. The spaghetti or pasta dishes are first-rate.

The Isle of Capri has a downstairs addition with lots of arches and brick and grillwork and an awful fake bust of Michelangelo's David. Upstairs, customers dine on plain marble tables.

Incidentally, the rum cake is delicious, although it

doesn't contain more than two drops of rum, if any.

Entrées on the à la carte lunch menu go from $3.00 to $5.75. At dinner, the range for à la carte main dishes is $3.75 to $6.50. A salad, vegetable or pasta is included in the price of entrée. *Cocktails, wines. Closed Sunday and major holidays.*
AE CB DC

★ ITALIANISSIMO
422 Third Avenue (between 29th and 30th Streets)
MU 4-8677

This pleasant little Italian restaurant has a garden in summer and a cozy atmosphere in winter. The food is good, but not inspired, and the service is friendly. The menu lists a wealth of pasta, seafood, and meat dishes and a variety of appetizers, including antipasto Italianissimo ($2.50), an assortment of hot stuffed vegetables. The veal scaloppine with peppers and mushrooms ($3.95) sampled on one occasion had good flavor, but the veal was not very tender. Portions are enormous. There is a $2.50 minimum at lunch. Dinner entrées range from about $3.50 to $7.50. *Cocktails, wines. Closed Sunday, New Year's Eve, Labor Day, and Christmas.*
AE DC MC

★★ ITALIAN PAVILION
24 West 55th Street   JU 6-5950

An agreeable décor, courteous service, and reasonably imaginative à la carte menus, at luncheon and dinner, mark the Italian Pavilion. Specialties, many of which show care in preparation, include crêpes Pavilion, osso buco milanese, and vitello tonnato, as well as gnocchi and fettuccine. Luncheon main courses from about $3.50 to $7.50; dinner entrées from about $4.50 to $8.50. The restaurant's garden (heated in winter) is open the year around. *Cocktails, wines. Closed Sunday, both Saturday and Sunday in*

summer, and major holidays.
AE   CB   DC

★★ JACK'S NEST
489 Second Avenue (at 27th Street)   889-6891

This is one of the nicest soul-food restaurants to open in Manhattan and the food is reasonably authentic. The menu is standard with such "Southern" dishes as fried chicken, barbecued ribs, pigs' feet, chitterlings or chit'lins, and, among the vegetables, collard greens and candied yams.

The chicken is well-seasoned and was on two occasions cooked in fresh fat, which in itself is a novelty in almost any Manhattan restaurant. The barbecued ribs are oven-baked with a tasty tomato sauce and, among the desserts one day, the peach cobbler was freshly made and excellent.

To use sugar or not in corn bread has been a point of contention among Southerners for generations. The corn bread at Jack's Nest is fresh, but it tastes like cake. The restaurant is a neat, bright place with dark wood paneling and an African mask on one wall.

All dishes are à la carte, with main courses from about $1.95 for ham hocks and collard greens to $3.50 for chit'lins and a split of champagne. *Cocktails, wines. Open from 11:00 a.m. to 11:00 p.m., Monday through Friday; 4:00 p.m. to 2:00 a.m., Saturday and Sunday.*

★ JADE PALACE
210 East 53rd Street   EL 5-5096

This is a spacious Chinese restaurant in midtown Manhattan. In keeping with the name, the Jade Palace is carpeted and upholstered in green, wall to wall. The food is generally good and the portions are copious. There are complete luncheons from about $1.45 to $3.95. The à la carte menu, available for luncheon and dinner, lists pleasant but ordinary main entrées from about $2.20 to $5.50. *Cocktails, wines. The restaurant opens at 5:00 p.m. on*

Saturday and at 4:00 p.m. on Sunday.
AE   CB   DC   MC

★★ JAI-ALAI
82 Bank Street (near Eighth Avenue between 11th and 12th Streets)   989-5826

There are numerous restaurants in Manhattan with Spanish kitchens, and, at their best, the food is very good. One of them is the Jai-Alai, and the dishes, whether a casserole of seafood, paella, or pork with almond sauce, are palatable. There is one reservation about dishes sampled at the Jai-Alai—those containing clams are slightly sandy. Otherwise, the preparations are cordially recommended, and the food is reasonably priced. At midday, main courses are from about $1.75 to $2.25. The à la carte menu is priced from about $2.50 for eggs Flamenca to $5.50 for sirloin steak. *Cocktails, wines. Open 7 days a week.*
AE   CB   DC

★★ JAMAICA ARMS
1315 Second Avenue (at 69th Street)   YU 8-5850

There is something solidly authentic in the Caribbean-inspired surroundings of the Jamaica Arms, which has weathered well. It has old bottles, rough beams, charts, ironwork chandeliers, dried corn in the husk, and tables with neat red and white napery. The tables are close together and there is lots of clutter, but it is all festive and hangs together. The menu shows admirable imagination and the food, for the most part, is well-prepared.

On Monday evenings, there is a small buffet (anchovies and sweet peppers, salads, a cold casserole of tomatoes and green peppers) that may serve as a first course, and there are also well-conceived appetizers on the menu, including a dish of chick-peas or garbanzos with creole sausages and shrimp de jonghe. Both of these arrived lukewarm on one occasion and were returned for reheating, but the end result was good. The chef had also omitted the sausages first time around.

The main courses include such island fare as lamb curry, roast loin of pork (well-seasoned, but sometimes on the chewy side), shrimp creole, and (for a minimum of 10 persons with 48 hours notice) roast suckling pig. There are exotic fruit garnishes for most of the dishes. The Jamaica Arms rum pie isn't bad, but the crust has been soggy. The service is far from remarkable.

All dishes are à la carte with main courses from about $4.60 to $7.75. *Cocktails, wines. Opens at 6:00 p.m. Closed Sunday and 3 weeks in August.*
AE DC

★★ JAPANESE MIE COOKING
196 Second Avenue (near 12th Street)   674-7060

This is a relatively worthwhile Japanese restaurant in a basement setting catercornered from the Eden Theater. The food is simply prepared, but excellent, whether it is sashimi or yakitori or the special Japanese dinner called o-teishoku.

The yakitori, or chicken on skewers, was tender and well-seasoned and served with that batch of shredded lettuce and cabbage with tomatoes and cucumbers and Russian dressing which may be a Manhattan innovation.

With the o-teishoku there was an interesting appetizer—cucumber rings with pickled mackerel seasoned with ginger and sesame; very good tempura; commendable broiled tuna; and a splendid and unusual steamed chicken dish with onion and a thin pancake. Among the side dishes, the cold yakinasu, or eggplant with lemon and stem ginger, was fascinating.

The décor of the Mie is nondescript, and the ventilation leaves much to be desired. There is a sushi bar in one of the two dining rooms.

Complete dinners are priced from about $3.25 to $4.25, with à la carte main dishes from about $2.00 to $3.75.

There is no bar. The restaurant opens at 5:00 p.m., 7 days a week.

★★ JAPANESE STEAK HOUSE
225 West Broadway   226-5915

One of the pleasantest innovations on the Manhattan dining scene in recent years is the Japanese restaurant. In a genre by themselves are the Japanese steak houses, in which guests are seated around large rectangular tables with solid metal slabs on which the food is cooked and served. The food at the Japanese Steak House is generally excellent, although the vegetables tend to taste a trifle overcooked. Complete luncheons from $2.75 to $6.00; complete dinners about $8.00. *Cocktails, wines. Luncheon is not served Saturday. Closed Sunday.*
AE CB DC MC

★★ JASPER'S
201 East 61st Street   688-9279

This is a rather dark, candlelighted, subterranean restaurant with a casual atmosphere.

The young men who wait tables are a pleasant lot, and one of them says, "Sure," to almost all questions. "Is the lasagne good?" "Sure." "How about the chili?" "Sure." And, once he added, "We do make great dishes here, if I say so myself."

Jasper's menu is basically Italian and the food at its best is quite edible, although the antipasto is no more nor less insulting than you'll find it in most Italian restaurants around town. The usual salami, anchovies, and peppers.

Jasper's has its rough edges, but it has atmosphere and it is open for snacks such as hamburgers and chili con carne after the theater.

All dishes are à la carte, but include vegetable or salad, with main courses at midday from about $1.45 to $3.75; in the evening, from about $1.75 to $6.75. *Cocktails, wines.*

Open 7 days a week, except in the spring and summer, when the restaurant is closed Sunday.

★ JENEDI'S
13 East 47th Street   688-0778

The surroundings in Jenedi's are a little haphazard —with wavy plastic banquettes, motley groupings of bright floral art on the walls and tables too close for comfort—but the food is a cut above that of the average Italian restaurant in the city. There are several excellent dishes on the menu, including very good fettuccine, excellent osso buco (but once accompanied by a watery rice), sautéed chicken breast with prosciutto and melted cheese. All dishes are à la carte. Main courses at midday from about $2.50 to $6.00; in the evening, from about $3.50 to $8.95. *Cocktails, wines. Closed Saturday, Sunday, and major holidays.*
All major credit cards.

★★ JIMMY'S GREEK-AMERICAN RESTAURANT
6 Water Street   269-9458

Jimmy's is one of the oldest-established and most-talked-about of Manhattan's numerous Greek restaurants. The dishes are long-cooked and well-seasoned and bear a welcome resemblance to the foods of small rustic Greek restaurants. The décor is rather sterile, American-cafeteria. Dishes include such fare as roast lamb, Greek macaroni with meat, lamb fricassee, stuffed vine leaves, meat balls, and the usual assortment of Greek pastries. Guests are served in the kitchen by the chef. The cost of main courses is about $4.50 to $5.00, with an additional charge for side dishes. *There is no bar, but guests may bring their own spirits, beer, or wine. The restaurant is open Monday through Friday for luncheon from noon to 2:00 p.m. Closed Saturday and Sunday.*

★★ JIMMY'S LA GRANGE
151 East 49th Street   PL 3-3899

This small, interesting restaurant boasts only one menu, and that is in the owner's head. On a first visit, chicken Kiev (chicken breast stuffed with butter and herbs) is almost mandatory, and it is very good. Other specialties include saltimbocca, which, as served at the restaurant, has a layer of spinach between the ham and the veal. Complete luncheons from about $5.25. Dinner is à la carte with entrées, including vegetable, from about $5.75. *Cocktails, wines. On Saturday the restaurant opens at 5:45 p.m. Closed Sunday.*

★ JOE ALLEN
326 West 46th Street   581-6464

There are numerous visitors to New York, frequently from abroad, who ask to be taken to a typical American restaurant, and this is in that category. The restaurant serves chili, shrimp creole, omelet, and chicken pot pie, and the food is very good. The kitchen offers an excellent black bean soup, and, when available and at its best, the chicken pot pie is cordially recommended. Faults to be found on visits to the restaurant include lukewarm dishes and service that is far too casual. The décor, with its exposed brick walls and photographs, is pleasant enough. All dishes are à la carte with main courses from about $2.75 to $6.25. *Cocktails, wines. Open for dinner only, 7 days a week, from 4:00 p.m. Closed Christmas.*

★ JOE AND ROSE
745 Third Avenue (at 46th Street)   EL 5-8874

A popular midtown restaurant with Italian food. There is no menu at luncheon, but the cost of the meal is from about $3.50 to $4.25. Dinners are à la carte with entrées from about $2.50 to $8.00. *Cocktails, wines. Lunch served Monday through Friday only. Closed Sunday and*

the first 2 weeks in August.
AE DC

★★ JOE'S RESTAURANT
79 Macdougal Street   473-9393

This is an Italian restaurant in Greenwich Village that is notably unpretentious and has food that is simply prepared and gratifying. It is also reasonably priced. At lunch and dinner the menu is à la carte with main courses from about $2.75 to $6.00 for steak. *Cocktails, wines. Closed Tuesday.*

★ JOE'S PIER 52
144 West 52d Street   245-6652

Although it is one of the handsomest fish houses on or off Broadway, Joe's Pier 52 is regrettably not a great fish house. Frederick Fox, the Broadway scenic designer, has produced an admirable setting with handsome 19th-century nautical prints, a mounted collection of 18th-century ship models, figureheads, oak tables, comfortable chairs on ball casters, and so on. The only trouble with the décor is that some of the tables are too close for comfort.

The menus are extensive and well planned, with broiled foods, steamed fish, curries, Newburgs, and salads. But the food is, for the most part, quite as ordinary as you're apt to find in less awesome surroundings around the Fulton Fish Market. Despite attractive concepts in the presentation of food both the service and reception leave much to be desired.

The food is neither bad nor inspired. The oversize crab cakes were wholly edible, although not as light as a well-made crab cake should be—too much binding for the quantity of crab—and it was necessary to ask for lemon as an accompaniment. And tartar sauce was not served with the crab cakes as it customarily is.

An assortment of deep-fried fish was passably good, but not delicate.

One of the best dishes sampled on another occasion at Pier 52 was simply broiled striped bass. Beautifully fresh, but it was served lukewarm and had to be returned to the kitchen for reheating.

Similarly, one of the least palatable dishes at Pier 52 recently was the broiled flounder, heavily sprinkled with paprika, as are most if not all of the broiled foods at the restaurant. Paprika, of course, gives the illusion to the untutored eye of proper broiling.

Luncheon without dessert costs from $3.95 to $7.50, and à la carte dishes at midday are priced from about $4.25 to $10.50. The evening menu is à la carte, with main courses from about $4.50 to $11.75. *Cocktails, wines. Open 7 days a week.*
AE BA CB DC MC

★ JOHNNIE'S
135 West 45th Street   CI 5-9667

This is a narrow, rectangular-shaped Italian restaurant in the Broadway area.

The food at Johnnie's is honestly and competently prepared, whether it is a simple dish of baked spaghetti with meat balls, beans with pasta soup, or pot roast with spaghetti.

The principal fault to be found with Johnnie's is the proximity of the tables. They are practically tablecloth to tablecloth.

The food is modestly priced and the menu is extensive. The cost of a complete luncheon is $2.50, with à la carte dishes from about $1.65 for spaghetti and $1.90 for sausage with peppers and spaghetti to $6.50 for steak. Complete dinners cost $4.95, with à la carte dishes from $1.75 to $6.25. *Cocktails, wines. Open 7 days a week, except Christmas.*
All major credit cards.

★ JOHN'S RESTAURANT
302 East 12th Street   GR 5-9531

The management's attitude may border on the lofty, but if one likes well-cooked Neapolitan cuisine, this small restaurant may be worth a visit. The tomato sauces and rum cake are excellent. Dinners are à la carte with main courses from about $2.10 to $6.75. *Cocktails, wines. Open for dinner only. Closed Monday, major holidays, and from July 1 through Labor Day.*

★★ JOLLY CHAN'S CHINESE KITCHEN
1069 First Avenue (at 58th Street)   486-1182

This is one in a long line of Chinese kitchens with take-home foods. It is in the Sutton Place area, and it may very well have the most extensive and best menu of them all. It is the enterprise of Robert Tsang, who owns the well-regarded Mon Sing restaurant on Mott Street in Chinatown.

There are nearly 200 dishes on the carry-home menu, including such usual things as wonton and eggdrop soup and lo mein dishes, as well as such unusual fare as clams in black bean sauce, spicy dishes like pepper chicken ding, and crabs Cantonese style.

In winter, when the crabs are rich with eggs, the Jolly Chan chef does admirable things with them. At times, the Jolly Chan offers Chinese buns filled with pork, and they are first-rate.

By most restaurant standards, the food is not inexpensive. Prices range from about $1.50 for a pint of chop suey to $6.00 for mushroom lobster kow. Representative dishes are in the $3.00 category.

The foods may be ordered and picked up in person, or will be delivered (within a 10-block area) for a 50-cent service charge. By the way, fortune cookies are available at 30 cents the package.

There is a small counter where no more than three or four customers may dine on the premises. *No alcoholic beverages, naturally. Sunday through Thursday, the restaurant is open from 11:30 a.m. until midnight; Friday and Saturday, 11:30 a.m. to 2:00 a.m.*

★ JOYCE'S MACAO
44 Trinity Place   425-3810

Despite a few negative points, one suspects that this Chinese restaurant in the financial district probably has a quite competent chef.

Among the appetizers, the walnut rolls (finely chopped shrimp with water chestnuts and almonds shaped into croquettes and deep-fried) came off very well and so did the steamed dem sem dumplings. The lobster Cantonese was tender and well-seasoned, and the chicken (in a black bean sauce seasoned with ginger) with watercress was good, even if the watercress was a bit stringy.

What didn't come off well was a platter of lobster ding, in which the main ingredient was less than fresh and had to be returned to the kitchen.

Joyce's Macao is a simply decorated restaurant, with tables close together. There are complete luncheons that cost from about $2.50 to $3.25. A la carte main courses from about $3.25 to $6.25. The restaurant does not as of now hold a liquor license. *Closed Sunday.*
Most major credit cards.

★★ JOY GARDEN
48 Mott Street   WO 2-9787

This small upstairs restaurant has one of the most interesting menus in Chinatown. Chop suey and chow mein are available, but more imaginative dishes, such as fried squabs and steamed whole sea bass, happily dominate the à la carte bill of fare. Complete luncheons cost from $1.45 to $1.95. The same à la carte menu serves for luncheon and dinner, with main dishes priced from about $1.25 to $4.95. *No alcoholic beverages. Only à la carte items are available on Sunday.*

★ JULIO RESTAURANT
129 East 15th Street   AL 4-1838

There is a remarkable honesty about the surroundings, food, and prices of Julio, a basement restaurant with an Italian kitchen in Greenwich Village. The food is, in fact, one of the best bargains in all of Manhattan, and there is a steady clientele who knows it.

Julio is decorated with new and obvious art that is nonetheless pleasant and wholly suited to the restaurant. The walls are plastered with Italian newspapers; and there is only one waiter, or at least there has been on one visit. The dining room is small.

You can dine here—fairly substantially at that—for as little as $1.40 for a main course with spaghetti and vegetable, and the most expensive item—filet mignon—is about $3.50. Don't expect virtuosity at those prices—the soups are a little watery, the antipasto on the skimpy side—but the food is more than merely edible and on a par with that of some Italian restaurants in the city that cost twice and three times the price. *There is no bar, but beer and wine may be brought in. Closed Sunday.*

★ KABUKI RESTAURANT
115 Broadway (near Cedar Street)   WO 2-4677

Most of New York's Japanese restaurants remind one of Clifton Fadiman's line about cheese. Provided it is well and truly made, he said, there is no such thing as a really bad cheese. Similarly, Japanese dining spots, provided they turn out a decent sukiyaki, fresh tempura, and teriyaki, are generally worth the visit.

The spacious Kabuki is all right, but it seems to be more routine than one remembers from former visits at another address. It seems more Westernized, from the commonplace pickled vegetables to the "donburi" lunches and the sukiyaki.

An "authentic" teishoku lunch has been a distinct disappointment. It included a soup; a small portion of red snapper cheeks (complete with eye, which might put some customers off) that still had some of the scales left on; pieces of rather tough octopus with lime, soy, and wasabi (horse-radish); a creditably fresh sashimi; and ice cream. That costs $4.50.

The waitresses in kimono have the usual charm, but the service is comically disoriented (pardon the word). There is difficulty finding place for service trays; an unrequested order of sukiyaki was served at one table; et cetera.

Complete luncheons cost from $3.75 to $4.25; complete dinners from $5.75 to $7.50. A la carte dishes from about $4.50 to $6.00. *Cocktails, wines. Luncheon is not served on Saturday. Closed Sunday, bank holidays, and Saturday during July and August.*
AE CB DC MC

★ KAMEHACHI
41 West 46th Street 765-4737

New Yorkers have taken to Japanese food with awesome enthusiasm. Restaurants that serve sushi, sashimi, and the like are increasing and flourishing. A very good one where food is concerned is the Kamehachi. There is a bar for sushi (raw fish with vinegar rice), and specialties include broiled eel and tempura. The prices are modest, in the vicinity of $1.25 to $3.25. There is one annoyance, and that is the limited staff. At times there are lengthy waits between courses. *American and Japanese beers. Closed Monday, New Year's Day, Labor Day, and Thanksgiving.*

★ KARACHI
144 West 46th Street CI 5-9643

This second-floor restaurant is easy to bypass, but curry lovers manage to seek it out. Prices, although inevitably not as low as they used to be, are modest. Curries are on the mild side and hot sauce is available. The usual assortment of meat, fish, poultry, and vegetable cur-

ries is served; also a variety of "bengal" breads, relishes, and chutneys. There is a small assortment of desserts, including a delicious rosewater-flavored custard. There is a special $1.45 luncheon and complete dinners are priced from $2.95 to $5.50. *No alcoholic beverages, but wine and beer may be brought in. Dinner is served from noon on Saturday and from 12:30 p.m. on Sunday.*
AE DC

★★ KASHMIR RESTAURANT
108 West 45th Street   247-8785

The atmosphere is plain and the service enthusiastic though slow at the Kashmir, but the food is gratifying. It should be noted that most of the dishes, whether beef kurma or tandoori chicken, are well-spiced and some of the condiments powerfully hot. The menu lists both à la carte dishes, from about $2.25 for chicken curry to $2.95 for chicken biriani, and complete meals from about $3.00 to $4.50. There is a special luncheon at $1.50 served Monday through Friday. *Cocktails, wines. Open 7 days a week.*
AE CB DC MC

★ KATZ'S DELICATESSEN
205 East Houston Street (at Ludlow Street)   AL *4-2246*

One of the best known of New York's delicatessens. The à la carte menu, which is available all the time, lists sandwiches from 95 cents (salami) to $1.50 (combination with turkey). Frankfurters, with mustard and sauerkraut, cost 35 cents. Combination platters start at $2.00. *Beers. Closed on Jewish holidays.*

★★ KEEN'S ENGLISH CHOP HOUSE
72 West 36th Street   WI *7-3636*

In recent years, English pubs and chop houses have sprouted in Manhattan like British primroses in spring. Keen's was perhaps the forerunner of them all, or, at least, it seems the most durable. There is an appropriate tavern décor dominated by thousands of "churchwarden" clay pipes that hang from the ceiling.

The menu relies heavily on steaks, roasts, and chops, generally well-prepared, with such typical English dishes as mutton chops, beefsteak, and kidney pudding (Monday only) and, on occasion, imported Dover sole.

Club luncheons are from about $3.25 to $6.50, with à la carte main courses from about $2.50 to $7.75. À la carte dinner main dishes from about $4.75. *Cocktails, wines. Open 7 days a week. Restaurant opens at 4:00 p.m. on Sunday. Closed weekends during the summer.*
AE DC

★★ KEGON
80 East 56th Street   421-8777

This Japanese restaurant may well boast the largest tempura bar in Manhattan. And, over-all, the place is reasonably handsome, with a large waterwheel (well, it looks like a waterwheel) at the entrance, lacquered panels, stone lanterns, and beautiful, young Japanese waitresses in kimono.

The seating in the various small dining areas (there are two floors) is unfortunately limited. Unfortunately, since that is where the six specialties of the house are served—tempura or fried things, principally shrimp; sukiyaki; shabu-shabu, in which beef and vegetables are cooked in broth; nabe, another boiled dish with seafood and chicken; ozen, which is a complete Japanese dinner; and steak served on a hot platter. The shabu-shabu is particularly tasty, with two sauces, one of sesame and bean paste, another of soy and lemon.

The tempura bar is a complete circle that can accommodate 40 guests at a time, and the meal there includes an appetizer of shrimp and small meat balls; onion soup in stoneware; and the various fried foods of shrimp, beef, eggplant, mushroom, and octopus with seaweed.

As to the quality of the Kegon's tempura, it is competently prepared—no more, no less. And the ventilation of the room could be improved on. Nonetheless, the Kegon is pleasant enough.

The cost of lunch at Kegon is about $3.50 to $4.75; dinner about $6.50 to $9.50. *Cocktails, wines, and Japanese beers. Lunch served Monday through Friday; only dinner, Saturday and Sunday.*
AE   DC   MC

★★ KENERET
296 Bleecker Street   OR *5-9587 and 691-8299*

This is a Syrian restaurant in Greenwich Village and the food is quite special. It may not appeal to the most fastidious palates, but for those who enjoy fairly robust salads, eggplant dishes, and the North African specialty called couscous, it is excellent. Keneret is, in fact, one of the few restaurants in New York that offers couscous—a buttery, tender cereal served with a hot or mild sauce containing meat and vegetables. The restaurant is a large, faintly illuminated place with a brick wall and fish-net décor, and the service is pleasant, if slow. All the dishes at Keneret are seasoned with creditable imagination, and a roof garden is open in the summer. The cost of main dishes at Keneret is from about $2.75 to $6.50 for veal fillet. *Cocktails, wines. Open for dinner only.*
AE   BA   CB   DC

★★ KENNY'S STEAK PUB
Lexington Avenue at 50th Street   EL *5-0666*

Kenny's Steak Pub is a large, dimly lit, and expensive steak house in midtown Manhattan. The restaurant is neat and the reception is warm, but the portions, whether of salad or a main course, may seem overly copious. The service is swift and efficient, perhaps a touch too much so. For those who dote on first-quality steaks, however, the restaurant should have great appeal. All dishes at Kenny's are à la carte, with main luncheon entrées from

about $2.95 to $6.95 and main dinner courses from about $5.95 for a salad platter to $9.50 for boneless sirloin steak. *Cocktails, wines. On Saturday and Sunday the restaurant opens at 5:00 p.m.*
AE CB DC MC

★ KING OF THE SEA
879 Third Avenue (between 53rd and 54th Streets)
EL 5-9309 *and* PL 3-9140

This is one of New York's largest and oldest seafood houses, and one always feels that it should be better than it is. The menu is elaborate, but the food, although appetizing enough, is generally not distinguished. There are a few unusual entrées, such as crab fingers with mustard dressing and, when available, Florida stone crabs. Complete lunches range from $4.25 for mackerel to $7.50 for lobster Thermidor. Complete dinners from $6.25 for snapper to $9.65. A la carte prices go from $4.50 to $9.75. *Cocktails, wines. Closed New Year's Day and Christmas.*
BA CB MC

★★ KING WU
18 Doyers Street   WO 2-8480

There are many restaurants in Chinatown, but few achieve the goodness and admirable authenticity of King Wu. The décor of the establishment is not elegant, just basic. A la carte dishes at both lunch and dinner from about $2.95 for shredded pork to $12.00 for Pekin duck, which must be ordered in advance. Complete lunches from $2.00 to $3.00. Full-course dinners for two from $6.00. *No alcoholic beverages, but excellent tea. Open 7 days a week.*

★ KIRBY ALLEN RESTAURANT, THE
797 Madison Avenue (between 67th and 68th Streets)
RH 4-9835

If anyone wishes to show a foreigner a restaurant that serves typical New York food, he should go no farther than the Kirby Allen. It has certain tearoom aspects, but the dishes are all there, from the molded salmon aspic salad and roast loin of pork with apple sauce to pineapple upside-down cake and chocolate pie with whipped cream. The food is prepared with reasonable care, but no special inspiration. The service, on the other hand, by waitresses, is about as pleasant as you will find in the city. The cost of luncheons with copious portions is from about $1.75 to $3.45; complete dinners from about $3.95 to $4.75. *No alcoholic beverages. Closed Saturday, Sunday, major holidays, and the last 3 weeks of August.*

★★ KITCHO RESTAURANT
103 West 44th Street   581-6670

There are numerous enthusiasts for Japanese food who say this is the best of the city's many Japanese restaurants. The dining room is physically no thing of beauty, but the kitchen is rewarding whether it offers such basics as sukiyaki and tempura or a notable pork and mushroom dish on skewers, kushikatsu. A la carte dishes at midday cost from about $1.25 to $4.00; special luncheons from about $2.50 to $4.50. Complete dinners are about $5.00 to $6.50; à la carte dinner main dishes from $2.50 to $7.00. *Cocktails, wines, Japanese beer, and sake. The restaurant opens at 5:00 p.m. on Sunday. Closed Saturday and major holidays.*

★ KLEINE KONDITOREI
234 East 86th Street   RE 7-7130

This is one of the smallest, neatest, and perhaps the best of the so-called German restaurants in the section of New York known as Yorkville. The menu, the same for lunch and dinner, lists such dishes as sauerbraten, pork, veal or beef wurst with sauerkraut, and schnitzel. The cost of each day's specialties is about $2.00. Dinners are à la carte, with main dishes from about $2.35 to $6.75 for steak. *Cocktails, wines. Open 7 days a week.*

★★ KOBE STEAK HOUSE
145 West 49th Street   765-3146 and LI 4-0094

Anyone who has never dined in one of the several Japanese steak houses in Manhattan is missing an exceptional opportunity to sample excellent international cookery. The dining rooms are equipped with large rectangular tables with heavy metal slabs in the center where the food is cooked. Guests, generally six, sit around the tables. The Kobe is typical, with a menu that offers a choice of steak, shrimp, pork, or chicken. The foods are quickly cooked, cut into bite-size pieces, and served with sauces containing soy and sesame seeds. Accompaniments include bean sprouts, green peppers, onions, and mushrooms, also quickly cooked on the metal slab. A complete steak house luncheon is priced from about $2.95 to $3.95, with à la carte dishes from about $3.95 to $7.95. Complete dinners cost from $5.25 to $8.25. *Cocktails, wines. Open 7 days a week.*
AE CB DC

★ KOON SHING TEA HOUSE
202 Canal Street   964-2410

One of the joys of the Chinese kitchen can be the assortment of appetizers with various fillings such as chopped chicken, shrimp, pork, or beef, most of them steamed. The brightly lit Koon Shing teahouse has an extensive menu of hors d'oeuvres and pastries, and some of them are a delight. The cost is from about 15 cents to 50 cents, and there is a special tea lunch with seven appetizers, enough for a complete meal, that costs $1.00. The lunch is served Monday through Friday from noon to 3:00 P.M. The restaurant also has noodle dishes, soup dishes, and the like that cost from about 95 cents to $2.75. The restaurant is, come to think of it, one of the biggest bargains in Chinatown. *There is no bar.*

★★ KYOTO STEAK HOUSE
148 West 46th Street   265-2345

Some of the most interesting Japanese restaurants in Manhattan are those that specialize in steaks. They follow a familiar pattern, of course: large tables with heavy metal slabs in the center that are fired with gas from below. Young chefs wearing toques blanches perform the cooking ritual at the table, quickly searing steak, chicken, shrimp, or whatever, then sautéing a mixture of bean sprouts, mushrooms, and onions as a vegetable course.

It is all served piping hot with two sauces and, at its best, it is first-rate. One of the best of these steak houses is the Kyoto, in the theater district. It is decorated with the usual Japanese understatement, and the foods are well-seasoned and of good quality.

The only fault found here is in the basic nature of all Japanese steak houses. On crowded days, unless you are with a party of six, chances are you will have to share a table with others, leaving little room for privacy. And please note that the service is leisurely—it is no place to dine for those on the run.

Luncheons are à la carte, with main dishes from about $1.98 to $5.00. Most dinners are à la carte, with main courses from $5.00 to $7.00. There is one complete and extensive dinner that costs $10.00. *Cocktails, Japanese wines, and beers. Open 7 days a week. Luncheon is not served on Sunday.*

★★ LA BIBLIOTHEQUE
341 East 43rd Street   689-5444

If all the dishes of La Bibliothèque measured up to the best of them, this restaurant would be something to cheer about. In any event, it is run by several young men who seem to care tremendously about the enterprise, and that is something to encourage.

One of the nicest luncheons included the chef's mixed grill with a tender, well-cooked lamb chop, a small piece of beef, sausage, and sprigs of watercress. Similarly, an order of broiled red snapper was fresh and not overcooked.

At one dinner, the veal cutlet Jean Paul Sartre, with fried egg on top plus anchovies and capers, was commendable. On the other hand, the petite marmite smacked of beef extract and was overly salty; a crab cocktail had good-quality crab, but came with the most ordinary cocktail sauce.

La Bibliothèque has pleasant surroundings—one wall paneled with books, and exterior views of the United Nations. There is piped-in music, at times a bit loud.

All dishes are à la carte, with main courses at midday from about $2.75 to $5.75; in the evening, from about $3.95 to $5.95. *Cocktails, wines. Luncheon is not served on Saturday. Closed Sunday.*
AE CB DC MC

★ LA BOURGOGNE
123 West 44th Street   JU 2-4230

One of the nicest things about La Bourgogne is its proximity to the Broadway theaters. The food is French, of course, and the specialty of the house is the cheese soufflé. The luncheon menu is table d'hôte and ranges in cost from $3.25 to $5.95. Dinners are both prix fixe and à la carte, with complete meals from $4.50 to $7.95. *Cocktails, wines. Closed Sunday and major holidays.*
AE BA DC

★★ LA CABANA
146 East 57th Street   758-3242

This is an Argentine restaurant with a brief, interesting menu and food that is fascinating. It has the taste of authenticity. There is, for example, excellent broiled chicken delicately flavored with cumin and garlic; grilled skirt steak of considerable merit; and, among the appetizers, Argentine turnovers and rolled beef stuffed with

hard-cooked eggs. The décor of La Cabana is also beguiling. There are potted palms, ceiling fans with globe lamps, a polished marble fireplace, and an expansive entrance. Some people may be put off by the service, which is casual in a Latin way, but the foods are grilled to order and that in itself is something to praise. The cost of luncheon main courses is from $2.75 to $4.50; a complete dinner, $9.95. *Cocktails, wines. Closed Sunday and major holidays.*
AE CB DC MC

★★★★ LA CARAVELLE
33 West 55th Street   JU 6-4252

This is the finest restaurant in New York on almost every count. The direction under Fred Decré and Robert Meyzen is enormously professional. The waiters have as much style and experience as you are apt to find in Manhattan; but, most important, perhaps, the chef, Roger Fessaguet, is a fiercely dedicated young man, and the food from his kitchen, whether it be sauces or dessert, is almost consistently outstanding. The cold dishes, such as salads, poached fish, and foods in aspic, are especially noteworthy. There is a comfortable décor, and the clientele represents, for the most part, the beau monde of New York and world society. The cost of a complete luncheon is $8.75; of a complete dinner $13.75. *Cocktails, wines. Closed Sunday and for several weeks during summer.*

★★★ LA COCOTTE
147 East 60th Street   832-8972

This is a modestly proportioned French restaurant directly across the street from Bloomingdale's. It is one of the nicest to open in the city in some while, and the menu, compared with those of some of its more ambitious counterparts, is modestly priced. The owners are Pierre Geneen and Ernest Guzmits, and they are, like their surroundings, admirably without pretense and chi-chi. Mr. Geneen will be familiar to long-time patrons of Le Poulailler, La Caravelle, and La Côte Basque; Mr. Guzmits to patrons of L'Escargot, Delmonico's Hotel, and Le Pavillon.

If La Cocotte's menu is not dazzlingly different from that of other French restaurants, the food seems to be prepared with uncommon care. The pâté maison has an excellent texture. It is well-seasoned, studded with pistachios, and not too dry—an excellent pâté de campagne. The jarret de veau, or veal knuckle baked with tomatoes and mushrooms, is first-rate. Almost as good is a tender rib of veal with a delicate sour cream sauce.

One also recalls with pleasure a luncheon dish of pork roast with puréed potatoes. Both the veal knuckle and the pork roast were plats du jour, which is to say, not listed on the regular menu, but specially prepared and available. There is, of course, a different plat du jour each day.

There is one thought about the chef's baked clams. They are exceptionally well-seasoned and buttery, but they are large cherrystones, not small littlenecks, as they should be. When this was mentioned to one of the owners, he said the public felt cheated if they didn't get the large cherrystones. Too bad.

Tables—placed close together, by the way—are hard to come by.

There is a seating capacity of 40, and reservations are almost imperative for both lunch and dinner. Complete luncheons at La Cocotte are priced from about $3.75 to $5.75; complete dinners from about $6.75 to $10.00. *Cocktails, wines. Closed Sunday and major holidays.*

★★★★ LA COTE BASQUE
5 East 55th Street   688-6525

For one man's taste, this is the most beautiful restaurant in America. The murals, painted on canvas by Bernard Lamotte, are captivating. Particularly enchanting is a view of the harbor at Saint Jean de Luz. The tiny fishing vessels, the cafés along the quay, and the tiled roofs of the town are executed with such perspective and such vivid colors that the scene is a tour de force. The cuisine at La Côte Basque is classic and at its best superb. The kitchen is at times wayward, a remark that can be applied to almost any in Manhattan. The table service is professional. The cost of a complete luncheon is $10.50; of a complete dinner $15.50. There is no à la carte menu. *Cocktails, wines. Closed Sunday and, during August, Saturday also.*

★★ LA CREPE RESTAURANTS

48 West 55th Street   247-1136
Wines and beers only. Open all day until 1:00 a.m. Closed Sunday, New Year's Day, and Christmas.

158 West 44th Street   246-5388
Cocktails, wines. Open 11:30 a.m. until 12:00 midnight. Closed Sunday and major holidays. Sidewalk dining in the summer.

15 Greenwich Avenue   CH 3-2555
Wines and beers only. Open all day until 1:00 a.m. Closed Labor Day and Christmas. Sidewalk dining in the summer.

1974 Broadway (at 68th Street, near Lincoln Center)
TR 4-6900
Cocktails, wines. Open all day until 1:00 a.m. Closed Labor Day and Christmas. Sidewalk dining in the summer.

59 Nassau Street (at Maiden Lane)   732-8680
Cocktails, wines. Open until 9:00 p.m. Closed Saturday, Sunday, and major holidays.

The first of these generally admirable establishments opened in 1965 and its success was instantaneous. The principal dishes are large, thin, Brittany-style crêpes, and there are more than 50 fillings, including snail butter, eggs, sausage, caviar, and cheese. They range in cost from about 40 cents for a plain crêpe to $2.75 for one with lobster Thermidor. If there are faults to be listed, it is that the service is at times slow, the crêpes are occasionally served lukewarm. In addition to the crêpes, there is a very good onion soup, although it is topped with a gummy bland cheese. Salads, desserts, brie, and roquefort cheese are all available and so is cider.

★★ LA CROISETTE
1063 First Avenue (at 58th Street)   PL 9-2630

La Croisette is in the genre of several local restaurants, with murals in bright colors evocative of various regions of France. The name comes from the boulevard that borders on the bay at Cannes, one of the most famous promenades in the world. The restaurant has a kitchen of general excellence that offers at times such dishes as duck with apples and chicken with woodland mushrooms. Both the luncheon and dinner menus at the restaurant are prix fixe. The cost of a complete meal at noon is from about $3.85 to $4.00 and in the evening from about $5.00 to $7.00. *Cocktails, wines. Closed Sunday.*
AE CB DC

★★ LAFAYETTE
202 East 50th Street   421-4640

One of the small, dignified, and relatively elegant restaurants in Manhattan. The name of the restaurant is celebrated with a flourish. There are tricolors vertically imprinted on the cloth wall-coverings, and above a functional fireplace framed with French tiles there is the Lafayette heraldic emblem. The menu is interesting and the kitchen is generally excellent. Both the luncheon and the dinner menus at the Lafayette are table d'hôte. The cost of complete luncheons ranges from about $8.00 for an omelet to $12.00 for an entrecôte. Complete dinners go from about $12.25 for veal kidneys in cocotte to $16.50 for tournedos. *Cocktails, wines. Closed Sunday.*

★★ LA FONDA DEL SOL
120 West 51st Street   PL 7-8800

This colorful restaurant closed temporarily because of certain real estate transactions and when it re-opened it was half the size of the original. But it is still expansive and handsome with highly stylized ceiling lamps with pinpoint lighting, handsome wood columns and banquette dividers, a feeling of openness throughout, and a few remnants of those folk treasures in wall recesses.

Some of the food is quite good, particularly the appetizers and the "tidbits" served at the food bar. There is a spicy guacamole with coarse chunks of avocado, a shrimp cocktail with a racy horseradish sauce, chilled clams on the half shell, an excellent bean soup with lemon, uncommonly good baked beef bones with barbeque sauce, and so on.

But much of the food is pedestrian, and, one suspects, adulterated (cultivated for the American palate) where national dishes are concerned.

The fillings for the tacos and enchiladas are too much on the same taste level, whether made with chicken, beef, or pork. And the tortillas seemed a bit soggy as of a recent tasting. The beef slices in a barbecued beef sandwich had too many streaks of fat and the chili with its untender chunks of beef was served lukewarm.

La Fonda del Sol offers enormously pleasant surroundings, including the young waiters and waitresses and perhaps in the future the food will be less of a compromise. One other thing—the "tenderloin" of pork turned out to be boneless loin with whole coriander seeds and a bland tomato sauce. It was good, but the seeds would be better crushed.

The menus are à la carte, with main courses at midday from about $1.50 for a chicken taco to $3.25 for a combination plate. In the evening, it is from about $3.95 for a small combination to $7.95 for sirloin steak. *Cocktails (the margaritas are excellent), wines. Open 7 days a week.*
AE CB DC

★★ LA FONDUE
43 West 55th Street   581-0820

New York was not too long ago thought of in

terms of French, Italian, and Chinese restaurants. But lately, the old town has become increasingly sophisticated. La Fondue specializes in cheese and, while longer on inspiration than execution, is still welcome.

The menu offers an assortment of such appetizers as quiche Lorraine, fillet of mackerel, and herring; main dishes such as sausage and cheese platters, cheese and meat fondues. The Cheddar cheese soup is interesting, and one luncheon dish, a croque monsieur—a sort of hot ham and cheese sandwich covered and baked with a Mornay sauce —is excellent.

Whether you like the sausage platters may depend on whether you like the smoky flavor of some German sausages. The cheese fondue tasted surprisingly grainy. There are numerous excellent fresh cheeses available for sampling. The French bread is excellent.

The menu is both à la carte and prix fixe. At noon one can have cheese, sourdough French bread, condiments, and salad for $1.95. More substantial lunches are about $2.25 to $4.95. Complete dinners in the evening from $4.95 to $7.95; à la carte dishes from $2.10 to $4.25. You can have a complete assortment of fresh cheeses for $2.75. *Cocktails, wines. Closed Sunday.*

★★ LA FORTUNA
16 East 41st Street   MU 5-4890

This Italian restaurant has gained a deserved popularity. It is a fairly handsome, comfortably appointed place with limited seating capacity. It may be a trifle expensive for some pocketbooks, but the food is prepared with care and sauces are good. All dishes are à la carte. The cost of main courses is the same at all times, from about $4.00 to $7.25. *Cocktails, wines. Closed Saturday, Sunday, and most major holidays.*
AE   CB   DC

★★★★ LA GRENOUILLE
3 East 52nd Street   PL 2-1495

In some respects, this is a strikingly beautiful restaurant, particularly as to the multicolored roses or other bouquets found there in abundance. La Grenouille also boasts a distinguished kitchen, and some of the specialties include littleneck clams Corsini and striped bass with beurre blanc (white butter sauce). The sauces are generally as good as you are apt to find in the city. A regrettable aspect, however, is that the tables are so close together, as it lessens the grandeur that the restaurant should have. The cost of a complete luncheon is $9.75; of a complete dinner $15.75. *Cocktails, wines. Closed Sunday and most major holidays.*
AE

★★ LA GRILLADE
845 Eighth Avenue (at 51st Street)   265-1610

The owners of La Grillade were formerly with the well-favored Le Caneton on the Upper East Side and the same high standards apply here. This is a fairly small, pleasant restaurant with jigsaw murals on the walls and friendly service by French waitresses. The menu is not startlingly original, but the food is generally good, whether it is the house pâté or roast lamb with flageolets. A walk from the restaurant to Lincoln Center is not unthinkable. A la carte items at midday range from about $2.15 to $6.50; in the evening, from about $3.75 to $6.50. *Cocktails, wines. On Saturday and Sunday, the restaurant opens at 5 p.m. Closed July 4 and Labor Day.*
AE CB DC

★★ LA GROCERIA
333 Avenue of the Americas (at West 4th Street)
CH 2-3200

This is conceivably the most colorful restaurant in

Greenwich Village, and the atmosphere is in conservative good style. The restaurant is triangular, and the walls are lined with boxes and tins of pasta, olive oil, tuna, and olives, all of which are for sale—thus the name La Groceria. The food is not altogether different from that found in a score or more small Italian restaurants in Manhattan. The food is good, nonetheless, and the veal francese is recommended in particular. There is one menu and it is à la carte. The cost of main dishes is from about $1.85 for spaghetti Valdostano to $4.15 for veal cutlet. *Cocktails, wines. The restaurant is open for dinner only. Closed New Year's Day, Thanksgiving, and Christmas.*
AE CB DC MC

★ LA HACIENDA
172 Bleecker Street   475-9230

This is a pleasantly decorated restaurant in Greenwich Village that specializes in both Argentine and Italian cooking. It is a neat, colorful place with whitewashed brick and walls hung with ponchos.

Some of the dishes come off reasonably well, including the empanadas, or pastry turnovers, filled with well-seasoned ground beef and spaghetti with pesto. That, of course, is the well-known Genoese sauce made with chopped basil.

The mixed grill is an Argentine specialty and at La Hacienda it seemed only so-so. The sweetbreads, thinly sliced and grilled, were excellent, but the other meats, including the skirt steak and blood sausage, were ordinary.

The veal for the veal French-style was a bit chewy even though it seemed to have been "tenderized" with a claw hammer. The sangria or wine with fruit beverage is fairly good.

All dishes are à la carte with main courses from about $1.90 to $5.25. *There is no bar, but wines are available. The restaurant opens at 5:00 p.m. every day except Monday, when it is closed.*

★★ L'AIGLON
13 East 55th Street   PL 3-7295 *and* PL 3-7296

This is a neat, air-conditioned, and comfortable restaurant that has the virtue of being open all summer. The menu is both French and Italian, and at its best the food is very good, although some of the portions may seem a touch too ample for discriminating appetites. Both the luncheon and dinner menus are prix fixe and à la carte. At midday the cost of a complete meal is from about $6.00 to $7.25; à la carte entrées from about $4.75 to $7.75. Complete dinners cost from about $9.00 to $12.00; à la carte dishes from about $5.75 to $8.50. The service corps at L'Aiglon is large, but it is at times inattentive. *Cocktails, wines. On Sunday, the restaurant opens at 5:00 p.m. Closed major holidays.*
AE DC

★★ LAIR, THE
1493 Third Avenue (near 84th Street)   861-0262

This is a dimly lighted, long, narrow restaurant that seats about 50. The rough stucco walls, fake beams, and escutcheons create a pleasant setting for intimate late dining except for the background music.

The menu offers the chef's imaginative interpretation of "continental cuisine." The garlic bread served before dinner was piping hot, fresh, and suitably aromatic. An asparagus quiche appetizer was good, but the sausage Parisienne was marred by a spoonful of poor-quality potato salad.

The chef's choice of soup on a recent evening was an unusual and pleasant purée of apple and celery. The Lair salad is a fresh spinach and mushroom combination. A baked breast of chicken with rice and Dijon mustard sauce was tender and moist but lacked character. The veal Cordon Bleu, scallops of veal stuffed with ham and Gruyère cheese, was excellent. The crêpe St. Julien flambé was a pyrotechnical triumph, but the flaming liquid imparted a slight sweetness. The filling of chicken, veal, and ham was different and good.

The urge to flambé extended to an otherwise good fruit cobbler and to the twist of lemon for espresso.

Complete dinners, including appetizer, soup, entrée, and dessert, run from $4.70 for manicotti or cannelloni to $7.95 for shell steak. A la carte entrées from $2.95 to $6.50. *Cocktails, wines. Dinner only is served at The Lair Tuesday through Saturday from 6:00 p.m. to midnight and Sunday from 5:00 p.m. to 11:00 p.m. Closed Monday. Reservations are recommended.*
AE   DC   MC

★ LA LOCANDA
228 East 45th Street   682-9307

An Italian restaurant that seems to have a potential not fully realized. There is no doubt in one mind that the chef has unusual skill; the menu is well-varied and the food is cooked to order. If you ask for spaghetti al dente, you get spaghetti al dente. The food is South Italian, and there is an apparent odor of garlic in the dining room. There are excellent seafood dishes at La Locanda, and the combination dish of veal and chicken is recommended. There is a single à la carte menu for lunch and dinner with main courses from $2.25 to $6.75. *Cocktails, wines. Closed Sunday.*
AE   CB   DC   MC

★ LAM KEE
3 Catherine Street   CA 6-9572

Let the fastidious be aware that the tiny Lam Kee restaurant in Chinatown will not be their cup of lapsang souchong. It is an unsanitary-looking little establishment tucked away on Catherine Street, but those who find adventure in searching out inexpensive and offbeat restaurants with a fairly good table will enjoy it.

There is no menu, so you are more or less at the mercy of the smiling waiter whose command of English approximates more or less the average customer's command of Chinese. Thus one falls back on old standbys like hot and sour soup, which he recommended and which was quite good. So was a platter of chicken lo mein or chicken strips with noodles.

An unusual dish that day was pork Shanghai-style, very small pork cutlets with bone, deep-fried, and served with seasoned salt, the same salt usually served with fried squab. Oddly enough, the pork tasted like what might be called poor man's squab and perhaps that's the idea.

The prices are rather vague, but all of it is inexpensive. Main dishes are about $2.00. The portions if anything are too generous. *There is no bar, but wine and beer may be brought in. Closed Wednesday.*

★★ LANTERN LIGHT
801 Second Avenue (between 42nd and 43rd Streets)
683-4306

In several respects, this is an admirable Chinese restaurant on the East Side. It is a good-looking place with upstairs and downstairs dining, a markedly pleasant serving staff, and one of the most ambitious menus in town.

One wishes that all the food came off as well as that of a recent luncheon that included what is listed as ocean-flavored spicy shrimp with tree ears, ginger, garlic, and water chestnuts, and a splendid braised fish fin with an outstanding dark sauce and scallions.

Another meal was a reasonably good dish of walnut chicken, the pieces of chicken (poorly cubed, by the way) quickly cooked with whole walnut meats and seasonings of scallions and ginger, and an above-average pork and cabbage soup.

A dish of Lantern Delight, a house special, was a mishmash of scallops and mushrooms, baby corn, lobster, sweet peppers, and shredded snow peas, and this, too, was acceptably good, if not particularly distinguished—except for the variety of ingredients. On a par was a fish casserole with bean curd and black mushrooms.

An order of assorted appetizers called merry-go-round was a genuine disappointment—the dem sem steamed far far in advance, meaning hours perhaps; too sweet and innocently flavored spareribs; and tough walnut rolls.

Complete luncheons are priced from about $2.75 to $3.25, with à la carte dishes throughout the day and evening from about $3.25 to $7.50. Pekin duck is priced at $16.00. *Cocktails, wines. Open 7 days a week, but luncheon is not served on Sunday.*
AE DC

★ LA PAELLA
3 Hamilton Place (136th Street and Broadway)
283-8439

A Cuban who had spent several years in Madrid surveyed the interior of La Paella restaurant one evening and reflected, "In Spain designs are stark. In this country, when they try to recreate Spain, it is always in bad baroque."

La Paella is a modern mass of ironwork, obvious art, and coats of arms. And music, which, whether live or recorded rock, seems ear-splitting.

There are many people who say that the restaurant produces a fine paella, and it is passable, although some of the components are chewy and there is no apparent use of saffron in the dish, although there should be.

La Paella's Galician soup, with its beans and pork and greens, is, by New York standards, a cut above average and the gazpacho, a bit garlicky and on the tart side, is spicy and good. The shrimp creole-style was chewy and the restaurant's special appetizer (including slices of tinned ham and supermarket yellow cheese among other things) an embarrassment.

All dishes are à la carte with main dishes at midday from about $1.85 for an omelet with sausages to $3.25 for steak; in the evening, from about $3.00 for rice with

chicken to $5.00 for the paella and $6.00 for steak. *Cocktails, wines. Open 7 days a week.*
AE   MC

★★ LA PETITE FERME
189 West 10th Street   242-7035

This is possibly (you have to qualify everything in Manhattan) the smallest restaurant in town. It is certainly one of the most cunning without being coy. It is the enterprise of Charles Chevillot, a son of the family that owns the well-known restaurant and Hotel de la Poste in Beaune, Burgundy.

There are only five tables with heavy pine tops—seating for no more than 21. There are bouquets of fresh flowers in corners and over the entranceway, and from the ceiling hang hams and sausages. And doves in a cage.

You can't see the kitchen, but through an open door you can hear the chef (the owner) whistle while he works. There is one waitress, a handsome French lass who doesn't speak English. The menu is quite limited, and in a restaurant of restricted size that is comme il faut. The cooking is bourgeois, and that, too, is all to the good.

The menu is printed on a blackboard, and one recent meal included freshly cooked mussels at room temperature with an admirably made vinaigrette sauce; and an impressive assortment of thinly sliced charcuterie—jambon de Bayonne and Swiss dried beef and salamis. Among the main courses, a steak with a Burgundy wine sauce and poulet au vin. And assorted cheeses.

A subsequent meal included a first course of fresh asparagus (not on the menu but available that day in the market) with a butter and shallot sauce; a good pot au feu with boiled beef, turnips, leeks, and carrots, served with horseradish, mustard, and coarse salt; excellent sautéed calves' liver. And with it all, freshly cooked, crisp vegetables, and that, for Manhattan, is a switch. Plus a laudable fresh salad.

The two dishes cooked with red wine—the coq au vin and steak with Burgundy sauce—were good, and yet the sauces with them left something to be desired. The raw wine taste was apparent in both.

But La Petite Ferme is an excellent idea and just about as French, along bourgeois lines, as you can come by in this city.

All dishes are à la carte, with main courses from about $3.75 to $6.00. *There is no bar, but wines may be brought in. Open for lunch from noon to 3:00 p.m.; dinner, 6:00 to 11:00 p.m. Closed Monday. Reservations are essential.*

★★★ LA PETITE MARMITE
5 Mitchell Place (49th Street and First Avenue)
JU 6-5237

It is always a major circumstance to discover one dish of exceptional merit in the French restaurants of Manhattan, and Le Petite Marmite has one. It is the clear soup for which the restaurant is named, the chef's petite marmite. It is freshly made, has an excellent body, and the meats and vegetables in it have a proper texture.

The food over-all here is very good, and it should be. The chef was a key figure in La Caravelle's kitchen for some time and is one of the partners here, according to a spokesman for the restaurant. He turns out some well-made appetizers, including moules à la moutarde (although it needs a garnish, a bit of chopped parsley, perhaps), artichokes vinaigrette, and pâté maison. The onion soup is good. The fricassee of chicken with sorrel is good, although on one occasion served lukewarm, and the daube of beef Provençale is excellent.

The décor of La Petite Marmite is somewhat sober but pleasant enough with non-objectionable art on the walls (landscapes and flowers) and arches and columns that look vaguely Venetian.

Unfortunately, the cheeses at La Petite Marmite, with the exception of the brie, have been mediocre, and the pastry assortment is limited. But the staff is trying.

Both the luncheon and dinner menus are prix fixe. The cost of a complete luncheon is $4.75; of a complete dinner $7.75. *Cocktails, wines. The restaurant opens at 5:30 p.m. on Saturday. Closed Sunday and major holidays.*
AE   CB   DC   MC

★★ LA PIAZZETTA
144 East 52nd Street   PL 3-3131 *and* 755-5260

At first glance, the menu of La Piazzetta does not look substantially different from those at scores of other Italian restaurants in the city. The menu lists the expected linguine with clam sauce, scampi marinara, and spaghetti dishes, but there seems to be someone in the kitchen who cares. The pasta dishes taste freshly made, and the fettuccine Alfredo, although not prepared at tableside, is worthwhile. The tables are small and close together, but the reception is warm and friendly. All dishes are à la carte at midday, from $2.25 to $6.50; in the evening the prix-fixe dinners are from $5.75 to $7.75. *Cocktails, wines. On Saturday the restaurant opens at 5 p.m. Closed Sunday and all major holidays.*
AE   CB   DC   MC

★★ LA POTINIERE DU SOIR
47 West 55th Street   CI 5-4266 *and* 245-4248

From some points of view, this is one of the pleasantest French restaurants in Manhattan. At its best, the cuisine is first-rate; it is also reasonably priced. One disquieting note, however, is the piped-in music, which is occasionally loud and distracting. Complete luncheons from $3.60 to $7.25; complete dinners from $6.00 to $9.25. A la carte prices start at $3.25. *Cocktails, wines. The restaurant is open until midnight Monday through Friday and until 1:00 a.m. Saturday. Luncheon is not served Saturday. Closed Sunday.*
AE   MC

★ LA POULARD
1047 Second Avenue (near 55th Street)   838-2970

When the owner of a restaurant takes charge of the kitchen he deserves encouragement. In spite of its flaws, La Poularde is a restaurant that is serious about the preparation of food. The veal chef's-style is cooked with vermouth and the chicken in the style of the chef has been perfected by him. The pâté is well above par and a platter of charcuterie included excellent thinly sliced sausages. The ventilation is not adequate, however.

Lunch is à la carte from $2.25 to $4.25. Complete dinners run from $6.25 to $8.95. *Cocktails, wines. Closed Sunday and major holidays.*
AE MC

★★ L'ARMORIQUE
246 East 54th Street   PL 3-3787 and EL 5-9086

Guests at L'Armorique are greeted by the chef and host in his toque blanche. Specialties of the house seem generally to be more the chef's creations than works of classic cuisine, but the results can be excellent. The restaurant's recommendations usually include snails ($2.25), though the coquille Nantaise ($2.25) is delicious. The à la carte lunch entrées start at $3.00. In the evening, entrée prices start at $4.75. *Cocktails, wines. Closed Monday and major holidays.*
AE BA CB DC

★ LARRE'S FRENCH RESTAURANT
50 West 56th Street   CI 7-8980 and CI 7-8557

The impressive things about Larré's are the prices and a few dishes that are a trifle out of the ordinary for Manhattan. There is a club luncheon (entrée, dessert, and coffee) for $2.25 and a complete dinner for $4.00. One of the unusual dishes is raie, or skate, served with black butter and capers, a specialty of the house. Like most of the dishes at Larré's, it is very good but not overly distinguished. *Cocktails, wines. Closed Sunday.*

★ LA SCALA
142 West 54th Street   CI 5-1575

A fairly pleasant Italian restaurant with a conventional menu. At lunch, à la carte entrées are $1.00 to $7.00 and there is a minimum charge of $2.50. The prices for à la carte dinner are from $3.50 to $8.00. *Cocktails, wines. Open from noon until midnight. Closed Thanksgiving and Christmas.*
AE CB DC MC

★ LA STRADA EAST
274 Third Avenue (between 21st and 22nd Streets)
GR 3-3760

A neighborhood restaurant with an interesting Italian menu. The food at times is excellent. All foods are à la carte, with main luncheon courses from $2.50 to $3.75; dinner entrées from $3.00 to $7.50. *Cocktails, wines. Lunch is served Monday through Friday only. Closed Sunday.*
AE CB DC MC

★★★ LA TOQUE BLANCHE
359 East 50th Street   PL 5-3552

This is a generally excellent and popular French restaurant with a menu that shows more imagination than most. On occasion such specialties as quiche Lorraine, tripe à la mode de Caen, and cassoulet Toulousain are available. The restaurant is larger than many in its class and the service is attentive. Complete luncheons from $4.25 to $5.50; complete dinners from $7.50 to $9.50. *Cocktails, wines. On Sunday the restaurant opens at 6:00 p.m. Closed major holidays. Reservations suggested.*

★★ LA VENERE WEST
117 West 58th Street   765-1427

For the most essential element, the food, this Italian restaurant is cordially recommended. The pasta dishes,

167

particularly the fettuccine, are prepared with considerable care, and so are the veal dishes. Recommended in particular is the veal alla chef with an excellent brown sauce. The walls of La Venere West are painted green, and there is aqua-colored Venetian glass on all the tables. Opera music is piped in, and the table service is not markedly efficient. The kitchen deserves patronage, but one wonders what would happen on a crowded night. Complete luncheons cost $3.70; complete dinners are $5.00, including wine. There is also an à la carte menu with entrées from $4.50 to $8.50. *Cocktails, wines. On Saturday, the restaurant opens at 5:00 p.m. Closed Sunday, and major holidays.*
DC

★ LA VERANDA
60 East 54th Street   758-5560

This is an Italian restaurant with a dining room conservatively decked out with soft murals, mirrored columns, and artificial roses on black iron grillwork.

There seems to be an uneven quality about the kitchen, starting with the hot antipasto, a sort of fritto-misto. The deep-fried scallops were tender, sweet, and good; the bits of deep-fried flounder just on the verge of not being fresh. A dish of linguine was cooked to the al dente stage (if you want your pasta here cooked well done, you'd better ask for it) and that was all to the good. The clam sauce was well-seasoned.

One serving of chicken called galaina impinida, stuffed with prosciutto and cheese, was creditable enough.

The cost of a four-course lunch at La Veranda is from $3.95 to $4.50. A la carte dishes in the evening from $3.00 to $6.35. *Cocktails, wines. Luncheon is not served Saturday. Closed Sunday and major holidays.*
AE BA CB DC MC

★ LE ALPI
234 West 48th Street   JU 2-7792

An Italian restaurant with, happily, more things plus than minus. The fettuccine is excellent, the veal is of good quality, and, although the staff seems small, the service in general is enthusiastic. On the negative side, soups have in the past lacked substance and the American-style coffee is dreary. There is a four-course luncheon that costs from about $3.00 to $5.50. There are two complete dinners at $6.50 each, plus an à la carte menu that lists main courses from about $3.25 to $5.75. *Cocktails, wines. Luncheon Saturday is à la carte. Closed Sunday and major holidays.* AE CB DC MC

★ LEBANON RESTAURANT
8810 Fourth Avenue, Brooklyn   745-8873

Brooklyn has a fair share of restaurants that offer Middle-East cookery, and this is one of the most recent. The food here is interesting and tastes rather like—by some rare stretch of language—mass-produced home-style cooking.

There are the usual appetizers such as humus bi tahini or chick-pea and sesame paste spread; baba ghannouj or eggplant and sesame paste spread; stuffed grape leaves; and tabbouleh made with much chopped parsley, cracked wheat, and tomatoes.

The kitchen offers a good individual spinach pie with pine nuts among the appetizers. Among the main courses there are, of course, shish kebab; kibbee made with ground lamb and served raw or baked; and an unusual dish called mouloukia, a spinach stew served on a bed of rice and orzo with shredded chicken on top. The rice for this dish, as well as for the shish kebab, was at one visit lamentably overcooked.

The food isn't bad, but the ventilation could be improved for those trying to concentrate on food. The Lebanon's desserts, incidentally, are generally excellent.

There are complete dinners priced at $3.75; à la carte dishes from about $1.50 to $2.50. *Cocktails, wines. Closed Monday.*
DC

★★ LE BIARRITZ
325 West 57th Street 245-9467

Several restaurants with chefs as proprietors have opened in New York, among them Le Biarritz. A. Vaillant was formerly chef of the Potinière du Soir, and his establishment is neat and comfortable. Specialties of the house include an excellent crêpe Biarritz, and other dishes remembered with pleasure are chicken à l'estragon and a crisp duckling Montmorency. At first glance, the restaurant's menu looks conventional, with its sole meunière, trout amandine, and so forth, but there is much to recommend the kitchen. Luncheon is à la carte, with main dishes from $2.50 to $5.25. Complete dinners cost from $5.75 to $9.50. *Cocktails, wines. On Saturday and Sunday the restaurant opens at 4:30 p.m.*
AE BA DC

★★ LE BISTRO
827 Third Avenue (between 50th and 51st Streets)
EL *5-8766 and* PL *9-5933*

One of the neatest of New York's small French restaurants, Le Bistro also boasts of a loyal French clientele. Both the hors d'oeuvres and main courses are of a high order, and the service is attentive. The tables are a fraction too close together and the restaurant is frequently crowded. Complete luncheons from $4.75 to $5.50; complete dinners from $6.50 to $9.25. *Cocktails, wines. Closed Sunday and major holidays.*
AE MC

★★ LE CHAMBERTIN
348 West 46th Street PL *7-2154*

This is one of the pleasantest restaurants in the thea-

ter district from the standpoints of the quality of the food and relative lack of hurly-burly. The menu at lunch seems commonplace, but at dinner it does have such less-than-inevitable dishes as poached turbot, short ribs, and duck with cherries. The sweetbreads maison are delicious, and the beef is rare and tender. Complete luncheons from $3.00 to $5.50; complete dinners from $5.50 to $8.75. *Cocktails, wines. Closed Sunday and the first 2 weeks of July.*
AE

★★ LE CHAMPIGNON
35 West 56th Street   245-6335

If you are among those who think that the "popular-priced" French restaurants in New York are just dandy, you will probably enjoy dining at Le Champignon. The principal thing that distinguishes these restaurants one from the other, anyway, is the décor; the chefs are all seemingly equipped with the same talent and imagination. Or lack of it.

The décor of Le Champignon is pleasant enough: a long, somewhat narrow room with a Victorian-style bar with black grillwork, a dining area with black patent leather banquettes, pink napery, and the mushroom motif everywhere from vases and small sculpture to, of course, mushrooms à la grecque among the appetizers.

As far as the menus go, if you are an habitué of "popular-priced" restaurants—those that offer a complete luncheon for about $3.95, complete dinners about $5.95 to $7.25, in addition to à la carte fare—you can go right down the line in quoting the menu: chef's pâté, céleri rémoulade, snails, eggs Benedict, sole meunière, beef bourguignon, and so on.

Some of the dishes at Le Champignon can be praised without reservation, including a recent specialty of the day: lamb curry in an excellent cream sauce. And the goujonettes of sole—small strips of fresh fish breaded and deep-fried and served hot with a tartar sauce. There is an interesting dish served as a main luncheon dish or in the evening as an appetizer: mushrooms with a stuffing of chicken liver and with a Madeira sauce.

In addition to the predictable nature of the restaurant's menu, the chief faults to be found are the routine nature of the food, the non-attention to seemingly small details, and the gross portions.

The cost of a complete luncheon at Le Champignon is from about $2.75 to $3.50; of a complete dinner from about $5.75 to $6.50. A la carte items at midday from about $3.85 to $4.75; in the evening from about $5.25 to $8.00. *Cocktails, wines. Closed Sunday and some holidays.*
AE CB DC MC

★★ LE CHANTECLAIR
18 East 49th Street PL *5-7731*

Where price is concerned, Le Chanteclair is less expensive than the grand-luxe category of Manhattan restaurants, and in its league it has a very good kitchen. There is a neat décor focused on a mural of the Place de la Concorde, and the service is above average. The problem is that the tables are too close for comfort, and, because of the restaurant's success, which is considerable, there may be a long wait for a table, particularly at midday. The assortment of cheeses at Le Chanteclair is, as it is in most New York restaurants, lamentable. Both luncheon and dinner are prix fixe, with complete luncheons from about $5.75 to $7.95; complete dinners from about $6.75 to $11.25. *Cocktails, wines. Closed Sunday and major holidays.*
AE BA CB DC MC

★ LE CHATEAU RICHELIEU
48 East 52nd Street PL *1-6565*

At its best, the food at Le Château Richelieu is inspired, but it is quite capable of being routine. The same may be said of the restaurant's wines. All dishes are à la carte, with main luncheon dishes from $5.00 for mushroom

omelet to $10.00 for sirloin steak. Main dinner dishes from $6.00; a complete dinner is $15.00. *Cocktails, wines. Closed Sunday.*
AE CB DC MC

★★ LE CHEVAL BLANC
145 East 45th Street MU 2-9695

This is one of the most active French bistros in the city, and although the menu is not burdened with inspiration, the food is of general excellence. One problem, however, is due to the popularity of Le Cheval Blanc. At peak dining periods both the restaurant's dining rooms are filled. It is best to go early or late for lunch. Complete luncheons from about $3.75 to $5.25; complete dinners from about $5.25 to $7.50. *Cocktails, wines. On Saturday, the restaurant opens at 5:00 p.m. Closed Sunday and major holidays.*
AE CB DC

★★★ LE CYGNE
53 East 54th Street PL 9-5941

This elegant, cheerful, and knowing establishment is owned by Gerard Gallian and Michel Crouzillat, who were formerly at La Caravelle. They are going about their business of pleasing their customers with style and grace. Their premises are pleasant, with mustard-colored walls hung with rather festive paintings of flowers.

As to the kitchen, some dishes have recently come off with uncommon distinction, among them an appetizer of tender mussels in a well-seasoned mustard sauce and a whole braised pigeon with olives in a sauce lightly flavored with cognac. The food, for the most part, seems extraordinarily well cooked and equal to that of the best of the restaurant's counterparts throughout the city—the chef's pâté, the squab chicken in champagne sauce, the kidneys in mustard sauce, and so on. There is a very good dessert, the crème caramel, mahogany-colored and served with a mahogany-colored sauce.

Both the luncheon and dinner menus at Le Cygne are of a fixed price, $7.00 for a complete luncheon; $10.75 for dinner. *Closed Sunday and major holidays.*
AE

★★★ LE MANOIR
120 East 56th Street   PL *3-1447*

This is a handsome restaurant with cheerful, comfortable surroundings and a menu of unpretentious dishes that are generally first-rate. Some of the fish dishes are outstanding, particularly the poached bass with whipped butter sauce. The meat entrées, such as sweetbreads in champagne and chicken with mushrooms and artichokes, are generally good. The menu is table d'hôte and à la carte with complete luncheons at $4.50 and dinners from $7.50. *Cocktails, wines. Closed Sunday, New Year's Day, and Christmas.*
AE   CB   DC

★ LE MARMITON
216 East 49th Street   MU *8-1232 and* MU *8-1355*

Le Marmiton is very well-known in New York. The décor is neat and standard French provincial, and the menu shows no more imagination than is found in a score of other restaurants around the city and the kitchen is not without minor flaws. The most interesting item sampled was the coquille of seafood with scallops and white wine as a first course. It was well-glazed and well-flavored. There are complete luncheons from about $4.75 to $5.75; complete dinners from about $6.50 to $9.25. *Cocktails, wines. On Saturday, the restaurant opens at 5:00 p.m. Closed Sunday and, during June, July, and August, Saturday also. Closed all major holidays.*
AE   BA   CB   DC   MC

★★★ LE MISTRAL
14 East 52nd Street   *421-7588 and 421-7589*

New York is host to several restaurants with stylish

interiors, but it is a compliment allowable to few to say that the food is on a par with the décor. Such praise may be accorded Le Mistral, however. One of the town's roster of luxury restaurants, it is a place of estimable charm with a kitchen of considerable merit. The cost of dining there is $8.75 for the complete luncheon and $12.75 for the complete dinner. *Cocktails, wines. Closed Sunday and all major holidays.*
AE DC

★★ LE MOAL
942 Third Avenue (between 56th and 57th Streets)
MU 8-8860

This is a well-established, frequently crowded French bistro with a bill of fare that is well rounded, if standard, for the city. There is the usual duck with orange sauce and grilled chicken, and the food is generally good, though at times overcooked. The maître d' is easily ruffled. A la carte entrées at midday are from about $3.25 to $5.25. The evening menu is à la carte, with main courses from about $3.75 to $6.50. *Cocktails, wines. Dinner is served from 1:00 p.m. on Sunday. Closed all major holidays.*
AE CB DC

★ LENGE-SAIMIN RESTAURANT
202 Columbus Avenue (near 69th Street)   874-8278

The word lengé is Japanese for lotus flower and saimin is the name of a Hawaiian soup with noodles. The Lengé-Saimin is an almost miniature restaurant that has achieved a considerable following.

The kitchen produces some interesting food, but if you go, go armed with patience. Even when the restaurant is half-full, the service seems innocently fragmented. One might not care so keenly about the poorer aspects of the Lengé-Saimin if it weren't for the good ones.

Luncheon dishes are à la carte, with main courses from about $1.50 for yakitori, or chicken on skewers, to $2.50

for lobster. Complete dinners cost from about $2.80 to $3.50, with à la carte dishes from about $1.00 to $1.85. *Beers and wines only. Closed Monday, New Year's Day, and Christmas.*

★ L'ENTRECOTE
1057 First Avenue (at 57th Street)   755-0080

An entrecôte is a rib steak and the best thing about this small restaurant, with its small tables set too close together, is the quality of its steaks. It is high.

There are 15 tables here, most of them round with marble tops. There is a minuscule kitchen and bar, brick and paneled walls, and two young Frenchmen who are notable among entrepreneurs for their energy and dedication.

The menu at the Entrecôte is Franco-American in concept. The meal may start with a crisp chicory salad with walnuts. There is the excellent-quality steak cooked to the proper degree of doneness and with an acceptable butter sauce. And there are french-fried potatoes as slender and crisp as you'll find in the city, although in some cases they may be cooked in less frequently used fat.

The cost of the steak dinner is $6.95. The Entrecôte's coffee leaves something to be desired. *Cocktails, wines. Open for dinner only. Closed Sunday.*
AE MC

★ LEONE'S
239 West 48th Street   JU 6-5151

Leone's offers quantities of food in a colorful setting, and the sheer abundance is most impressive on an initial visit. Thereafter, it may begin to pall. A fine place, nonetheless, for visitors to the city. The cost of an extensive dinner is $7.50 to $9.50. *Cocktails, wines. The restaurant is open for dinner only: weekdays, 4:30 p.m. to 12:30 a.m.; Saturday, 3:30 p.m. to 12:30 a.m.; Sunday, 2:00 to 10:00 p.m.*
All major credit cards.

★★★ LEOPARD, THE
253 East 50th Street   EL 5-8213

This restaurant, in a building that was formerly a private residence, seemed a trifle naïve and pretentious when it first opened. It has, however, matured into something both responsible and honestly worthwhile, with food that is prepared with exceptional skill and care. There is no printed menu; for each meal, a limited but well-chosen selection of entrées is outlined by a captain or maître d'hôtel. This might include a choice of grilled filet mignon with Choron sauce (béarnaise flavored lightly with tomato); chicken with tarragon; sirloin au poivre; and stuffed fillet of striped bass. These were preceded by a gossamer pie that the captain promised as a quiche but was in truth an onion tart and smoked salmon. There was also a choice among first courses of prosciutto with melon or eggplant caviar. Next, a choice of soups, a consommé with claret, or a purée of sweet peas, both of which were excellent. There was salad and dessert. In a critical sense, a dish of braised leeks came off poorly. The flatware on the table was slightly tarnished and the wines—which are included in the price of the meal, incidentally—were nothing remarkable. The over-all atmosphere is that of a plush bistro that could, like the flatware, do with a bit of polish. The cost of a complete luncheon at The Leopard is $8.00; a complete dinner from $15.00 to $17.50. *Cocktails, wines. Closed Sunday and major holidays.*
AE   DC

★★★ LE PAVILLON
111 East 57th Street   PL 3-8388

In the days of its glory Le Pavillon was the ultimate French restaurant on this continent. It was, in fact, the model and principal training ground for hundreds of chefs, waiters, and the like, and the man responsible was the legendary Henri Soulé, who opened the restaurant in 1939. When he died in 1966 the spirit of the place went with

him. The next year Le Pavillon was taken over by another management under the direction of Claude C. Philippe. It is now operated by Stuart Levin and remains a place of certain elegance and luxury. But however much one might devoutly wish it, Le Pavillon does not exist in all its former grandeur. In its finest moments the kitchen perpetuates to a great extent the cuisine for which the restaurant was celebrated. But even that is not without fault, and the service today falls short of its former mark. Luncheon is prix fixe at $9.00 to $15.00. Dinner is à la carte, with main courses from $4.25 to $11.00. *Cocktails, wines. The restaurant is open from noon to 3:00 p.m. for luncheon, 6:00 p.m. to 10:00 p.m. for dinner, and 10:00 p.m. to 11:30 p.m. for supper. Closed Sunday, Monday, major holidays, and the month of July.*
AE CB DC

★★ LE PERIGORD
405 East 52nd Street   PL 5-6244

This is far and away the best French restaurant in the Beekman-Sutton Place area. Several of the dishes are distinguished, including the duck pâté, the langoustines au gratin, and the various preparations of striped bass. The turbot sampled on one occasion was dry. The décor of Le Périgord is nondescript, with bright, almost fluorescent murals, grillwork, potted plants, and low ceiling. The cost of a complete luncheon is $5.50; of a complete dinner $9.50. *Cocktails, wines. On Saturday and Sunday the restaurant opens at 6 p.m. Closed New Year's Day, Thanksgiving, and Christmas.*
AE CB DC

★★★ LE PERIGORD PARK
575 Park Avenue (at 63rd Street)   752-0050

Someone has remarked that, in writing about restaurants, if the writer dwells in the beginning and at length on the décor, the kitchen is apt to be suspect. It is not true in the case of Le Périgord Park, for the décor here is something special and the kitchen can measure up to some of the major cuisines in the city.

First off, Le Périgord Park has one of the prettiest, most elegant main dining rooms you're apt to find anywhere, with its airy murals—some in trompe l'oeil patterns, some elegant caricatures of strolling musicians, fantasy figures with lyres and flutes. There are crystal chandeliers, richly upholstered banquettes, and, recently, fresh wind flowers throughout the room. There are two smaller dining areas, a bit more somber but handsome enough.

Where food is concerned, there are numerous things to recall with pleasure—an excellent, well-seasoned terrine of duck; delicate, minuscule clams on the half-shell baked quickly with butter and herbs; a masterfully roasted squab, not overdone as it too often is in Manhattan; a very good gratin of sweetbreads with a duxelles or purée of mushrooms; first-rate veal beau séjour, lightly seasoned with bay leaf and garlic; and numerous desserts of special merit, including eggs à la neige—gossamer ovals of meringue with custard; and prune tarts.

One dish, a disappointment, was goujonettes of sole. These are small fingers of sole, breaded and deep-fried. At one luncheon, they had a rather tough crust as though they had not been made with freshly made bread crumbs and they were overly salty. And so was the mustard sauce that accompanied them.

The wine list at Le Périgord Park (it is related, by the way, to the long-established Le Périgord on 52nd Street) offers very few bottles.

The menus at Le Périgord Park are fixed prices. The cost of a complete luncheon is $6.50; of complete dinners about $10.50 to $13.00. *Cocktails, wines. The restaurant is not open for lunch on Saturday and Sunday. Closed major holidays.*

★★ LE PONT NEUF
212 East 53rd Street   751-0373

At this French restaurant the food is both reasonably good and reasonably priced. The décor consists of murals that will give many diners the feeling of déjà vu, but the surroundings are pleasant enough. Luncheon is prix fixe at $4.75; dinners are à la carte with main courses from $4.50 to $8.00. *Cocktails, wines. Luncheon is not served Saturday and Sunday. Closed Sunday, major holidays, and two weeks in July.*
AE CB DC MC

★★ LE POULAILLER
43 West 65th Street   799-7600

This is an enterprise of the owners and chef of New York's esteemed La Caravelle restaurant. Le Poulailler means "the poultry coop," and it is a handsome, spacious place with an airy, delicate décor by Jean Pagès. It is next door, more or less, to Lincoln Center, and that is a point in its favor. As to the atmosphere, on the walls there are linear drawings of the Paris opera, views of Paris bridges, and sketches of game birds in cages. The menus for lunch, dinner, and supper are wholly adequate, although not as dazzling, perhaps, as dedicated patrons of La Caravelle might have hoped. Much of the food at lunch is of an à la minute sort, with such dishes as omelets, poached eggs, chicken in cream sauce, and sauerkraut in champagne. The food is generally well-prepared, and remembered with special favor on one occasion were the bay scallops in a light wine sauce with mushrooms and a ragout of beef. The cost of a complete luncheon is $5.25; of a complete dinner, $9.00. There is a supper menu with a variety of dishes to suit all ranges of after-theater appetites. *Cocktails, wines. Closed Sunday and major holidays.*
AE DC

★★ LE PROVENCAL
21 East 62nd Street　TE 8-4246

A small but rewarding French restaurant with the same familiar menu (coq au vin, boeuf bourguignon, and so on), but a thoroughly competent kitchen. The service is just a cut above par, but the chef seems to care. The restaurant is popular and therefore crowded. Both luncheon and dinner are table d'hôte, with midday meals from about $4.75 to $8.50, dinners from about $7.00 to $9.75. *Cocktails, wines. Closed Sunday, most major holidays, and from August 1 through Labor Day.*
AE DC

★★ L'ESCARGOT
987 Third Avenue (near 59th Street)　PL 5-0968

Pleasant is the word for this L-shaped, pint-size French restaurant. It applies equally to the décor, the service, and the food. The snails for which the restaurant is named are subtly seasoned and are served as an appetizer or as a main course. The menu is somewhat predictable, but it is extended daily by two plats du jour. Such dishes as calf's brains are rewarding; the pâté is robust and good. Complete luncheons (entrée, dessert, and coffee) from about $3.50 to $5.25; dinners from about $5.25 to $8.75. *Cocktails, wines. Closed Sunday and major holidays.*
AE

★ LES CHAMPS
25 East 40th Street　LE 2-6566

This is a large, modern, and popular restaurant. Although the name is French, the menu offers a mélange of dishes, such as curried chicken, goulash, and broiled fish. The food is reasonably well prepared. Luncheons are à la carte with main courses, including vegetables, from about $2.75 to $4.50. Dinners are à la carte with entrées from about $4.50 to $6.50. *Cocktails, wines. On Saturday the restaurant opens at 5 p.m. Closed Sunday, New Year's Day,*

Christmas, and Jewish holidays.
All major credit cards.

★★ LES PYRENEES
251 West 51st Street   CI 6-0044 and CI 6-0373

Les Pyrénées, with its neat and pleasant ambience, has long been established as one of the better middle-class French restaurants in New York. The composition of the menu offers few surprises, but the food, such as roast lamb and poulet chasseur, is generally well-prepared. Complete luncheons from $3.50 to $4.25; complete dinners from $5.50 to $7.50. *Cocktails, wines.*
AE DC

★★ LE STEAK
1089 Second Avenue (near 57th Street)   421-9072

This is a steak house, purportedly French, that enjoys an enviable fault, an excess of success. At the peak of the dinner hour, there are masses of people at the bar waiting for tables. It is crowded, with a noise level at times like that of Bedlam, but the food is good. There are only 20 tables in this neat, L-shaped restaurant, and a single menu serves from day to day. The meal consists of a very good, crisp salad as a first course; grilled steak with a maître d'hôtel sauce faintly flavored with tarragon; and a choice of dessert or frommages (sic). The steak is of prime quality and the desserts are excellent. The cost of dinner is $7.95. The wines are reasonably priced. *Cocktails, wines. Open for dinner only. Closed Sunday.*
AE DC

★ L'ETOILE
Sherry Netherland Hotel, Fifth Avenue and 59th Street
PL 1-7025

This is an elegant-looking brasserie whose décor offers a welcome change from the stale and all-too-frequent murals of provincial scenes with which the walls of most

French restaurants hereabout have been garnished in recent years. To call it a brasserie is to say that the food is of a casual sort as opposed to haute cuisine. Unfortunately, both food and service here leave much to be desired. For example, the jambon persillé, or ham in parsley aspic with a vinaigrette sauce, may arrive without the sauce. But one should be persistent in one's efforts to have the sauce produced, as it is excellent—more distinguished than other more complicated dishes, including a cheese soufflé and a stuffed striped bass. A paillard of veal, a thin, flattened steak of excellent quality, quickly grilled over charcoal, is well-remembered. The best dishes to be had, in fact, seem to be those that are the least complicated to prepare. Luncheons are à la carte; à la carte dishes cost from about $2.75 to $4.95. Complete dinners cost from $8.75. Supper dishes from $3.75 to $7.75. *Cocktails, wines. Luncheon is not served on Saturday and Sunday during July.*
All major credit cards.

** LE VEAU D'OR
129 East 60th Street   TE 8-8133

In its finest moments this is the ultimate restaurant with bourgeois cooking in Manhattan. The chef, Rolland Chenus, is a master of his art, whether it is in turning out a lobster américaine, tripe à la mode de Caen, or a simple dish of boiled beef. There is frequently a long wait for a table, even though the tables for some tastes are already too close together. The atmosphere is wholeheartedly French. During the summer, when there are vacation periods for the staff and owners, Le Veau d'Or does not function as smoothly as it should. Complete luncheons cost from about $4.90 to $6.40 for lobster; complete dinners from $7.10 to $12.00 (lobster). *Cocktails, wines. Luncheon is not served on Saturday during the summer; closed Sunday and for 3 weeks at the end of August.*

★ LIBORIO
150 West 47th Street   JU 2-6188

A popular and interesting restaurant with Latin-American food, including such novel dishes as stuffed pot roast and stewed goat meat on special occasions. Complete lunches are $3.25 to $3.95. Complete dinners are $5.75 to $8.25; à la carte entrées from $4.50 to $9.25. There is entertainment in the evening. *Cocktails, wines. Closed Monday.*
AE   CB   DC

★ LICHEE TREE, THE
65 East 8th Street   GR 5-0555 and GR 5-0959

This is a Chinese restaurant in the heart of Greenwich Village. The décor is Chinese modern and the menu is well-varied. The cuisine is, on occasion, very well-prepared; the service is so-so. Luncheons and dinners are both prix fixe and à la carte. Complete luncheons from about $1.85 to $3.50; complete dinners from about $5.00 to $7.00. A la carte dishes from about $3.75 to $8.00. *Cocktails, wines. Open 7 days a week. Dinner is served Sunday from 1 p.m. Reservations accepted.*
AE   CB   DC   MC

★★ LIMERICKS
573 Second Avenue (between 31st and 32nd Streets)
683-4686

The nicest thing about Limericks is the warm and friendly ambience. It has a neighborly bar at the entrance, a dining room, and, with the onset of warm weather, an outside dining area with shade trees. One is rarely impressed with the service in Manhattan, but at Limericks it has seemed uncommonly attentive and considerate. The food may not be the greatest thing that ever happened to the city, but it is done with obvious care and seems to be reasonably priced.

There are such dishes as steak and kidney pie, pork and mushroom pie, shepherd's pie, and Irish stew. The mixed grill—with steak, chicken livers, pork sausage, and blood sausage—is copious and freshly cooked. It is topped with sautéed green peppers and onions. The restaurant does seem to use a concentrated chicken base in its soups, rather than fresh chicken stock, which is too bad. The soups actually are interesting—a cock-a-leekie with leeks and barley and a mulligatawny with raisins and vegetables.

All dishes at Limericks are à la carte, with main courses at noon from about $2.25 to $6.95; in the evening, from about $3.25 to $7.50. *Cocktails, wines. Open 7 days a week. Closed major holidays. The restaurant opens at 5:00 p.m. on Saturday.*
AE BA CB DC MC

★ LIN HEONG
69 Bayard Street   WO 2-8195

This is a small but burly and popular restaurant in Chinatown. Customers frequently share tables with other customers, and the food is generally excellent. The fish and seafood dishes, such as the poached sea bass with fermented black beans, are particularly recommended. All dishes are à la carte, with main courses from about $1.10 for soft-noodle dishes to $3.60 for lobster preparations. *Open 7 days a week, 24 hours a day. No alcoholic beverages, but customers may bring their own wine or beer.*

★ LINO'S U. N. RESTAURANT
547 Second Avenue (near 30th Street)   MU 4-8257

That there is a certain amount of talent in Lino's kitchen is obvious from a couple of dishes sampled there. Most notably in a dish called chicken à la Florentina, which is boneless chicken dipped in a delicate batter and deep-fried.

The chef's chicken Vesuvio, a sauté in tomato sauce, is quite edible and the veal Marsala has been improved since they started using a Marsala that is less sweet. The restaurant's antipasto is New York standard. The broths with

185

escarole, pastina, broccoli, and so on taste as though they had been "given body" with meat extract. There is piped-in music and it is insistent.

On the other hand, the prices at Lino's are modest and the owner is genuinely concerned about the quality of his kitchen. All dishes are à la carte, with main courses at midday from about $1.60 to $3.75; in the evening, from about $2.50 to $7.00. *Cocktails, wines. Open 7 days a week.*

★ LITTLE KITCHEN, THE
243 East 10th Street   477-4460

Part of the wonder and pleasure of dining in New York is the extraordinary variety of its restaurants. The Little Kitchen is a place that has been much publicized for "soul food." This embraces such dishes as fried chicken, barbecued spareribs, chitterlings, candied yams, and various greens such as mustard and collards. The Little Kitchen is presided over by a woman known as Princess Pamela, and her kitchen produces an interesting table with the tasty and well-seasoned spiritual fare listed above, plus baking-powder biscuits, corn bread, bread pudding and fruit sauce, "old-fashioned" shortcake. The cost of a copious meal is from about $2.95. *Open for dinner only, every day except Monday.*

★★ LITTLE PEKING RESTAURANT, INC.
1 Doyers Street   267-8290

This is a new, small, and welcome restaurant in Chinatown. The food is Peking and Szechuan, and the chef quite obviously knows what he's about.

A recent menu began with fried dumplings (some of the dumplings had split, which shouldn't happen, but they were of good texture) and continued with subgum fried noodles (that are tender but crisp and a bit smoky-flavored from frying) crowned with a mélange of chicken, shrimp, and pork; kung po chicken, cubed chicken with fiery hot red peppers; and shredded pork in hoi-sin sauce.

It was one of those ice cold days in Manhattan, and that could account, to some degree, for some of the food coming to the table a bit on the lukewarm side. Then, too, the kitchen is downstairs and that could be accountable.

In any event, there are only 12 tables and the food at noon for a complete lunch is priced from $1.25 to $2.40. The à la carte menu is priced from about $2.00 to $3.75. *There is no bar, but customers may bring their own beer or wine. Open 7 days a week.*

★★ LITTLE PLACE, THE
174 West Fourth Street CH 2-1764

In the first place, The Little Place is not so little, and it has no lack of customers. The foot-in-the-door, crowded condition is, in fact, part of the ambience, so ochlophobes beware. The waiters treat the clientele, mostly neighborhood people, with friendly abuse, and the guests seem to like it, in that it makes them feel like part of a family.

The attraction of the restaurant also includes the prices of the food, which range from about $1.80 for spaghetti with tomato sauce to $4.75 for filet mignon. The antipasto is simply made, but it is fresh and good; the tortellini Bolognese is excellent. Some of the dishes can be a trifle overcooked, including a recent order of chicken sauté with olives and the fish in a cacciucco Livornese, but, by and large, this can be an agreeable place to dine. *Cocktails, wines. Closed Monday, New Year's Day, and Christmas.*

★★ LITTLE ROYAL HUNGARIAN RESTAURANT
1606 Second Avenue (near 83rd Street) RH 4-9508

There are several engaging things about this European-flavored restaurant. One evening, the soup du jour turned out to be a delectable, hot, full-bodied, paprika-flavored cauliflower soup with bits of the vegetable as garnish. Cold cherry soup is frequently on the menu.

There is tremendous honesty in the food preparation.

Among the appetizers, the roast chicken livers are excellent. The Little Royal's veal shanks are tender, meaty, and well-seasoned, and so is the lamb paprikás with spätzle. The desserts are also worthwhile and they include palacsinta, or Hungarian pancakes, and cherry strudel.

The restaurant is small and the owner and his wife do most of the cooking and serving. The tables are so close together there is no room for two persons to pass abreast. There is piped-in music, but most of it is on the quiet side and in the genre of opera and operetta.

In the evening, à la carte dishes are priced from about $2.40 to $3.10; complete dinners from $3.40 to $4.00. *There is no bar, but wines and beers may be brought into the restaurant. Closed Monday.*

★★ LONG RIVER
10 West 45th Street   867-6496

This relatively handsome Chinese restaurant is conveniently close to Broadway theaters. There are beaded room dividers, framed embroidery, and Chinese art, and the service is pleasant. The food is competently prepared. The portions are vast, and the combination platters, piled to overflowing with chow mein, chop suey, and the like, look almost unappetizing. The platters, served with tea, are priced from about $1.45. At lunch, à la carte dishes cost from about $1.95 to $3.95 for moo shee with pork, shrimp, and chicken. Entrées at dinner cost from $2.15 to $5.00 for a seafood dish. *Cocktails, wines. Closed Sunday.*
AE DC

★ LORD & TAYLOR'S SOUP BAR
Fifth Avenue at 38th Street (10th floor)   WI 7-3300

Men and women shoppers alike crowd the two dozen chairs here for one of the most limited menus in town. But shoppers who enjoy the man-size bowl of excellent Scotch broth rarely hunger for more. In hot weather, the broth gives way to chilled vichyssoise. Dessert the year round is deep-dish apple pie, with hard sauce or cheese. With milk or coffee, the total tab comes to $1.30. *Open daily from 11:00 a.m. to 3:30 p.m., Saturday to 4:00 p.m. Closed Sunday.*

★★ LOTUS EATERS
880 Third Avenue (near 54th Street)   688-1410

This is a reasonably handsome and corking good Chinese restaurant in midtown Manhattan. It is best to order from the à la carte menu, rather than rely on the spareribs–fried rice–chow mein format of the luncheon menu. Such a menu is available, however, from about $1.50 for roast pork–fried rice to $3.75 for lobster Cantonese. The à la carte items cost from about $2.75 for fried shrimp balls to $4.50 for hot spiced lobster out of the shell or five-flavored fried squab (both of which are excellent, by the way). There is one minor distracting note and that is the ventilation in the dining room. It is not perfect. *Cocktails, wines.*
AE CB DC

★★ LOTUS EATERS EAST
155 East 79th Street   734-2320

This is one of the generally commendable chain of Chinese restaurants called Lotus Eaters. At its best, this East Side annex is of high order, particularly in such well-spiced Szechuan dishes as hot spiced shredded beef, spiced ginger shrimp, chicken with peanuts, and the less peppery shrimp with green peas.

Among the appetizers, the pan-fried dumplings (the pastry was torn on two servings) might rate 50 out of 100, while an order of Szechuan-style fish served lukewarm with overcooked, dried out rice would rate zero. The Lotus Eaters chicken in two kinds of sauces with broccoli is interesting and good. Please note that many Szechuan dishes are cooked in a considerable amount of oil, and if you are put off by such cooking, don't bother.

Combination plate lunches of the chow mein, egg roll variety are $1.75 to $2.40. A la carte dishes from about $2.75 to $4.75. *Cocktails, wines. Open 7 days a week. Closed Thanksgiving.*
AE DC MC

★★ LOTUS EATERS FIFTH
182 Fifth Avenue (between 22nd and 23rd Streets)
929-4800

Anyone who is fascinated by Chinese cooking that is far from run-of-the-mill should find much to admire in this restaurant. There are numerous insidiously good dishes, such as a hot and sour soup, chicken with special sauce (a thin soy sauce with scallions and ginger), ginger-flavored shrimp, and spiced shredded chicken. The chef makes much use of oil and spices, and, for those who ask, the dishes will be made quite hot, Szechuan-style. Lotus Eaters Fifth is a big restaurant, largely undecorated and with piped-in music. The service is friendly, but with no particular style. Complete luncheons cost from about $1.40 to $3.60; à la carte main dishes are priced from about $1.80 to $3.60. *Cocktails, wines.*
AE CB DC

★★★ LOTUS EATERS PARK
119 East 23rd Street   GR 3-4447

This is probably the best of the Lotus Eaters restaurants in New York, and most of them specialize in Szechuan or well-spiced cooking. The Lotus Eaters Park specializes more in northern and perhaps more subtle dishes.

It does have, of course, the usual moo goo gai pan and pork fried rice and they may or may not be superior. Like several other good Chinese restaurants, the Lotus Eaters Park offers an assortment of dem sem or appetizers served on Saturday and Sunday only and they are excellent.

For example, there are steamed Tien-Tsin-style dumplings filled with vegetable and pork; Yangchow dumplings

with pork alone. One of the most appetizing of all these
dishes is called silver strips roll, and it is served with
tender, succulent, soy-braised pork, vaguely sweet and
sesame-flavored.

There are good bean curd dishes, one of them with snow
peas and black mushrooms and ham, plus ginger, scallions,
and garlic. Also fried dumplings.

Please note that the dem sem dishes are listed in Chinese, and it may take some persuasion to convince the
waiters that you know what you want. If you should go
for these, it is best to have a party of at least 4 persons.
The dem sem are generally cooked 10 to a portion.

There is a luncheon menu available Monday through
Friday, priced from about $1.40 to $3.60. The principal
menu, available throughout the week, offers a complete
dinner for two priced at about $3.50 to $7.25 per person.
A la carte items from about $2.10 to $12.95 for Pekin
duck. *Cocktails, wines. Open 7 days a week.*
AE DC MC

★★ LOTUS EATERS ROYALE
59 East 56th Street   421-5580

There are so many dishes of outstanding quality at
this newest and most ambitious of the Lotus Eaters assortment of restaurants, there is no questioning the talent of
the chef.

Consider the chicken dishes alone. Both the Mandarin
chicken with pine nuts, green peppers, and celery and the
delicate, most gossamer chicken velvet (available on special order) are as fine as you'll find anywhere in the city
and perhaps the Orient.

The shredded beef is good and the fried wonton are
excellent. The assorted appetizers, on the other hand, are
generally commonplace.

Many of the dishes, including one serving of frogs'
legs, are too bland and some of the dishes, such as fish
with a fermented rice sauce, are a bit too sweet, but that
is a personal taste.

In sum, the Lotus Eaters Royale can be superb, but it can also disappoint. In any event, it is a fairly handsome restaurant with bright colors and an excellent bar.

Complete luncheons are priced from about $1.75 to $4.25. Dinners are à la carte, with main courses from about $3.00 to $6.00. *Cocktails, wines. Open 7 days a week.*
AE DC MC

★★ LOU G. SIEGEL
209 West 38th Street WI 7-1262

Lou Siegel calls itself "America's foremost kosher restaurant," and it is certainly one of the best and most interesting in New York. Actually there are two dining areas—one large, high-ceilinged affair with mirrored columns, and a less formal setting around the bar known as the grill room. There are numerous dishes on the menu not commonly found elsewhere including lungen and miltz stew (the lung and other parts of the beef), steamed calf's feet, and stuffed derma (stuffed beef casings).

The food is generally excellent, particularly such dishes as stuffed green peppers, stuffed cabbage, and stuffed breast of veal. The soups, such as mushroom and barley or kasha, are rich and first-rate. Some of the sauces are sweet and sour, but they are deftly seasoned. Stuffed derma is a great favorite at Siegel's.

Another interesting item is the tender, well-seasoned potted meat balls with kasha on the side. The restaurant offers numerous delicatessen plates such as various assortments of tongue, corned beef, and turkey leg or turkey wings. The pastries at Siegel's are acceptable, but they taste bakery-made. The coffee is commendable.

All dishes on the luncheon menu are à la carte, with main courses from about $2.10 to $4.75. Complete dinners cost from about $4.95 to $7.95, with à la carte dishes in the evening from about $3.50 to $7.75. *Cocktails, wines. Closed Saturday and Yom Kippur.*

★ LOUISE
225 East 58th Street   EL 5-8133

A great favorite with many New Yorkers. The Italian menu is familiar, but the kitchen is generally competent. The cost of dinner is from about $7.00 to $9.50. *Cocktails, wines. Open for dinner only. Closed Sunday, all year, also Saturday in summer, Thanksgiving, Christmas, and the first 2 weeks in July.*
AE DC

★★ LOUISE JR.
317 East 53rd Street   EL 5-9172

The food is generally good at this restaurant with the odd name, and the portions are copious. There is also plenty of noise, particularly near the kitchen. The antipasto in itself is sufficient for a meal, and the table d'hôte menu adds soup, a main course, dessert, and fresh fruit. The menu is à la carte and table d'hôte with complete luncheons from about $5.50 to $6.75 and complete dinners from about $7.50 to $8.50. *Cocktails, wines. On Saturday, the restaurant opens at 5:00 p.m. Closed Sunday.*
AE CB DC

★★★ LUCHOW'S
110 East 14th Street   GR 7-4860

Lüchow's is a landmark of more than 80 years, and, as such, it has a special eminence. It smells profoundly at times of red cabbage and sauerkraut, and it is one of the noisiest restaurants in the city. It is also one of the most colorful. At times there are German bands playing oompah-pah, and children love it. There are festivals galore, numbering among them the bock beer festival, the venison festival, and the goose festival. The food at its best is excellent. One of the major faults is that the portions are enormous and sometimes arrive at the table lukewarm. Lüchow's is schmaltzy enough to border on the sophisticated, and the beer is cold. There are few places in town

where one can dine as well on a limited budget. Complete luncheons from $2.35 to $4.75; complete dinners from $3.95 to $6.50. There is also an à la carte menu. *Cocktails, wines. Closed Monday.*
AE BA CB DC MC

★ LUCY JUNG
206 Canal Street   349-7880

There's a grandmother who lives near the eastern tip of Long Island, who rarely gets to New York more than twice a year. She thought everything at Lucy Jung in Chinatown was just grand.

Among the appetizers, she found the shrimp toast (in truth, dry and overcooked) delicious; the dem sem (rubbery and lukewarm) insidiously good, and the chicken in cellophane exceptional.

She found equal delight in the Triple Delight made with chicken, roast duck, and crab meat and the shrimp with black bean sauce very much to her taste.

All of which makes one conclude that Lucy Jung is certainly a nice enough place to take visitors. There is no danger of anyone's palate being offended with exotic seasonings. The food, like the surroundings, is, in short, highly conventional. Not bad, not distinguished. The service leaves something to be desired; you ask for chopsticks 3 times, the soup is served before the appetizer, and so on.

The luncheons are reasonably priced, with main courses from about $1.50 to $2.75; à la carte dishes from about $1.85 to $6.50. *Cocktails, wines. Open 7 days a week, from 2:00 p.m. on Saturday and Sunday.*
AE DC MC

★★ LUNA'S RESTAURANT
112 Mulberry Street (one block north of Canal Street)
CA 6-8657

Luna's Restaurant on Mulberry Street is as much of an institution in Little Italy as the annual Feast of San

Gennaro. It is a lusty place, where waiters are not above giving you a certain amount of abuse if you do something to displease them. Like putting on airs and letting them know you're one of those cats from uptown; that you dig better restaurants than the one you're surrounded by.

Come to think of it, there may not be a better Neapolitan restaurant in the city, and it is certainly no secret. There is almost always a line of customers waiting.

The tomato sauces are robust and for that genre of cooking, excellent, whether they be with lasagne, manicotti, shrimp, spaghetti, ziti, or whatever. The bitter broccoli at the Luna is special and so are such odd dishes as tripe Neapolitan-style, squid, and scungilli. When lobster fra diavolo was ordered, the waiter asked, "Would you like to know what it costs now or later?" It was expensive but worth it.

All dishes are à la carte, with main courses from about $1.50 for spaghetti with butter sauce to $9.50 for lobster dishes. *Wines, beers. Open 7 days a week.*

★★★ LUTECE
219 East 50th Street   PL 2-2225

There is an indisputable charm about this small restaurant which, in some ways, seems the most Parisian of New York's restaurants. The kitchen has improved since it opened years ago, and some of the specialties show great taste and imagination. Count among them a pâté of fresh fish in crust, a combination of fish in a mosaic pattern. There is a cunning small bar here, in the summer a pleasant outdoor garden, and, when the restaurant is crowded, over-all it seems more festive than jammed. There is a complete luncheon at $9.75 prix fixe. The dinner menu is à la carte, with main courses from about $8.50 to $18.50 for two. *Cocktails, wines. Luncheon is not served on Saturday. Closed Sunday during the winter, Saturday and Sunday during the summer.*

MACARIO'S
145 West 58th Street   PL 7-5913

Macario's is the sort of dining spot known in New York as a neighborhood restaurant, and that says a lot. It has a steady clientele and the food, while not distinguished, isn't bad. There are good stuffed baked clams and a recent copious dish among the appetizers, the peppers with anchovies, was excellent (it should be, too, since it costs $1.25 on the dinner).

The menu states that only plume de veau, veal grown in upstate New York, is used and that it is the best veal available. It may be true, but a recent order of veal française, while tender, did not have the snowy whiteness normally associated with plume de veau. An order of ziti with tomato sauce was acceptable enough, and so was an order of boneless breast of chicken parmigiana.

There are plastic flowers on the table, but that is not nearly so disconsoling as the sight of the chef on two separate occasions walking through the dining room in soiled apron and trousers.

The menus are à la carte, with main courses at midday from about $1.60 to $2.95; in the evening, from about $2.60 to $7.50. *Cocktails, wines. In summer the restaurant closes at 3:00 p.m. on Saturday. Closed New Year's Day, Thanksgiving, and Christmas.*
AE CB DC MC

★★ MME. ROMAINE DE LYON
32 East 61st Street   758-2422

This is a revered and worthwhile New York institution which specializes in omelets. Mme. Romaine's omelets bear such names as Rond Point, Bordelaise, Talleyrand, and Mozart. And her menu with several hundred omelets, ranging from plain ($2.55) to one called Périgord ($9.00) with foie gras, truffles, Madeira, and Pernod, is just as impressive as ever. Physically, Mme. Romaine's omelets may not be invariably things of beauty, but they are excellent to the taste. The only off-note in the small, two-room restaurant is the ventilation. At times, the odor of cooking is evident. The menu, which also offers salads, brioches, and croissants, is à la carte. *There is no bar, but wines and apéritifs are served. Open for lunch only, 11:30 a.m. to 4:30 p.m., Monday through Saturday. Closed Sunday and most major holidays.*

★ MADISON DELICATESSEN AND RESTAURANT, THE
1175 Madison Avenue (at 86th Street)   EN 9-6670

This is a bustling delicatessen and restaurant, and the most commendable thing about it is the sandwiches, which are comparable with some of the best in Manhattan. There are excellent chopped chicken liver, pastrami, and sturgeon. The prime brisket of beef is freshly cooked and good.

Sandwiches are priced from $1.20 to $2.35. A la carte items on the main menu go from about $3.50 to $7.95. *There is no bar, but there is an extensive collection of domestic and imported beers. Open 7 days a week.*

★ MAMA LAURA RESTAURANT
230 East 58th Street   MU 8-6888

There are numerous faithful customers who consider this one of the best Italian restaurants in Manhattan. Many of the dishes, such as the boneless chicken Dorato, are very good, but the over-all quality of the kitchen is uneven. Luncheons are à la carte, with entrées from $3.00 to $5.75. A la carte main courses in the evening from $4.75 to $8.25. *Cocktails, wines. On Saturday and Sunday, the restaurant opens at 5:00 p.m. Closed Thanksgiving and Christmas.*
AE   CB   DC

★ MANANA
1136 First Avenue (at 62nd Street)   838-9847

This is a busy, ambitious little Mexican restaurant

with food that its customers fairly rave about. It is good, more El Paso than Mexico, and its seasonings are not for shy palates. Much of it is muy caliente. There are 8 combination plates, embracing such dishes as tacos, enchiladas, tamales, tostadas, and chilies rellenos. The interior, with its exposed bricks and overhead pipes, is pleasantly shabby, the service friendly. The disturbing thing about Mañana is the ventilation, which is poor and particularly noticeable at the point of arrival. A la carte dishes are priced from 90 cents to $1.75, $1.80 to $2.25 at lunch and from $2.95 to $3.25 at dinner. A pitcher of sangria—the iced Mexican wine drink—costs $4.95. The restaurant, incidentally, also caters at-home parties. *It is open from noon to 3:00 p.m. and 5:00 p.m. until midnight. Cocktails, beers. Open 7 days a week.*

★★ MANDARIN HOUSE
133 West 13th Street   WA 9-0551

This is an excellent Chinese restaurant and one of the best in the city outside Chinatown. It will rarely disappoint. There are complete luncheons from about $1.85 to $2.50; complete dinners from about $4.00 to $5.50. A la carte main dishes from about $3.25 to $16.00 (Pekin duck). *Cocktails, wines. Dinner is served Sunday from noon.*
AE CB DC MC

★★★ MANDARIN HOUSE EAST
1085 Second Avenue (at 57th Street)   PL 5-9631

There are some residents of the fashionable East Side who declare that they have gourmandized on every entrée of the Mandarin House East, and for a very good reason. The food is prepared with particular excellence; to name a few of the delicacies, there are the sliced chicken in fish-flavored sauce, the river shrimp in hot spiced sauce, a delectable North China egg dish made with shredded pork and wrapped in thin pancakes, and the vari-

ous chicken dishes. The décor of the Mandarin House East is a curious combination of Indian and Chinese. There are complete luncheons that cost $2.35. The à la carte menu lists main courses from about $2.75 to $4.75. *Cocktails, wines. Luncheon is not served Saturday and Sunday.*
AE CB DC

★★ MANDARIN INN
15 Mott Street   962-3830

This has long seemed to be one of the best restaurants in Chinatown.

There are excellent fried dumplings with a self-made sauce of soy, vinegar, and hot sauce; delicious crisp duck with a delicate smoked tea-leaf flavor; appetizing and tender pieces of lean lamb, seasoned lightly with ginger and garlic, and sautéed quickly with scallion pieces; and very good small shrimp in an interesting, thickened sauce that tastes lightly fermented or "cheesy" and is made with a mixture of three bean sauces.

Other specialties of the house include moo shee pork, the shredded pork dish with pancakes, and the Mongolian hot pot, made with various meats, to be cooked at the table. The latter is not on the menu.

The Mandarin Inn, heaven knows, is in no sense pretentious in its décor. It is, if anything, a bit on the sleazy side, but the food is worthwhile. And the new host is a young Chinese full of enthusiasm who is a "ball of fire."

Complete luncheons are priced from about $1.50 to $2.25. A la carte main dishes throughout the day are priced from about $2.25 to $4.75 with Pekin duck (to be ordered one day in advance) priced at $15.00. *There is no bar. Open 7 days a week for lunch and dinner.*
AE DC MC

★★ MANGANARO'S AND MANGANARO'S HERO-BOY RESTAURANT

488 and 492 Ninth Avenue (between 37th and 38th Streets)   LO 3-5331

There is considerable distinction in the food served both in Manganaro's vast and fabled grocery store and in the Hero-Boy Restaurant next door. First-rate "heroes" are served in both, but there is, in addition, an excellent assortment of hot Italian dishes served in the rear of Manganaro's. The menu varies each day, but there are spaghetti and other pasta with various sauces, soups, and so forth. Entrées are about $1.15. The sauces in both establishments are made on the premises, and they are interesting and good. The ingredients for the heroes include salami, cheese, prosciutto, peppers, pickled eggplant, tuna, meat balls, and eggs scrambled with green peppers. They cost from about 65 cents to $39.50, and that's no joke. They do prepare a special six-foot hero for the latter price and it serves 30 people. *Only beer and soft drinks are available. The restaurant is open until 7:30 p.m. Closed Sunday.*

★★ MANNY WOLF'S

Third Avenue at 49th Street   355-5030

The food at this septuagenarian steak house is almost consistently of high quality, whether it is a charcoal-broiled chateaubriand or chicken in the pot with matzoh balls. The tables are too close together, and the noise level is notably high. Luncheons are prix fixe and à la carte, with complete luncheons from about $3.95 to $5.95; à la carte prices go from about $3.50 to $7.95. Dinners are à la carte, with main courses from $4.95 to $9.00. *Cocktails, wines. Dinner is served from 2:00 p.m. on Sunday. Most major credit cards.*

★★ MARCHI'S

251 East 31st Street (near Second Avenue)   OR 9-2494

One of New York's most unusual North Italian restaurants, Marchi's has no sign outside and no printed

menu inside. There is an extensive antipasto, homemade lasagne, a fish course, a roast course (generally chicken and veal), vegetables, salads, cheese, fruits, dessert, and espresso. One price: $7.75. *Cocktails, wines. Open for dinner only: 5:30 to 10:00 p.m. weekdays; 5:00 to 11:00 p.m. Saturday. Closed Sunday, except Mother's Day, Easter, and Father's Day.*
AE

★ MARIA CIN CIN
224 East 53rd Street   EL 5-0520

To give this restaurant the benefit of a doubt, there are many who recommend it and they rave with most enthusiasm about the chef's mussel soup. There are several interesting ideas on the menu, but they lack something in execution.

The hot shrimp pâté, for example, seemed like a well-seasoned but somewhat soupy dip with chopped shrimp and lettuce. So did the clam appetizer, with celery in lieu of lettuce.

One dish that came off very well, however, was the house scaloppine with smothered mushrooms. An order of chicken breast with champagne sauce was adequate. As to the mussel soup, which is served during the mussel season only; it is thin, served with one or two mussels, and, to re-use a phrase, well-seasoned. It would have been better if it had been served piping hot, rather than lukewarm.

There is lots of piped-in music at Maria Cin Cin and, according to a waiter, the specialty of the house among drinks is a purple martini. The blackboard menu of the restaurant is displayed on artists' tripods.

Lunch with dessert and coffee is priced from $2.50 to $3.75. Dinners are à la carte, with main courses with pasta or vegetable from about $4.25 to $7.75. *Cocktails, wines. Closed Saturday, Sunday, and major holidays.*
AE CB DC MC

★ MARIA'S PATIO
415 West 50th Street   265-9681

This is an inexpensive Mexican restaurant and a place of frustrating contradictions.

On one occasion, one indulged in a first-rate guacamole; excellent chicken enchiladas; tender, well-seasoned shrimp with hot chili sauce; and equally savory tacos filled with cubes of pork and lettuce. The chef seemed to be dedicated but the one apparent problem at Maria's was the service, which may be friendly but rushed.

On a subsequent evening, two orders of a combination plate seemed notably commonplace, with tough tortillas.

There are only 11 tables, but there was recently only one waitress who doubled as bartender.

There is only one menu, and all the dishes are à la carte, with the main courses from about $2.25 for tacos to $5.00 for paella. *Cocktails, wines. Open only in the evening. Closed Monday.*

★★ MARIO
140 West 13th Street   WA 9-1850

One of those very good small Italian restaurants, this one in Greenwich Village. It is inexpensive and friendly. The tomato sauces are down-to-earth, but excellent. Complete luncheons from $2.75 to $4.00; complete dinners from $4.50 to $7.50 for lobster. *Cocktails, wines. AE CB DC MC*

★ MARIO'S VILLA BORGHESE
65 East 54th Street   PL 1-2990

This is a spacious and pleasant Italian restaurant with a menu that is principally Italian, but has a few Yankee entrées. The quality of the food ranges from pedestrian to excellent. Luncheons are prix fixe and cost $4.75. Dinners are prix fixe and cost from about $8.00. *Cocktails, wines. Closed Sunday and major holidays. Most major credit cards.*

★ MARIO'S VILLA D'ESTE
58 East 56th Street   PL 9-4025

There is an extensive menu here, and the feeling is that, if the chef would concentrate on fewer dishes, it would be improved over-all. The food is acceptably good, but not distinguished. There is a cold seafood appetizer with a piquant sauce that can be recommended. The scampi, however, on one visit were tough and overcooked, and the veal kidneys had not been cored. The London broil was New York typical. There are excellent rum cake and good coffee. Complete luncheons cost $4.75. Complete dinners are priced from about $7.75 to $9.50. *Cocktails, wines. Open 7 days a week. Luncheon is not served on Sunday. Closed Christmas.*
All major credit cards.

★★ MARK TWAIN RIVERBOAT
Empire State Building (Fifth Avenue at 34th Street)
PL 9-2444

This stationary riverboat, paddlewheel and all, boasts a somewhat flamboyant décor by Oliver Smith, the Broadway set designer. It is, in truth, a Longchamps Restaurant; the quality of the food is generally high. The luncheon menu is à la carte, with main courses from about $2.95 to $6.25. There are complete dinners including liquor for $10.95. Supper including liquor is $7.95. *Cocktails, wines. Dinners are served on Sunday from noon.*
AE CB DC

★ MARSH'S STEAK PLACE
112 Central Park South   CO 5-2470

This is a popular and colorful steak house. The most interesting aspect of the restaurant is the serving of spirits. Waitresses bring the bottles and water or soda to the tables and customers serve themselves. This does not apply to mixed drinks such as martinis and Manhat-

tans. Other than that, Marsh's is a friendly place, the steaks are generally excellent, and that's about the sum of all praise. On the reverse side of the coin, such dishes as chopped chicken liver, the salads with various dressings, the shrimp cocktails, and so forth are edible but far from distinguished. Three lamb chops, ordered medium rare, were brought to the table grossly overcooked. All dishes are à la carte, with main courses at midday from $2.50 to $6.95. In the evening, main courses cost from $5.25 to $8.95 for broiled filet mignon. *Cocktails, wines. Open 7 days a week. Luncheon is not served Saturday and Sunday.*
Most major credit cards.

★★ MARTA RESTAURANT
75 Washington Place   GR *3-9077*

The kitchen at Marta makes more of an effort than many of its competitors. The hot antipasto, compared with that of many small Italian restaurants in town, is impressive, with excellent broiled shrimp, stuffed mushrooms, and mussels Posillipo. The pastas are cooked with care and the marinara sauce is excellent. The veal rolls seem overcooked, but tasty. Luncheon dishes are à la carte, with main courses from about $2.50 to $4.75. Complete dinners cost from about $5.25 to $7.00 for steak. A la carte dinner entrées from about $4.75 to $6.50 including side dishes of pasta and salad. *Cocktails, wines. Open 7 days a week.*
AE   CB   DC

★★ MARTA'S
249 West 49th Street   CO *5-4317 and 247-8829*

Many of the dishes on Marta's menu will seem familiar to those who know New York's Italian restaurants, but the kitchen here is above average. The restaurant is in the theater district, and, although the staff is limited, the service is pleasant. The veal dishes are good,

but the fish dishes and vegetable dishes seem to have special excellence. All food is à la carte. Main dishes at lunch cost from about $1.65 for spaghetti with butter sauce to $5.50 for steak. At dinner, the entrées cost from $3.45 to $6.50 for lobster. *Cocktails, wines. Closed Thanksgiving and Christmas.*
AE DC MC

★ MARY ELIZABETH'S
6 East 37th Street MU *3-3018*

Mary Elizabeth's is something of a landmark in New York. It has a tearoom atmosphere and is divided into three parts—a main dining room, a men's grill, and, downstairs, what is called the Soup Tureen. The food is simply prepared, modestly priced, and generally good. Recommended in particular is the Soup Tureen, which specializes in soups and salads. An adequate meal there costs $1.25. It is open Monday through Friday for luncheon only. The dining room and men's grill, open Monday through Saturday at midday and on Thursday only for dinner, offer complete luncheons from about $2.25 to $2.70. A la carte dishes at midday cost from about $1.90 to $2.85. A complete dinner costs about $4.05 to $5.00. *Cocktails, wines. Closed Sunday and major holidays.*
AE CB DC MC

★★ MARY'S
42 Bedford Street CH *2-9588*

Mary's has one of the best pasta dishes ever encountered outside Italy. It is a spaghetti carbonara with the spaghetti cooked to the proper degree and bathed in an elegant and melting cream and cheese sauce with flecks of ham.

As a matter of fact, most of the dishes eaten here are above the New York average—mussels Posillipo (on the menu only when fresh mussels are available); another pasta dish, a basic, earthy matriciana with tomatoes and bacon and onions; a couple of elaborate stuffed veal dishes, one called granadin, another called imperiale. Even a simple minestrone had been cooked with great care.

Mary's is on two levels, with a kitchen downstairs that opens onto a small dining room with only 4 or 5 tables. The dining room above is not much larger. All dishes are cooked to order.

All dishes are à la carte, with main courses at midday from about $1.75 to $3.25; in the evening, from about $2.80 to $5.50. *There is no bar, but wines are available. The restaurant is open 7 days a week from 11:30 a.m. to 2:00 p.m. for lunch, 5:00 to 11:00 p.m. for dinner.*

★ MAUD CHEZ ELLE
40 West 53rd Street   CI 5-3350

A rather stylish dining room with a kitchen that has its moments of grandeur, such as the chocolate mousse, but fleetingly. At times, too, there is confusion over the wine service. The cost of luncheon is from about $5.00 to $8.00; of dinner from about $6.00 to $13.00. *Cocktails, wines. Dinner only served Saturday. Closed Sunday. AE CB DC*

★ MAX'S KANSAS CITY
213 Park Avenue South (between 17th and 18th Streets)
777-7870

This is one of the most switched-on restaurants in Manhattan. Max's is a large, angular, two-level restaurant. At the moment it is fairly popular, and consequently there is at times a wait for tables. The service is a bit disorganized, but the simply grilled steaks and lobsters are good. Complete lunches are about $1.75 to $3.50. The à la carte prices are about $2.25 to $4.95. At dinner, the à la carte entrées are $4.50 to $5.50. Complete dinners are $3.50 to $5.50. *Cocktails, wines. The house wine ($2.75)*

served in a pichet, or pitcher, is dreadful. On Saturday and Sunday, dinner is served from 1:00 p.m.
AE DC MC

★★ MAXWELL'S PLUM
64th and 1st Avenue   628-2100

One of the most impressive successes among New York's restaurants is Maxwell's Plum. Ever since it arrived on the scene, there has been S.R.O. It comes as something of a surprise to an aging member of the sedentary set to learn that Maxwell's is not merely a place for bird watching *et seq.*, but a serious and handsome food enterprise.

Serious diners such as Louis Vaudable, owner of Maxim's, and Claude Terrail, owner of Tour d'Argent, generally sit in the large and splendid open dining room to the rear with its impressive Tiffany glass ceiling and dine on the likes of hamburgers and chili con carne or Burgundy snails. Iranian caviar and stuffed squab can be washed down with anything from a dollar mug of draft beer to a magnum of champagne. On the second level, there is a sidewalk café. On the third level, those citizens at the rear tables can munch on their chateaubriand or cold half-lobster and peer down on one of the best shows in town: the swinging singles that mill (very slowly mill) around one of the most substantial and elegant bars in town.

It must be said that the food at Maxwell's Plum is not the hautest of haute cuisine, but much of it is amusing (the oversized hamburgers of excellent-quality meat, the chili con carne, the spareribs) and much more of it is more than merely palatable (the seafood crêpes, the sirloin chunks in sour cream and chive sauce). The chef is a young man named Jean Brecq, who formerly worked at the Pré Catelan and Fouquet's in Paris.

There are several menus, but prices in general range from about 95 cents for chili con carne to $7.85 for filet

mignon with béarnaise sauce. *Cocktails, wines. Open 7 days a week.*
Most major credit cards.

★ MAYFAIR, THE
964 First Avenue (at 53rd Street)   EL 5-9259

In the strictest sense, perhaps, any restaurant in Manhattan is a neighborhood restaurant. They're all in one neighborhood or another. But some restaurants seem more neighborly than others, more patronized by local residents. The Mayfair has two things going for it: It is a friendly sort of neighborhood restaurant, and the prices are reasonable.

The food, which is typically American, is reasonably good. It includes broiled fish and chops, shrimp creole, roast beef, London broil, and so on. At noon, there are sandwiches. One evening the roast beef was well-seasoned and rare but a bit chewy. The shrimp in the cocktail had a decent texture, but seemed to have been cooked without seasoning. There are specialties of the house each evening, including fried chicken, sauerbraten, and boiled beef.

All dishes are à la carte, with main courses at midday from about $1.50 to $2.40; in the evening, from about $3.75 to $6.25 for steak. *Cocktails, wines. Open 7 days a week. Luncheon is not served on Sunday.*

★ MAYHEWS
1178 Third Avenue (near 68th Street)   LE 5-9222
785 Madison Avenue (near 66th Street)   BU 8-3781
774 Broadway (near 9th Street)   GR 3-0370

These are decidedly informal restaurants with quick, casual service. They are worth noting if only for their hamburgers, which are lean and neatly cooked to order. The food is generally good, if not remarkably distinguished. The à la carte dishes cost from about 95 cents for steakburger to $2.75 for a steak platter. *No alcoholic beverages at Madison Avenue; beer only at Third Avenue;*

cocktails, wines at Broadway. There is great variance in the hours during which the Mayhews restaurants are open. On weekends and for late evening dining it is best to telephone.

★★ McSORLEY'S OLD ALE HOUSE
15 East 7th Street GR 7-9363

This is one of the most engaging saloons in America. It is a man's world and women aren't encouraged. The story goes that a woman named Mother Fresh Roasted, a peanut peddler whose husband had died of a lizard bite during the Spanish-American War, was welcomed in her day for an occasional ale. The bedraggled atmosphere includes portraits of George Washington, a pot-bellied stove, tables with a distressed appearance, and the smell of beer and ale. The bill of fare consists of roast beef, fresh ham, Virginia ham, hamburger steak, corned beef hash, and chili. The most famous dish, and it is worth the visit, is a platter of ripe Liederkranz cheese, thick slices of sweet Bermuda onion, and bread or crackers. The cost of most dishes is from about 60 cents to $1.75. *The bar serves only beers, porter, and ale. Hot lunch served from 11:30 a.m. to 2:30 p.m. Sandwiches and cheese all the time. Closed Sunday.*

★★ MERCURIO
53 West 53rd Street JU 6-4370

A popular Italian restaurant with an attractively uncluttered décor. Service is generally excellent and the food varies from only fair to extremely good. The wine list includes some of the less well-known Italian imports. The fettuccine Alfredo is above average. Main dishes include everything from veal scaloppine to rognoncino trifolato (veal kidney with mushroom, truffles, and sherry). Table d'hôte luncheons from about $3.75 to $9.00; à la carte dinner with entrées from about $4.00 to $9.50. *Cocktails,*

wines. Closed Sunday, summer Saturdays, major holidays, and the month of July.
AE

METROPOLITAN OPERA HOUSE
Lincoln Center

Grand Tier Restaurant (799-3400). Nothing can be all bad in a restaurant that has murals by Marc Chagall, and the Grand Tier Restaurant has two. If you sit at the right table, you can see them both; if not, from almost any table you can see one of them reflected in the towering windowpanes out front. On the other hand, the room is crowded and noisy, and customers are rushed through the meal that consists for the most part of mediocre food. Composed dishes, such as breast of capon opera or sweetbreads financière, taste flat when cold or lukewarm. Guests are advised that simple dishes, such as chops or roast prime ribs of beef, are the preferable choices from the menu. There is an à la carte menu with main courses from $5.25 to $9.75. *Cocktails, wines. Dinner only. Only guests holding tickets to the opera may dine at the Grand Tier on the evening of their performance. Open according to opera schedule. Reservations are essential.*
AE CB DC MC

★★ MEXICAN VILLAGE
224 Thompson Street   677-9706

There are several things commendable enough about the kitchen of the Mexican Village to compensate for some fairly obvious faults. In the first place, the specialties of the house—tacos and enchiladas with beef, chicken, sausage, and so on—are competently seasoned and served hot on thin, well-made, crisp or soft tortillas, depending on the dish. The chicken mole—or braised chicken in a dark sauce with mildly hot spices and a touch of chocolate—is above average for similar restaurants in the city. The difference is that in most restaurants the chicken tastes cooked in advance and reheated. Here it tastes freshly made and the sauce is good.

Some things at the Mexican Village seem neither inspired nor dull, and this would include the guacamole and the seviche. The watery tequila cocktails, flavored with bottled lemon juice and something that makes them froth, are terrible. If you like Mexican food with Texan overtones, however, you will probably like the restaurant.

A la carte dishes are priced from about 90 cents to $3.00. Combination platters are from $1.65 to $2.15. *Cocktails, wines, and Mexican beers. The restaurant is open from 4:00 p.m. to 1:00 a.m. Closed Tuesday and Christmas.*

★ MEXI-FROST SPECIALTIES COMPANY
220 West 13th Street   CH 3-0922

Note well that this is a decidedly offbeat dining spot. It is a little place, whose floor at times is littered with paper napkins. There are fading Pepsi-Cola signs here and there, and one cat with a very long tail. Mexi-Frost supplies numerous restaurants around town, some of them well-known, with Mexican and Latin-American specialties including tamales, empanadas with various fillings, and so forth.

One point of interest is the daily soup specialty. On Monday, for example, there is the Spanish caldo gallego, a bean soup; on Tuesday, the Caribbean sancocho with vegetables; on Wednesday, the Mexican mondongo made with tripe. The foods are well-seasoned and good.

Tacos and tostadas are 60 cents; combination plates are $1.65 to $2.15; chicken in mole sauce is $2.50. The counter accommodates 6 or so customers; small tables only 8 or so additional. *No alcoholic beverages. Lunch is served Monday through Friday; dinner, Tuesday through Friday.*

★ MICHAEL'S PUB
1919 Third Avenue (at 55th Street)   PL 8-2272

This was one of the first pubs in Manhattan. It has

a gregarious atmosphere and is crowded and noisy at luncheon. There are some very good dishes available, including the chops, calf's liver, and Irish bacon. The pub's trifle is ordinary, but the Stilton is good. Main luncheon dishes from about $2.75 to $6.00; main dinner entrées from about $3.50 to $6.80. *Supper is served from 11:00 p.m. to 1:00 a.m. Cocktails, wines. Closed Saturday and Sunday.*
AE DC

★★ MIKADO
21 West 39th Street   563-1660

A modestly decorated but handsome enough Japanese restaurant with a kitchen that is a cut above average. Guests should be pleased with the standard entrées on the menu including well-seasoned and tender teriyaki, tempura, and table-cooked sukiyaki.

The teishoku multiple-entrée Japanese formal meal may be more interesting, however. It changes from day to day, but might include a choice of clear or bean paste soup, both of which are worthwhile; sashimi or raw fish, including tuna and cuttlefish with wasabi and soy sauce; an exceptionally good dish of grilled, boneless fresh salmon with fresh ginger; and a cold dish of excellent shredded jellyfish in sesame paste. As the man said, don't knock it until you've tried it. The Mikado is far more pleasant at noncrowded hours because the tables are close together.

Complete luncheons are priced from about $3.50 to $4.25; à la carte main courses from about $2.30 to $5.75. Complete dinners cost from $5.00 to $8.50; à la carte main courses in the evening from $4.00 to $5.75. *Cocktails, wines. Luncheon is not served Saturday. Closed Sunday and all major holidays.*
AE BA DC MC

★★ MIKE MANUCHE
150 West 52nd Street   JU 2-5483

This is a colorful restaurant with a pleasant and

masculine atmosphere. At midday, in particular, it is a favorite dining spot of businessmen. The menu is primarily Italian and quite palatable. Both luncheon and dinner are à la carte, but the price of the entrée includes spaghetti and salad. Luncheon main dishes range from about $3.00 to $6.75; main dinner courses from about $3.25 to $8.50. *Cocktails, wines. Luncheon is not served on Saturday. Closed Sunday.*
AE CB DC

★ MILLER'S
233 Broadway (at Park Place)   CO 7-3156

A large, old, solidly established restaurant on the ground floor of the Woolworth Building. It has an interesting menu with such dishes as lobster meat Vallauris, a sautéed dish awash with butter; numerous fish dishes; and such down-to-earth fare as chicken pot pie, corned beef hash, and corned beef and cabbage. One of the best-known dishes is listed as côtelette de veau de l'empereur. It is sautéed veal with a light cream sauce, and is quite tasty. Miller's is crowded with businessmen at midday. All dishes are à la carte, with main courses from $2.25 to $7.50, and a complete meal is $1.20 more. *Cocktails, wines. Closed Saturday, Sunday, and major holidays.*
AE

★ MINETTA TAVERN
113 Macdougal Street   GR 3-9119

A neat and frequently crowded neighborhood restaurant in Greenwich Village. It has a loyal, genteel clientele, and the quality of the food, which is Italian, ranges from the ordinary to the excellent. The portions for almost all the foods are overly copious and the table service is only average. The restaurant is generally pleasant, nonetheless. At lunch and dinner, all dishes are à la carte, from about $2.00 for spaghetti with tomato sauce to $5.50

for steaks. *Cocktails, wines. Closed Monday.*
AE BA DC MC

★★ MINOTAUR, THE
875 First Avenue (at 49th Street)   *752-9252*

Where restaurants are concerned, the 12-table Minotaur is one of the nicest things to have happened to the Beekman-Sutton Place area. It is not just one more addition to the lengthening roster of Greek restaurants in the city; it is a place with intimate style and generally excellent food. The kitchen is at the entrance and is open for all to see—the chef with his various baked and roasted dishes including moussaka, the ground meat and eggplant dish; pastitsio, the ground meat and macaroni dish; roast lamb; and so on.

The menu is not vastly different from that of numerous other Greek restaurants hereabouts, but the dishes are expertly seasoned. There are excellent salads, appetizers, and broiled fish.

Some guests may complain that one or two dishes are too oily, but that's the nature of bourgeois Greek cooking, and most Greek cooking is bourgeois.

All dishes are à la carte and main courses are priced from about $1.75 for spinach and cheese pie to $3.75 for lamb shish kebab. *Cocktails, wines. Open noon to 11:00 p.m., Monday through Friday; from 4:00 to 11:00 p.m. Saturday. Closed Sunday and major holidays.*

★★ MR. AND MRS. FOSTER
242 East 81st Street   *535-1234*

This restaurant seems to have most of the ingredients for local success. It is small (there are only 10 tables) and seating is by reservation only. The public likes that. If you can maneuver a table where the food is appreciably priced and the tables are in demand you somehow seem select.

The food at Mr. and Mrs. Foster isn't bad at all. It is

cooked to order; all the dishes show imagination and some of them are excellent. When you telephone, Mrs. Foster outlines the main dishes available for the day. You make a selection and, when you arrive, a dinner of several courses begins.

One dinner started with broiled chicken livers in a ramekin with heavily buttered herb toast on the side. It proceeded through very good buckwheat crêpes with caviar and sour cream and a creamy green pea soup that improved with the twist of a pepper mill.

One main course was a tender lobster whose cavity was stuffed with crab meat and coral (a simply broiled lobster would have been preferable; the crab meat was dry), a broiled (overcooked) split scampi, and a broiled sliced sea scallop. Another main course was boneless chicken stuffed Polynesian-style and overly sweet. The cornstarch-thickened sauce that accompanied it contained pineapple chunks. The salad was well-seasoned, but too cold. The desserts—a lemon custard in meringue shell and a thick, rich chocolate mousse—were notable, the latter in particular. The menu changes from day to day.

A pleasant asset of the restaurant is the price of the wines, and the selection, though limited, is good. Mrs. Foster is a birdlike woman in a smock. Certain aspects of Mr. and Mrs. Foster are like a tearoom. In any event, it is different.

The décor is severely plain and brightly lighted. The tables are cloth by cloth.

The cost of a complete dinner is $7.00 to $15.00. *Only wine is served. Seatings are at 6:30 and 9:00 p.m. Closed Sunday, major holidays, and for several weeks in July.*

★ MI TIERRA
668 Amsterdam Avenue (at 93rd Street)   *874-8292*

This is the sort of place with such a disheveled, if not to say disreputable, look that a fastidious gourmet would not only pass it by, but also conceivably cross the street. There are a refrigerator for beer and soft drinks at the entrance, and catsup bottles on the table. The chef wears a plaid flannel shirt and a golf cap, and the cat follows him around. It has a counter and only 4 tables.

But the food—a blend of Mexican and Cuban—is robust, interesting, and good. For what it is, it is expertly seasoned —and a bit oily. There are several kinds of tortilla dishes, including shrimp or lobster enchiladas and chalupas; chicken, beef, or pork tacos; tortillas as bread; picadillo made with ground beef and peppers; fried bananas; and, of course, black beans with rice.

One of the most interesting dishes is the shrimp chalupa made with chopped shrimp, tomatoes, onions, and cheese on a crisp tortilla smeared with refried beans. The same menu serves throughout the day. Main courses are accompanied by side dishes of fried bananas and salad and are priced from $2.35 to $3.50. A combination of six different dishes runs from $3.75 to $4.50. *Beer is available. Open 7 days a week.*

★ MIYAKO
20 West 56th Street   CO 5-3177

This was one of the first of New York's Japanese restaurants. It is a three-story place with a large, crowded dining room and food that is agreeable enough for anyone with only a casual interest in Japanese food. New Yorkers may have become spoiled by a wealth of adventurous Japanese restaurants, and at the Miyako the food seems more Westernized than in some of the more recent ventures. The menu includes the usual tempura, sukiyaki, teriyaki, or fish shioyaki, and it is good enough although, by and large, unremarkable. There are complete luncheons from $2.50 to $5.00; complete dinners from $3.95 to $6.50. A la carte items cost from $3.00 to $4.25. *Cocktails, wines. Luncheon is not served on Sunday. Closed Monday and New Year's Day.*
AE   CB   DC

★ MOLFETAS CAFETERIA
307 West 47th Street   JU 6-9278

What Molfetas lacks in elegance it more than makes up for with good Greek food. There are roast lamb and braised lamb, stuffed vine leaves and excellent rice, and the cost of any main dish is rarely more than $2.10. Desserts are along the lines of baklava. The food is hearty, the portions are large, the staff helpful and good-humored, and the cafeteria neat. *Cocktails, Greek wines and beers. Open 7 days a week, from 10:00 a.m. to 1:00 a.m.*

★★ MONA LISA
71 Macdougal Street   473-9804

This is a well-established and decent restaurant in Greenwich Village with honest, conscientiously cooked Italian food. And it's a bargain to boot.

There is, for example, an excellent chicken dish called Mona Lisa, breaded chicken breast, deep-fried and baked with ham and cheese and crowned with a freshly cooked tomato sauce. A dish of flounder was fresh and so was an appetizer of the chef's baked clams with a bread and garlic topping. Other relative pleasures included the sautéed escarole, an order of eggplant parmigiana, and a crisp green salad.

The Mona Lisa has a small, friendly bar and a large, brightly lighted dining room with the usual décor.

The cost of a complete three-course luncheon is $2.35, including coffee, tea, or milk. Complete four-course dinners cost from about $4.00 to $6.75. A la carte dishes from about $1.60 for spaghetti with tomato sauce to $5.00 for steak. *Cocktails, wines. Closed Sunday.*

★ MONA LISA EAST
936 Second Avenue (near 50th Street)   753-0290

This small Italian establishment is the happy victim of success. At peak meal times, there is standing room only for seating on one of the 26 chairs. There are the usual red-checked tablecloths, a sandwich bar, a pizza bar, and, on the wall, a reproduction of Mona Lisa wearing a smile more crooked than ever.

There is one outstanding thing on the small menu and that is the homemade antipasto. It is a well-varied, well-seasoned assortment of cold foods including baked green peppers with a bread and caper stuffing; cooked sweet sausages in an excellent Neapolitan tomato sauce; excellent white bean salad; small artichokes; imported black olives; baked eggplant with oil; eggplant parmigiana; and so on.

One portion, which costs $2.00, is sufficient for a meal. A subsequent cannelloni with ricotta was acceptable, but indifferently seasoned. A large portion of veal parmigiana was well-cooked, but the meat was tough and not white enough to be first-rate. A portion of meringue-covered rum cake was tender and good.

All luncheon dishes are à la carte, with main courses from about $1.75 for spaghetti bolognese to $5.50 for steak. At dinner main courses are from $2.00. There are dinners with first course, main course, and coffee priced from $6.00. *Cocktails, wines. Closed Sunday and major holidays.*

★ MONA TRATTORIA
567 City Island Avenue, the Bronx   885-1366

There is a certain raffish charm about City Island and its views of boats and boatyards. There is a similar charm about the Mona Trattoria, a small, largely unadorned Italian restaurant near the waterfront. The chief virtue of the restaurant is its pasta dishes, although the turkey breast with prosciutto and white truffles is also rather special. The service staff of the Trattoria is small, and, when the restaurant is crowded, the service is disorganized. The same menu serves throughout the day. The cost of à la carte dishes is from about $2.85 for homemade noodles with meat sauce to beef in wine and marsala at

$6.50. There is a complete dinner that costs $7.25 to $8.25. *Cocktails, wines. Closed Monday.*

★★ MONK'S INN
35 West 64th Street   874-2710

The concept of this restaurant near Lincoln Center is admirable. Its specialty is cheese—disks, wedges, pyramids, and tunnels, plus fondues, rarebits, and omelets. There are also Alsatian and Swiss dishes, such as sauerkraut, bratwurst, and pigs' knuckles. The décor is contrived without apology—stained-glass windows, wine butts, candles, and waiters in flowing monks' robes. The works.

Monk's Inn is worth a visit, although it is better in concept than in execution. Judgment of most of what it offers can be summed up in a commentary on the snails. Escargots at their best are sublime, but must be assertive in both flavor and temperature. One order at Monk's Inn was wholly edible, but bland and less than fiery hot.

The pigs' knuckles were good, but not melting in texture as they should be and were garnished not only with sauerkraut but also with tomato slices and a leaf of lettuce, of all things. The garnish should be sauerkraut and boiled potato.

In any event an original and well-motivated restaurant in New York deserves patronage, and Monk's Inn seems to fit that category. Monk's Inn's raclette—or scraped cheese dish—was brilliantly hot and excellent. A bottle of Dole, a red Swiss wine, was corking good.

All dishes are à la carte, with main courses at midday from about $2.50 for an international assortment of cheeses to $11.00 for fondue bourguignonne; in the evening, from about $3.00 to $12.00 for the same dishes. *Cocktails, wines. Open 7 days a week.*
AE   CB   DC   MC

★★★ MON PARIS
111 East 29th Street   MU 4-9152

Although Mon Paris has enlarged, it has not lost the qualities that have made it one of the finest small French restaurants in New York. The food is prepared with remarkable finesse and the service is attentive, even friendly. Mon Paris is generally crowded at main dining periods. All dishes on the restaurant's menus are à la carte. Main dishes at midday cost from about $3.00 to $5.00 and in the evening from about $3.75 to $7.00. *Cocktails, wines. On Saturday and Sunday the restaurant opens at 5:00 p.m. Closed major holidays, Saturday, and Sunday and for 4 weeks in summer.*

★ MONT D'OR
244 East 46th Street   OX 7-5668

A plain, pleasant, and popular restaurant with a Franco-American kitchen. The menu ranges from spaghetti bolognese to filet mignon with bordelaise sauce. A la carte main luncheon dishes from $3.50 to $4.50; complete luncheons from $3.75 to $4.75. Complete dinners only, from $5.75 to $7.50. *Cocktails, wines. On Saturday, the restaurant opens at 5:00 p.m. Closed Sunday.*
AE CB DC

★★ MONTE'S RESTAURANT
97 Macdougal Street   OR 4-9456

Monte's is far from being the most elegant Italian restaurant in New York, but it is one of the neatest bargains in the Italian genre. It is popular with many of the budget-minded and substantial citizens of Greenwich Village, and at times it is difficult to obtain a table. All dishes are à la carte with main courses from about $1.25 to $3.75 for pork salscia. *Cocktails, wines. Closed Tuesday, Thanksgiving, Christmas, and several weeks in summer.*

★★ MONT ST. MICHEL RESTAURANT
326 West 57th Street   LT *1-1032*

This is a pleasant French restaurant with a menu that is tried and true and a kitchen that is competent. The trump and triumph of the Mont St. Michel, however, is available on Thursday and Friday and it is couscous, that extraordinary cereal of North African celebrity. There is probably no finer couscous served in America than that at the Mont St. Michel. It is steamed to perfection and served with an assortment of excellent accompaniments including chicken, lamb, and cumin-flavored meat balls. There is bouillon, too, and a hot sauce served on the side. The cost of the couscous with salad is $5.00. There are complete luncheons that cost from $2.95 to $3.95; complete dinners from $5.00. *Cocktails, wines.*
AE CB DC

★ MOON PALACE
2879 Broadway (at 112th Street)   *666-7517 and 666-7518*

At its best, the food at the Moon Palace ranks with the best to be had in any Chinese restaurant in Manhattan. A dish of shredded chicken with abalone and another of pork shreds with soft bean curd were enjoyed with uncommon relish, and they will long be remembered. Both the boiled and fried dumplings are first-rate. The problem here, as it is in many Chinese restaurants, is to persuade the management that you have an authentic appetite for food that is leagues removed from chow mein and chop suey. This is a large, unpretentious restaurant, near Columbia University, and it seems vastly popular with the students. The luncheon menu is inexpensive and mundane with complete meals from $1.20 to $3.15. The à la carte menu, available at all hours, lists main courses from about $1.00 to $10.00 for Pekin duck. *Cocktails, wines. Dinner is served Sunday from 11:30 a.m. Closed Chinese New Year's Day, only.*

★ MORGEN'S EAST
34 East 52nd Street   HA *1-1331*
★ MORGEN'S RESTAURANT
141 West 38th Street   BR *9-7420*

These are neatly-run restaurants from dining room to kitchen, and the food is agreeable. The chopped chicken liver, the brisket of beef, and the corned beef are excellent. The fresh seafood is good. The luncheon menu is à la carte, with main courses from about $3.25 to $5.00. There is a complete dinner that costs $6.75. A roast beef dinner is $7.75. *Cocktails, wines. Morgen's East is closed for lunch on Saturday and all day Sunday. The restaurant at West 38th Street is closed Saturday and Sunday.*
AE   CB   DC

★★ MYKONOS
349 West 46th Street   *265-1590*

There is nothing in the Greek islands more ornate and—at the height of an evening's revels—noisier than this taverna on West 46th Street. The main dining room has recessed arches with murals in colors so brilliant they seem luminescent, and if you are like most good Athenians who enjoy sound and color, you will probably find your money well-spent here, particularly after 9:15 P.M., when a trio comes on with piano, accordion, bazookas, drums, and flute.

The Greek food is on a par with some of the best in Manhattan. There are several interesting hot hors d'oeuvres, including sautéed sweetbreads, cubes of chicken livers, hot stuffed grape leaves with lemon sauce, and spinach and cheese pastries. The cold hors d'oeuvres, with shrimp, taramosalata, feta cheese, and so on is good, if standard fare.

A roast rack of baby lamb, characteristically cooked until well done, was excellent, if tepid; a broiled squab lightly seasoned with orégano, first-rate; and there are good traditional dishes such as moussaka and pastitsio, or macaroni with ground meat.

The vegetable accompaniments are generally overcooked and the desserts, including a dry baklava and a chewy rice pudding, something less than interesting. The service by young Greeks is friendly.

A 4-course luncheon is $4.00. There is a complete 6-course dinner priced at $9.50. A la carte dishes are from about $2.50 to $8.75. *Cocktails, wines. Closed Sunday.*
AE CB DC MC

★★ NATARAJ
112 West 45th Street   586-9680

Some of New York's most engaging restaurants are small, wholly unprepossessing places that are likely to escape the notice of the casual passer-by. One of these is the Nataraj, which has Indian cooking and a simple décor.

The executive lunch at Nataraj is one of the best buys in the city. For $1.25 there is a choice of 6 curries, including chicken, shrimp, lamb, beef, vegetable, and koofta, or meat ball curry, all differently and interestingly seasoned.

The portions of each curry are small, but there is, in addition, a large platter of buttered rice; dahl sauce, which is a thin purée of curried lentils; an onion relish; and a small side dish of vegetable curry, which may be with potatoes and black-eyed peas. The food at the Nataraj is not refined at all, but it is interesting and good and the price is right.

There are complete dinners that cost from about $2.75 to $6.95 (a rijsttafel with 16 different dishes). A la carte dishes are priced from about $2.00 to $6.50. *There is no bar, but beers are available. Open 7 days a week.*
All major credit cards.

★ NAT SIMON'S PENGUIN ROOM
21 West 9th Street   777-2670

A candle-lit, subterranean rendezvous that in some respects may seem a trifle gauche. There are blackamoor candelabra and piped-in music and a room that the man-

agement calls a "romantic library." The specialties of the house are the steaks. They are quite good, if not extraordinary. All dishes are à la carte, with main courses from about $4.25 to $7.95. *Cocktails, wines. Luncheon is not served.*
AE CB DC MC

★★ NEAR EAST RESTAURANT
138 Court Street, Brooklyn   624-9257

This is another of those small, unpretentious, and generally excellent Middle Eastern restaurants where one may dine well for one or two dollars. Lamb is the principal meat, and it is cooked at the Near East with numerous vegetables, such as green beans, eggplant, and okra. There are also several excellent appetizers—for example, the traditional homus, a purée of chick-peas, and baba gannough, a purée of eggplant. There is one menu for lunch and dinner, and all dishes are à la carte. Main dishes cost from about $1.25 for stuffed cabbage to $2.50 for shish kebab. *No alcoholic beverages. Closed Monday, major holidays, and a month in summer.*

★ NEW HANKOW
130 West 34th Street   OX 5-4972

It is pure speculation, but at midday this may be the busiest Chinese restaurant in Manhattan. Customers queue up to await their turns at table, and you might suppose from the crowds that the food was wildly fantastic. It isn't, but it is more than adequate and the appetizers show considerable imagination.

The lobster and chicken roll ($1.00), for example, has a sizable chunk of lobster wrapped in a flat layer of chicken breast, coated with batter and deep-fried. Very good, but the batter is too thick. The main dishes are mostly meats with coarsely chopped vegetables—nothing subtle, but palatable.

The cost of complete luncheons is from about $1.85 to $4.25. Complete dinners from $2.80 to $5.60. A la carte dishes are priced from about $2.85 to $5.75. *Cocktails, wines. Closed Sunday and major holidays.*
AE DC

NEW KOREA
9 East 40th Street   MU 3-7775

The food of Korea is among the most fascinating in the Orient. It is not, for the most part, noted for its subtlety, but the Korean kitchen offers vivid contrasts in flavor. Many of the dishes are based on garlic, and a meal without kimchi, that hot and salty delectable pickle, is unthinkable, morning, noon, or night.

There are several interesting dishes on the New Korea's menu, including the sinsullo, the national soup; the bul go ki, the national grilled beef dish; and the dak chim, chicken with mushroom sauce.

The menu states that the bul go ki is made with top sirloin beef, but I found it a bit chewy. The sinsullo, with its numerous ingredients, including gingko nuts, hard-cooked eggs, small meat balls, and mushrooms, was good, but the broth was a bit thin. The chef concocts several stir-fried dishes with many vegetables—celery, cabbage, mushrooms, and so on—and they are tasty.

There are complete luncheons priced at $2.25; complete dinners at $5.50. A la carte dishes from about $3.00 to $4.00. *Cocktails, wines. Open 7 days a week.*
AE DC MC

★ NEW MOON INN
2824 Broadway (between 109th and 110th Streets)
AC 2-2653

In its best moments, this is an excellent Chinese restaurant, but at times both the service and the food can be indifferent. Complete luncheons from $1.80 to $2.40.

Cantonese family dinners range from $6.20 to $6.80 for two to $13.80 to $17.00 for five. *Cocktails, wines.*

★★ NEW PORT ALBA
208 Thompson Street   473-9735

This is one of those small, family-run Italian restaurants with home-style cooking that New Yorkers like to discover on their own. The food is Neapolitan, tastes as if it were cooked by someone's mother in the kitchen, and is at its best excellent.

The spaghetti sauces, even the most basic tomato, are freshly made and, if you stir in a pat or two of butter, above average. One of numerous pasta dishes is spaghetti alla matriciana made with tomatoes, cooked onion rings, and prosciutto, and it is typical—robust, a bit peasanty, and more than palatable. There is much to recommend about the boneless breast of chicken Alba-style, stuffed with cheese and ham and served with a well-made fresh mushroom sauce.

The same menu serves throughout the day, and all dishes are à la carte. They range in price from about $2.25 for homemade lasagne to $4.95 for mignonette of beef cognac. *Cocktails, wines. Open 7 days a week.*
AE DC MC

★★ NEW WAH DOR
43 Bayard Street (at the Bowery)   732-6946

A gentleman from Hong Kong has recommended this as one of the best restaurants in Chinatown. It is a particularly good source for such finger foods as crabs Cantonese style, clams with black bean sauce, and snails in the shell with a peppery coating of oil, ginger, and garlic. Or more usual dishes such as lobster Cantonese and steamed sea bass.

One dish was a disappointment. It was the mushroom chicken pan with black mushrooms, snow peas, bamboo shoots, and water chestnuts. Dullsville. If you've never tried Chinese snails and the other finger foods, please take note that they are tedious to eat, albeit delectable.

A la carte dishes cost from about $1.05 to $5.75. *There is no bar. Open 7 days a week, 11:30 a.m. to 4:30 a.m.*

★★ NEW YORK EXCHANGE RESTAURANT
541 Madison Avenue (between 54th and 55th Streets)
PL 3-2330

If anyone wants the name of a restaurant that has a typical, if not to say classic, American menu, it is the restaurant of the New York Exchange for Woman's Work. It has at times codfish balls; grilled sausage with Southern waffles; chicken salad; New England striped bass with stewed tomatoes; deep-dish apple pie with cheese; and orange marshmallow layer cake. The food is not bad.

How joyous it would be if the Woman's Exchange offered not just competent food, but an altogether memorable American kitchen as well as menu. For, the food, while acceptable, is more or less of tearoom quality.

A shrimp cocktail was served on one occasion with an ordinary catsup sauce; the crab meat cocktail in thin shreds; a grilled chicken half was fresh and well-seasoned, but overcooked; a wedge of Camembert was brown and tired; and the coffee was weak. What came off well was broiled liver that appeared at the table hot and expertly done. A dish of zucchini was lukewarm, but at least it was fresh.

Physically, the New York Exchange dining room has a quarry tile floor and the walls are aquamarine. There are Formica tables topped with rectangular doilies that serve as place mats.

This is by no means the city's least expensive restaurant. There are complete luncheons priced at $2.95, with à la carte entrées at midday from about $1.65 to $3.25. Complete dinners cost from about $4.00 to $6.50, and there are additional charges for various items. *Cocktails, wines,*

Lunch is served from 11:30 a.m. to 2:30 p.m., Monday through Saturday. Dinner is served from 5:00 to 8:00 p.m., Monday through Friday. Closed Sunday and major holidays.

★ NICK'S TOPKAPI PUB
517 Avenue of the Americas (between 13th and 14th Streets)   691-7780

The menus proclaim that this is "The Only Turkish Pub in the U.S.A." Or in the world, for that matter, Istanbul included. It is a pleasant place, somewhat small, and with a bar, of course.

The owner is a man tremendously alert and with an intense desire to please, and that is uncommon in New York. The food isn't bad, if you consider that the cost of a complete lunch is $2.25 with a free beer. It isn't distinguished either, but the management stresses that it's a pub, doesn't it?

There is a nice assortment of appetizers, particularly the imam biyaldi or baked eggplant with onions and tomatoes in olive oil, and the stuffed grape leaves. The taramosalata or carp roe salad leaves much to be desired.

Then there are main dishes like moussaka, which is the baked eggplant dish with chopped meat and pine nuts, the tas kebab or braised lamb cut into thin bits, and Turkish-style chicken.

The dishes are well-seasoned, but a bit too oily.

In addition to the complete lunch, the pub offers hamburgers at 95 cents and, on some days, a Turkish buffet priced at $2.75. The evening menu is à la carte, with main courses from about $2.50 to $3.95. *Cocktails, beers. Open 7 days a week. Luncheon is not served on Sunday.*

★★ NICOLA PAONE
207 East 34th Street   889-3239

Inasmuch as there are few very good Italian restaurants in New York City, there are several things to admire at Nicola Paone. The menu shows much imagination, although some of the best dishes have curious names like Boom Boom and Nightgown, both rolled-veal dishes, one with mushrooms, the other with eggplant. For New York, the service is sufficiently enthusiastic and efficient to marvel at. On the negative side, the restaurant's banquettes are not notably comfortable and the antipasto is dull. Paone's is no recent discovery, and the tables are frequently filled, particularly at midday. All dishes are à la carte, with main courses from about $2.75 to $6.00 at noon; $4.00 to $8.50 in the evening. *Cocktails, wines. On Saturday the restaurant opens at 5:00 p.m. Closed Sunday. AE DC*

★★ NINGPO RESTAURANT
83 Second Avenue (between 4th and 5th Streets)
473-9761

At the Ningpo, the food is obviously prepared by a first-rate Chinese hand, whether it is lobster Cantonese or almond dice-cut chicken. The food is reasonably priced. The cost of main dishes à la carte is from $1.40 to $4.50. There is also a thriving take-out section. *No alcoholic beverages. Closed Monday.*

★★ NIPPON
145 East 52nd Street   EL 5-9020

This is one of the finest Japanese restaurants in Manhattan—and they have proliferated within recent years. The restaurant is stylish in concept, and service is by handsome kimono-clad young women. There is a tempura bar, where guests may sit at a counter to dine on a variety of seafoods and vegetables dipped in batter and deep-fried; also a sushi bar, where the traditional kinds of various raw fish are served with soy, ginger, and wasabi, which is grated horseradish. There are special luncheons at the Nippon that include a clear soup or a bean soup, pickled vegetables, a principal dish, rice, and dessert, such

as melon. The cost is from about $4.50 to $5.50. Complete dinners, which are more elaborate, cost from about $6.00 to $15.00. *Cocktails, wines. On Saturday, the restaurant opens at 5:30 p.m. Closed Sunday.*
AE CB DC

★★ NIRVANA
1193 Lexington Avenue (at 81st Street)   288-9097

This restaurant subtitles itself the "India Pakistan International Gourmet." There is an interesting menu and a pleasantly gaudy interior: fabric-covered poles and billowing canopies overhead to simulate a terribly Old Empire tent.

Indian- or Pakistani-style food is among the world's most difficult for a Westerner to judge, because that kind of cooking is the most complicated where seasonings and flavors are concerned, sometimes dry, sometimes oily. It ranges from the marvelously subtle to the wildly condimented. The chef at the Nirvana is no coward in his use of spices, and the food is, over-all, quite tasty.

There are interesting appetizers, including samosas, which are turnovers made with curried meat or mixed vegetables, and chopped meat patties. The main courses include tandoori chicken and various curries, which seem competently made. There are assorted chutneys on the menu, including lemon and onion (one guest at another table ordered these and complained loudly that they weren't chutneys, when what he meant was they were not the Major Grey chutney that he is accustomed to).

There is a splendid dessert, a creamy rich dahi, which is a thickened yogurt; and a most indifferent, pallid, and uninteresting (to this Westerner's palate) roshogolla, which are "milk spheres in rose water." The waiters are most pleasant, but the service is slow. The food at the Nirvana is assertive in its flavors, and if you do not like spiced foods (an elaborate use of peppercorns and cloves and so on) and foods a bit on the oily side, do not bother.

The restaurant is open evenings only. A la carte dishes are priced from about $2.95 to $4.95; complete dinners from about $5.95 to $7.95. *Cocktails, wines. Open 7 days a week.*

★★ NOM WAH TEA PARLOR
13 Doyers Street   wo 2-8650 *and* wo 2-6047

Numerous restaurants are a vital part of the color of Chinatown. One of the best for Chinese tea lunches is the Nom Wah Tea Parlor, which serves a large assortment of exotic dumplings and other oriental appetizers ranging in cost from about 15 cents to 50 cents. A representative luncheon for two is usually about $3.00. The restaurant is generally crowded shortly after noon, so it is best to get there early, particularly on Saturday and Sunday. *No alcoholic beverages. Open 10:00 a.m. to 4:00 p.m. on weekdays and 10:00 a.m. to 6:00 p.m. on weekends.*

★ OCEAN, THE
521 Third Avenue (at 35th Street)   889-3889

This small seafood house that calls itself a seafood boutique is built around an interesting idea—quickly prepared seafood and fish dishes with tray service, plus retail orders to take out. It has, as might be expected, a nautical décor complete with portholes, tables in the shape of boat hulls, and a gunwale-shaped ceiling. There are a few small tables and customers sit on small stools. The menu does not change from day to day.

What is good and unusual is an appetizer of chilled, absolutely delicious large crab legs, already cracked and ready to be eaten with cocktail sauce. A characteristic dish is the batter-fried shrimp tempura. The shrimp are edible and seem to have been cooked in fresh fat, but they still seem a bit oily. Many of the dishes are fried, such as scallops and a version of crab claws. The lobster tails are precooked, brushed with butter, then cooked again under a salamander. Quite obviously, they dry out in the process.

The french-fried potatoes are no bargain.

All dishes are à la carte, with main courses from about 75 cents for a fried scallop sandwich to $3.25 for the lobster tails. *There is no bar, but there is very good beer on tap served in a paper cup. Closed Sunday.*

★ O. HENRY'S STEAK HOUSE
345 Avenue of the Americas (at West 4th Street)
CH 2-2000

Butcher blocks for cocktail tables, gas lamps that formerly illuminated the streets of Baltimore, and sawdust on the floor help make this one of New York's most colorful restaurants. It has a solid mahogany bar, waiters in butcher coats, and stained-glass windows. The draft beer is excellent, and the food is just reasonably good. The charcoal steaks, for example, have a good flavor, but the texture can be flaccid and chewy. All foods are à la carte, with main luncheon dishes from about $1.75 to $6.75. The dinner menu ranges from about $3.75 to $7.50. *Cocktails, wines, beer on draft. A sidewalk café for outdoor dining is open April through November. Closed Christmas.*
AE BA CB DC MC

★ OLD DENMARK
135 East 57th Street   PL 3-5856

The Old Denmark is first and foremost a purveyor of Scandinavian delicacies for the retail trade, but it also boasts one table where customers may dine on Danish specialties. There is a seating capacity for 8 persons at a time and the table is shared by other customers. The food consists primarily of salads, such as cucumber, mushroom, crab, beet, and herring, but there is also liver pâté and smoked salmon. The meal also includes bread, lemon cake, and coffee. The cost of the lunch is $2.95. *Open for luncheon only. No alcoholic beverages, but the restaurant serves a sugar-free Swiss grape juice, both red and white. Closed Sunday and major holidays.*

★ OLD FORGE STEAK HOUSE
200 East 17th Street (at Third Avenue)   GR 3-1767

A neat and comfortable steak house with good food and some of the most accommodating waiters in town. Charcoal-broiled dishes are the principal fare. Complete luncheons cost from about $2.85 to $4.50; complete dinners from about $4.95 to $6.95. A la carte dishes throughout the day cost from $3.50 to $6.95. *Cocktails, wines. On Saturday and Sunday the restaurant opens at 3:00 p.m.*
AE CB DC MC

OLD GARDEN, THE
15 West 29th Street   LE 2-8323

The several rooms of this landmark are divided by natural brick walls with arches. The food is mostly Yankee-style, with such dishes as creamed chicken, breaded veal cutlets, steaks, and chops. There is nothing elegant about the menu, but it is well-varied; the portions are large and inexpensive. Luncheons are à la carte, with main courses from about $1.45 to $2.05; complete dinners from $2.95 to $5.95. *Cocktails, wines. Open for lunch Monday through Friday. Closed Sunday and major holidays.*

★ OLD MEXICO RESTAURANT
115 Montague Street, Brooklyn   MA 4-9774

Where the food is concerned, this is an especially good Mexican restaurant in Brooklyn. There are the usual specialties such as tostadas, enchiladas, and tamales, but there are the spiced mole dishes as well. There is also an excellent pasta. The restaurant is small. On the negative side, the ventilation is poor and the service is indifferent. For aficionados of Mexican food, however, it can be rewarding. All dishes are à la carte, with main courses from about $2.75 for tacos and enchiladas to $4.50 for Costena, shellfish in wine sauce. *Wines, beers. Open for dinner only, from 5:00 p.m. Closed Sunday and major holidays.*

★★ OLD SEIDELBURG
542 Third Avenue (at 36th Street)   689-3384

The menu of the Old Seidelburg notes that the restaurant serves "The best beer in town in ice cold steins," and it may be true. At least the customer has a choice of 12 imported and domestic beers on draft. And, all things considered, the price in particular, the food is as acceptable as it is predictable.

There is a choice of bratwurst, or pigs' knuckles, or knockwurst with sauerkraut; goulash with noodles; and sauerbraten with potato dumplings and red cabbage. All dishes are à la carte, with main courses from about $1.65 for chicken and potato croquettes to $6.75 for filet mignon.

The Old Seidelburg has been around for a long time, and it is now in a new location. The waiters are in black tie, the service is friendly, and there are two dining rooms with conventional murals. The head cheese is made from odds and ends, some of them smoked, but it is quite good. The pigs' knuckle is not, or recently was not, as moist and melting as it should have been, but, on the other hand, it wasn't bad. *Cocktails, wines. Open 7 days a week from 11:00 a.m. to 11:00 p.m.*

★★ OMAR KHAYAM
945 Second Avenue (near 50th Street)   752-9631

The chef of this new restaurant is Indian. The canopy outside says "Persian" cooking, and the menu lists the dishes of several nationalities, including Indonesian. Whatever the circumstances, the dishes are impressive, far from run-of-the-mill, and seasoned subtly without compromise. As a matter of fact, there is probably no better Indian or Persian cooking in any New York restaurant.

The appetizers include an excellent filled pastry triangle listed as pirashki; the main courses include a first-rate chelow kebab—two kinds of skewered meats, one cubed, another ground, with rice and an egg yolk; a hot, spicy Indonesian dish, nasi goreng, with rice and meat; and an outstanding curry dish, khoreshte bademjan, made with lamb and eggplant.

Among the appetizers, something called meygou and pofak—shrimp in a tomato sauce—was ordinary. The rice in the chelow kebab was good, but without the typical crustiness found in Iran.

There are good breads at the Omar Khayam, including the Persian fried bread called non; and there are excellent side dishes, including must and rhiyar (cucumber and raisins in yogurt) and chutneys and other condiments.

The restaurant was quite obviously decorated on a budget. It is neat, but plain. And the service staff has been limited. But inasmuch as no more than two tables have been occupied at any one visit, the service has been adequate.

Complete meals at Omar Khayam are priced from $5.00 to $7.00. A la carte dishes are priced from about $3.00 to $4.50. *There is no bar, although a license has been applied for. Open 7 days a week for lunch and dinner.*
AE DC MC

★★ O'NEAL'S BALOON
48 West 63rd Street   765-5577

Take O'Neal's for what it's worth, a saloon-type, light snack place with no pretension to be anything else. There are small, rickety tables and on the menu things like chili con carne and hamburgers and salads and steak tartare, and for this type establishment the food comes off very well.

They put horseradish in the Bloody Marys so that they taste just like shrimp cocktail sauce. The meat for the steak tartare is straight from the grinder, spaghetti fashion, not pressed together and scored on top as it is at the Ritz, but then this isn't the Ritz. And, rather than anchovies and egg yolk and other separate seasonings, they serve the same vinaigrette sauce for the tartare that they do for the spinach, bacon, and raw mushroom salad, and that's inventive and time-saving in a busy restaurant.

By the way, a bowl of lentil soup was excellent, and the various kinds of hamburger are good. O'Neal's is a popular place, located directly across from Lincoln Center.

One menu serves throughout the day, and it is à la carte with prices from about 75 cents for the soup to $3.95 for shish kebab. *Cocktails, wines. Open 7 days a week. Closed Christmas.*

★ ORIENTAL PEARL
211 Pearl Street (between John Street and Maiden Lane)
WH 3-6490

When the Chinese food is good at the Oriental Pearl it is capital. The good food includes the pressed duck. The menu also boasts such dreary items as chop suey and chow mein. The restaurant is frequently crowded and the tables are close together. A la carte dishes from about $1.75 to $4.00. *Cocktails, wines. Closed Saturday and Sunday.*

★★ ORSINI'S
41 West 56th Street   PL 7-1698

This restaurant is a joy to behold, the most European-looking of all New York restaurants, and it numbers among its clientele some of the most stylishly dressed men and women you're apt to find in the city. There are fashion designers and models and countless members of the international set. The dining room is on the second floor, above a handsome entrance room below. The dining tables are of inlaid tile, presumably Italian; the walls are of exposed brick and rough stucco; and good-looking fabrics serve as wall hangings. The service staff is neatly turned

out. The menu is long and far more interesting than you will find in most of the city's Italian restaurants. The pasta dishes, particularly those simply made with butter sauces—the noodles Alfredo, for example—are excellent. The veal dishes are good but shrimp and clams may be overcooked. The restaurant's elvetia or rum cake, like that you find almost everywhere in town, smacked of rum flavoring rather than rum, and why that should be is one of the mysteries of the century. All dishes are à la carte with main luncheon dishes from about $3.50 to $5.50; main dinner courses from about $5.25 to $8.50. *Cocktails, wines. Closed Sunday.*
AE CB DC MC

★ OSCAR'S DELMONICO
56 Beaver Street   BO 9-1180

New York's old Delmonico Restaurant at the turn of the century was at 494 Pearl Street, and it was one of the world's most celebrated dining rooms. The present Delmonico's is said to have many of the trappings of the original, including the front entrance. The food is Continental, primarily of North Italian inspiration, and, although it may not be in its predecessor's league, it is very good. The menu offers such dishes as breast of chicken Valdostana with cheese and tomatoes, and sliced breast of chicken with noodles in a rich cream sauce. Luncheons are à la carte with main dishes from about $4.50 to $10.95. Dinner à la carte entrées are from $5.50 to $10.95. *Cocktails, wines. The kitchen closes each evening at 10:30 p.m. Closed Saturday and Sunday, major holidays.*
AE

★ OSCAR'S SALT OF THE SEA
1155 Third Avenue (between 67th and 68th Streets)
TR 9-1199

This is at the moment New York's reigning fish and seafood emporium, and with very good reason. It is one of the most reasonably priced restaurants in town and the food is honest—no substituting of paprika for improper broiling. Oscar's has recently expanded and has a brand-new front. There is still frequently a wait for tables, at times half an hour or longer, and the people noise is something to contend with. A la carte dishes from about $2.95 to $7.50. *Cocktails, wines. Open 7 days a week.*

★ OVIEDO
202 West 14th Street   WA 9-9454

For better or for worse, this is one of the best-known Spanish restaurants in New York, and it has the usual offerings of paella, saffron rice, and seafood dishes in green sauce. The kitchen is competent, but not distinguished, and, to coin a phrase, it is a colorful restaurant, from the oil-on-velvet paintings recessed in the walls to the jukebox music that blares forth from the bar. The menu is à la carte and main courses are priced from about $1.50 for a Spanish omelet to $4.25 for the paella with lobster. *Cocktails, wines.*

★ PAGANO'S
1269 Lexington Avenue (between 85th and 86th Streets)
722-7617

With a few rare exceptions, if you've seen one Italian restaurant in Manhattan, you've seen them all, and Pagano's fits the mold.

It has the usual menu with the usual veal dishes and shrimp scampi (redundant usage, of course). Don't mistake me. This is a neighborhood restaurant, and much of the food, even if predictable, isn't bad.

Pagano's turns out a creditable spaghetti alla carbonara—indecently rich in calories—with its bacon or pancetta, egg yolk, and cheese; and an acceptable dish of rigatoni with marinara sauce. The stuffed mushrooms are well-seasoned, if a bit oily, and a dish of saltimbocca, delicately seasoned with rosemary, was tender but served with far too much sauce. The restaurant's salad is tart and good, but the shrimp in a marinara sauce was overcooked and dry.

All dishes are à la carte, with main dishes from about $2.50 to $7.50. *Cocktails, wines. The restaurant is open for lunch Monday through Friday; open for dinner 7 days a week. Closed Sunday in the summer.*

★★ PAK-INDIA CURRY HOUSE
130 West 45th Street   586 9614

There is tremendous variety in the numerous curries available at the Pak-India Curry House. The special luncheon, priced at $1.65 and available on weekdays, represents one of the best bargains in the city. There is a markedly friendly atmosphere about the Pak-India and a pleasant quaintness about the décor, wallpaper murals of Pakistani and Indian scenes, arches and gilded twist columns. The menu lists about 10 beef curries, 3 shrimp curries, 6 chicken curries, and so on, and there is a note that any Indian or Pakistani curry not on the menu is available if requested in advance. Complete dinners cost from $3.50 to $6.00. A la carte dishes cost from about $2.75. *Cocktails, wines.*
AE DC

★★★ PALM RESTAURANT
837 Second Avenue (near 45th Street)   MU 2-9515

This is a friendly, rough-and-tumble restaurant with cartoons on the walls and a checkroom attendant who reads the racing forms. It is, nonetheless, one of the finest steak houses in Manhattan. There is no written menu, but it is recited by the waiters and runs along the lines of chicken, chops, and roast beef, in addition to steaks and lobster. Steaks and lobster cost in the vicinity of $8.00 to $14.00. The home-fried potatoes at the Palm are extraordinarily good. All dishes are à la carte, with luncheon and dinner entrées from about $3.00. *Cocktails, wines. On Sat-*

urday the restaurant opens at 6:00 p.m. Closed Sunday and, during the summer months, Saturday also, and for 2 weeks in July.
AE

★★ PAMPLONA RESTAURANT
822 Avenue of the Americas (between 28th and 29th Streets)   683-4242

This bright, Spanish restaurant (a notice in the window says the chef was with the Spanish Pavilion at the World's Fair) has so much to recommend it that it is regrettable it is not better than it is.

The menu offers, for example, a creamy, if not to say, silken, black bean soup. One seafood cocktail was notable for the quality of its ingredients. An appetizer of creamed mushrooms on toast was excellent. Both a chicken riojana (with mushrooms and pimientos in a tomato sauce) and a chicken with lobster were interesting. A serving of paella at one luncheon was acceptable, but far from exceptional. The so-called saffron rice on the menu does not smack (nor does it have the color) of saffron. It is, nonetheless, well-cooked.

What disturbs one customer more is that some of the tomato sauces (for an appetizer of clams and for one chicken dish) seem too obviously thickened with flour. Maybe that's the way they do it in Spain.

The desserts are freshly made and generally excellent.

In any event, the Pamplona is a cheerful place, simply decorated with Spanish posters, plastic garlands here and there, and a jukebox in the bar area.

All dishes are à la carte with main courses from about $3.00 to $5.25 at noon and from about $3.00 to $6.00 in the evening. *Cocktails, wines. The restaurant opens at 4:30 p.m. on Saturday. Closed Sunday and major holidays.*
AE   DC   MC

★★ PANCHO VILLA'S
1501 Second Avenue (corner 78th Street)   734-9144

This is welcome in Manhattan's roster of Mexican restaurants. The surroundings are neat and interesting, but, unfortunately, the seating capacity is limited. The chef does a commendable job with such dishes as cheese enchiladas, both dark and green mole sauces, and the usual assortment of tacos, enchiladas, and tostadas. The cost of main courses is from about $2.50 at lunch; $3.25 to $5.50 at dinner. *Cocktails, wines. Open 7 days a week from noon to 1:00 a.m.*

★★ PANTHEON RESTAURANT
689 Eighth Avenue (near 43rd Street)   JU 6-9672

This is one of the oldest of New York's numerous Greek restaurants, and it seems to improve as years go by. It is a friendly place with casual service, and the food is better than you'll find in many small, well-known restaurants in Athens. The menu runs along the traditional lines of well-done lamb dishes with rice or vegetables or both, roast veal, and chicken and macaroni dishes, but innovations such as lamb with dandelions are listed. One delight is the avgolemono, or egg and lemon soup made with chicken broth. It is especially good at the Pantheon. The Greek antipasto with its taramosalata, or cold, lemon-flavored red caviar salad, anchovies, and feta cheese, is simple and good. All dishes are à la carte, with main courses from about $1.25 to $4.25 for a combination plate. *Cocktails, wines. Open 7 days a week.*

★ PAPARAZZI
964 Second Avenue (at 51st Street)   PL 9-7676

There is something bright and alive and what's happening, baby, about the Paparazzi, a place where people go more for atmosphere than for food. There are blow-ups of color photographs (for those who tuned in late, paparazzi are the news photographers of Italy); fresh brick; Tiffany lamps; and lots of traffic noises from without. Lots of jukebox noises from within.

Some of the dishes are creditable, including the sautéed chicken and veal francese and the veal dishes in general. The main fault found with the kitchen is the generally bland nature of the foods, from the pasta with white clam sauce to the beef rollatine. The over-all atmosphere—from the ventilation in the dining room to the waiter with his napkin in the soup—is casual. Oh, well, it's a friendly place.

The dishes are à la carte and the prices are right. The cost of main dishes at midday is from $1.20 to $2.85; in the evening from $3.25 to $6.50. A specialty of the house, incidentally, is crêpes stuffed with any of 19 fillings; they cost from 40 cents plain to $1.95 for chicken and ham. *Cocktails, wines. Brunch is served Saturday and Sunday. Closed Monday and major holidays.*
AE CB DC

★★ PAPPAS
14th Street and Eighth Avenue   WA 9-9421

The atmosphere of this 60-year-old restaurant is bourgeois, but the seafood, particularly the broiled lobster, can be rated with some of the best in the city. The menu also lists casseroles and grilled meat dishes. Luncheons are à la carte, with main courses from about $2.50 to $7.35. Complete dinners cost from about $4.50 to $7.75 for broiled whole lobster. *Cocktails, wines. Closed Sunday and major holidays.*
AE BA DC MC

★ PAPRIKA
1529 York Avenue (at 81st Street)   RH 4-9227

This is a small Hungarian restaurant on the Upper East Side. There are only 12 tables, and all the food is cooked in a small kitchen. The food at its best is excellent, and this would include a giblet soup, an enormously tasty ragout with sausages, and a sampling of freshly made

chopped chicken livers. Many of the main courses, including the stuffed cabbage, roast pork, and potted steak, are well-seasoned, but they also seem overcooked. Among the desserts, the Hungarian pancakes called palacsinta are very good and the rich chocolate cake with three textures is admirable. There are complete meals that cost from about $3.50 to $5.30; à la carte items from about $2.50 to $4.30. *Closed Monday and 3 weeks in summer.*
AE MC

★★ PARADISE INN
347 West 41st Street   LO 3-2581

This is one of New York's most peripatetic restaurants. It has just settled down at this address with lusty, carnival-bright walls, Greek music at night, and, happily, the same reasonably priced menu. The food is bourgeois Greek and one of the best-cooked bargains in the city.

There is the usual well-made antipasto with stuffed vine leaves, taramosalata, which is carp roe salad, feta cheese, olives, and anchovies. The meats are mostly lamb, and the choicest may be the roast shoulder. There is also excellent moussaka and pastitsio, or baked macaroni, plus numerous vegetables, predictably long-cooked in the Greek manner.

The portions are copious. A complete lunch is $1.85; à la carte main dishes with rice and generally a vegetable from about $1.75 to $3.25 for shish kabob. *Cocktails, wines. Open 7 days a week.*
AE BA

★ PARIOLI, ROMANISSIMO
1466 First Avenue (at 77th Street)   734-9951

This is a pleasant Italian restaurant with a maître d'hôtel who seems thoroughly professional. The foods are cooked to order and include such dishes as a meat-filled cannelloni Rossini with cream sauce, rolled breast of chicken Eleanora Duse, and veal Quo Vadis with artichokes and peas. The tables are too close for total comfort,

a recent bottle of Valpolicella was too tart for pleasure, and the restaurant's ventilation leaves something to be desired. All dishes are à la carte, with main courses from $3.75 for spaghetti Bolognese to $7.00 for sliced steak alla Parioli. *Cocktails, wines. Open for dinner only. Closed Sunday and major holidays.*
AE CB DC

★ PARKWAY EAST
163 Allen Street   GR *5-9815 and* GR *3-8704*

A fascinating unroutine restaurant with Jewish cuisine, Romanian style. There are chopped liver and borscht. There is also a lengthy list of charcoal-broiled meats, chicken in the pot, and boiled beef flanken. The food is generally excellent. The menu is à la carte, with main courses from about $4.50 to $7.50. *Cocktails, wines. Open for dinner only. Closed for Yom Kippur. Reservations are recommended for Saturday and Sunday.*

★★ PASSY, THE
28 East 63rd Street   TE *8-0094*

The Passy has maintained its feeling of elegance relatively well during its many years in Manhattan. The service is attentive but leisurely, and the food varies from ordinary to excellent. As in several of the city's restaurants of a certain class, there is an inexplicable and annoying charge on the menu for bread and butter—70 cents at luncheon, 90 cents at dinner. Luncheon entrées run from about $3.25 to $6.00; dinner entrées from about $4.25 to $8.00. *Cocktails, wines. Dinner is served Sunday from noon. Closed Saturday and major holidays.*
AE CB DC

★★ PATRICIA MURPHY'S CANDLELIGHT RESTAURANT
12 East 49th Street   *421-6464*
1 Fifth Avenue   *533-1800*

Patricia Murphy's may look a trifle prim and proper

to some guests, but the quality of the food is excellent and
it is cooked with care and some sophistication. There are
salads, of course, and sandwiches, but there are also very
good dishes on the order of striped bass with a mustard
and hollandaise sauce, chicken liver pâté with walnuts, and
caviar aspic. Luncheon à la carte dishes are from about
$2.00 to $3.25. Dinners are prix fixe from about $2.95 for
fruit salad to $6.95 for steak or lobster tails. *Cocktails,
wines. Dinner is served from noon on Sunday. Closed
Christmas.*
AE CB DC

★★ PAUL AND JIMMY'S PLACE
54 Irving Place OR 4-9463

Paul and Jimmy's Place is usually crowded because
it is one of the best small Italian restaurants in Manhattan.
La cucina is Neapolitan. The sauces are good and the
striped bass livornaise-style is generally excellent. All
dishes are à la carte, with main luncheon dishes from about
$2.50; main dinner courses from about $6.00. *Cocktails,
wines. Closed major holidays. Reservations are frequently
essential.*
AE DC

★ PAUL REVERE'S TAVERN AND CHOP HOUSE
Lexington Hotel, Lexington Avenue at 48th Street
PL 5-4400

There is more atmosphere here than you could
shake a lantern at, and the dark bar might do well with
more illumination. The menu is weighted on the side of
seafood, steaks, and chops, with odd curry and flamed
dishes. The fresh oysters and clams are first-rate, and the
steaks and chops are generally good. But, to choose at ran-
dom, a couple of orders of salad, made with that most undistinguished of salad greens, iceberg lettuce, were tossed
with a white dressing best not described. The portions, including desserts, are about as large as you'll find in New

York, and that is saying something. The menus are à la carte, with main dishes at midday from about $2.95 to $8.50 for steak; in the evening, from about $4.50 to $8.50 for steak. *Cocktails, wines. Open 7 days a week. Dinner only on Saturday and Sunday.*
All major credit cards.

★ PEARL'S CHINESE RESTAURANT
149 West 48th Street   586-1060

Pearl's is the perfect Chinese restaurant for people who don't really like Chinese restaurants. The proprietor is Mrs. Pearl Wong, better known to a devoted following as Miss Pearl. As to the décor, there are freshly painted, brightly lighted orange and salmon walls, and the over-all feeling is one of simple elegance. There is an impressive clientele, including numerous luminaries of Broadway. Miss Pearl offers exceptional variety in her establishment. Two of the most popular dishes are the moo shee pork with pancakes and the beef with lotus root, snow peas, and tree mushrooms. Among the appetizers, dem sem, or white flour dumplings, and the steamed dumplings made with rice flour are particularly good. The wor wonton, a large bowl of soup with numerous ingredients, is excellent and sufficient for a meal. Complete luncheons are priced from $2.50 to $6.75. A la carte dishes are $3.00 to $6.95. Pearl's has one drawback—its size. There are only 20 tables, and at times there is a wait to get one. *Cocktails, wines. Luncheon is not served on Sunday. Closed on Saturday and major holidays.*

★★ PEKING HOUSE
845 Second Avenue (at 45th Street)   MU 7-6636

This is one of the friendliest of the city's Chinese restaurants, and some of the dishes, particularly the quick-sauté dishes and steamed dumplings (listed on the menu as ravioli Chinese style), are excellent. At one meal, however, an order of braised squab tasted as though it had been cooked too far in advance and reheated. The Peking

House is fairly small and modern in décor. There are complete luncheons from about $2.75 to $2.85. A la carte dishes on the main menu cost from about $1.55 for pork fried rice to $15.00 for Pekin duck. *Cocktails, wines.*

★ PEMBLES
330 East 56th Street   688-6945

As someone who is turned off by noise, we were ready to flee Pembles after one cocktail, but a loaf of praiseworthy bread and butter came and the ears seemed to become more inured to din with dinner as the evening progressed.

If you can ignore the clangor from the dance floor (the sounds are both live and recorded), there are some things to admire on the menu. Considering the price of the sirloin steak—$5.95—it was of very good quality and quite decently cooked. The veal French-style was of excellent quality and flavorful, and the shish kebab on an enormous bed of rice wasn't bad at all.

An appetizer of avocado with sauce vinaigrette was good, and the salad, tossed by the captain to the beat of the music (a few pieces of lettuce dropping here and there), contained feta cheese and black olives and lots of garlic and it was robust but worthwhile.

The wines are, by New York standards at least, reasonably priced.

What didn't please was an appetizer of smoked salmon with the most extraordinary soft, flabby texture and the overcooked linguine with the veal. The napoleon was too cold, too old, and its filling was too thick. And, oh, that din.

The restaurant opens at 5:00 P.M. and supper is served from 10:30 P.M. All dishes are à la carte, with main courses from about $3.50 to $5.95. *Cocktails, wines. Closed Sunday. All major credit cards.*

★★ PEN AND PENCIL, THE
205 East 45th Street　　MU 2-1580

Bruno's Pen and Pencil is a popular and frequently crowded midtown restaurant that specializes in steaks, chops, and roasts, catering to a largely male clientele at luncheon. The à la carte menu is largely the same each day, with some Continental and curry dishes at luncheon, such as Vienna schnitzel Holstein and curry of lamb Singapore. Luncheon main courses are from about $3.15 to $4.25; entrées at dinner are from about $4.25 to $9.00. *Cocktails, wines. On Saturday and Sunday, the restaurant opens at 5:00 p.m. Closed many major holidays.*
AE　BA　CB　DC

★ PERGOLA DES ARTISTES
252 West 46th Street　　*245-9779 and* CI 7-8726

This is an agreeable small French restaurant in the Broadway area. The reception is cordial, the food is modestly priced, and the service is reasonably good, although the staff is small. The menu, with duck in orange sauce and fish meunière, is not overly original, but the food is well-prepared. Luncheons are à la carte with main courses from about $2.00 to $3.50. Complete dinners from about $5.00 to $7.00; à la carte entrées from about $3.00 to $5.50. *Cocktails, wines. Closed Sunday and major holidays.*
DC

★★★★ PETER LUGER
178 Broadway, Brooklyn　　EV 7-7400

This is a motley, raffish place with the atmosphere of a respectable neighborhood restaurant. The premises are neat and the bare tables are of polished oak. The important thing, however, is that the steaks at Peter Luger's are exceptional from the standpoint of both quality and grilling. There may be none better in all New York. Luger's is no sudden discovery. It has been around since 1887 and has a faithful clientele. The restaurant is frequently crowded and at times it is necessary to stand in line to wait for a table. There are special luncheons, with such dishes as prime ribs of beef, beef stew, and pot roast, that cost from about $2.65 to $3.15. The cost of steaks is from about $7.50, according to weight. Two large grilled lamb chops are $5.95. *Cocktails, wines, beer on draft. Open 7 days a week.*

★★ PETER'S BACKYARD
64 West 10th Street   GR 3-2400

This is a busy, noisy, pleasant place and one of the best steak houses in Greenwich Village. The quality of the beef is excellent, and the meat is cooked to a turn over a massive open charcoal pit. The atmosphere is neat and comfortable. The salads, on the other hand, with a sweet tomato dressing, are awful, and, although the waiters are friendly enough, their style is largely mechanical. All the dishes are à la carte, with main courses from about $3.50 for chopped steak to $9.50 for a T-bone. *Cocktails, wines. The restaurant opens at 4:00 p.m. Tuesday through Saturday; at 2:00 p.m. Sunday. Closed Monday and major holidays.*
AE   CB   DC

★★ PHILIPPINE GARDEN, THE
455 Second Avenue (near 26th Street)   MU 4-9625

This is a colorful, friendly restaurant that offers, particularly at noon, some of the biggest culinary bargains in town. The cooking is good, if slightly robust at times, and vaguely resembles Chinese cuisine. The menu lists such dishes as fish with vinegar, green peppers, and ginger; chicken and pork with cabbage, scallions, bananas, sausages, and onions. There are 7-course luncheons with copious dishes for about $3.00; complete dinners from about $4.00. The evening menu is also à la carte, with main courses from about $6.50. *Cocktails, wines. Dinner is served on Saturday from 3:00 p.m. and on Sunday from 5:00 p.m.*

★ PICCOLO MONDO
1269 First Avenue (between 68th and 69th Streets)
249-3141 and 249-3142

In some aspects, this is an admirable Italian restaurant with gauche modern décor, warm reception, and service that is generally commendable. The fettuccine Alfredo is excellent, and the soups, which include vichyssoise, minestrone, and onion, are worthwhile. The medallions of beef with truffle sauce are very good, the veal Florentine pedestrian. The veal is served on a bed of spinach, and why the chef would serve a dish of spinach as an accompaniment is the kitchen mystery. The hors d'oeuvres at Piccolo Mondo look ravishing, but all the flavors are generally on the same level. There are complete dinners from about $5.50 to $8.00. A la carte dishes at midday from about $1.95; in the evening from about $3.50 to $7.50. *Cocktails, wines. Dinner is served Saturday and Sunday from 1:00 p.m. Closed Monday.*
AE   DC   MC   UC

★★ PIERRE'S
52 East 53rd Street   EL 5-4074

This is a deservedly popular restaurant with French cuisine. The tables, however, seem uncomfortably close together, and at peak dining periods the noise level tends to be high. There are complete luncheons from about $5.45 to $7.77; complete dinners from about $7.77 to $10.00. *Cocktails, wines. Closed Saturday, Sunday, holidays, and 3 weeks at the end of the summer.*
AE   BA   DC   MC

★★ PIETRO'S
201 East 45th Street   MU 2-9760

This is physically one of the least pretentious Italian restaurants in town. The food—whether pasta or chicken parmigiana—is prepared with admirable care and simplicity in an all-butter kitchen that is small but equipped with a sizable staff. The food is generally first-rate. And awesomely expensive. Both luncheon and dinner menus are à la carte with main courses at midday from about $3.75 to $5.75 for minute steak; in the evening, from about $5.00 for spaghetti to $13.00 for lobster. *Cocktails, wines. On Saturday the restaurant opens at 6:00 p.m. Closed Sunday and, during the summer months, Saturday also.*

★ PINE GARDEN RESTAURANT
79A Mott Street   227-8559 and 233-9568

If you want an interesting change from the routine bill of fare of New York's Chinese restaurants, you might try the shiny bright Pine Garden Restaurant. The really interesting dishes are, however, for those who enjoy Chinese food in depth—crab in the shell with a kind of lobster sauce, snails in black bean sauce ($1.95), and clams Chinese-style. These are finger foods, and the snails in particular require some dexterity with both the fingers and the mouth to eat.

Among other dishes sampled, the noodles with roast pork was excellent and the beef with Formosa mushrooms special. There are only 12 tables at the Pine Garden, the décor is typical Chinatown, and the service is friendly.

The menu is à la carte, with main courses from about 85 cents for lo mein to $3.55 for lobster. *No alcoholic beverages. Open 7 days a week, 24 hours a day.*

★ PINK FOOT, THE
1053 Lexington Avenue (near 75th Street)   861-7725

The best thing about The Pink Foot, a small enterprise run, we are told, by a young couple from Belgium, is the desserts. There is a scrumptious thing called dame blanche with chocolate sauce and vanilla ice cream and tender cream caramel, and a good meringue glacé with ice cream and whipped cream.

A few other courses have been known to come off less well. A wedge of quiche Lorraine, for example, was spongy and overcooked; an order of snails would have been good if it had been seasoned with less salt.

The Pink Foot has a pizza parlor in front, and the main restaurant looks like an American version of a brasserie. There is limited seating—only 10 tables. The Pink Foot's pizza, in the opinion of one amateur, is better than most around town.

All dishes are à la carte, with main courses from about $1.25 for scrambled eggs to $4.50 for a steak maître d'hôtel. *No alcoholic beverages. Open 7 days a week.*

★ PIP'S
164 West 48th Street   582-1166

A few things about Pip's have come off so well, it is all the more annoying to note the things that haven't.

What did appeal were an appetizer of crisp, freshly cooked mushrooms; a pair of splendid, thick lamb chops, cooked to perfection; and a beautiful slice of rare roast beef. The green beans with almonds tasted as fresh and freshly cooked as anything encountered this side of a well-run home kitchen.

What jolted, among other things, was the ventilation, all the more apparent since most of the clientele (on one evening, at least) smoked cigars of such encompassing fumes and belligerent bad odor you rather wished for instant and merciful asphyxiation.

The salads were crisp but watery (improperly shaken); at one lunch, the corned beef with the overcooked cabbage tasted pre-sliced and dry; while the baked breast of chicken with sauce supreme accompanied by frozen peas and carrots and corn seemed catered by some airline.

Pip's is sort of Olde English or Olde Monke down to the stained-glass window in the rear.

All dishes are à la carte, with main courses at midday from about $2.25 to $7.95; in the evening, from about $3.95 to $7.95. *Cocktails, wines. Closed Saturday and Sunday.*
AE CB DC

★★ PIRAEUS, MY LOVE
117 West 57th Street   757-8847 and 757-8848

This is a seemingly fashionable Greek restaurant. The décor simulates the deck of a rather large yacht, including a gangplank entrance with rope and a dining deck with genuine glass-centered portholes illuminated with lights in nautical blue. The waiters wear blue and white jerseys, and there is piped-in Greek music and the pleasant scent of cucumber. Some of the dishes are interesting, including lamb in pastry with tomatoes, feta cheese, and tomatoes. The octopus in oil is excellent. If you like Greek dishes cooked in much oil, you will certainly enjoy the cold imam baldi, or eggplant goulash with onions and tomatoes. A vital disappointment at the restaurant was a main course of barbounia mesogiou, listed on the menu as a fish flown in by the Greek airline. At one dinner, it was overcooked and tasted as though it had been frozen. There is an à la carte menu, with main courses from about $3.50 to $5.50. *Cocktails, wines. Open 7 days a week. Lunch is served Monday through Friday only.*
AE BA CB DC

★ PIRO'S
1350 Madison Avenue (between 94th and 95th Streets)
534-3016

This is a neighborhood restaurant with an Italian menu. At its best, the food is very good. There is, for example, an excellent eggplant dish stuffed with a soft creamlike cheese, and the scampi are appetizing. On the debit side, the antipasto is uninspired. Piro's has a seating capacity of about 25. The cost of main dishes is from about $2.50 for spaghetti with garlic and oil to $5.00 for breast of chicken dishes. *There is no bar, but guests may bring their own wine or beer. Open for dinner only. Closed Sunday, Monday, and major holidays. Reservations are frequently essential.*

★★★ P. J. CLARKE'S
915 Third Avenue (at 55th Street)   PL 9-1650

Demolition and skyscraper construction is going on up to the walls of Clarke's but the two-story stone landmark still stands. It is a friendly, colorful place with original turn-of-the-century furnishings, and many New Yorkers regard it as a second home. It is celebrated as the setting for that old movie classic, *The Lost Weekend*, with Ray Milland. Some of the best hamburgers and chili in town may be had at noon in the barroom, and the food in the rear dining room is, considering the small kitchen, very good. The blackboard menu lists such diverse fare as steak Diane; spinach and mushroom salad; zucchini Benedict, which is to say with hollandaise; and chili and meat balls. The cost, à la carte, is from about $1.00 to $4.00. *Cocktails, wines. Open 7 days a week.*

★ P. J. MORIARTY
42 West 33rd Street (near Pennsylvania Station)
LO 3-3453

50 East 54th Street (between Park and Madison Avenues)
MU 8-6060

Third Avenue at 61st Street   TE 8-2438

1690 York Avenue (at 88th Street)   249-7555

Yankee and Irish cuisine, with steaks and chops as specialties of the house. All dishes are à la carte, with main luncheon courses from about $3.25 to $3.90; main dinner entrées from about $4.50 to $7.50. *Cocktails, wines. The restaurants on 33rd and 54th Streets are closed Saturday and Sunday. York Avenue branch is closed Sunday.*
AE CB DC

★★ P. J. O'HARA
869 Third Avenue (at 53rd Street)   EL *5-8122 and*
PL *5-8825*

The name may sound Irish, but the menu has such entries as veal parmigiana, curries, and an English mixed grill. The food is simply done and generally very good, whether it is roast beef or a basic tomato sauce for spaghetti. The fish and seafood dishes, in particular, are creditable. On the other hand, O'Hara's antipasto is dull and woefully overpriced. The restaurant's décor is pleasant, with a long bar and a good deal of nouveau-art stained glass. Luncheons, including main courses with dessert, are from about $2.85 to $3.05. Dinners are à la carte, with main courses from about $3.25 for half a broiled chicken to $7.50 for sirloin steak. *Cocktails, wines. Open 7 days a week. Closed Christmas.*
AE BA CB DC MC

★★ PLAKA EAST
208 East 60th Street   *371-4851*

An arched entrance, stucco walls, and a fake fireplace create a plain, modest atmosphere at this pleasant Greek restaurant.

Someone in the kitchen is obviously competent, but seems to have been told to use a light hand with oil and seasonings. As a result, the avgolemono soup was thin and tasted more of chicken broth than of lemon and egg yolks. A salad of excellent crisp greens, feta cheese, and Greek olives needed retossing with more seasonings.

A good representative assorted appetizer plate included taramosalata (the fish roe spread), scordalia (garlic salad), melitzanosalata (eggplant salad), and dolmades (stuffed vine leaves).

The roast loin of lamb did not come off so well. It was overcooked, a fault noted in several offerings, including an otherwise good barbecued spring lamb. Both the sautéed sweetbreads and liver dish, and capama (loin lamb chops in a tomato sauce), were tasty.

The Formica-topped tables, bare at luncheon, are close together, and the service tends to be casual, but friendly.

Luncheon and dinner menus are à la carte, with main courses at noon ranging from $1.95 for feta-tomato omelet to $3.50 for shish kebab. At dinner, the moussaka (eggplant and lamb) is $2.95 and barbecued spring lamb, $4.25. *There is no bar, but guests may bring their own wine. The restaurant is open 7 days a week from noon to midnight.*

PLAZA HOTEL
59th Street and Fifth Avenue PL 9-3000

★★**Trader Vic's** see page 318

★★**Oak Room** is a fine-looking room with a masculine appeal, and the food is of the same quality as that found in the Plaza's **The Green Tulip.** That is to say, it is, by and large, competently prepared. The less complicated dishes come off best. A prix fixe dinner is $10.50. Main courses at midday go from about $3.90 for an omelet to $10.40 for sirloin steak. Entrées in the evening from about $4.75 for half a broiled chicken to $10.40 for the sirloin. *Cocktails, wines. Open 7 days a week. Luncheon is not served Saturday and Sunday during July and August.* **Oyster Bar.** At first glance, it seemed all there: the handsome Victorian décor, turn-of-the-century murals, comfortable banquettes, and a spacious bar in the center where customers may dine on oysters and whatever else the menu provides. The menu is interesting. And one hastens to add that the oysters, either the blue points or Cape Cods, are as chilled and fresh and fine as you'll find anywhere in the city. But, alas, that about sums up the praise. Almost all the tables are woefully close together. The service, if you can call it that, is ponderous and clumsy. A curry of seafood was so highly salted it was returned to the kitchen to be replaced by shrimp jambalaya.

All dishes at the Oyster Bar are à la carte, with main courses at noon from about $2.75 to $6.50; in the evening, from about $2.90 to $7.25. *Cocktails, wines. Open 7 days a week.*
CB

★★ PONTE'S STEAK HOUSE
39 Desbrosses Street   226-4621

To speak of out-of-the-way restaurants is to speak of Ponte's Steak House, but the food is worth the maneuvers to get to this restaurant on the West Side waterfront. The easiest access is perhaps via the IRT-Seventh Avenue subway, ascending at Canal Street and walking two blocks south.

There is no printed menu at Ponte's, but rather a blackboard where the day's specialties are listed. Steaks are anchor (and praiseworthy) items, but one remembers with great pleasure a lentil soup as a first course, an outstanding dish of broiled sea bass with freshly cooked green broccoli, and an excellent dish of manicotti with ricotta filling and an expertly made tomato sauce.

Ponte's is upstairs, and access to the dining room is by a staircase with flowing, hanging plastic ferns. The dining room has a masculine look. The walls are decked out with reproductions of paintings whose subjects include gypsies, flowers, and clowns.

All dishes are à la carte, with main courses at midday from about $2.75 to $6.75; in the evening, from about $4.25 to $9.00. *Cocktails, wines. Luncheon is not served Saturday. Closed Sunday, Christmas, and New Year's Day.*
AE CB DC MC

★ PORT ARTHUR
7 Mott Street   WO 2-5890

The best thing about the Port Arthur, one of the oldest restaurants in Chinatown, is the décor. It is heavy and antique, with much use of mother-of-pearl, hand-carved wood, and stained glass. The menu may seem on the stereotyped side, but the food is competently prepared. There is excellent shrimp broiled with bacon, for example, and boned duckling with almonds. The sauces seem a trifle thick. There are complete luncheons that are a bargain, costing from 90 cents to $1.25. A la carte dishes cost from $2.50 to $4.95. *Cocktails, wines. Only à la carte items are available Saturday, from 11:00 a.m. Closed Sunday.*

★ PORTOFINO
206 Thompson Street   GR 3-9752 *and* 475-9241

The Portofino is a three-room Italian restaurant, one of several passably good ones in Greenwich Village. The food here is relatively inexpensive and served in abundance. The antipasto dishes tend to be robustly flavored, but the main courses, such as boneless chicken Portofino or scaloppine with butter and lemon, are very well-cooked. The menu is à la carte, with main courses from about $1.75 to $5.50 for steak. *Cocktails, wines. Open 7 days a week. Closed Thanksgiving and Christmas.*
AE BA CB DC MC

★ PRESS BOX
139 East 45th Street   YU 6-4565

Predominantly American cuisine with steaks and chops as the prime entrées. Complete luncheons from about $4.50 to $7.00. The à la carte menu, available for luncheon and dinner, lists entrées from about $3.50 to $6.50. *Cocktails, wines. Lunch served Monday through Friday only; dinner, 7 days a week.*
Most major credit cards.

★ PRIME BURGER

536 Madison Avenue (between 54th and 55th Streets)
PL 3-4214
5 East 51st Street   759-4730

In a city the size of New York, it is remarkable how few enterprises offer first-rate hamburgers. The Prime Burgers' hamburgers are small but very good, and so is most of the other food. The menu lists such foods as eggs in several styles, salads, steak tartare, and chili con carne. The two restaurants are frequently crowded and there is often a wait for a counter seat. The cost of the principal dishes ranges from about 95 cents for a hamburger to $1.55 for English-style fish and chips. The restaurants offer a take-out service. *No alcoholic beverages. Closed Sunday and all legal holidays.*

★★ PROMENADE CAFE

Rockefeller Center   PL 7-5730

As someone was saying for the dozenth or so time recently, New York is not the ideal city for open-air dining. Too much soot and grime, carbon monoxide, heat, and humidity. A rare exception is this spa where food and drinks are served to the sound of a gushing fountain beneath the statue of Prometheus plus music groups on a bandstand. You know. It's at Rockefeller Center, where they skate in winter.

Unfortunately, even the Promenade Café isn't spared on exceptionally muggy days or when it rains. In any event, it's certainly a pleasant place to dine when the temperature is right. And the menu shows imagination. International more or less. Greek things such as an appetizer of carp roe with lemon (taramosalata) and baked lamb moussaka with eggplant. There are curried chicken, at times, and stuffed breast of veal like a galantine. And salmon steak with dill mayonnaise and a fish fry. And sandwiches and omelets.

There are views of skyscrapers and you sit under umbrellas with floral patterns listening to mariachi music or whatever. The management makes a very good sangria, the chilled wine drink, and the wine list is fairly priced.

The Promenade Café is joined by two indoor cafés with the same menu. The indoor cafés also offer a special luncheon priced at $3.95. Otherwise, all dishes are à la carte, with main courses from about $2.95 for an omelet to $6.95 for roast prime ribs of beef. *Cocktails, wines. Open 7 days a week.*
Most major credit cards.

PROOF OF THE PUDDING
1165 First Avenue (at 64th Street)   421-5440

For want of a better word, you might call this edition of the Proof of the Pudding a "fun" restaurant. It has a modern look, with shiny plastic banquettes, marble table tops, mirrors and sconces and miniature candles. When the young and attractive owners describe the food, it sounds like heavenly relish, but the food itself is of a fantasy sort. For example, one dish, so help me Hannah, was made with shrimp, lemon, dill, noodles, and a maraschino cherry in a cream sauce. How does that strike you as an ice cream sundae? The portions are large. When a waiter produced one order of overcooked lamb, it was with the greeting, "If you get through that, I say 'bon voyage' to you." Giving credit where it's due, a salmon steak with béarnaise at one lunch was good and in beautiful contrast to a rather tough shrimp appetizer, at the same table, with a lime sauce that smacked strongly of commercial mayonnaise. The cocktails, served in wine glasses, are gigantic. There is an outdoor dining terrace. A complete lunch is around $3.00. Prix fixe dinner is $5.50 before 6:30 weekdays and $7.50 on weekends. *Cocktails, wines. Open 7 days a week.*
Most major credit cards.

★★★★ QUO VADIS
26 East 63rd Street   TE *8-0590 and 838-0591*

The Quo Vadis not only has one of the finest kitchens in Manhattan, but the management maintains the most rigid standards for the conduct of its admirable enterprise. The menu is scrupulously put together, from the fondue bruxelloise (fried cheese) and the exceptional specialty, eels in green sauce, through entrées and roasts, crêpes suzette, and soufflés. The service is generally polished at Quo Vadis, and, if there is to be the slightest criticism, it may be that the acoustics in the main dining room permits a certain din at peak dining periods. All dishes are à la carte, with main courses at midday from about $3.25 to $4.00; in the evening, from about $6.75 to $9.00. *Cocktails, wines. Closed on Saturday and Sunday in the summer. Closed holidays.*
AE   CB   DC

RAINBOW ROOM
30 Rockefeller Plaza   PL *7-9090*

There is one thing to be said for certain about the Rainbow Room. The windows on a clear night open onto some of the most glorious views of the city. The food is another matter. The menu is broad and offers an extensive assortment of four courses for one fixed price, $11.75. *Cocktails, wines. Open 7 days a week for dinner. Brunch, at $6.50, is served Saturday and Sunday from noon to 3.00 p.m.*
All major credit cards.

★★ RAJMAHAL RESTAURANT
124 Fourth Avenue (between 12th and 13th Streets)
473-9086

This is markedly unpretentious Pakistani-Indian restaurant in the East Village. Specialties include bhunda dishes, thickened curries made of beef, lamb, chicken, or shrimp; birani dishes with a somewhat more

delicate sauce; kurma dishes made with sweet spices and yogurt; and kebab dishes. The Rajmahal has a kitchen that is generally excellent and offers in addition to main courses an assortment of breads and condiments. There is a complete luncheon that costs $1.50; complete dinners from $3.25 to $5.00. A la carte dishes are priced from $2.00 to $3.50. *Wines, beers. Luncheon is not served Sunday.*
AE DC

★ RATTAZZI
9 East 48th Street   PL *3-5852*

This is a worthwhile and popular Italian restaurant. All food is à la carte, with main luncheon dishes from about $3.45 to $8.00 for steak; dinner entrées from about $4.00 to $8.25. *Cocktails, wines. Closed Saturday, Sunday, and major holidays.*
All major credit cards.

★★ RED COACH GRILL
784 Seventh Avenue (at 51st Street)   CI *5-2500*

This grill, in the City Squire Motor Inn, has a pleasant atmosphere contrived to resemble an English rustic inn. The roast beef is of excellent quality, and the lobster and shrimp dishes are recommended particularly. There are special luncheons with soup, main course, salad, and beverage that cost about $2.50. Most of the items are à la carte with main courses from about $2.10 to $5.45. Complete dinners cost from about $5.80 to $6.35; à la carte main dishes from about $4.60 to $8.25. Supper, served from 11:00 P.M. to 1:00 A.M., is à la carte with entrées from about $1.95 to $5.95. *Cocktails, wines. Closed Christmas.*
AE CB DC MC

★ REIDY'S RESTAURANT
22 East 54th Street   PL *3-2419*

The most impressive thing about Reidy's Restaurant is the honesty of the establishment. It is a long, narrow, informal place, with watercolors, portraits, and caricatures on the wall.

The tables are close together and some of the banquettes are not for solid comfort. Nevertheless, the welcome is courteous and warm, the food is reasonably priced, and in a town like Manhattan that has its virtues.

The portions are copious, Irish pub style. The dishes are along the lines of corned beef and cabbage, prime ribs of beef, calf's liver, roast turkey, and steaks. It is one of the few places in the city where you can get a shrimp cocktail for 95 cents.

All dishes are à la carte, with main courses at midday from about $2.35 to $4.50 for steak; in the evening, from about $2.25 to $4.50. *Cocktails, wines. Closed Sunday and major holidays.*

★★ RENE PUJOL RESTAURANT
321 West 51st Street 246-3023

When the name Pujol is connected with a theater district restaurant, one expects a small, bistro-style place with personal, courteous service, and competently prepared French food. The René Pujol Restaurant is no exception. Various members of the family also run Du Midi, Au Tunnel, and Les Pyrénées.

Wooden beams, bare brick walls, a fireplace, and antique accessories create an attractive and comfortable country atmosphere in the main dining room. A small tiled and stuccoed rear area is good for small private groups, but is the passageway to the kitchen.

The choice of appetizers and soups is essentially the same at luncheon and dinner and has included a creditable country pâté; a first-rate coquilles St. Jacques (scallops in wine sauce); a delightfully aromatic, creamy-smooth lobster bisque; and a pleasant tomato and bean soup.

The à la carte specials, which change at every meal, seem to be chosen and prepared with extra care. For example, a striped bass in fresh tarragon wine sauce at luncheon was superb. Late diners may find the first special of the evening gone, but a piquant l'escalopine de veau aux chanterelles, veal scallops with French mushrooms, is tasty, and it is always on the menu. The lobster in whisky sauce was disappointing, but a fillet of sole with almonds came off very well.

The chocolate mousse had a strange consistency and resembled partly melted chocolate ice cream. Perhaps desserts are not the chef's forte, because an apple tart and a portion of Paris Brest (cream-filled choux pastry ring) were only fair.

Complete luncheons are $3.50 to $5.00; complete dinners are $5.50 to $8.00. *Cocktails, wines. Open for lunch and dinner Monday through Saturday. Closed Sunday. AE*

★ RESTAURANT TOKYO
342 Lexington Avenue (between 39th and 40th Streets)
697-8330

This Japanese restaurant seems to be having growing pains, particularly with its menu. On one visit at midday, the Tokyo pot and sukiyaki, both of which are cooked on portable electric grills, were available. On the next visit at noon, the waiter explained that no dishes would be cooked at the table during the main luncheon period because it is too time-consuming. Thus, one had a choice of such dishes as broiled dumplings with pork fillings, chicken or pork with eggs on rice, fried shrimp on rice, and noodles in soup. Where Japanese restaurants are concerned, New Yorkers have a right to be spoiled. There are so many good ones. The new Tokyo is pleasant enough, and the food quite edible. But it is, for the most part, conventional.

One dish that didn't come off well recently was that Tokyo pot, apparently the Japanese version of fondue bourguignonne: meats, seafood, and vegetables on skewers to be cooked in hot oil at the table. The meat for the dish was raggedly cut, and the beef was chewy. On the other hand, the soup with noodles, garnished with tender slices of roast pork, shrimp, spinach, and slices of brown bamboo shoot, was excellent.

Complete luncheons are priced from $3.00 to $4.50; complete dinners from $4.00 to $5.00. A la carte dishes are priced from about $2.00 to $3.00. *Closed Saturday.*
AE DC

★★ REUBEN'S
6 East 58th Street   PL 9-5650

This celebrated landmark is best-known for its cheesecake and sandwiches, both of which are inspired. Frequent entrées on the menu include cold gefüllte fish with pickled beets and horseradish, hot turkey drumstick, and roast beef hash with poached egg. The main dining room is spacious, with a conservative décor. Sandwiches from $3.10 to $4.65. Dinners are à la carte with main dishes from about $2.65 to $8.10. *Cocktails, wines. The restaurant is open Friday from 9:00 a.m. until 5:00 a.m., Monday through Thursday from 9:00 a.m. to 5:00 a.m. Reservations are accepted.*
AE DC

★ RIGHT BANK PROVINCIAL, THE
822 Madison Avenue (at 69th Street)   RH 4-9256

This is the upstairs, more polished, and more expensive version of the Right Bank Restaurant. The auberge-style décor is simple and handsome. The walls are covered with fabric in floral patterns. There are swag draperies and oval-backed chairs.

There is a curious fact about the kitchen. The quality of the food preparation seems to swing like a pendulum. One recalls an excellent beurreck, a French-style stuffed Turkish pastry, with chopped shrimp and mushrooms in waferlike phyllo pastry; and an excellent toulousaine preparation in a nest also made with phyllo pastry rather than puff pastry and served, oddly, with rice. The soups, too, seem generally excellent, including one soup du jour, a watercress, and the onion soup gratinée.

There is less enthusiasm for a quiche Lorraine with a spongy filling; one noontime dish of goujonettes of sole, vividly overcooked; an undistinguished veal scallop zingara served with canned or bottled petits pois; and so on.

The waiters seem to know next to nothing about wines and how to pour them. But the surroundings are pleasant and the food at its best is quite good.

Luncheons are à la carte, with main courses from about $2.25 to $4.50. There are complete dinners priced from about $5.75 and up. *Cocktails, wines. Closed Sunday, July 4, and Labor Day.*
AE CB DC MC

★ RIGHT BANK RESTAURANT, THE
822 Madison Avenue (at 69th Street) RH 4-9630

There is a nice ambience in this downstairs bistro with its checked tablecloths, modern art on the walls, and a clientele—particularly at midday—that seems happily endowed with a joie de vivre, albeit that of Madison Avenue rather than the Rue de Rivoli. There is piped-in music, French, of course, and the menu is laudably brief, with 8 or so main dishes, sandwiches, and salads.

One of the most commendable dishes sampled was the pâté maison, from a nice-textured, freshly made, and well-seasoned loaf. The main dishes seem wholly edible, although largely lackluster, including a minute steak ordered rare and served medium-well and a scaloppine of veal with tomato sauce. There are only 18 tables at the Right Bank and the waitresses are comely.

All dishes are à la carte, with main courses at midday from about $2.00 to $3.50. In the evening, from about $3.75 to $6.50. *Cocktails, wines. Closed Sunday.*
AE CB DC MC

★ ROCCO RESTAURANT
181 Thompson Street   GR 3-9267

This restaurant, near several off-Broadway theaters in Greenwich Village, is of the genre sometimes referred to as "family-style Italian." The menu is South Italian-style, and some of the dishes are industriously spiced with herbs and spices, such as garlic and orégano. The dishes are à la carte and include a very good but plain antipasto at $1.75, a special antipasto at $2.00, steamed clams marinara at $2.00 and—the most expensive entrée—sirloin steak at $5.50. *Cocktails, wines. Open noon until 11:30 p.m. every day.*
All major credit cards.

★ ROMA NOVA
171 East 33rd Street   683-8745

It seems fairly obvious that the chef of this small restaurant has more talent and inspiration than some of his colleagues who head the kitchens of Italian-restaurant hideaways in Manhattan. The fault here seems to lie largely in the service, which vacillates between smiles and casual indifference.

On one evening, a hot antipasto, a course of pasta, and two main courses were ordered. The hot antipasto was hot, well-seasoned, and embraced stuffed mushrooms, eggplant, shrimp, baked clams, and so on. But the fettuccine Roma Nova—ordered à la carte—was not served as a separate course, as it would be in any conscientious Italian restaurant. It was brought to the table simultaneously with boneless chicken parmigiana and a scaloppine with lemon. By the time the pasta had been eaten, the other dishes were tepid, the cheese on the chicken congealing. What a bore.

In any event, there is a seating capacity for 32 and the décor is pleasant enough with fake brick walls and bamboo.

Most dishes are à la carte. Main courses at midday are

priced from $2.50 for spaghetti with meat sauce to $4.50 for steak. A complete lunch is around $3.50. In the evening, prices range from $3.75 for pasta to $5.95 for sirloin. *Cocktails, wines. Luncheon is not served Saturday. Closed Sunday.*
Most major credit cards.

★★ ROMEO SALTA
30 West 56th Street   CI 6-5772

Romeo Salta is now in its new quarters. It is doubtful that you will find finer, more conscientiously made pasta dishes anywhere in America today.

On the other hand, the restaurant leaves much to be desired; but more about that later.

At a dinner, one meal included a superb fettuccine; an outstanding veal dish, "Mont Blanc," with small white chops lightly sautéed and delicate, served with polenta (a bit too sweet for my palate), artichoke hearts (cooked from a frozen state, but good), and sautéed mushrooms. Another main course included an excellent chicken dish, called Scarpariello, the chicken in small pieces, delicately seasoned and sautéed—the chicken livers, too—and served with the artichoke hearts.

The veal Villa d'Este with eggplant is regarded by some as the restaurant's finest dish.

The cannelloni Anna Maria Sabatini may be the kitchen's most popular dish but it is sometimes served with crusty edges and a none-too-distinguished meat filling.

Physically, the new Romeo Salta is nondescript, large, and with some of the tables a bit too close for comfort. The restaurant also has certain vulgar aspects, including the plastic plants at the entrance.

And the service can best be termed confused. When the captain was asked for his recommendation on wine, he came back with a perfectly dull, patronizing, and salesmanlike suggestion that he offer us a nice bottle of Chianti. When a napkin fell to the floor, the waiter, rather than replacing it with a fresh one, picked it off the floor and handed it to the customer.

If Romeo Salta were not priced in the luxury class category of New York restaurants, such matters would seem incidental, such criticism niggling. In any restaurant where the food is in all respects consummately prepared and the service impeccable, the cost is, for those who can afford it, incidental. But a dinner for two at Salta's with one cocktail each, one order of fettuccine, two main courses with a decent bottle of Bardolino, one order of cheese and two orders of coffee cost in excess of $38.00.

Luncheons are fixed price, with complete meals priced from about $7.50 to $8.50. Dinners are à la carte, with pasta dishes from about $5.75 to $6.50; main courses from about $7.50 to $12.00. *Cocktails, wines. Closed Sunday.*
AE DC CB

★ ROSETTA'S RESTAURANT
502 Avenue of the Americas (near West 12th Street)
YU 9-9442

This is a small, fairly pleasant Italian restaurant in Greenwich Village. The food may not be distinguished, but it is nonetheless palatable and reasonably priced. Complete luncheons from about $2.75 to $3.50; à la carte dinner entrées from about $2.50 to $5.50. *Cocktails, wines. Closed Monday.*

★★ RUC RESTAURANT
312 East 72nd Street   RH 4-9185

A small, frequently crowded Czechoslovak restaurant with a kitchen that is generally commendable. The veal goulash, pork chops à la Bratislava, and roast duckling are well-prepared. The palacinky, or Czechoslovak version of crêpes suzette, are distinctive and consequently very popular. The menu is prix fixe, with complete meals from about $3.50 to $6.50. *Cocktails, wines. Open from 4:00 p.m. to 10:00 p.m., Monday through Friday; and from noon until 10:00 p.m., Saturday and Sunday. From May through September, a garden is open.*

★★ RUGANTINO
55 West 56th Street   581-5615 and 581-5725

This is a dimly lit, neat, and simply decorated dining spot with food better than that found in most small Italian restaurants. The cannelloni, tender noodles stuffed with meat vaguely seasoned with nutmeg, is especially good. And the osso buco, or veal bone, is recommended. Luncheon is à la carte, with main courses from about $2.50 for green noodles and meat sauce to $5.00 for filet mignon. A la carte entrées at dinner range from about $3.25 to $7.00. *Cocktails, wines. Closed Easter, July 4, and Christmas.*
AE   CB   DC   MC

★★ RUNNING FOOTMAN, THE
133 East 61st Street   838-3939

This is a fashionable restaurant, the enterprise of Michael Pearman, the former owner of Michael's Pub. The décor is bright, interesting, and offbeat. It is a three-level restaurant with a bar opening into a small dining area. This leads into a main dining room with walls painted "hot salmon" color. The lighting is dim, with chandeliers and globe lamps mounted on steer horns. The steaks and chops are excellent, and one of the most interesting dishes is listed as a chickenburger. The menus are à la carte. Main courses at dinner are priced from about $4.75 to $8.50; luncheon and supper dishes from $2.80 to $5.80. *Cocktails, wines. Closed Sunday.*

★★ RUSSIAN TEA ROOM
150 West 57th Street   CO 5-0947

This is not a tearoom in the usual sense of the word, and it is probably the best Russian restaurant in the city. The kitchen does not have extraordinary merit and yet

the food is generally good. Specialties of the house include such familiars as borscht with sour cream, blinis with red caviar, and beef à la Stroganoff. One of the best dishes, served only at Wednesday luncheon, is the Siberian Pelmeny. These are ground beef balls flavored with dill, wrapped in pastry, and cooked in broth, the Russian version of wonton or ravioli. They are available either served in broth or with a mustard sauce and sour cream. The cost of main luncheon dishes with dessert and beverage is from about $3 to $6.50. There are complete dinners from about $5.50 to $6.75; à la carte entrées from about $3.50. Supper is served from 9:30 P.M. to 1:00 A.M., Saturday to 2:00 A.M. *Cocktails, wines.*
AE   CB   DC

★★ SAKURA CHAYA
198 Columbus Avenue (at 69th Street)   874-8536

An evaluation of this laudable Japanese restaurant will need an explanation. We were taken there by a Japanese photographer who dines there frequently and is well-acquainted with the management. On other visits there have been no more than 6 other customers, and the food and service have been leisurely, if not to say devoted.

The chef—a man with pride in his profession—is a genius in shaping sashimi or raw fish to resemble roses and chrysanthemums. The Sakura Chaya is conceivably the best source for sashimi in the city today. The chef also makes at times fascinating appetizers with a white bean paste and scallions.

The menu is for the most part predictable with its sukiyaki, teriyaki, tempura, and yakitori dinners. None of the dishes such as sukiyaki are cooked at table, as they are under the best of circumstances, but rather in the adjoining kitchen. But the chef prepares special dishes each day, on one occasion poached cod in a broth that was excellent.

The point is that the Sakura Chaya is at present an uncommonly good restaurant.

There is one menu, with complete dinners priced from $2.30 to $4.95; à la carte dishes from about $1.75 for kushi katsu, or skewered pork with vegetables, to $3.25 for sukiyaki. *There is no bar, but customers may bring in beer or wine. Closed Monday.*

★★ SAM BOK
127 West 43rd Street   582-7944

This is a large, unprepossessing, but interesting Korean restaurant in the theater district. The food is both unusual and good, although it will certainly not appeal to all palates. Much of it is highly spiced and there is a liberal use of garlic.

The menu includes sinsullo ($5.00), perhaps the most famous of Korean dishes. It involves beef, mushrooms, green vegetables, shellfish, and so forth, simmered at the table. There are charcoal grilled dishes, skewered dishes, and noodle dishes, all well if not subtly seasoned. The kimchi, pickled cabbage, is powerfully hot with pepper and good. The broth for the soups is freshly made and excellent.

The menu also lists numerous Japanese dishes. The Sam Bok's service is by sweet-faced, smiling young Korean women in traditional native gowns.

Main courses at midday cost from about $2.00 to $4.00; in the evening, a complete dinner is about $6.95. *Cocktails, wines. Open 7 days a week.*
DC

★★ SAM PAM
45 West 33rd Street   239-4127

The number of Chinese restaurants of superior quality in Manhattan sometimes seems too good to be true. This is a large, modern place of plastic and paneled wood décor and fairly somber.

All of the dishes sampled here have had a certain merit: the deep-fried crab hors d'oeuvre; the dem sem; the chicken wing appetizer; and, among the main courses, the hong shue fish, whole and batter-fried, was excellent; the roast pork with bean curd was tender and had good flavor.

One order of young chow wonton, an elaborate wonton soup with several kinds of meat and fish, was too bland in all respects, but it was acceptable. One stronger criticism, although the food is good, is that the kitchen does seem to use more cornstarch than is absolutely necessary.

There are complete luncheons at the Sam Pam and the cost is from about $1.85 to $4.25. All dishes on the principal menu are à la carte, with main dishes from about $1.90 to $5.95. *Cocktails, wines. Closed Sunday.*
AE DC

★ SAM WO
39 Mott Street   WO 2-8750

There is no apparent end to the good restaurants in Chinatown with a clean but frowsy atmosphere. What would the place be without them? The Sam Wo is cordially recommended for all categories—noodles, pork, beef, poultry, or fish. The restaurant is open day and night and guests might be asked to share their table. The menu is à la carte with main dishes from about $1.00 for roast pork lo mein (with noodles) to $5.00 for lichee duck. *There is no bar. Closed for Chinese New Year.*

★★★ SAN MARCO
52 West 55th Street   CI 6-5340

Some of the personal ambience once enjoyed by the San Marco has been lost. Dishes that deserve it are not invariably prepared tableside these days, and one plate of pasta requested with truffles was returned for want of a truffle flavor. The San Marco remains, however, possibly the best Italian restaurant in New York. It has a well-rounded menu and the food is generally first-rate, whether it is pasta, meat, or fowl. It has been said that you can judge the quality of a restaurant by its veal, and judged

on that alone the San Marco would be remarkable. The chef would do well, on the other hand, to make his own soup stock. The soups taste altogether as though they were made from a commercial base. There are complete luncheons from about $4.75 for vermicelli with tomato and garlic to $7.25 for various steaks Italian-style. Dinners are à la carte, with main dishes from about $4.75 to $8.00. *Cocktails, wines. Closed Sunday and, during July and August, for luncheon on Saturday. Closed major holidays and 2 weeks in August.*
AE CB DC

★★ SAN MARINO
236 East 53rd Street   PL 9-4130

At its best, and the best would include the marinara sauce for imported langoustine and the broiled jumbo squab, the food at San Marino is excellent. And if the food in the main is very good, it is in contrast to the reception, which is at times indifferent, and the service, which, when the restaurant is crowded, is impatient and hurried. The cost of a full-course luncheon is from about $4.50 to $5.00. The dinner menu is à la carte, with main courses from about $3.25 to $8.50. *Cocktails, wines. On Saturday, the restaurant opens at 5:00 p.m. Closed Sunday, legal holidays, and 3 weeks in August.*

★★ SAN REMO
393 Eighth Avenue (between 29th and 30th Streets)
565-6161

The things one admires here are an excellent cold seafood salad made with squid and mussels and shrimp; well-cooked chicken Florentine—the chicken batter-cooked and served with mushrooms in a lemon sauce; and genuinely excellent pork chops Milan-style, breaded and served with a light wine sauce. The red snapper in green sauce (made with spinach) was interesting and fresh, although the texture of the fish was a bit soft.

The things one deplores at the San Remo are the side dishes of spaghetti or spaghettini that have invariably been overcooked; the fact that the waiter assures you they serve espresso that turns out to be filter coffee; and there is harp and accordion music in the evening that is painfully loud in such close quarters, although the combo plays with talent and enthusiasm. The tables are tablecloth to tablecloth.

Complete luncheons are priced from $3.25 to $6.25; complete dinners from about $4.50 to $6.95. *Cocktails, wines. Luncheon is served from noon to 3:00 p.m., Monday through Friday. Dinner is served from 5:00 to 11:00 p.m., Tuesday through Saturday; 5:00 to 9:00 p.m. on Sunday.*
AE DC MC

★★ SANTA LUCIA
160 West 54th Street 586-2484

This is another of the noteworthy, small Italian restaurants of Manhattan with an interesting menu. Among the unusual first courses, for example, there are warm, sautéed escarole and cold, fried tripe with lemon. The sauces here are excellent. Three-course luncheons are from about $3.50 to $4.25; dinners are à la carte. The à la carte menu is available at all times, and main courses are priced from about $4.25 to $8.00. In summer, an open-air garden is in use. *Cocktails, wines. Closed Saturday, Sunday, and major holidays.*
AE CB DC

★★ SARDI'S
234 West 44th Street LA 4-0707

This is almost without question the nation's most famous restaurant for celebrity-watching. The atmosphere is convivial, and, all things considered, it is a reasonably priced restaurant with moderately good food. The best-known specialties are, perhaps, the cannelloni à la Sardi, hot shrimp à la Sardi, and deviled beef bones. A la carte

items at luncheon are $3.00 and up; at dinner, from about $4.50 to $9.75. *Cocktails, wines. Closed Sunday.*
AE   CB   DC

★ SAVOIA
519 Second Avenue (at 29th Street)   MU 6-5848

This is a simple, earthy, and honest Italian restaurant of the "neighborhood" variety, and, if you like that kind of place, it is altogether pleasant. The menu itself—with its pasta dishes, various veal dishes, and so forth—will seem familiar, but the sauces are well-seasoned and the food in general is cooked with care. Pizza is one of the most popular specialties of the Savoia, and it is very good. The menu is à la carte, with main courses at lunch from about $1.50 for ziti; in the evening, entrées go from $2.00 to $7.00. *Cocktails, wines. Open 7 days a week.*
AE   DC   MC

★★ SAYAT NOVA
91 Charles Street   OR 5-7364

At Sayat Nova there is a garden dining area that is illuminated, even in winter, and offers a handsome view for those sitting near the rear windows. The food is Armenian, interesting, and generally excellent.

There are well-made cold appetizers like the boureg or flaky turnovers filled with cheese, stuffed grape leaves, stuffed mussels, and so on. There are good soups, some with meat balls and lemon, others of yogurt, and a hearty one of lentil. Then there are the eggplant and lamb dishes for main courses, including the moussaka with eggplant and ground lamb.

A la carte dishes are priced from about $6.25. The cost of complete meals is from about $9.00. *Cocktails, wines. Open only for dinner, 7 days a week. Closed major holidays.*

★★ SAY ENG LOOK
1 East Broadway   732-0796

Almost all the restaurants of New York's Chinatown can claim one distinction or another. This one, however, has more than the accustomed share. Two excellent dishes are tiny shrimp cooked with sesame oil and crab with egg sauce. The crab dish is tedious to eat, but delicious. There is a single menu for lunch and dinner; all dishes are à la carte, with main courses from about $1.95 for shredded pork Shanghai-style to $2.95 for sea cucumber with crab meat. Sea cucumber is a long, forbidding-looking ocean creature sometimes called sea slug. The service at the Say Eng Look wavers between friendly and indifferent. *No alcoholic beverages.*

★★ SCANDIA
227 West 45th Street (in the Piccadilly Hotel)
CI 6-6600

New York does not boast a Scandinavian restaurant to equal those of Denmark or Sweden, but this is one of the best the city has to offer. The restaurant is in the heart of the theater district. Before dining, guests should read the explanation on the back of the menu on how to enjoy a smorgasbord. Complete smorgasbord at luncheon is $3.95; at dinner, $6.50; at supper (10:00 P.M. to 1:00 A.M.), $4.50. A la carte entrées from $2.10 at lunch. Prix fixe dinners go from $5.50 up. *Cocktails, wines, akvavit, and Danish beer. Open 7 days a week.*
AE   DC   UC

★ SCHAEFER'S
1202 Lexington Avenue (between 81st and 82nd Streets)
734-9887

This German-American restaurant may not be much to look at, but it has "home-style" cooking that is inexpensive and good. The menu at times offers such bourgeois fare as homemade head cheese, oxtail ragout, pigs' knuckles, spätzle, and potato pancake. Main dishes cost from about $1.45 to $3.10, and the portions are copious. Schaefer's is a small restaurant with only 4 tables. There is also a dining counter. Breakfast is served from 7:00 A.M. *There is no bar, but domestic and imported beers are available. Closed Saturday, Sunday, and major holidays.*

★ SCHRAFFT'S RESTAURANTS

There are 28 Schrafft's Restaurants in the New York area, with many foods that should appeal to the young set—particularly the ice cream, which, over the course of a year, comes in about 40 flavors. The sundaes, notably hot fudge and butterscotch, seem to be special favorites. A day at the Central Park Zoo might include a visit to Schrafft's at 625 Madison Avenue. The Stock Exchange is next door to the restaurant at 48 Broad Street. The Schrafft's at 990 Madison Avenue is around the corner from the Metropolitan Museum. Luncheon is à la carte, with main courses from about $1.35 to $2.50. Club dinners, without appetizer, are about $3.95 to $4.50; à la carte entrées from about $2.75 to $6.95. *Cocktails, wines. Closing days differ for the various restaurants; all are closed Christmas.*
AE DC

★ SCOOP, THE
210 East 43rd Street   MU 2-0483

The Scoop is a steak house and Italian restaurant, and at noon and evening it is as festive as a Roman candle. Patrons at times seem willingly to wait for tables for as long as half an hour. There must be something to justify such popularity. There are pleasant surroundings with wine-red walls hung with obvious art.

The antipasto is well-made-standard and enormous enough for two. The breast of chicken parmigiana is tasty, although a top layer of cheese became a trifle dry as the dish approached room temperature. The flavor of a broiled sirloin steak was excellent and the meat was admirably grilled, but certain bites were chewy. A dish of spaghetti was well-cooked and its tomato sauce good.

A la carte entrées at noon are about $4.00 to $7.50. In the evening main courses run from $6.75 to $9.25. *Cocktails, wines. Luncheon is not served Saturday. Closed Sunday and major holidays.*
AE DC

★★ SEA-FARE OF THE AEGEAN
25 West 56th Street LT 1-0540

In view of the considerable financial outlay for this restaurant, the décor is disappointing. All dishes are à la carte, with main courses from about $4.45 to $10.75. There are also daily specials. *Cocktails, wines. Closed Thanksgiving.*
AE CB DC MC

★ SHALIMAR
39 East 29th Street 889-1977

This is a nice-looking, Indian restaurant, and, if all the food were equal to the best, it would be excellent indeed. There's a very good appetizer called samosa, a pastry filled with well-spiced meat or vegetable; an interesting tandoori chicken; and commendable desserts. The décor of the Shalimar is honest and pleasant with white rough stucco walls.

There are two faults that seem basic to the Shalimar: The various curries are bland and have a sameness of flavor, and some of the dishes seem woefully overcooked, particularly the shrimp. Even the tandoori chicken—marinated in spices and baked—seemed to have been left in the oven too long. Among the desserts, the firni (a custard-like, rose-water-flavored affair with pistachios) and the gulab jaman (deep-fried pastry balls in honey syrup) seemed special.

There is a special luncheon (without dessert) priced at $1.45. Complete dinners, which may be ordered throughout the day, are priced from about $3.25 to $4.50. The price of an à la carte main course includes pilaf, vegetable, and condiments. At lunch, entrées range from $1.99 to $3.25; at dinner, from $2.95 to $4.85. *Cocktails, wines. Open 7 days a week.*
AE BA CB DC MC

★ SHANGHAI CAFE
3217 Broadway (between 125th and 126th Streets)
MO 2-1990

The luncheon menu at the Shanghai is as stereotyped as chop suey, but the à la carte dishes can be excellent. Complete luncheons from about 90 cents to $1.40; à la carte dishes throughout the day from about $1.50 to $3.50. Family dinners for 2 persons begin at $4.95. *No alcoholic beverages. Closed Thanksgiving.*

★ SHANGHAI D'OR
2519 Broadway (at 94th Street)   AC 2-5500

In the most essential thing, the food, the Shanghai d'Or ranks high. The menu is interesting, with its beef or pork with mustard greens and chicken with peanuts and mushrooms in mustard sauce. There is a good relish too—pickled cabbage with a touch of sesame oil. The service is willing, but, particularly at noon, the restaurant seems understaffed. Main courses at noon cost from about $1.10 for chicken chow mein to $3.00 for lobster with black bean sauce. There are complete dinners from about $2.00 to $4.00. *Cocktails, wines.*

★ SHANGHAI GARDEN
140 West 4th Street   982-7670

In some respects this is a laudable Chinese restaurant and it is within walking distance of Washington

Square. The food at its best seems exceptionally good. On one occasion, the hot and sour soup, the fried dumplings, and the chicken in hot sauce all had special merit. On another evening, the soup came off far less well and an order of scallion pork was brought to the table cold. It should be added that the dishes are reasonably priced. Family dinners are $6.50 for two. A la carte dishes cost from $1.50 to $4.25. *No alcoholic beverages, but wine and beer may be brought in. Only à la carte items are available Saturday and Sunday, from noon.*

★★ SHANGHAI TOWN
1 Mott Street   732-7270

At its best, this is a very good Chinese restaurant, a small and angular place with tables close together.

One dish of special excellence is the subgum brown noodles, an elaborate dish with shrimp, chicken, bamboo shoots, black mushrooms, Formosa mushrooms, spinach, and, of course, noodles, partially fried to give them two textures.

The bean curd in hot sauce, the chicken with peanuts, and the shredded chicken are all good, and among the appetizers there is an interesting cold dish of shredded lettuce with shredded chicken skin. The fish in brown sauce, a carp, was overcooked and bony. A platter of fried dumplings was well-seasoned, but the dough was on the heavy side.

All dishes are à la carte with main courses from about $1.95 to $3.50. *There is no bar. Open 7 days a week.*

★ SHANGHAI VILLAGE
23 Pell Street   CO 7-2092

The Shanghai Village is an upstairs place with indifferent service, a menu with commendable variety, and a good kitchen. Even the spring rolls have something to recommend them. There are endless listings of uncommon dishes in the $2.00 to $3.95 range. A la carte dishes cost from about $1.45 to $12.00 for Pekin duck at midday; from $1.75 to $12.00 in the evening. *Cocktails, wines.*

★ SHAVEY LEE
32 Mulberry Street   BE 3-7747

The people who praise Shavey Lee's are legion, and there are those who deem it the best Chinese restaurant in or near Chinatown. For one man's taste, however, the food is palatable and substantial, yet dull and unadventurous.

Most of the dishes have a bland nature and seem to beg for more ginger, more shredded scallion, fresh coriander, or whatever. This goes for such specialties as the tungsai special chicken made with ham and vegetables, the shrimp cashew ding, and the subgum joy wonton. Oddly enough, the wonton soup, perhaps by contrast, is a standout.

On the dinner menu, main courses are priced from $2.50 to $5.50. *Cocktails, wines. Closed Thanksgiving.* AE DC MC

★★ SHEIK RESTAURANT, THE
132 Lexington Avenue (between 28th and 29th Streets)
MU 4-9143

Some of the most gratifying restaurants in New York are the small ones, like The Sheik, that specialize in Middle-Eastern cookery. The menu here includes appetizers made with sesame paste, such as baba ganough, which is mashed eggplant, and humus, which is puréed chick-peas. The main courses, such as the shish kebab, are made principally with lamb, and there are excellent stuffed vegetables. The restaurant is relatively inexpensive. A complete luncheon costs $1.85; a complete dinner, $4.95. The same menu, with à la carte main courses from about $1.85 to $5.50, serves throughout the day. *Cocktails, wines. Closed Sunday and all major holidays.*

★ SHUN LEE
119 East 23rd Street   GR 3-4447

A large, bustling, and physically colorless Chinese restaurant with unadorned walls and artificial flowers. The food, however, even at its most conventional, is almost invariably appetizing, and with expert guidance it is possible to dine extremely well. There are run-of-the-mill luncheons priced from about $1.70 for chicken chow mein to $4.00 for lobster Chinese-style. The à la carte menu is recommended. Dishes cost from about $1.50 for chicken yat gaw mein to $4.95 for lobster in spicy sauce. *Cocktails, wines.*
AE DC MC

★★★★ SHUN LEE DYNASTY
900 Second Avenue (at 48th Street)   PL 5-3900

This is a consistently excellent Chinese restaurant and decidedly one of the best in Manhattan. It has a décor by Russel Wright that becomes more and more agreeable with subsequent visits. There are shiny gold streamers that serve as room dividers and a Fongling, a circular device made with Chinese wind chimes, overhead. The menu doesn't change from one visit to the other, but the variety is admirable, from the assorted hot appetizers and hoisin chicken to Szechuan dishes. The latter, incidentally, may not be as highly spiced as they should be—a concession to public taste. The management will provide a hot sauce on the side on demand. Complete luncheons cost from about $1.85 to $2.75; complete dinners are $6.75. A la carte dishes at midday from $1.45 to $4.75; in the evening, from $3.50 to $15.00 for Pekin duck. *Cocktails, wines. Open 7 days a week. Luncheon is not served Saturday and Sunday. Closed Thanksgiving.*
AE CB DC

★ SIGN OF THE DOVE
1110 Third Avenue (at 65th Street)   UN *1-8080*

From the standpoint of décor, this is one of New York's most enchanting restaurants. There are gas lamps, antique grillwork, Venetian glass, and a garden. The menu includes cheese soufflé ($4.50 at lunch), fish dishes, and charcoal-broiled meats, and the quality ranges from mediocre to very good. The table service at worst is lamentable. A la carte main courses at luncheon range from $3.50 to $6.50; à la carte dinner entrées from $7.25 to $10.50. *Cocktails, wines. Luncheon is not served Monday. Closed most major holidays.*
AE CB DC MC

★★ SIXTY-EIGHT RESTAURANT
59 Fifth Avenue (between 12th and 13th Streets)
255-8744

This restaurant has reportedly reverted to the original management of several years ago, and the change seems all to the good. Some of the dishes sampled came off remarkably well, including the very simply made broiled jumbo shrimp à la "68," which are tender and cooked with a lemon butter and herb sauce. Equally good were a rollatin of chicken—braised, rolled chicken with a well-seasoned filling—and green tagliarini with marinara sauce. The service is not polished, but it is done with some care. There are complete luncheons priced from $2.75 to $7.25. Complete dinners cost from $4.75 to $8.25. A la carte dishes from $2.85 to $7.50. *Cocktails, wines. Open 7 days a week.*
AE

★★ SKEWER ON THE TABLE
150 West 49th Street   *246-4877*

New York has several score restaurants of certain charm simply because they are not duplicated anywhere else in the city. One of these is the Skewer on the Table, which was once the Brazilian Club. There are still the murals with views of Rio, a bar with a thatched roof, and service that is pleasant, if markedly detached.

The menu is interesting. There is a choice of 8 to 10 meats, all skewered, that are cooked over charcoal, and the lightly smoked flavor that evolves is excellent. So is the quality of the marinated meats.

There is a choice of steaks, chicken, pork, lamb, sausage, shrimp, and so on, and, to begin, a large bowl of onion rings and mixed greens (predominantly iceberg lettuce leaves) with three sauces, one mayonnaise, one tomato, one oil and vinegar with herbs. The latter is astringent and most agreeable.

The main dishes are served with well-cooked rice and a raw onion and herb relish as an accompaniment for the meats.

The cost of complete luncheons is from $2.95 to $4.85; complete dinners, from $3.85 to $8.25. *Cocktails, wines. Closed Monday.*

★ SLATE RESTAURANT, THE
852 10th Avenue (at 56th Street)   581-6340

There is a certain charm about The Slate Restaurant. It has a "neighborhood" feel, the welcome is warm, and there is good will upstairs and down. It is in an old building with a naïve but, nonetheless, pleasant décor; wood and brick and mock-marble frescoes in high relief.

Some of the food is quite good, and that goes for the shrimp cocktails, steaks, and tomato sauces—the specialties of the house are steak and Italian dishes. But there is so much that is commonplace—the overcooked (and, one suspects, not cooked to order) spaghetti; the sautéed veal with peppers, also too-long simmered so that it tastes more like beef stew; the routine blue cheese dressing called Roquefort. But, as we were saying, the herbed tomato sauce is excellent.

The cost of the entrée includes vegetable and salad,

with main courses at midday from about $1.50 to $7.95; in the evening, from about $3.95 to $9.95. *Cocktails, wines. Luncheon is not served on Saturday. Closed Sunday.*
AE DC MC

★★ SLOPPY LOUIE'S
92 South Street   BO 9-9821

There are a few restaurants in town that are legends in their own time, and one of them is Sloppy Louie's, near the Fulton Street Market. Devotees of the place will be happy to know the fish is just as fresh and the service just as casual and the surroundings just as raffish as ever.

The restaurant (first owned by John Barbagelata and known as Sloppy John's) was bought by Louis Morino about 40 years ago, and the tawdriness—bare tables, painted metal walls, wall hangings askew—is not contrived. It is simply there like Mount Everest.

The fish is freshly cooked and that, apparently, is the important thing. There are the usual listings of striped bass, scallops, and swordfish, and in spring you can find shad and shad roe and excellent squid, fried or cooked in butter and wine.

All dishes at Louie's are à la carte and main dishes at midday cost from about $1.75 to $3.50; in the evening, from $1.75 to $3.75. The restaurant closes at 8:00 P.M. *There is no bar, but wine and beer may be brought in. Closed Saturday, Sunday, and major holidays.*

★ SMOKEHOUSE, THE
7 West 8th Street   260-0400
71 West 47th Street   CO 5-5620
957 Third Avenue (between 57th and 58th Streets)
421-4040

New York is probably the delicatessen capital of the world. The Smokehouse rates average marks where the food is concerned, but it is unusually attractive physically, with its wood paneling, high ceilings, and odd-shaped, four-square counters. The flavor of the foods, whether corned beef, chopped liver, or sauerkraut, is good, but notably bland, and thus without marked distinction. The cost of the food is from about $1.15 for a meat loaf sandwich to $3.25 for a delicatessen platter. *Draft beer at the Third Avenue and West 8th Street branches; cocktails from a computerized bar at 47th Street. The 47th Street restaurant is closed Sunday; the others are open 7 days a week.*

★★ SOUL EAST
317 East 79th Street   534-9820

The best soul food in the world is to be found in the home, and, the closer the kitchen of a soul restaurant comes to tasting like that, the finer it is. The food at the Soul East on the Upper East Side comes reasonably close. It has several things worth recommending and is as good as this reporter has found in the city. At least one of the dishes there is positively triumphant and that is the lightest, most delicately flavored sweet potato pie you could hope to find anywhere.

The rest of the menu varies from fork-tender, well-seasoned, smothered pork chops and spareribs to acceptable but un-moist, overcooked fried chicken; from very good vegetables, including black-eyed peas and collard greens, to good-flavored but lukewarm macaroni and cheese. The chitterlings—the small intestines of pork, cut into pieces and cooked in a seasoned broth—were peppery, as they should be, and tasted first-rate, but they, too, seemed a bit dry.

The restaurant is a friendly, noisy, swinging place with what may be the loudest jukebox in town.

The Soul East is open for dinner only. All dishes are à la carte, from about $2.95 for chicken giblets and peppered pork to $5.50 for T-bone steak or lamb chops. *Cocktails, beers. Closed New Year's Day and Christmas.*

★★ SOUTH PACIFIC PORTS
Taft Hotel, 769 Seventh Avenue (near 51st Street)
265-0107

This is a venture of the Longchamps chain, which owns various dining establishments about town, including the Cattleman restaurants. The chain's trademark seems to be showmanship, and there's lots of it in South Pacific Ports. There are ship riggings, upturned boats, tapa cloth wall hangings, and giant clam shells in nets. The whole thing has a deliberately seedy aspect, and the only trouble is it doesn't look quite seedy enough. Or, to put it another way, somebody stinted in striving for the seedy effect. (Comparisons may be odious, but the dècor over-all really looks like a poor man's Trader Vic's.)

What is interesting is that much of the food comes off remarkably well, and the fish dishes are impressive in their freshness. A platter of sashimi—the traditional Japanese specialty—made with raw tuna and raw striped bass, came off well. A dish listed as sea bass Taipei (poached bass served in a sweet and ginger sauce with scallions and soy) was excellent. The assorted appetizers, called puu puus, were interesting, particularly the skewered chicken called sate.

The food is, for the most part Chinese, and the chef turns out a very good dish called sesame chicken, filled with ham (they should use Virginia ham but don't) and with pea pods and bean sprouts. The pressed duck is acceptable. A dish of chicken with peppery sauce seems to have gotten its heat from a bottle of hot sauce rather than fresh chilies.

The menus are à la carte, with main dishes at midday from about $3.75 to $5.75; in the evening, from about $3.95 to $7.75. *Cocktails, especially exotic drinks; beers. Open 7 days a week.*
AE CB DC MC

★ SPAIN
113 West 13th Street   929-9580

There are two things particularly impressive about this unpretentious Spanish restaurant—the paella and the prices.

The paella is an abundant and carefully conceived blend of chicken, sausages, clams, mussels, and shrimp, with, of course, rice, peas, and pimientos. It is $2.90 at dinner. Good, too, is the Spain's thinly sliced ham as a first course and an excellent but simple gazpacho.

A crisp salad with a well-seasoned dressing accompanies each main course. There are two dishes on the Spain's menu in green sauce. The sauce isn't bad, but the crab meat at one lunch, although served characteristically in too great quantity, was not sublimely fresh.

In any event, one can dine at the Spain at midday on main dishes priced from about $1.50 to $4.00; and in the evening from about $2.50 to $4.50. All dishes are à la carte. *Open 7 days a week. The restaurant opens at 4:00 p.m. on Sunday.*

★★★ SPANISH PAVILION, THE
475 Park Avenue (near 57th Street)   421-5690

This is one of the most beautiful restaurants in Manhattan. It is as elegant and grand as a Spanish grandee, and the menu and the food are generally a delight. The restaurant is more or less rectangular in shape, one wall hung with a large 16th-century tapestry and a life-size portrait of the Spanish King Felipe IV. There are rich red banquettes and square-cut Jacobean chairs with handwoven wool backs. The menus are printed on stiff parchment, and from appetizer to dessert the food is interesting. There is, for example, an excellent appetizer consisting of three egg halves neatly shaped to resemble whole eggs, but capped with minced seafood and various sauces, including mayonnaise and vinaigrette; an unaccustomed and interesting soup, castilla la vieja, made with slivers of almonds and

bread. But best of all perhaps, there is a classic zarzuela de mariscos Costa Brava, which is made with an assortment of fresh seafood, including lobster, langostinas, mussels, clams, and shrimp, in a delicate sauce vaguely flavored with tomato. Wonder of wonders, some of the most palate-seducing dishes are the desserts—the rich, fluffy natillas à la española, or Spanish custard, and the pine-nut cake in particular. There is less enthusiasm for a flaming banana with spirits. The banana was both undercooked and underripe. The Spanish Pavilion is substantially priced, along the lines of the town's luxury French restaurants. There is a complete luncheon that costs $7.50. A la carte dishes in the evening cost from about $6.25 for broiled fish to $8.50 for the partridge in grape sauce. *Cocktails, wines. The restaurant is closed Sunday and for lunch on Saturday. Reservations are recommended.*
AE CB DC

★ SPARK'S PUB SOUTH
123 East 18th Street   GR 5-9696

If you have a taste for art nouveau there might be much to your liking at Spark's Pub South. It is a long, narrow restaurant with dim lighting and posters pinned to the wall and a jukebox, which seems, oddly enough, appropriate to the mood of the place. If you sit close to the kitchen you will find it noisy. Salad and french fries are included in the price of an à la carte entrée. At lunch prices are from $1.60 to $1.75; at dinner, from $2.50 to $5.95. *Cocktails, wines. On Saturday and Sunday the restaurant opens at about 5:00 p.m.*

★★ STAGE DELICATESSEN AND RESTAURANT
834 Seventh Avenue (between 53rd and 54th Streets)
245-7850

This is a relatively small restaurant with genuine character, an understandable favorite with men and women in the entertainment world. The sandwiches, whether a single-decker corned beef or a triple-decker with chopped liver, turkey, and pastrami, are excellent. The delicatessen has such Jewish specialties as matzoh ball soup and stuffed derma. The menu is à la carte, with sandwiches from 50 cents to $2.40; hot main entrées from about $1.55. *Soft drinks, beers. Open 8:00 a.m. to 4:00 a.m. Closed for the Jewish New Year.*

★ STAGE DELICATESSEN AND RESTAURANT
Lexington Avenue Branch, 593 Lexington Avenue (at 52d Street)   935-9480

This is an operation based on the original and for several decades celebrated Stage Delicatessen a few blocks over on Seventh Avenue.

Where atmosphere is concerned, this version is not even a pale imitation. Part of the charm of Max Asnas's original Stage (and even that is no longer what it used to be) was the brusque treatment by the waiters and the quaintly rude seating master, the frenzied wait for a table, the mixed bag of people.

Except for the name (and the menu, which is a reproduction of the original), the Lexington Avenue Stage Deli is much like numerous other sandwich emporiums in Manhattan. You can get the same matzoh ball soup here as elsewhere; excellent breast of beef if you get it lean enough; a very good pastrami on seeded roll; chopped chicken liver on rye; and so on.

All dishes are à la carte, with sandwiches priced from about 95 cents (cream cheese) to $3.55 for an Eddie special (three-decker with sturgeon and salmon). Main courses from about $2.25 (frankfurters with individual can of beans) to $3.95 (breast of beef). *Beers, soft drinks. Open 7 days a week.*

★ STEAK AND BREW
400 East 57th Street   593-0990
1655 Broadway (at 51st Street)   889-5100
55 Fifth Avenue   889-5100
2005 Broadway (at 68th Street)   799-6768
1015 Madison (at 79th Street)   861-4678

The big lure in these restaurants is an "inexpensive" steak plus all the salad you wish to make and all the beer you wish to drink.

The 57th Street version of Steak and Brew is a shadowy and rambling retreat where the walls are lined with fish nets and copper kettles, life preservers and copper-rimmed kegs marked Scotch, rye, bourbon, and so on. There are pewter mugs hanging overhead.

There is a large salad bar with the various components for mixed greens—crisp bacon bits, chopped olives, croutons, and the usual dressings, green cheese, chef's, oil-and-vinegar, and Russian. The greens are mostly iceberg, but at least they are chilled and the green cheese dressing is edible. The steaks here seemed of common quality—a boneless sirloin quite chewy, nonjuicy, and lukewarm.

It is a source of constant amazement, too, that steaks in most of the city's restaurants are rarely served with melted butter (or even the less expensive spread) and chopped parsley, both of which add so much to grilled meats. On the evening in question it was necessary to ask for butter on the side. In any event, the restaurant's cheesecake is quite respectable.

The menus are printed on small slates, and all the dishes are à la carte, with main courses that include steak and beer from about $4.50 for a 12-ounce steak to $5.50 for a 16-ounce boneless sirloin steak. *Cocktails, wines. The restaurant opens at 4:00 p.m. every day.*
AE   BA   CB   DC   MC

★★ STEAK CASINO
33 University Place (at 9th Street)   AL 4-7499

This is a comfortable, well-run steak house in

Greenwich Village, a neighborhood place, with paneled walls hung with replicas of various games of chance and an odd assortment of chandeliers. There is a cooper-hooded charcoal grill, and the steaks and chops are, by and large, of good quality. The menu is typical, with its seafood cocktails, grilled foods, baked potatoes in foil, and salads with the usual choice of dressing—French, Russian, or blue cheese. The blue cheese, incidentally, is good. All dishes are à la carte with main courses at midday from about $1.95 to $2.75; in the evening, from about $4.50 to $8.25. *Cocktails, wines. Closed Christmas.*
AE CB DC

★ STEAK JOINT, THE
58 Greenwich Avenue   CH 2-0009

The quality of the steaks at Don Stampler's Steak Joint remains unchanged and their grilling is almost scientifically perfect.

Each table has a full-color brochure illustrating the color and texture of "rare, medium rare, medium, and medium well," and that's the way the steaks arrive at table. As far as one long-time admirer of The Steak Joint is concerned, the busy and circus-like décor with shiny gold wallpaper and red coach booths is a distraction rather than an asset.

The french-fried or shoestring potatoes are crisp and fried in fresh fat, and the baked potatoes and green salad are good. The shrimp for a cocktail were overcooked (why? why? why?) and fibrous. The grilled chicken, while edible and freshly cooked, did not taste farmhouse fresh.

Dinners are à la carte, with main courses from about $3.95 to $7.95. *Cocktails, wines. Open 7 days a week for dinner only.*
AE BA CB DC MC

★ STEAK PLACE, THE
112 Central Park South (near the Avenue of the Americas)
CO 5-2470

In the most essential thing, steak, The Steak Place ranks as excellent. The meat is of first quality, and it is grilled over charcoal with considerable expertise. The Steak Place smells like a New York steak place with its odor of smoke and charred meat. The décor is all red flocked wallpaper and poor lighting, and, in a word, it doesn't swing. The service, such as it is, is friendly but wishy-washy, and the restaurant seems to be understaffed. With its faults, The Steak Place is, nonetheless, recommended. The dinner menu is à la carte with main courses from about $5.25 to $8.25. *Cocktails, wines.*
AE CB DC

★★ STEINWAY BRAUHALL
28-26 Steinway Street, Astoria, Queens   RA 8-9780

This is a plain, honest German restaurant and bar with a kitchen that is considerably superior to those bourgeois beer and bratwurst eateries on 86th Street in Manhattan. In fact, some of the dishes at Steinway Brauhall are as impressive as they are simple.

You can find a very good head cheese among the appetizers, and the soup with liver dumplings is made with genuine meat broth cooked on the premises. Most of the soup broths in local restaurants are made from a powdered base, some of them synthetic. The roasted veal shanks are fresh, tender, and well-seasoned and served with light potato dumplings. Typical luncheon dishes include boiled beef with pickled beets, beef goulash with spätzle (dumplings), and meat balls with caper sauce.

There is a no-nonsense décor with deer antlers dangling from the ceiling and beneath them plastic tulips in various manmade hues. The tables are sometimes three abreast with one tablecloth, and they may be shared with strangers.

The cost of main dishes is from about $1.75 to $5.50. On

Sunday, there are complete dinners priced from about $3.75. *Cocktails, wines. Closed Monday.*

★★ STOCKHOLM RESTAURANT
151 West 51st Street   CI 6-6560

The décor of this restaurant is nondescript and uninspired, but the smorgasbord, or Scandinavian feasting board, is one of the most interesting in New York. There is, of course, an assortment of herring, which is very good, as well as lobster, shrimp, salads, cold meats, and hot dishes. Guests may return to the buffet as often as the spirit moves them. The cost of the smorgasbord with dessert and coffee is $3.50 at midday and $6.50 in the evening. The restaurant's menus also list complete luncheons from about $3.00 to $5.75; complete dinners from about $5.95 to $8.75. *Cocktails, wines. Dinner is served Sunday from 1:00 p.m.*
AE BA CB DC MC

★★ STOUFFER'S
666 Fifth Avenue, downstairs (between 52nd and 53rd Streets)   PL 7-6662

Among New York's reasonably priced restaurants this is one of the best. The menu is plain, but it shows imagination, and the food is almost consistently first-rate. There are many rooms in the restaurant, the surroundings are pleasant, and the waitresses are courteous. A typical menu might include chicken pot pie with dumplings, or fillet of fish with lemon, and excellent vegetable accompaniments, particularly the eggplant and spinach. There are special luncheons priced from about $1.40 to $2.75. A la carte entrées at dinner are from about $3.35 to $6.70. *Cocktails, wines. Closed Christmas.*
AE DC MC

★ SUEHIRO RESTAURANT
35 East 29th Street   MU 4-9187

New York has enjoyed a rash of Japanese restaurants for years, and the Suehiro upstairs at this address has been here for many a moon. It is a simply decorated place, if it can be called decorated at all, but it is popular because the food is quite good and it is relatively inexpensive. One criticism of the restaurant could be that the tempura, although tasty, is a trifle oily. There are complete luncheons from about $2.25 to $4.50 and complete dinners from about $3.75 to $4.95. The à la carte menu throughout the day is priced from about $1.00 to $3.50. *Cocktails, wines. Luncheon is not served Saturday. Closed Sunday.*

★★ SUM HEY RICE SHOPPE
66 Bayard Street   226-8530 and 966-6078

Someday, it would seem, they must inevitably run out of space in Chinatown to open new restaurants, but not, happily, in the predictable future. The Sum Hey is a bright and typical restaurant where they trim the snow peas and fill the wonton in the rear of the dining room.

There is chow mein, to be sure, but there is also an assortment of not-too-common dishes such as Formosa mushrooms—delicious, by the way—with crab meat, snails Chinese-style, and clams Chinese-style. The lo mein or soft noodle dishes and the chow mai fon or fine rice noodle dishes, too, are commendable.

There is one menu with family dinners that cost $2.50 a person. A la carte dishes are priced from about 85 cents for beef and bean sprouts on rice to $4.50 for steak kew. *There is no bar, but beers and wines may be brought in. The restaurant is open 24 hours a day, except for the Chinese New Year.*

★ SUN HOP KEE
13 Mott Street   349-9831

It is still possible for 3 people to dine in Chinatown for about $12.00 in a plain-style restaurant such as the Sun Hop Kee. Sun means new, but the place is run by the same family who operate the original Hop Kee farther down the street.

This is a storefront restaurant; it is clean, brightly lighted, and has Formica-topped tables that at a busy time may have to be shared with a stranger (tablecloths are reserved for groups of 10 to 12 who plan to eat family-style).

The clientele is mainly Chinese and there is a Chinese menu. If you wish dishes prepared Cantonese-style, it is necessary to say so; otherwise they will be Americanized. Service is polite but distant, if you don't speak Chinese.

At a lunch hour, one portion of shredded chicken yat gaw min, a delicately flavored soup with noodles, was ample for two. A roast duck appetizer was tasty, as was an order of wor shu opp, crisp-skinned duck with toasted almonds and bean sauce. The snails Cantonese-style were good, once the knack of holding them firmly in chopsticks and sucking out the meat without embarrassment was acquired.

A delicious bean sauce, with no starch thickener, was the bonus with lobster Cantonese-style made with first-rate fresh lobster. Steamed chicken, ordered with two kinds of Chinese sausage, was an interesting combination of textures and flavors.

Main dishes from $1.00 to $4.75. *There is no bar. Open 11:30 a.m. to midnight, 7 days a week.*

★ SUN LUCK EAST
75 East 55th Street   PL 3-4930

A vast and somewhat lavish Chinese restaurant in midtown Manhattan. The menus for both luncheon and dinner are better than average for midtown. The cost of a complete luncheon is from about $1.95 to $4.25. The cost of main dishes on the à la carte menu is from about $2.00 to $15.00 for Pekin duck. *Cocktails, wines.*
AE   CB   DC   MC

★ SUN LUCK GOURMET
157 West 49th Street   JU 2-8182

A neat, serviceable Chinese restaurant in the Broadway area. The kitchen is not invariably distinguished, but it is competent. There are complete luncheons from about $1.60 to $3.75. Main courses on the à la carte menu range from about $3.50 to $6.25. *Cocktails, wines. Luncheon is not served on Sunday.*
AE   CB   DC

★ SUN LUCK IMPERIAL
935 Lexington Avenue (at 69th Street)   LE 5-4070

This edition of the Sun Luck restaurants is spacious and handsome with interiors of rich gold. The Chinese food, on the other hand, is more or less run-of-the-mill. The restaurant is also relatively expensive. There are complete luncheons from about $1.50 to $3.85. Dinners are à la carte, with most main courses in the $3.75 to $6.00 category. *Cocktails, wines. Dinner is served Sunday from 1 p.m.*
AE   CB   DC

★★ SUN LUCK QUEENS
91-16 59th Avenue, Elmhurst, Queens   446-1166

It seems that the farther Chinese restaurants are from Manhattan, the less Chinese they are in spirit. Long Island does not have a wealth of Chinese dining establishments, and this one is welcome. The chef prepares food cued to what the management obviously considers local taste, but it is palatable, nonetheless. The restaurant, frequently crowded, consists of two levels, but the service is willing. There are complete luncheons from about $1.30 up; complete dinners from about $1.90. A la carte dishes cost from about $1.60 to $4.75. *Cocktails, wines. Dinner is served Sunday from 1 p.m.*
AE   CB   DC

★★ SUN LUCK TIMES SQUARE
200 West 44th Street 524-4707

Considering the extent of the Sun Luck enterprise, particularly where food is the vital issue, there may be room for skepticism. On the other hand, the food at the Sun Luck Times Square restaurant—which in itself is vast—comes off surprisingly well.

Among numerous dishes remembered with pleasure were a very good hot and sour soup; excellent dem sem of steamed dumplings; delicate chicken rolls made with minced chicken in a thin bread crust, deep-fried; a first-rate fried sea bass with pork and vegetables; and minced duck.

The Sun Luck Times Square is a nice looking restaurant in a leaden sort of way. Its Chinese opulence includes lacy red lanterns, high relief paneling, and artificial flowers. There are several rooms, and on several visits the restaurant was never half-full and even with that there was some confusion about getting the food to the table.

There are complete luncheons priced from about $1.60 to $3.75. The à la carte menu available for lunch and dinner has main courses from about $3.50 to $4.75. *Cocktails, wines. Open 7 days a week.*
AE CB DC

★★ SUN YAH
1341 Third Avenue (between 76th and 77th Streets)
BU 8-2886

A simply, tastefully decorated Chinese restaurant on the Upper East Side, with a limited menu, but food that is well prepared. There are several well-made appetizers including the dem sem or steamed, meat-filled dumplings; and the paper-wrapped chicken, coated in a savory sauce, enclosed in parchment, and deep-fried. An order of fried squabs with spiced salt came off exceptionally well. The piped-in music is not an agreeable addition.

There are complete luncheons priced about $2.15. The

à la carte menu entrées cost from $2.35 to $7.55. *Cocktails, wines. The restaurant opens at 1:00 p.m. on Sunday.*
AE CB DC

★ SUSHI GINZA RESTAURANT
167 West 45th Street   247-5543

Like many another restaurant in New York, this Japanese restaurant is strong enough in one or two items and regrettably weak in others. It has excellent, admirably fresh sushi, which is, of course, raw fish, and seafood on rice delicately seasoned with vinegar and wasabi, a green horseradish paste.

The menu offers a preponderance of sushi dishes, but you can find a creditable tempura or batter-fried shrimp entrée. The sukiyakidon, a bowl of beef sukiyaki on rice, is tasty, but the beef is on the skimpy side. And on one occasion, two of the meat dishes on the menu were not available.

The service both in front of and behind the sushi counter is slow. But if you have patience and like fresh sushi, the Ginza is well worth a visit.

Most main courses are served with soup and all the dishes are à la carte from about $1.75 for the sukiyakidon to $3.25 for a de luxe sushi. *Cocktails, wines. Open 7 days a week.*

★★ SWEET'S
2 Fulton Street   WH 4-9628

It is quite possible—indeed, part of the game of dining out in New York—to wink at certain negative aspects of restaurants provided there are compensations. At Sweet's, a Manhattan landmark that probably serves the freshest fish in Manhattan, you may close your eyes to the fish odors—sometimes ripe of an evening—outside the restaurant because this is Fulton Street. You might even find the wet fluke on the sidewalk—the one on which you almost slipped—amusing, for this, too, is local color. What cannot be ignored, however, is discourtesy and abuse from any member of the staff.

Sweet's is, of course, incredibly crowded with, at times, a 20-minute wait on the stairs leading to the restaurant not uncommon. The tables are situated almost cloth by cloth, but the simply baked or broiled fish is excellent. Sweet's has, of course, been roundly praised in these pages in years past, but, how the mighty have fallen!

All dishes are à la carte, with main courses from $3.00 to $7.00. *Cocktails, wines. Closed Saturday and Sunday and the first 2 weeks in July for vacation.*

★★★ SWISS CENTER RESTAURANTS
4 West 49th Street   247-6545 (for Swiss Pavilion Restuarant) and 247-6327 (for Fondue Pot)

This is a conglomerate of Swiss restaurants, all connected, and together they comprise—with certain faults—the finest Swiss restaurants ever to exist in Manhattan and, therefore, probably, in America. They really do have the feel of Switzerland and they are:

The Swiss Pavilion. This is the most "formal" of the Swiss restaurants in the center and, all things considered, it boasts the most impressive menu. It offers various regional specialties, some Suisse Alemanique, some Suisse Romande; some from Tessin; and some from the Grisons.

Among the appetizers can be found an exceptional baked snail dish—the snails bathed in a splendid, rich, curry-flavored butter sauce; and vitello tonnato or cold, thin-sliced veal with a tuna, mayonnaise, and caper sauce.

Among the main courses, an excellent veal Engadinaisa (like cordon bleu), the breaded, sautéed veal stuffed with ham and cheese and with a wild mushroom garnish; and good osso buco or braised veal knuckle.

Among the desserts, the walnut torte is special; the Black Forest cake, pure joy. Snobs to the contrary, I happen to feel enthusiastic about Swiss wines and they are good here.

The Swiss Pavilion is a fairly large restaurant, with

rough-textured white walls, modern sculptured lamps, and vivid cloth crests on the walls. The service is Swiss-inspired and generally good. All dishes are à la carte, with main dishes from about $4.50 to $7.25. *Cocktails, wines. Reservations are recommended.*

The Fondue Pot. This is a restaurant in the Swiss Center "cellar." At least, you walk one flight down to get there, and it is a pleasant place with somewhat less "classic" dishes than are to be found in the Pavilion, although numerous of the Pavilion's dishes are duplicated here, including the snails, and vitello tonnato.

There are typical regional dishes like the quiche made with Gruyère cheese, onions, and bacon; and the émincé of veal Zurichoise, choice pieces of veal sautéed with shallots in a cream sauce. The rösti potatoes are well-seasoned and crisp.

Among the appetizers, the cheese ramequin is delicate and the mehlsuppe made with brown flour and cheese is fascinating. The restaurant derives its name, of course, from the fondues served here—one, oddly enough, flavored with bourbon whisky. The cheese fondues are all to the good, but the beef fondue—generally listed as fondue bourguignonne—needs lots of ventilation, more than is apparent at the Fondue Pot Restaurant. The odor of cooking fat—however light—pervades the premises.

All dishes on the fondue pot menu are à la carte, with main courses from about $2.50 to $5.95. *Cocktails, wines. Reservations are recommended.*

The Bell Bar. The littlest restaurant of the Swiss Center is called the Bell Bar, and it is situated immediately above the entrance bar, which is dominated, as the name implies, by cow bells.

There are light dishes here of the sort found in many Swiss terrace restaurants. Among them are cold meat dishes, the slices of meat served on wooden platters and garnished in great style. Among them is the Grisons platter with the famed air-dried beef and dried ham from the

Swiss Alps. They are served with small cornichons and pickled white onions in the best Swiss fashion. The salads here, as in the other restaurants, have an excellent dressing.

Dishes in the Bell Bar are à la carte, with platters from about $2.50 to $2.75. *Cocktails, wines.*

The restaurants of the Swiss Center are closed Sunday. All major credit cards.

★★ SYMPOSIUM
544 West 113th Street   749-9327

This is a colorful, offbeat, and fascinating Greek restaurant near Columbia University. What's more, the food is as good as you're apt to find in any other Greek restaurant in town.

It is a notably informal place with place mats and friendly, young waiters who make up with their attitude what they may lack in expertise.

Among the dishes there is a good egg and lemon soup; good tender roast lamb; well-seasoned moussaka and pastitsio (overcooked, but that does seem to be routine); spinach pie; and stuffed zucchini with avgolemono sauce. And very good taramosalata and salad.

The Symposium at times (noted on posters) has poetry readings. There is a garden in the rear beyond the kitchen, and it is too warm on very hot and humid days. The main dining room is poster-covered, and the tables are close together. And there is recorded Greek music.

All dishes are à la carte, with main courses from about $1.75 to $3.50. *There is no bar, but beers and wines may be purchased close by. Open 7 days a week.*

★★ SZECHUAN
2336 Broadway (at 95th Street)   663-8150

As everyone must know by now, Szechuan is the province of China where the food is characterized by its spicy, fiery hot nature. To judge by the number of restaurants in New York that now serve Szechuan-style food, it has a great appeal for many customers in this area.

The Szechuan restaurant on upper Broadway offers, in its best moments, some of the best Szechuan cooking in town. The diced chicken with hot pepper sauce is splendid; the Szechuan dumpling with red hot oil is excellent; and the eggplant with garlic sauce—it is cooked in oil with garlic and hot pepper—is extraordinary.

There are very good noodle dishes, too, including the braised beef with noodles.

If any of this should tempt you, remember that this is a cuisine hot enough to bring tears to some eyes and, also, most of the dishes are cooked in what will seem to some people an unusual amount of oil. The Szechuan is a large restaurant with a décor of no special distinction and service that is largely indifferent.

A la carte dishes are priced from about $2.05 to $5.95. *Cocktails, wines. Open 7 days a week.*

★ SZECHUAN TASTE
23 Chatham Square   267-0672

The Szechuan school of cookery is noted mainly for the spicy, peppery, and sometimes fiery seasoning of its food. On different visits to the Szechuan Taste, the reaction to the food was almost wildly enthusiastic. But, alas, the food can also be ordinary.

The better meals have included diced chicken sautéed with chili paste; it was excellent and equal to the baby shrimp cooked with bean cake. The sautéed hot beef shreds were very good and on a par with the noodle soup with sesame paste.

Faults include two sauces that seemed overly thickened, one for a specialty of the house, Ta-chien chicken, another for hot prawns sauté. The chicken seemed otherwise undistinguished and the hot prawns were tough. In any event, if your taste runs to spiced dishes, the Szechuan Taste is probably worth a visit.

All dishes are à la carte, with main courses from about

$2.00 for minced beef with bean cake, which is very good, by the way, to $3.50 for the Ta-chien chicken. *There is no bar. Open 7 days a week.*

★ TACO VILLA
350 West 46th Street 541-7260

This is a new restaurant and it is chockablock with wayward charm. It is like a Mexican music circus in the evening—a very loud Mexican music circus—and just how you respond to the place may depend on your tolerance for mariachi music. It is a small, friendly restaurant with red napery and woven place mats and a décor like a Latin festival cake (the ceiling looks like meringue).

The food isn't bad, although it seems naïvely seasoned. Which is not to criticize an absence of fiery spices, but rather to say the foods aren't distinguished by any flavors.

The chef does have a fine hand in his use of fresh coriander, and that is all to the good. Some of the most interesting dishes include a seviche of shrimp; a nice assortment of tidbits called nachos, with refried beans and cheese and chilies; the Mexican noodle soup called sopa de fideo; and the tamales.

A few dishes generally good if not overly distinguished were the mole verde and a combination of enchiladas, tacos, and tostadas.

One problem is that almost every dish intended to be hot was at room temperature or thereabouts. One order of black bean soup was too thin and tasted burnt. And the mole verde, which specified double chicken breasts on the menu, turned out to be chicken legs and thighs. The waiters are nice, but the service is desultory.

There is at present one à la carte menu for lunch and dinner. At midday, the cost of any dish is $3.00. In the evening, main courses range from about $4.50 to $6.50. *Cocktails, wines. Open 7 days a week.*

★★ TAMURA RESTAURANT
106 Liberty Street   964-2247

This is a very pleasant Japanese restaurant in the Wall Street area. It is a long, simply decorated place with a well-conceived menu. The kitchen produces excellent kushikatsu made with deep-fried pork and vegetables; a delicious shiwoyaki, or salt-broiled salmon; and there are numerous dishes cooked at the table including, of course, sukiyaki. Complete meals are priced from $2.80 to $3.50. *Cocktails, wines. Closed Sunday.*
DC

★★ TANDUR, THE
1402 Lexington Avenue (92nd Street)   831-2106

This is an odd Indian restaurant in Manhattan and the food comes off remarkably well. It is as good, in fact, as you may find in any other Indian or Pakistani restaurant around.

The Tandur is in a small bar with the name of Georgie Jay's Lounge. The restaurant has been visited only under the best of circumstances. There were few others dining there. And that is all to the good, because there was only one waiter, and it would be difficult to predict what would happen if the restaurant had a sudden influx of new customers.

The rather somber restaurant and/or bar has few tables and there is dining by candlelight (don't mistake that for elegance).

There are very good curries, including chicken, lamb, beef, and meat balls, although the curried lamb may seem a bit oily to some palates. The tandoori (oven-roasted) chicken seemed a bit bland, but it was good.

All dishes are à la carte, with main courses from about $3.00 to $6.50. *Cocktails, wines. The restaurant opens at 6:00 p.m. 7 nights a week.*

★ TANPOPO
139 East 52nd Street   935-9241

This Japanese restaurant will probably be far better when it acquires a steady clientele. The dishes on the menu—the teriyaki, tonkatsu, sukiyaki, and so forth—are wholly predictable, but they are well-prepared.

It is a small restaurant and the service is on the hesitant side. Among various dishes sampled, the clear soup is excellent; the yakitori or chicken broiled on skewers tasty; the sukiyaki very good. But best of all is the tonkatsu, or breaded veal cutlet, which is outstanding. There is also a good sesame-flavored salad.

The surroundings of the Tanpopo are plain but pleasant enough, but the piped-in music, at times from a radio, is a bit distracting.

The cost of a complete luncheon is $2.50 to $4.50; of a complete dinner $5.50 to $7.00. The à la carte menu lists entrées from 85 cents to $3.50. *Cocktails, wines. Lunch and dinner are served Monday through Friday. The restaurant opens at 5:00 p.m. on Saturday and Sunday.*
AE DC MC

★ TASTE OF INDIA
206 Sullivan Street   473-9420

A consummately made curry is one of the best of dishes, and if the cook doesn't resort to commercially made curry powder, their flavors can be endlessly varied.

The curries of Taste of India are both reasonably good and reasonably modest in price.

The restaurant offers curries of chicken, lamb, beef, and vegetable, with the usual chutneys, condiments, and breads. Taste of India is a somewhat seedy-looking establishment with one large dining room and recessed dining spaces for from 2 to 4.

There is a special luncheon served Monday through Friday and the cost is $1.75. Complete dinners cost from $3.25 to $5.25. *There is no bar. Luncheon is served from noon to 3:00 p.m., dinner from 5:30 p.m. to midnight. Open 7 days a week.*

★★ TASTE OF TOKYO
54 West 13th Street   691-8666

This is an agreeable, one might even say cunning, Japanese restaurant that has in a brief time found an audience. It has a counter with chairs and half a dozen or so small tables that are generally filled shortly after the noon hour. Taste of Tokyo has been decorated simply and with taste; color slides of Japanese scenes are flashed soundlessly onto one of the walls. The service staff on several visits has consisted of one comely, slender young lady in kimono with obi.

The menu is quite simple, which, considering the size of the work space, is all to the good. A lunch of tempura, chicken yakitori, beef or pork costs $2.50, with soup included. A more elaborate meal at midday costs $3.75; this is for kushiyaki—an assortment of skewered dishes such as shrimp, chicken, and beef—or for salmon teriyaki, which is to say "shiny-broiled."

Dinners with similar entrées plus salad and dessert cost $3.75 to $7.00.

The ventilation of Taste of Tokyo is not vividly distracting, but some of the cooking odors are apparent.

Cocktails, wines. Open 7 days a week. Luncheon is not served on Saturday and Sunday.

TAVERN ON THE GREEN
*Central Park at 67th Street   *TR *3-3200*

The best thing to be said of the Tavern on the Green is that it has the physical feel of Manhattan. There is an open terrace for dining, and it is pleasant enough on a cool night in midsummer. The kitchen and service are something else again. Among other regrettable items samples list ordinary chopped liver, roast chicken served in lieu of broiled chicken that had been ordered (with the

waiter or captain insisting that it was broiled chicken with stuffing), and a cold wedge of brie cheese on the way to petrifaction. Luncheons without dessert cost from about $2.65 to $5.50. Complete dinners range from about $7.25 to $9.50. *Cocktails, wines. Open 7 days a week.*
AE CB DC

★ TEACHER'S
2249 Broadway (between 80th and 81st Streets)
787-3500

The simple, but effective, décor at this neighborhood restaurant is a cross between an old Pullman coach and a poker saloon. There is narrow, dark brown wall paneling and orange shaded lights hang low over the tables. Butcher-block tables are bare at lunchtime.

Several items on the menu proved to be unavailable one evening. "Chef's gone," the busy waiter explained in an offhand manner, as though it were not the first time.

The salad was served before the appetizer, and the excellent homemade herbed dressing almost made up for the iceberg lettuce in the greens. A melon and Belgian ham appetizer would have benefited from the ham's being sliced thinner. A shrimp rémoulade had five excellent shrimp around a mundane mayonnaise sauce. The clams casino were tender and tasty.

The roast lamb and steak au poivre listed were unavailable, but a special-of-the-day, seafood au gratin, when it came, was acceptable, but big on fish fillets. A sautéed, whole, boned breast of chicken was enormous, tender, moist, and redolent with tarragon. Two orders of "boned roast duck with Burgundy cherries" at the next table arrived with bone and without cherries.

The luncheon menu is limited and recently included a first-rate black bean and meat soup and an excellent chicken liver and bacon combination served with crisp french fries and crusty Italian bread.

Main entrées at lunch from $1.25 to $2.00 and at dinner

from $2.25 to $5.25. *Cocktails, wines. Open for lunch, dinner, and supper 7 days a week. Brunch is served on Saturday and Sunday.*
AE DC

★ TEDDY'S RESTAURANT
219 West Broadway   WO 6-2180

The best-known features of this restaurant are the bountiful six-course dinners. In the evening there is no printed menu and the captain recites the main-course dishes. These determine the price of the meal, which is Italian throughout. The cost of the entire meal ranges from $10.50 to $13.50. There is an à la carte luncheon menu with entrées from about $2.75. The décor is modern, neat, and quite stylish. *Cocktails, wines. Closed Christmas and New Year's Day. Reservations are recommended.*
AE CB DC MC

★ TEMPLE GARDEN, THE
16 Pell Street   BE 3-5544

The food is good at this Chinatown restaurant, and, although it is large and overly illuminated, it is worth a visit. Complete luncheons from about $1.25 to $1.75. A la carte dishes from about $1.95 to $2.00 for Pekin duck or cold cuts. *No alcoholic beverages, but customers may bring their own wine and beer.*

★★ 37th STREET HIDEAWAY
32 West 37th Street   947-8940

Although the quality of the kitchen at this dimly lit rendezvous still seems inconstant, there has been an improvement over the years. The Hideaway, said to have been patronized in former years by John Barrymore, is a study in red and shadows with flocked wallpaper, a large chandelier, and a smoky mirror.

Among the good things remembered are the simply broiled fish dishes, which are excellent, and the veal

Hideaway, rather like cheese-stuffed veal parmigiana plus green noodles and tomato sauce. The crêpes Finlandaise on the luncheon menu are edible, but average. The ungarnished pâté on one evening was sliced out of a tin, and both a Napoleon and an éclair were soggy. In any event, the Hideaway, one flight up, is pleasant enough, if you don't mind tables that are all but cloth-by-cloth together.

Complete luncheons are priced from about $3.50 to $6.50. Complete dinners cost from about $7.50 to $8.50, with à la carte items from about $5.50 to $9.50. *Cocktails, wines. Lunch is served Monday through Friday; dinner, Monday through Saturday. Closed Sunday.*
AE CB DC MC

★★ THREE SIX NINE RESTAURANT
12 Elizabeth Street   267-0265

This is one of the smallest restaurants in town, and, obscure though it may appear, you may have a long wait, especially at midday, for a table. The menu is Chinese regional: a cold chicken (Canton); an excellent hot soup with fresh and cured pork plus bean curd skin and bamboo shoots (Ningpo); a fantastic steamed, flaked fish dish with egg yolk sauce and fresh coriander (Peking); and a spiced chopped bean curd dish with peas and hot pepper (Szechuan).

The staff is smiling, affable, and efficient. Except for the size of the place, there is not a complaint to be uttered. And that's a switch.

All the dishes are à la carte, with main dishes from about $1.65 to $3.95. *There is no bar, but customers may bring in their own wine or beer. Open 7 days a week.*

★ THURSDAY'S
334 East 73rd Street   628-8670

There are several things to admire about Thursday's and one of them is the décor. This restaurant is not, as the name might imply, a place for swingers, like Tuesday's,

Wednesday's, and Friday's, which are under the same management. It is, rather, on the conservative side, but with a sleek elegance that is all black and wood and glistening electric bulbs.

The service at Thursday's is generally admirable and the food at its best can be impressive. The smoked salmon is good and one recalls with pleasure an appetizer called shrimp Jacqueline with Russian dressing. The chef's pâté, coarse and well-seasoned, is good and an order of rare roast beef one evening was exceptional.

By contrast, one order of roast duck was dry and stringy and an order of veal chops Barcelonette, that is, topped with a Mornay sauce, had a pronounced and disagreeable acid flavor. A captain stated that, "The chef always adds lemon juice to his Mornay sauce," which is, to say the least, extraordinary, if not bizarre.

A chilled green salad was served on warm plates and a bottle of Chambertin would have, if combined with a little mother of vinegar, produced in short order a very nice vinegar.

All dishes at Thursday's (the menu is printed on all sides of wooden blocks that look like oversized black dice) are à la carte. Prices range from about $3.35 for an omelet to $8.00 for beef. *Cocktails, wines. The restaurant opens at 6:00 p.m. every day except Sunday, when it is closed.*
AE CB DC MC

★★ TIEN TSIN
569 West 125th Street　　MO 6-5710

A pleasant, bright Chinese restaurant in uptown Manhattan. The à la carte menu has a tempting range of dishes prepared with excellent taste, whether boiled dumplings as an appetizer or strips of chicken with preserved turnip. The cooking here is generally more exotic than is customary in most of the Chinese restaurants in town. There is, to be sure, a lot of chop suey and chow mein available. All the dishes are à la carte with main courses at noon from about 99 cents to $1.75; at dinner, from about $1.50 to $11.00 for Pekin duck. *No alcoholic beverages. Closed for the Chinese New Year.*

★★ TIK TAK HUNGARIAN
1477 Second Avenue (at 77th Street)   RH 4-9699

This is another Manhattan restaurant that is extraordinary in that the food is both prepared with exceptional care and reasonably priced. The menu lists such Hungarian foods as goulash and paprikás, roast pork and an excellent braised veal shank. The cost of a complete luncheon is $2.25. Dinners are à la carte with main courses from about $3.05 to $4.25. *Cocktails, wines. Dinner is served Saturday and Sunday from noon.*

★★ TIN LIZZIE RESTAURANT, THE
140 West 51st Street   JU 2-3535

If you are fascinated by "fun" places, camp surroundings, and art nouveau, you will no doubt be enchanted with The Tin Lizzie. It is an amusing restaurant with assorted tongue-in-cheek trappings that include an antique automobile, a whole stuffed peacock with feathers, a giant simulated stained-glass window between the lengthy bar and the main dining room, a polished barber chair, and photographs and art held over from the nineteen-thirties. The menu lists ask-the-waiter soup and drinks like W. C. Fields' mother used to make. That will give you an idea of The Tin Lizzie. The dishes are along the lines of grilled foods, oversized salads, omelets, and eggs Benedict. The food is competently prepared, although one order of Tin Lizzie special steak with freshly grated horseradish left a little to be desired. The steak had an excellent flavor and was cooked to a turn, but the meat, alas, was chewy. All dishes are à la carte with main courses at midday from about $2.50 for an open club sandwich to $4.25; in the evening from about $4.25 for barbecued

spareribs to $7.50. *Cocktails, wines. Closed Sunday.*
AE CB DC MC

★★ TOKYO-BANGKOK RESTAURANT
217 West 79th Street   799-8430

This may be the only restaurant serving Thailand cooking in all of Manhattan.

There is Japanese cooking as well, but the Japanese menu on the whole seems somewhat conventional with the usual sukiyaki, tempura, teriyaki, and tonkatsu or pork cutlet. The Thai cooking, on the other hand—provided you like highly spiced foods—is memorable and as good as you're apt to find in any restaurant in Bangkok.

An appetizer of batter-fried eggplant with a soy sauce on the side was crisp, tender, and delicious. A peppery shrimp soup (made hot with a special oil) and seasoned with ginger was unusual; a beef curry, which might have contained ground nuts, was good and was fiery as brimstone; a chicken dish (pat king) with onions and chilies was fascinating; and so was a shrimp concoction that tasted somewhat like deep-fried coriander leaves and a few unfamiliar Thai herbs.

This is a very plain restaurant with plastic flowers and piped-in music, and it seems to be the brainchild of young men and women from Japan and Thailand who know what they are about. Complete luncheons are priced from about $1.50 to $2.95, dinners from about $3.80 to $6.00. A la carte dishes are from about $2.70 to $3.15. *Wine and beer only. Closed Monday.*

★ TOMALDO'S
230 East 51st Street   755-1862

The trouble with restaurant criticism in New York is that the defects in most places are too obvious to make the task yeasty and interesting. And there are none that an astute and conscientious management couldn't overcome.

Take Tomaldo's Italian restaurant. It is an overly bright place (dim the lighting), with tables almost cloth by cloth (why can't they remove a couple?) and such a predictable menu one could recite it sight unseen (isn't there more to the Italian repertoire than eggplant parmigiana, shrimp marinara, veal with peppers, and you know the rest?).

The food at Tomaldo's isn't bad, but it certainly isn't inspired. But speaking of specifics, the saltimbocca was made with the usual slices of veal and ham, but where was the sage between? And why was the sauce so liquid?

It must be said that the chef's chicken breast with melted cheese and a gelatinous mushroom sauce came off very well, but an à la carte antipasto was what one has come to accept with resignation in New York. And when a bottle of Valpolicello was ordered, the waiter (very compliant, by the way) volunteered that he didn't have any full bottles, but he'd be happy to supply two half-bottles. How's that for merchandising?

All luncheon dishes are à la carte, with main courses from about $2.15 for "tuna fish" salad to $3.50 for chicken à la Tomaldo. Complete dinners cost $5.75, with à la carte dishes from about $3.25 to $6.75. *Cocktails, wines. Closed Sunday and major holidays.*
AE CB DC

★★ TOM'S SHANGRI-LA
237 Madison Avenue (between 37th and 38th Streets)
MU 3-0996

One of the handsomest Chinese restaurants in all of Manhattan. The luncheon menu can be as dreary as an egg roll, but the à la carte menu, by contrast, can be rewarding. A la carte luncheon entrées from about $1.75 to $4.25; main dinner courses from about $2.85 to $16.50 (Pekin duck). *Cocktails, wines. The restaurant is open 7 days a week.*
AE DC

★ TONKATSU
9 East 52nd Street   889-5385

The customers at the Tonkatsu are primarily young Japanese businessmen, and that in itself is an indication that the restaurant must be worthwhile. The food is commendable, whether it is sashimi, tonkatsu (a breaded pork cutlet dish), noodle soup, teriyaki, or sukiyaki. The service at times is disoriented, but the waitresses are bright and smiling. The cost of a complete lunch is around $2.75, with à la carte dishes priced from about $2.25 to $2.50. Complete dinners are around $3.25; à la carte dinner entrées, from about $2.75 to $3.25. *Wines, beers. Closed Saturday, Sunday, and major holidays.*

★★ TONY'S ITALIAN KITCHEN
212 West 79th Street   TR 4-9017

The best thing to be said about Tony's is that the pasta is freshly made and the vegetables are freshly cooked. And that is saying a lot. The tomato sauces are good, the meat sauce standard. The food on the whole is competently prepared, whether it be lasagne or boneless chicken parmigiana. The portions are enormous. There is an extensive hot and cold antipasto table. At noon, all dishes are à la carte, and the à la carte menu has dishes from $2.90 to $6.25. Complete 4-course dinners cost from $6.50 up. *Cocktails, wines.*
AE   DC

★★ TONY'S WIFE
150 East 55th Street   EL 5-4506

Tony's Wife is a New York institution with a host of devoted patrons, and the enthusiasm is not misplaced. It is a small, intimate restaurant with a kitchen that is at times outstanding, particularly in grilled dishes such as royal squab and mutton chops. It may also have more waiters per capita than any other restaurant in the city. Nevertheless, the restaurant falls short of perfection.

There are plastic flowers, pictures hung askew, and a serving of prosciutto on one occasion was sliced from the impoverished side of the ham. There are complete luncheons from about $4.25 to $5.25. Dinners are à la carte, with main courses from about $3.50 for half a broiled chicken to $7.75 for sirloin steak. *Cocktails, wines. Closed Saturday, Sunday, major holidays, and 3 weeks in summer. AE MC*

★★ TOPKAPI PALACE
18 West 56th Street   765-8782

This is an unusually pleasant Turkish restaurant with a commendable kitchen. With one possible exception, the food is better than you'll find in the best-known restaurants of Istanbul. The exception is the absence of fresh grilled fish other than swordfish on the menu.

As might be expected, most of the dishes on the menu are made with lamb—on skewers, pot-roasted, spit-cooked, and so on. And, of course, moussaka.

The Turks have always had a way with appetizers, and they are good at the Topkapi Palace: the boereks or cheese in phyllo pastry; the tarama or red caviar paste; cucumbers in yogurt and so on. The imam bayildi or baked eggplant with onion and tomato is delicate and excellent. The stuffed mussels, on the other hand, are indifferent, and one order of tripe soup was badly in need of salt.

More serious, the food has on occasion been served on cold plates, and they do use canned green beans. The desserts are reasonably good, and, if you try them, ask for the kaymak (40 cents additional) made with heavy cream.

The cost of a complete luncheon is from $2.65 to $2.95, with à la carte dishes at midday from about $2.50 to $4.25. Dinners are à la carte, with main courses from about $2.50 to $4.50. *Cocktails, wines. Open 7 days a week. Luncheon is not served on Sunday.*

★ TOP OF THE SIX'S
666 Fifth Avenue (near 53rd Street)   PL 7-6662

For a city that towers architecturally, Manhattan has astonishingly few restaurants that swing aloft to take advantage of the views. The Top of the Six's offers breathtaking vistas and is therefore well worth a visit. The décor displays trappings from a French château, and it has lost some of its luster in the past few years. The food varies in quality, although it is rather simply prepared, with such dishes as grilled chops and steaks, french-fried shrimp, and broiled fish. Luncheons are à la carte with entrées from about $2.50 to $3.55. A la carte entrées at dinner range from about $5.75 to $8.75. Supper is served from 10:30 P.M. to 1:00 A.M., with entrées from $2.75 to $7.50. *Cocktails, wines. On Sunday, the restaurant opens at 4:00 p.m. Closed major holidays.*
AE DC MC

★★ TOWER SUITE
Time and Life Building, Rockefeller Center   JU 6-2100

The view from this restaurant at the top of the Time and Life Building is spectacular. The quality of the cuisine varies, but Sunday brunch, served until 3:00 P.M., is a joy. It offers fresh juices, fine breads, smoked fish, oysters, clams, soups, a fine assortment of main courses, and desserts. The cost for the entire menu is $7.50. The single price for dinner is $11.50. Theater suppers are $9.50. The Tower Suite has a fine collection of wines that are reasonably priced. *Cocktails, wines. Open for dinner 7 days a week; for brunch on Sunday.*
AE BA CB MC

★★ TRADER VIC'S
Plaza Hotel, 59th Street at Fifth Avenue   PL 9-3000

There is an undeniable appeal about Trader Vic's, the first of the big-time Polynesian restaurants. In its present location in the Plaza Hotel, it may seem a touch less

lush and overblown than formerly, but there is still an amplitude of fishing nets, hunting spears, tapa cloth and the like, and a garden in summer. The food, principally of Chinese inspiration, is competently prepared and the public loves it. All the menus are à la carte, with main courses at noon from about $2.95 to $4.75; in the evening, from about $3.95 to $8.50. *Cocktails, wines. Open 7 days a week. Closed major holidays.*
AE MC

TRATTORIA
45th Street entrance to the Pan Am Building MO 1-3090
and MO 1-3091

If only it were possible to eat the scenery and ignore the kitchen of a few Manhattan restaurants! This is a handsome place with its candy-striped Venini globes overhead, its multicolored posters on the wall, mahogany bar, and mosaic-faced rotunda. The menu is extensive, and the food is hopelessly mediocre. There is a vast assortment of appetizers, including stuffed artichokes, stuffed mushrooms, and the like, and it is amazing how the chef makes everything taste alike. The pasta dishes are ordinary and so are the sauces that grace them. The mozzarella in carrozza is a poor and overcooked joke. The desserts at the Trattoria, however, are excellent. All dishes are à la carte. During the day, the cost of main courses is from about $1.75 to $3.95. In the evening, entrées are priced from about $1.60 to $7.35. Open for breakfast, as well as after theater. *Cocktails, wines. Closed New Year's Day.*
AE CB MC

★ TREFNER'S RESTAURANT
619 Lexington Avenue (at 53rd Street) PL 9-6527

The menu at Trefner's is as down-to-earth as homemade apple pie. The food is Yankee-style and good and most reasonably priced. The menus are table d'hôte. The cost of a complete luncheon is from about $1.85 to $2.50;

of a complete dinner, $2.25 to $3.50. *No alcoholic beverages. Closed major holidays.*

★★★ "21"
21 West 52nd Street   582-7200

This New York institution founded by Jack Kriendler and Charlie Berns dates from Prohibition days and is adored by many of the world's elite. It is as much of a club, without formal membership rites, as a restaurant can be: One chronicler of the New York scene bull's-eyed the establishment in noting that "21" "is now run by relatives of Jack and Charlie . . . , who also possess the founders' talent for gemütlichkeit and for making the simple act of being admitted seem an enviable achievement." The atmosphere of "21" is primarily masculine, with its dark paneling and silver, a gregarious bar on the main floor, and an elegant dining room above. The menu at "21" has some excellent dishes including terrapin Maryland and, on occasion, fresh game. The kitchen is first-rate and is complemented by the service. The man at the door of "21," whose favor should be curried for entrance into the hallowed halls, is Chuck Anderson. The menus are à la carte. The cost of main courses at midday is about $15.00; in the evening from about $25.00; at supper (11:00 P.M. to 1:00 A.M.) about $18.00. *Cocktails, wines. Closed Sunday and, during the summer months, Saturday also. Closed New Year's Day, Memorial Day, July 4, Labor Day, and Christmas.*

★★ UNCLE TONOOSE RESTAURANT
2159 Broadway (at 76th Street)   799-2060

This Middle-Eastern restaurant with the unconventional name (Uncle Tonoose was a character on TV's "Danny Thomas Show") has an unconventional atmosphere; but it is highly agreeable where the food is concerned. There are excellent appetizers, including cold hummus bi tahina made with a purée of chick-peas blended with sesame paste; baba ganough, a purée of eggplant with sesame paste and lemon; tabooleh salad, a bit garlicky, made with cracked wheat, parsley, and tomato; and a first-rate cold brain salad.

Among the main courses are an interesting dish called shawerma, made with tender beef marinated in wine and cloves and broiled; delicious broiled shish kebab; and traditional keebeh, or kiba naya, which is raw ground lamb with wheat germ.

The menu is principally à la carte, with entrées from about $1.50 to $4.50. A complete lunch is $1.95. A "complete" Uncle Tonoose dinner is priced at $6.50. *Cocktails, wines. Open 7 days a week, from 11:00 a.m. to 3:00 a.m.*

★★ UN COIN DE PARIS
310 East 86th Street 744-8778

Although the name translates as A Corner of Paris, you're not likely to mistake it as a bistro near Les Halles or in the heart of Montmartre. The atmosphere smacks of Manhattan. On the other hand, the food is French, there is a nice ambience, and in midsummer there is open a small garden with picket fence, weeping willow, ailanthus tree, and fountain, a choice place to dine when the evening is cool. The quality of the food varies.

One recalls an acceptable coarse pâté. The artichokes had a canned citric acid flavor, although they were in a good vinaigrette sauce. An order of cassoulet was rich with beans, lamb, and Alsatian-style sausages, but the dish that came off best was veal chops in cream sauce, well made and served, mirabile dictu, with freshly cooked honest-to-garden fresh vegetables: green beans, carrots, and potatoes. The foil-wrapped cheese was edible, and that's the most you can say for that.

In all, there are only about a dozen tables at Un Coin de Paris, and reservations are, more often than not, essential.

The cost of a complete dinner is about $7.00. The restaurant is open evenings only. *Cocktails, wines. Closed Sunday, Thanksgiving, and Christmas.*

★★ UNICORN, THE
324 East 57th Street   751-4455

This is one of the fashionable restaurants that seem to reflect the mood, if not the madness, of Manhattan. If you can accept the decibels (and you certainly can't ignore them), the Unicorn is not an unattractive restaurant from a standpoint of décor, food, or service. In the center of the main dining room is a massive statue, and the walls are hung with oils. There are red-checked tablecloths, a unicorn tapestry, and leaded glass hurricane lamps that illuminate the tables. Among the appetizers, there are excellent hot stuffed mushrooms and scampi Lucienne, tiny, tender shrimp sautéed quickly in a butter sauce lightly flavored with garlic and parsley. The steaks and many of the main courses Italian-style are good. All dishes at the Unicorn are à la carte and the cost of main courses at dinner is from $4.25 to $7.50. Supper dishes cost from about $4.25 to $6.25. *Cocktails, wines. Closed Sunday. Most major credit cards.*

★ UN RINCON ARGENTINO
1626 Broadway (near 50th Street)   CI 5-2580

There is an undeniable appeal about the informal nature of this Argentine restaurant, and the price is right. There are, for example, platters of grilled luncheon dishes (available Monday through Friday) that include pork sausages and empanadas (listed as gaucho pie) for 40 cents. A grilled half chicken with salad is $1.39. The à la carte menu, available throughout the day, has entrées from about $2.50 for skirt steak cooked on skewers to $3.95 for "assorted typical Argentine broilings." The flavor of the steak is good, but it may be a trifle chewy. *Beers, wines. Open 7 days a week, noon to midnight.*

★ VALENTINO'S
355 West 39th Street   LO 5-8710

Anyone who enjoys "discovering" small, pleasant, so-called family-style restaurants may well be pleased with Valentino's. The dishes are made with basic sauces in a small kitchen and are simply prepared. There is no menu. The restaurant's soups are outstanding. One of the nicer specialties of the house is chicken breast stuffed with ham and cheese. A complete lunch runs from $2.75 to $3.25. The price of a representative dinner entrée is $3.75. There are fewer than a dozen tables, and the walls are adorned with photographs and memorabilia of the motion-picture actor. *Cocktails, wines. Lunch is not served on Saturday. Closed Sunday and major holidays. All major credit cards.*

★★ VASATA
339 East 75th Street   RH 4-9896

This is perhaps the best Czechoslovak restaurant in New York. The atmosphere is crisp and clean and the dining room is well-staffed with waiters who seem anxious to please. The food is of a high order, with such entrées as roast duck, roast pork, chicken paprika, and various schnitzels. The schnitzels, which are veal, are recommended in particular. The cost of complete dinners is from about $3.95 to $7.95. *Cocktails, wines. Open for dinner only. Dinner is served from noon on Sunday.*
AE

★★ VESUVIO RESTAURANT
163 West 48th Street   CI 5-6138

The Vesuvio has a commendable Italian kitchen, certainly one of the best in the Broadway area, where there are many. The fish and seafood dishes are particularly interesting. The service, on the other hand, is, on occasion, disheveled, slow, and frustrating. All dishes are à la carte, with main luncheon entrées from about $2.75

to $3.50; complete dinners from about $6.25 to $9.50. *Cocktails, wines.*
AE   CB   DC

★★ VIA MARGUTTA
24 Minetta Lane   AL 4-7630

There are numerous Italian restaurants in Greenwich Village, and the Via Margutta is one of the best. It has a bit more sophistication than some of the others, and the menu is well varied. The cannelloni Via Margutta is recommended in particular. There are complete dinners from about $4.75 for the cannelloni to $10.00; lunches, about $3.95. *Cocktails, wines. Open for lunch, Tuesday through Saturday; for dinner, Tuesday through Sunday. Closed Monday, New Year's Day, and Christmas.*
AE   CB   DC   MC

★★ VIA VENETO
56 West 56th Street   CI 5-8969 *and* JU 6-7812

The chef of the Via Veneto seems to exercise more care in the preparation of his menu than many other chefs in small Italian restaurants. The pasta, whether it is linguine with clams or fettuccine with truffles, seems special. A fault in the restaurant is that it is crowded and the tables are almost touching. There is a complete luncheon priced from $3.25 for homemade lasagne to $6.00 for minute steak. Complete dinners cost from about $4.50 to $8.00. *Cocktails, wines. On Saturday, dinner is served from noon. Closed Sunday and major holidays.*
AE   CB   DC

★★ VICTOR'S CAFE
240 Columbus Avenue (at 71st Street)   TR 7-7988

Anyone with a passion for Cuban food would look hard in this city to find a more auspicious source than Victor's. This is a neat, friendly place, and the food is generally excellent, whether arroz con pollo, arroz con mariscos marinera (rice with seafood), or shredded beef à la Cubana. The soups are excellent, including the fabada asturiana, or white bean soup. On Saturday and Sunday there is roast pig. The menu is à la carte, with main dishes from about $1.75 to $5.00. *Wines, beers. Open 7 days a week, 8:00 a.m. to 2:00 a.m.*

★ VILLA DORIA
1460 Second Avenue (between 76th and 77th Streets)
LE 5-9310

This is a pleasant enough Italian restaurant, neatly decorated with wine vats, heralds, shields, crossed swords, and the like. The food is reasonably good, and care is put into the evening meal. The Villa Doria has a very good dish called cannelloni gastronomica, made with ground meats, spinach, and cheese, and a creditable osso buco, when it is available. There are complete dinners from about $5.50 to $9.25; à la carte dishes are from about $3.25 to $7.50. *Cocktails, wines. Closed Monday during the winter. Open Monday, closed Sunday in summer. Closed major holidays.*
AE CB DC

★ VILLA MARBONA
55 East 10th Street   477-9928

If you like casual Italian restaurants with friendly service and food somewhat robustly flavored, you may find things to admire at the Villa Marbona. In the evening it has, in fact, an antipasto wagon that displays more imagination on the part of the chef than can be found in similar restaurants in the city. It includes prosciutto, of course, and cheese and salamis, but there are also interesting cold zucchini, baked eggplant, and stuffed mushrooms. The pasta includes a good but largely undistinguished fettuccine with cream and cheese made in the kitchen, and a very good if assertive spaghetti with anchovies.

The food in the evening at Villa Marbona seems to

come off better than food at midday. A distinct disappointment one noon was a veal scaloppine made with overaged veal pounded with one of those tenderizing claw hammers. First-rate veal doesn't need such sorry abuse. Luncheons are about $2.25 to $2.85. In the evening, à la carte prices go from about $2.50 to $6.75. *Cocktails, wines. Luncheon is not served Saturday. Closed Sunday and major holidays.*
Major credit cards.

★★ VILLA PENSA
198 Grand Street   226-8830 and wo 6-5620

This is an engaging, popular, and colorful Italian restaurant near the heart of Little Italy. It is also one of the best Neapolitan restaurants in town. The food is robust, and, although it may not appeal to the most fastidious palates, it is exceptionally good. There are numerous hot appetizers, many of them garlic-scented, including shrimp, stuffed clams, and eggplant. The mussels, when available, are excellent in a rich tomato sauce. The main dishes are very good, too, particularly those made with chicken. All dishes are à la carte, with main courses at midday from about $1.95 to $3.50; in the evening, from about $2.00 to $4.00. *Cocktails, wines. Closed Wednesday, Thanksgiving, and Christmas.*
DC

★★ VILLA VIVOLO
8829 26th Avenue, Brooklyn   ES 2-9860

An old Brooklyn hand has for years hailed the merits of the Villa Vivolo, a long-established Italian restaurant in the Bensonhurst section of the borough. It is in a house that is an entity unto itself, and the atmosphere is informal. The keyhole-shaped dining room is small, the service is casual, and the guests hang up their own coats. But all the foods are cooked to order and both the pasta and fish dishes, the specialties of the house, can be excellent.

To begin, there is a fascinating cold appetizer of mixed seafood with oil and lemon. The kitchen produces first-rate linguine with clam sauce; spaghetti with marinara sauce; squid with tomato sauce; and fritto misto, or mixed fry containing lobster, squid, octopus, smelts, asparagus, zucchini, and cheese balls. One wine there, a Soave Bolla, is well remembered.

The Villa Vivolo is not a place of ceremony or refinement, but the chef has imagination and pride, and the people enjoy themselves.

One large, well-organized menu serves throughout the day, and all dishes are à la carte. Main courses cost from about $1.75 for spaghetti with tomato sauce to $7.50 for lobster fra diavolo. *Cocktails, wines. Opens at 1:00 p.m. every day.*

★★ VINCENT PETROSINO
100 Greenwich Street (near Rector)   BA 7-5398

Petrosino's has for many years enjoyed a certain fame among people who enjoy fresh seafood cooked to order Italian style. The restaurant is located at the rear of Petrosino's fish market, where customers may stand at the counter and eat shrimp in the shell or other seafoods with cocktail sauce. The main dining room is a casually run, friendly place, and the food, some of it robustly seasoned, can be excellent. There are chowders, broiled fishes, fish fries, sautés, and salads. The specialties include lobster, shrimp, or crab meat marinara, creamed finnan haddie, and oyster broil. All dishes are à la carte, with main courses from about $2.50 to $3.75. *There is no bar, but beers are available. The restaurant closes at 5:30 p.m. Closed Saturday and Sunday.*

★ VINCENT'S CLAM BAR
119 Mott Street   CA 6-8133

This is a raffish, offbeat, and curiously compelling restaurant noted for a single specialty, a hot and peppery tomato sauce that may be too hot for some palates. On weekends, there may be a line of customers waiting for a seat at the bar or in the nondescript dining room. Vincent's serves the hot sauce with wonderfully fresh steamed scungilli (conch), squid, mussels, and clams. The accompaniment is a hard roll dipped quickly into boiling water to soften it. The cost of one serving of any specialty is about $1.00. *Cocktails, wines.*

★★ WAH KEE RESTAURANT
16 Doyers Street BE *3-8582*

Wah Kee has remained through the years one of Chinatown's consistently good restaurants. Like most of its counterparts in the area, it is physically nothing fancy, but the chef seems to know what he is doing. One of the most interesting dishes is lemon chicken. It is breaded and fried and has a lemon flavor. The cost of main courses ranges from about $1.10 for pork fried rice to $4.25 for squab with oyster sauce. There are also Chinese family dinners from $5.90 a person. *Cocktails, wines. Open 7 days a week.*

WALDORF-ASTORIA
301 Park Avenue (between 49th and 50th Streets)
EL *5-3000*

The Bull and Bear. A masculine, handsome décor and a club-like atmosphere at noon on weekdays, when the restaurant is open to men only. Women are invited after 3:00 P.M. and all day Saturday and Sunday. The portions are hearty and the bill of fare lists grilled dishes, stews, and generous sandwiches. All dishes are à la carte, with main dishes at both luncheon and dinner from about $2.50 to $14.00. *Cocktails, wines.*
CB

★★ WALLY'S
262 West 46th Street *582-0460*

This is a small and pleasant restaurant in the theater

district, with a tiny bar and sawdust on the floor.

The food at its best is conspicuously good. That would include the steaks, of first-rate quality and cooked with care, and the veal piccata, white, tender, and well-seasoned.

Wally's spaghetti is competently made and so are the salads. By contrast, the shrimp cocktail, priced at $2.50, was notably lacking in salt or other favorable character; an order of broiled chicken was ordinary; and the rum cake was grainy.

The gentleman whom one assumes to be the proprietor is admirably cordial and his friendly nature almost makes up for his too small wine glasses, in which was served recently a too warm bottle of Pommard.

Wally's is far from being the least expensive place in town, but what steak house is? All dishes are à la carte, with main courses from about $4.50 for that chicken to $14.00 for the largest lobster available. *Cocktails, wines. Open from 4:30 to 11:00 p.m. Closed Sunday. AE.*

★ WHYTE'S
344 West 57th Street   JU 6-7900

Whyte's menu offers a wide selection of fish dishes, including the restaurant's year-round specialty of finnan haddie, prepared in three different ways. There are two dining areas here, one in a high-ceilinged main dining room with an Edwardian atmosphere and, during warm weather, one on a covered terrace. The à la carte menu is essentially the same at luncheon and dinner, with main courses from about $3.25 to $8.00. *Cocktails, wines. Closed Sunday; in July and August closed weekends. All major credit cards.*

★ WINE AND APPLES
117 West 57th Street   582-8754

This is an interesting little restaurant with a rustic, European look, and it smells like cider (hot cider is one of the specialties).

The menu is a mixed bag of Greek and Austro-Hungarian cooking, and one of the chief assets of the place is the modest prices. It is close to Carnegie Hall, and much of the clientele looks arty, whatever that means.

The food over-all misses excellence, but it is certainly palatable. The main courses, such as beef goulash—paprika-colored and lightly flavored with juniper and orégano—and veal pot roast, are what one frequently calls "home-style," and good, if a bit overcooked.

There are a shish kebab and various sausages grilled and served with warm potato salad and sauerkraut. There are steaks and, best of all, perhaps, a good palachinka, the rolled pancake with apricot sauce and sour cream on top.

The chicken and rice soup (like the Greek avgolemono) was too thick with rice and lukewarm. The lentil soup was not thick enough with lentils and lukewarm. The service is ordinary.

The restaurant offers an interesting late-evening special —wine, apples, and cheeses at $3.75 for two. A la carte dishes are priced from about $1.75 to $2.95 for lunch and dinner. *Open 7 days a week, noon to midnight, Saturday and Sunday noon until 2:00 a.m.*
AE CB DC

★ WINE CELLAR, THE
531 Hudson Street (between Charles and 10th Streets)
242-6769

This informal, split-level dining-pub gets its name from the wine-rack décor against bare brick, old wood, and antiques, rather than from any outstanding offerings on the wine list. A few steps up from the entrance is an extensive bar with a few tables and down a few steps is the dimly lit main dining area with private booths and tables.

If the eyes function well in low candle power, the limited, cosmopolitan menu can be read from a wall blackboard. The soup of the day one evening was a good, robust Russian cabbage offering, but the pickled mushroom appetizer was too acid and lacked seasoning. A coarse liver pâté with a wedge of lemon was ordinary. A wedge of lemon in the iceberg lettuce salad can be a surprise.

Three fondues are offered. The beef with 3 sauces was creditable. A helpful waiter advised against the shrimp. No more than 5, he said. The cheese fondue has to be ordered for two. The sweet and sour shrimp was made with good shellfish but lacked character. Steak kebabs and rice were both chewy. A chef's special of chicken Kiev with a big baked potato was good.

It is pleasant to find a relaxed, friendly atmosphere for dining where conversation is the only background noise. Entrées range in price from $3.50 to $6.50. *Cocktails, wines. Open 7 days a week for dinner until midnight or later. Sunday brunch is served.*
Most major credit cards.

★ WISE MAN, THE
91 Bayard Street (at Mulberry Street) BE 3-9456

Chinese characters on the menu spell out "champagne," and the wise man pictured is holding a glass of it, but this restaurant is no different from many other Chinese-American establishments specializing in Cantonese food.

A beaded curtain separates the busy bar from booths and tables seating about 40 amid an abundance of plastic plants. For those who read Chinese, or have Chinese friends, there is a menu in the language with some exotic offerings. Some of these surely find their way to a tiny private room for special groups.

The luncheon menu follows the eggdrop soup, chow mein, shrimp with lobster sauce pattern, but it is a bargain. Diners may order from the regular menu throughout the day.

The wintermelon soup was excellent, but a watercress

soup with the traditional poached egg was interesting, but bland and difficult to eat, even with chopsticks. The egg roll was indistinguishable from others in similar places. The Chinese roast pork was good.

Fung wong gai, batter-dipped and deep-fried slices of chicken breast with Virginia ham between, was unusual and excellent. The chow steak kew was generally tender and tasty. The triple dragon with chicken, pork, really fresh lobster meat, and vegetables, and the house speciality, sizzling go ba with shrimp, pork, chicken, and mushrooms, were good.

Complete luncheons from $1.40 to $2.95. Dinner entrées from $2.00 to $4.95. *Cocktails, wines. Open from 11:30 a.m. to 2:00 a.m. 7 days a week.*

★ WO KEE
11 Doyers Street   WO 2-8155

This is another of those abundant, small, downstairs restaurants in Chinatown with food that is generally excellent. True, the menu is stereotyped, but even such standards as Cantonese lobster and shrimp with mushrooms (canned) are appealing. The fried squab, not listed on the menu, is delicious, with its spiced salt served on the side and a squeeze of fresh lemon. The chef at Wo Kee enjoys preparing meals to order. Some of the champions of the Wo Kee declare that it has the best wonton in town. It is good. The same menu serves throughout the day and it is all à la carte. The cost of main dishes is from $1.25 to $3.75. *No alcoholic beverages.*

★ WOLF'S DELICATESSEN
799 Seventh Avenue (between 51st and 52nd Streets)
586-4070

The menu of Wolf's is very much like that of numerous other delicatessens about Manhattan, and it is a small, pleasant enough place.

There is stuffed cabbage, of course, and old-fashioned

beef stew, and chicken in the pot, and sandwiches. The latter, the backbone of New York delis, are fat and the ingredients of good quality.

On the other hand, Wolf's doesn't share that brassy-with-Gemütlichkeit flavor for which the best of the city's delicatessens seem famous.

All dishes are à la carte, with main courses from about $1.60 for chopped sirloin steak to $3.95 for twin lobster tails. Sandwiches from 60 cents to $1.85. *Beers, soft drinks. Closed Sunday.*

★ WOLF'S DELICATESSEN
180 Broadway (between Maiden Lane and Dey Street)
267-9150

If you can ignore a few more than trifling details about this small delicatessen in the financial district, you will find some of the best sandwiches in Manhattan. The fresh brisket of beef, the pastrami, corned beef, and so on are first-rate and stuffed pillow-like into a choice of breads. The quality of the merchandise is first-rate and the service, mostly by waitresses, is with a smile.

The things to ignore are the incredibly soiled tiles on the floor, strewn with match-sticks, wrappings for straws, paper napkins, and whatever. It isn't the management's fault that the restaurant is jam-packed with customers, and, at peak dining periods, there may be a long wait for a table. There are many things on the typical delicatessen menu besides sandwiches, including salads, dairy dishes, side dishes, main courses, and desserts.

The cost of main dishes is from about $1.95 to $2.50. *Closed Sunday.*

★★ WO PING
24 Pell Street   RE *2-0847 and* WO *2-8172*

Wo Ping in Chinatown is noisy as a gong and earthy as a ginger root, but the restaurant is a great favorite with those who enjoy snails, crabs, and other seafood Chinese-style. The snails and crabs, in particular, can be delicious, if a trifle inelegant to eat, since they both demand fingers in the sauce. There are complete luncheons from 90 cents to $1.50. Main courses on the à la carte menu go from $1.50 to $4.55. *No alcoholic beverages. Dinner is served Sunday from 1:30 p.m. Open 7 days a week.*

★★ XOCHITL MEXICAN RESTAURANT
146 West 46th Street   PL 7-1325

One of the best-known and best of New York's Mexican restaurants. The kitchen offers a typical assortment of tamales, enchiladas, tacos, and tostadas, and the dishes are generally made with care. The Xochitl has fewer than 20 tables, and at peak dining hours there may be a wait for a seat. The service is of the smiling but take-it-or-leave-it category. The same à la carte menu serves throughout the day with entrées from about $1.50 for chili con carne without beans to $4.25 for a combination plate. *Cocktails, wines, Mexican beers. Closed Sunday.*

★ YAMASHIRO
307 Fifth Avenue (between 31st and 32nd Streets)
725-9241

This Japanese gift shop and garden restaurant—with a traditional teahouse and 12-foot-high cliff and waterfall—appeals to all of the senses in a relaxed, away-from-the-bustle atmosphere. The restaurant is in the rear and it is approached over a curved red bridge.

Named after the china that is used, and for sale, the restaurant has functional and attractive modern furnishings set against murals and calligraphy. Each table has a telephone for business and social calls. Kimono-clad waitresses serve with grace and charm even when their English is poor.

The menu is limited, but there are four different sushi,

artistically arranged raw fish, rice, and egg combinations served on china plaques.

Tiny scallion rings made an eye-catching garnish for a good chicken soup. Green tea is served with all dishes.

Two kamameshi dishes, the gyu with beef, and the ebi with shrimp, served on rice in wooden-covered casseroles, were pleasant and came with the traditional pickled radish and Chinese cabbage. Tori meshi, tender pieces of chicken breast in a tasty sauce over rice with a salad, was attractively arranged in a wooden box. The iceberg lettuce was the only jarring note.

A Commodore Perry casserole of shrimp and rice with cheese and mushrooms topped with a creamy sauce offered an unusual mélange of flavors. Only a few of the teatime desserts listed were available at noon, but included novel versions of a parfait and fruit in syrup over agar (jelly-like) cubes.

Luncheon entrées, with soup and tea, are from $2.50 to $3.00; complete dinners, $4.00 to $5.00. *There is no bar, but patrons may bring in wines and beers. Open Monday through Saturday. Luncheon served 12:00 noon to 3:00 p.m.; dinner, 5:30 to 9:00 p.m.*

★ YANGTZE RIVER
250 West 57th Street　CI 6-3659

If you happen to be in the vicinity of the New York Coliseum and have an hour or so to spare, lunch or dinner at the Yangtze River might not be a bad idea. While it is true that many of the items on the fixed price luncheon or dinner menus may be fairly commonplace, the kitchen is capable of better things.

The double prosperity, for example, is an appetizing combination of stir-fried shredded chicken at one end of a platter, pork shreds in hoisin sauce on the other. The lobster soon, with lobster, snow peas, water chestnuts, and so on in an egg sauce, is competently made, and the filling for the boiled dumplings is worthwhile. The dough for the dumplings is wholly edible, but on the tough side.

The hot and sour soup offers a clue to what seem to be the faults of the kitchen. It is bland. The other dishes seem to be in need of more seasonings. The dining room is large at the Yangtze River and, when crowded on one occasion, there were only three dexterous waiters.

A la carte dishes are priced from about $1.45 to $4.50. *Cocktails, wines. Open 7 days a week.*

★★ YANO
50 West 72nd Street   787-2300

One of the most phenomenal trends where New York restaurants are concerned has been the advent and surge in popularity of Japanese restaurants. Yano is in the Ruxton Hotel on West 72nd Street, within walking distance of Lincoln Center. It has a creditable kitchen.

There are numerous Japanese dishes that have an immediate appeal for the American palate, and the Yano menu is tailored to these—tempura or batter-fried seafood and vegetables; tonkatsu or breaded, deep-fried boneless pork; teriyaki; sukiyaki; and so on.

The Yano's sashimi of raw tuna is fresh and excellent, the tonkatsu particularly tasty. The sukiyaki is well-seasoned and made with first-rate beef.

The surroundings of the Yano are more or less hotel-dining-room basic with a bit of bamboo here and there. It is a large restaurant, and on one evening the bar was piled high with used glassware. There were two waiters and one waitress, and they were, to say the least, busy. But they've got a good chef and that's important.

Complete dinners cost about $3.50 to $5.50. *Cocktails, wines. Open 7 days a week.*
AE   DC

★ YELLOWFINGER'S BUTCHERIA
60th Street and Third Avenue   752-1460

This is a bustling restaurant that is far more interesting in concept than in execution. There are tables on the sidewalk and, inside, counters where guests may stand and dine while sipping beer or soft drinks. The dining and service areas are strikingly designed with inlaid Mexican tile. The Butcheria's menu is well-varied with grilled hot and sweet Italian sausages, white sausages, hamburgers, and shish kebab. There is one station where excellent Brittany crêpes are made and filled with such oddments as cheese, ham and cheese, or jelly. The quality of the food over-all is first-rate. There are two faults with the restaurant: The ventilation is poor and the service behind the counters is disorganized, desultory, and generally lacking in efficiency. Prices of entrées run from $1.75 to $3.00. *Wines, beers. Open 7 days a week.*

★★ YE OLDE CHOP HOUSE
111 Broadway   RE 2-6119

A restaurant in the city's financial section that is well worth remembering, particularly for lunch. The establishment has a chop house atmosphere, and at their best the grilled dishes, such as English mutton chop ($6.25), are excellent. This is also one of the few places in town where genuine Smithfield ham ($4.50), hot from the grill, is available. For the unaccustomed, the ham may be overly salty, but for the initiated it is delicious. The same menu serves for luncheon and dinner, and all dishes are à la carte. Main courses cost from $4.35 to $7.75. When in season, game is available. *Cocktails, wines. Open until 7:30 p.m. Closed Saturday, Sunday, and all major holidays.*
AE CB DC

★ YE WAVERLY INN
16 Bank Street   CH 3-9396

Visitors to New York or even the natives would be hard put to find a restaurant more typically American than Ye Waverly Inn. It is atmospheric, too, with low ceilings, antique floors, and an outdoor garden. The restaurant is said to date from the 19th century. The food is what is commonly called "home-style," and entrées include such dishes as roast beef, baked meat loaf, broiled fish, chicken pot pie, and grilled ham steak. Complete luncheons from about $1.25 to $2.50. Dinners cost from about $3.50 to $4.75. *Cocktails, wines. Luncheon is not served Saturday and Sunday. Open 7 days a week.*

★ YING'S
108 Fifth Avenue (at 16th Street)   929-0842

This is a brightly lighted and routine-looking Chinese restaurant on lower Fifth Avenue. The menu is rather heavy in the chop suey-chow mein department, but the chef can prepare some very good dishes, including Ying's boneless chicken and various noodle dishes. The food is, by and large, reasonably priced. There are complete luncheons from $1.30; complete dinners from $1.90 to $4.50. A la carte items are from about $1.60 up. *Beer only. Luncheon is not served on Sunday.*

★ Z
117 East 15th Street   254-0960

This Greek restaurant has a rather pleasant ambience and a bright and colorful décor that is not overly coy nor fussy. A fairly agreeable lunch might include a well-rounded antipasto with very fresh hard-cooked eggs, good melitzanosalata, the cold mashed eggplant salad, grape leaves, and so on. With that course, one could also sample two well-made Greek pie squares, one of cheese, the other of spinach.

The avgolemono soup is on the thin side and lukewarm.

A dish of moussaka finds the custard on top a bit heavy (too much flour, too few eggs). The salad is a minor masterpiece, not only in its freshness but in its presentation.

One evening, an order of baked baby lamb was a triumph, but Z's taramosalata, the fish roe blend, was too bland or too oily to hold together properly. The salad, limp onion rings and tomato on a bed of emaciated lettuce, had collapsed from sitting around all afternoon. The souvlaki, cooked meat from a spit, was dry and as uninteresting as the sauce that came with it. The tables are rickety.

The menu is à la carte, with main courses from about $1.75 to $2.25. *Beers, wines. Open 7 days a week.*

★ ZAPATA RESTAURANT
330 East 53rd Street   752-9738

The chef of this Mexican restaurant cooks with care and knowledge, and he deserves an audience. He turns out a first-rate guacamole, very good dishes such as tacos, enchiladas, and chili rellenos, and one of the best chicken moles (pronounced mo-lays) north of the border.

The chicken was freshly cooked, tender, and served with a mahogany-red mole sauce made with chilies and sesame seeds and—oddly, but traditionally—chocolate. Purists may argue that his sauce isn't authentic, but it is excellent.

The Zapata is a small restaurant with Mexican-inspired décor. One wishes the management well.

All dishes are à la carte, with main courses from about $3.25 for beef tamales to $4.00 for steak and chicken mole. *Cocktails, wines, beers. Open 7 days a week, for dinner only.*

★ ZOE CHASE
115 East 60th Street   TE 8-6983

The cuisine of Zoe Chase is as emphatically plain

as the décor. The over-all atmosphere of the restaurant is like a tearoom, but the food is appetizing and moderately priced. Single guests are asked at times to share tables. Luncheons with dessert and beverage cost from about $1.15 to $2.50. Complete dinners cost from about $3.65 to $5.50. *No bar, but customers may bring in wine and beer. Closed Saturday and Sunday.*

★★ ZUM ZUM
45th Street entrance to the Pan Am Building   974-6786
Lexington Avenue at 45th Street   974-4876
74 Broad Street   269-2955
142 Fulton Street   962-4005
463 7th Avenue (at 35th Street)   974-6836
1290 Avenue of the Americas (at 54th Street)
974-6828
1627 Broadway (at 51st Street)   974-6834
24 East 42nd Street   974-6685
722 Lexington Avenue (at 58th Street)   974-6698
17 University Place   974-6853
44 Court Street, Brooklyn   974-4856

The first of these agreeable beer-and-wurst establishments opened several years ago in the Pan Am Building. It is a casual restaurant, standing room only at peak dining periods, with white tile and chopping-block décor, and many kinds of sausages hanging from the ceiling. You can dine rather well for a very small sum, and a typical lunch with soup, sandwich, and dessert can be had for $1.50. The specialties are various kinds of sausages from 50 cents. Most are served on a bun with either sauerkraut or onion sauce, and the cost is from about 40 cents. The soups are, incidentally, made with first-class ingredients and they are generally outstanding. *There is no bar, but the cold beer, both light and dark, in steins is delicious. Hours and days open vary.*

Index

Acapulco Restaurant, 3
Acropolis Restaurant, 3
Act I, 4
Adams Rib, 4
Agra India and Pakistan Restaurant, 5
Akasaka, 6
Aki Dining Room, 6
A La Fourchette, 7
Alamo Chile House, The, 7
Al Cooper's Herald Square Restaurant, 7
Alda's, 8
Aldo and Eddie Rapallo Restaurant, 9
Alfie's, 9
Alfredo of New York, 9
Algonquin Hotel
  Oak Room, 10
  Rose Room, 10
Allen, Joe, 136
Allen, Kirby, Restaurant, The, 146
Allen's, 10
Allis' Restaurant, 11
Al Mounia, 12
Alpi, Le, 169
Amato's Italian Restaurant, 13
Angelina's, 13
Angelo's, 14
Angelo's Italian Restaurant, 14
Antica Roma, 15
Antolotti's, 15
Aperitivo, 16
Ararat, 17

Argenteuil, Café, 36
Argentino, Un Rincon, 322
Arigato, 17
Arirang House, 18
Armorique, L', 166
Artist and Writers Restaurant, 19
Assembly Steak House, 19
Asti, 20
Athenian Restaurant, The, 20
Au Canari d'Or, 20
Au Steak Pommes Frites, 21
Autopub, 21
Au Tunnel, 22
Azteca, El, 80

Balkan Armenian Restaurant, 22
Ballato Restaurant, 23
Bambino, Il, 125
Barbetta Restaurant, 23
Baroque, 24
Beirut Restaurant, 24
Bell Bar, The (Swiss Center), 302
Benihana of Tokyo East, 24
Benihana of Tokyo West, 25
Benihana Palace, 25
Bernstein-on-Essex-Street, 26
Biarritz, Le, 170
Bibliothèque, La, 149
Billy's, 26
Bistro, Le, 170
Black Angus, 27
Blossom Restaurant, 27
Blue Mill Tavern, 28

341

Blue Sea, 28
Blum's, 29
Bo Bo, 29
Bok, Sam, 272
Borghese, Mario's Villa, 202
Bourgogne, La, 150
Brasero, 30
Brasil, Casa, 43
Brasserie, 31
Brass Rail, The, 31
Brazilian Coffee Restaurant, 31
Brew's, 32
Brittany, Café, 37
Brittany du Soir, 32
Broadway Joe Steak House, 33
Brochetteria, 33
Brown's, Charlie, 53
Brownstone, The, 34
Brussels Restaurant, 35
Budapest Hungarian Restaurant, 35
Bull and Bear, The (Waldorf-Astoria), 328

Cabaña, La, 150
Cabaña Carioca, 35
Ca d'Oro, 36
Café Argenteuil, 36
Café Brittany, 37
Café de France, 37
Café du Soir, 37
Café Europa, 38
Café Nicholson, 39
Café Renaissance, 39
Camelot, 39
Canari d'Or, Au, 20
Canton Restaurant, 40
Canton Village, 41
Cape Cod, 41
Capri, Isle of, 129
Captain's Table, The, 42
Caravelle, La, 151
Cardinale, Chez, 53

Carioca, Cabaña, 35
Carmen's, 42
Carnegie Delicatessen and Restaurant, 43
Casa Brasil, 43
Casa di Pre, 44
Casa Laredo, 44
Casa Mario, 45
Casey's, 45
Castalia, 46
Castilian, The, 47
Cattle Baron, The, 47
Cattleman East, The, 48
Cattleman West, The, 48
Cedars of Lebanon, 49
Ceylon India Inn, 49
Chalet Suisse, 50
Chambertin, Le, 170
Champignon, Le, 171
Champs, Les, 181
Chan, House of, 123
Chandler's, 50
Chan's, Jolly, Chinese Kitchen, 139
Chanteclair, Le, 172
Charles à la Pomme Soufflé, 51
Charles French Restaurant, 51
Charley O's Bar and Grill, 52
Charlie Brown's, 53
Charro, El, 81
Chase, Zoe, 339
Château Richelieu, Le, 172
Cheshire Cheese Restaurant, 53
Cheval Blanc, Le, 173
Chez Cardinale, 53
Chez Napoleon, 54
Chez Renée, 54
Chez Vous, 55
Chez Yvonne l'Escargot, 55
Chi Mer, 55
China Bowl, The, 56
China Fair, 57

342

China Pavilion, 57
Chinese Rathskeller, 58
Chin-Ya, 58
Chock Full O'Nuts, 59
Christ Cella, 59
Christo's, 59
Chuan Hong Restaurant, 60
Cin Cin, Maria, 201
Clarke's, P. J., 254
Cleopatra, 60
Clos Normand, 61
Coach House, The, 61
Cocotte, La, 151
Coin de Paris, Un, 321
Colony, The, 62
Cooper's, Al, Herald Square Restaurant, 7
Copenhagen, 62
Copter Club, 63
Coq au Vin, 64
Côte Basque, La, 152
Crêpe, La, Restaurants, 153
Crêpes Suzette, 64
Croisette, La, 154
Cuisine of Szechuan, 64
Cygne, Le, 173
Czechoslovak Praha, 65

Daly's Dandelion, 65
Damon's, 66
Danny's Hide-a-Way, 66
Dardanelles Armenian Restaurant, 67
Daruma, 67
Dawson's Ha-Penny Bar, 68
Delmonico, Oscar's, 237
Delsomma, 69
Denmark, Old, 232
Deno's Place, 69
Derby Steak House, The, 70
Dewey Wong, 70
Dilluvio, 71
Dionysos, 72
Dogwood Room, 73
Doria, Villa, 325

Doriental Restaurant, 74
Double Dolphin Fish House, 74
Downing Square, 75
Dresner's, 75
Duck Joint, The, 76
Due Mondi, 77
Duff's, 77
Du Midi, 78
Dynasty, The, 78

Eduardo's, 79
Elaine's, 79
El Azteca, 80
El Charro, 81
Electra, 81
El Faro, 82
Elizabeth's, Mary, 205
Elizabeth White, 82
El Mirador, 83
El Parador, 83
El Quijote, 84
El Radiante, 85
El Rincon de España, 85
Emiliana's Restaurant, 86
Empire Chinese Restaurant, The, 87
Eng, Esther, 88
Entrecôte, L', 176
Escargot, L', 181
Esplanade, The, 87
Este, Mario's Villa d', 203
Esther Eng, 88
Estia, 88
Etoile, L', 182
Europa, Café, 38
Eva Hungarian Restaurant, 89

Faro, El, 82
Faro, Il, 125
Fedora, 90
Filippo Restaurant, 90

343

Fisherman's Net, 91
500 on 8th Restaurant, The, 91
Fleur de Lis, 91
Flower Drum Restaurant, 92
Fonda del Sol, La, 154
Fonda La Paloma, 92
Fondue, La, 155
Fondue Pot, The (Swiss Center), 302
Foo Chow Restaurant, 93
Forge, Old, Steak House, 233
Forlini's, 93
Fornos, 94
Fortuna, La, 156
Forum of the Twelve Caesars, The, 94
Foster, Mr. and Mrs., 214
Fourchette, A La, 7
Four Five Six, 95
Four Seasons, The, 96
France, Café de, 37
Frankie and Johnnie, 96
Fraunces Tavern, 97
French Quarter, The, 97
French Shack, The, 98
Friar Tuck, 99
Frini, 99
Fu Shin Restaurant, 100

Gaetano's, 101
Gage and Tollner, 101
Gaiety East, 102
Gaiety West Restaurant and Delicatessen, 102
Gallagher's, 33, 103
Garden, Old, 233
Gatti's, 103
Gauguin Room, The, 104
Gene's, 105
Georges Rey, Restaurant Français, 105
Giambone, 106
Gim Beck, 106
Ginger Man, The, 107

Gino's Restaurant, 107
Giordano Restaurant, 108
Giovanni, 108
Girafe, 109
Gloria's Restaurant, 109
Gloucester House, 110
Gold Coin, 111
Golden Coach, 111
Gold Full Restaurant, 111
Gondola, 112
Goodale's, 112
Granados Restaurant, 113
Grand Central Terminal Oyster Bar and Restaurant, 114
Grand Tier Restaurant (Metropolitan Opera House), 210
Grange, Jimmy's La, 136
Great Shanghai, The, 114
Greensleeves, 114
Green Tulip, The (Plaza), 256
Grenadier, 115
Grenouille, La, 157
Grillade, La, 157
Groceria, La, 157
Grotta Azzurra, 116

Hacienda, La, 158
Hankow, New, 224
Hanover Square Restaurant, 116
Ha-Penny Bar, Dawson's, 68
Happy Garden, 116
Haymarket Pub, 117
Heidelberg Restaurant, 117
Henry, O., Steak House, 232
Henry Stampler's Filet Mignon, 118
Herald Square Restaurant, Al Cooper's, 7
Hickory Pit Restaurants, 118
Hide-a-Way, Danny's, 66
Hide Sukiyaki, 119

Hime of Japan, 119
Hole in the Wall, 120
Hong Fat Restaurant, 121
Hong Kong Inn, 121
Hong Ying, 122
Horn and Hardart Automats, 122
Ho Shun, 122
House of Chan, 123
Hoy Kung, 124
Hyde Park Restaurant, 124

Il Bambino, 125
Ile de France, 125
Il Faro, 125
India House East Restaurant, 126
Inn of the Clock, 127
International Cheese Club Restaurant, 127
Irish Pavilion, The, 128
Irori, 128
Isle of Capri, 129
Italianissimo, 130
Italian Pavilion, 130

Jack's Nest, 131
Jade Palace, 131
Jai-Alai, 132
Jamaica Arms, 132
Japanese Mie Cooking, 133
Japanese Steak House, 134
Jasper's, 134
Jenedi's, 135
Jimmy's, Paul and, Place, 245
Jimmy's Greek-American Restaurant, 135
Jimmy's La Grange, 136
Joe Allen, 136
Joe and Rose, 136
Joe's Restaurant, 137
Joe's Pier 52, 137
Johnnie, Frankie and, 96
Johnnie's, 138
John's Restaurant, 139

Jolly Chan's Chinese Kitchen, 139
Joyce's Macao, 140
Joy Garden, 140
Julio Restaurant, 141
Jung, Lucy, 194

Kabuki Restaurant, 141
Kamehachi, 142
Kansas City, Max's, 206
Karachi, 142
Kashmir Restaurant, 143
Katz's Delicatessen, 143
Keen's English Chop House, 143
Kegon, 144
Keneret, 145
Kenny's Steak Pub, 145
Khayam, Omar, 234
King of the Sea, 146
King Wu, 146
Kirby Allen Restaurant, The, 146
Kitcho Restaurant, 147
Kleine Konditorei, 147
Kobe Steak House, 148
Koon Shing Tea House, 148
Korea, New, 225
Kyoto Steak House, 149

La Bibliothèque, 149
La Bourgogne, 150
La Cabaña, 150
La Caravelle, 151
La Cocotte, 151
La Côte Basque, 152
La Crêpe Restaurants, 153
La Croisette, 154
Lafayette, 154
La Fonda del Sol, 154
La Fondue, 155
La Fortuna, 156
La Grange, Jimmy's, 136
La Grenouille, 157
La Grillade, 157

345

La Groceria, 157
La Hacienda, 158
L'Aiglon, 159
Lair, The, 159
La Locanda, 160
Lam Kee, 160
Lantern Light, 161
La Paella, 162
La Petite Ferme, 163
La Petite Marmite, 164
La Piazzetta, 165
La Potinière du Soir, 165
La Poularde, 166
Laredo, Casa, 44
L'Armorique, 166
Larré's French Restaurant, 166
La Scala, 167
La Strada East, 167
La Toque Blanche, 167
Laura, Mama, Restaurant, 197
La Venere West, 167
La Veranda, 168
Le Alpi, 169
Lebanon Restaurant, 169
Le Biarritz, 170
Le Bistro, 170
Le Chambertin, 170
Le Champignon, 171
Le Chanteclair, 172
Le Château Richelieu, 172
Le Cheval Blanc, 173
Le Cygne, 173
Le Manoir, 174
Le Marmiton, 174
Le Mistral, 174
Le Moal, 175
Lenge-Saimin Restaurant, 175
L'Entrecôte, 176
Leone's, 176
Leopard, The, 177
Le Pavillon, 177
Le Perigord, 178
Le Perigord Park, 178
Le Pont Neuf, 180

Le Poulailler, 180
Le Provençal, 181
L'Escargot, 181
Les Champs, 181
Les Pyrénées, 182
Le Steak, 182
L'Etoile, 182
Le Veau d'Or, 183
Liborio, 184
Lichee Tree, The, 184
Limericks, 184
Lin Heong, 185
Lino's U.N. Restaurant, 185
Little Kitchen, The, 186
Little Peking Restaurant, Inc., 186
Little Place, The, 187
Little Royal Hungarian Restaurant, 187
Locanda, La, 160
Long River, 188
Lord & Taylor's Soup Bar, 188
Lotus Eaters, 189
Lotus Eaters East, 189
Lotus Eaters Fifth, 190
Lotus Eaters Park, 190
Lotus Eaters Royale, 191
Lou G. Siegel, 192
Louie's, Sloppy, 286
Louise, 193
Louise Jr., 193
Lüchow's, 193
Lucy Jung, 194
Luger, Peter, 248
Luna's Restaurant, 194
Lutèce, 195

Macao, Joyce's, 140
Macario's, 196
Mme. Romaine de Lyon, 196
Madison Delicatessen and Restaurant, The, 197
Mama Laura Restaurant, 197
Mañana, 197

Mandarin House, 198
Mandarin House East, 198
Mandarin Inn, 199
Manganaro's and Manganaro's Hero-Boy Restaurant, 200
Manny Wolf's, 200
Manoir, Le, 174
Manuche, Mike, 212
Marbona, Villa, 325
Marchi's, 200
Maria Ciu Ciu, 201
Maria's Patio, 202
Mario, 202
Mario, Casa, 45
Mario's Villa Borghese, 202
Mario's Villa d'Este, 203
Mark Twain Riverboat, 203
Marmiton, Le, 174
Marsh's Steak Place, 203
Marta Restaurant, 204
Marta's, 204
Mary Elizabeth's, 205
Mary's, 205
Maud Chez Elle, 206
Max's Kansas City, 206
Maxwell's Plum, 207
Mayfair, The, 208
Mayhews, 208
McSorley's Old Ale House, 209
Mercurio, 209
Metropolitan Opera House Grand Tier Restaurant, 210
Mexican Village, 210
Mexico, Old, 233
Mexi-Frost Specialties Company, 211
Michael's Pub, 211
Midi, Du, 78
Mikado, 212
Mike Manuche, 212
Miller's, 213
Minetta Tavern, 213
Minotaur, The, 214

Mirador, El, 83
Mr. and Mrs. Foster, 214
Mistral, Le, 174
Mi Tierra, 215
Miyako, 216
Moal, Le, 175
Molfetas Cafeteria, 217
Mona Lisa, 217
Mona Lisa East, 217
Mona Trattoria, 218
Mondi, Due, 77
Monk's Inn, 219
Mon Paris, 220
Mont d'Or, 220
Monte's Restaurant, 220
Mont St. Michel Restaurant, 221
Moon Palace, 221
Morgen's East, 222
Morgen's Restaurant, 222
Moriarty, P. J., 254
Mounia, Al, 12
Murphy's, Patricia, Candlelight Restaurant, 244
Mykonos, 222

Napoleon, Chez, 54
Nataraj, 223
Nat Simon's Penguin Room, 223
Near East Restaurant, 224
New Hankow, 224
New Korea, 225
New Moon Inn, 225
New Port Alba, 226
New Wah Dor, 226
New York Exchange Restaurant, 227
Nicholson, Café, 39
Nick's Topkapi Pub, 228
Nicola Paone, 228
Ningpo Restaurant, 229
Nippon, 229
Nirvana, 230
Nom Wah Tea Parlor, 231

347

Oak Room (Algonquin), 10
Oak Room (Plaza), 256
O'Hara, P. J., 255
O. Henry Steak House, 232
Old Denmark, 232
Old Forge Steak House, 233
Old Garden, The, 233
Old Mexico Restaurant, 233
Old Seidelburg, 234
Omar Khayam, 234
O'Neal's Baloon, 235
Oriental Pearl, 236
Orsini's, 236
O's, Charley, Bar and Grill, 52
Oscar's Delmonico, 237
Oscar's Salt of the Sea, 237
Oviedo, 238
Oyster Bar (Plaza), 256
Oyster Bar and Restaurant (Grand Central Terminal), 114

Paella, La, 162
Pagano's, 238
Pak-India Curry House, 239
Palm Restaurant, 239
Paloma, Fonda La, 92
Pam, Sam, 272
Pamplona Restaurant, 240
Pancho Villa's, 241
Pantheon Restaurant, 241
Paone, Nicola, 228
Paparazzi, 241
Pappas, 242
Paprika, 242
Paradise Inn, 243
Parador, El, 83
Parioli, Romanissimo, 243
Paris, Mon, 220
Parkway East, 244
Passy, The, 244
Patio, Maria's, 202
Patricia Murphy's Candlelight Restaurant, 244

Paul and Jimmy's Place, 245
Paul Revere's Tavern and Chop House, 245
Pavillon, Le, 177
Pearl's Chinese Restaurant, 246
Peking House, 246
Pembles, 247
Pen and Pencil, The, 248
Penguin Room, Nat Simon's, 223
Pensa, Villa, 326
Pergola des Artistes, 248
Perigord, Le, 178
Perigord Park, Le, 178
Peter Luger, 248
Peter's Backyard, 249
Petite Ferme, La, 163
Petite Marmite, La, 164
Petrosino, Vincent, 327
Philippine Garden, The, 249
Piazzetta, La, 165
Piccolo Mondo, 250
Pierre Au Tunnel *see* Au Tunnel
Pier 52, Joe's, 137
Pierre's, 250
Pietro's, 250
Pine Garden Restaurant, 251
Pink Foot, The, 251
Pip's, 252
Piraeus, My Love, 253
Piro's, 253
P. J. Clarke's, 254
P. J. Moriarty, 254
P. J. O'Hara, 255
Plaka East, 255
Plaza Hotel
  The Green Tulip, 256
  Oak Room, 256
  Oyster Bar, 256
Plum, Maxwell's, 207
Pomme Soufflé, Charles à la, 51
Ponte's Steak House, 257

Pont Neuf, Le, 180
Port Alba, New, 226
Port Arthur, 257
Portofino, 258
Potinière du Soir, La, 165
Poulailler, Le, 180
Poularde, La, 166
Pre, Casa di, 44
Press Box, 258
Prime Burger, 259
Promenade Café, 259
Proof of the Pudding, 260
Provençal, Le, 181
Pujol, René, Restaurant, 263
Pyrénées, Les, 182

Quijote, El, 84
Quo Vadis, 261

Radiante, El, 85
Rainbow Room, 261
Rajmahal Restaurant, 261
Rapallo, Aldo and Eddie, Restaurant, 9
Rattazzi, 262
Red Coach Grill, 262
Reidy's Restaurant, 262
René Pujol Restaurant, 263
Renée, Chez, 54
Renaissance, Café, 39
Restaurant Tokyo, 264
Reuben's, 265
Revere's, Paul, Tavern and Chop House, 245
Rey, Georges, Restaurant Français, 105
Right Bank Provincial, The, 265
Right Bank Restaurant, The, 266
Rincon Argentino, Un, 322
Rincon de España, El, 85
Riverboat, Mark Twain, 203
Rocco Restaurant, 267
Roma, Antica, 15

Romaine, Mme., de Lyon, 196
Roma Nova, 267
Romeo Salta, 268
Rose, Joe and, 136
Rose Room (Algonquin), 10
Rosetta's Restaurant, 269
Ruc Restaurant, 269
Rugantino, 270
Running Footman, The, 270
Russian Tea Room, 270

Sakura Chaya, 271
Salta, Romeo, 268
Salt of the Sea, Oscar's, 237
Sam Bok, 272
Sam Pam, 272
Sam Wo, 273
San Marco, 273
San Marino, 274
San Remo, 274
Santa Lucia, 275
Sardi's, 275
Savoia, 276
Sayat Nova, 276
Say Eng Look, 277
Scala, La, 167
Scandia, 277
Schaefer's, 277
Schrafft's Restaurants, 278
Scoop, The, 278
Sea-Fare of the Aegean, 279
Seidelburg, Old, 234
Shalimar, 279
Shanghai Café, 280
Shanghai d'Or, 280
Shanghai Garden, 280
Shanghai Town, 281
Shanghai Village, 281
Shangri-La, Tom's, 315
Shavey Lee, 282
Sheik Restaurant, The, 282
Shun Lee, 283
Shun Lee Dynasty, 283
Siegel, Lou G., 192

Sign of the Dove, 284
Simon's, Nat, Penguin Room, 223
Sixty-Eight Restaurant, 284
Skewer on the Table, 284
Slate Restaurant, The, 285
Sloppy Louie's, 286
Smokehouse, The, 286
Soir, Café du, 37
Soul East, 287
South Pacific Ports, 288
Spain, 289
Spanish Pavilion, The, 289
Spark's Pub South, 290
Stage Delicatessen and Restaurant, 290
Stampler's, Henry, Filet Mignon, 118
Steak, Le, 182
Steak and Brew, 292
Steak Casino, 292
Steak Joint, The, 293
Steak Place, The, 294
Steak Pommes Frites, Au, 21
Steinway Brauhall, 294
Stockholm Restaurant, 295
Stouffer's, 295
Strada East, La, 167
Suehiro Restaurant, 295
Suisse, Chalet, 50
Sum Hey Rice Shoppe, 296
Sun Hop Kee, 296
Sun Luck East, 297
Sun Luck Gourmet, 298
Sun Luck Imperial, 298
Sun Luck Queens, 298
Sun Luck Times Square, 299
Sun Yah, 299
Sushi Ginza Restaurant, 300
Sweet's, 300
Swiss Center Restaurants, 301
Symposium, 303
Szechuan, 303
Szechuan, Cuisine of, 64
Szechuan Taste, 304

Taco Villa, 305
Tamura Restaurant, 306
Tandur, The, 306
Tanpopo, 307
Taste of India, 307
Taste of Tokyo, 308
Tavern on the Green, 308
Teacher's, 309
Teddy's Restaurant, 310
Temple Garden, The, 310
37th Street Hideaway, 310
Three Six Nine Restaurant, 311
Thursday's, 311
Tien Tsin, 312
Tierra, Mi, 215
Tik Tak Hungarian, 313
Tin Lizzie Restaurant, The, 313
Tokyo-Bangkok Restaurant, 314
Tollner, Gage and, 101
Tomaldo's, 314
Tom's Shangri-La, 315
Tonkatsu, 316
Tonoose, Uncle, Restaurant, 320
Tony's Italian Kitchen, 316
Tony's Wife, 316
Topkapi Palace, 317
Topkapi Pub, Nick's, 228
Top of the Six's, 318
Toque Blanche, La, 167
Tower Suite, 318
Trader Vic's, 318
Trattoria, 319
Trefner's Restaurant, 319
Tunnel, Au, 22
Twain, Mark, Riverboat, 203
"21," 320

Uncle Tonoose Restaurant, 320
Un Coin de Paris, 321
Unicorn, The, 322

350

U. N. Restaurant, Lino's, 185
Un Rincon Argentino, 322

Valentino's, 323
Vasata, 323
Veau d'Or, Le, 183
Venere West, La, 167
Veranda, La, 168
Vesuvio Restaurant, 323
Via Margutta, 324
Via Veneto, 324
Victor's Café, 324
Villa Borghese, Mario's, 202
Villa d'Este, Mario's, 203
Villa Doria, 325
Villa Marbona, 325
Villa Pensa, 326
Villa Vivolo, 326
Vincent Petrosino, 327
Vincent's Clam Bar, 327
Vivolo, Villa, 326
Vous, Chez, 55

Wah Doi, New, 226
Wah Kee Restaurant, 328
Waldorf-Astoria
  Bull and Bear, The, 328
Wally's, 328
Waverly Inn, Ye, 338

White, Elizabeth, 82
Wine and Apples, 329
Wine Cellar, The, 330
Wise Man, The, 331
Wo, Sam, 273
Wo Kee, 332
Wolf's, Manny, 200
Wolf's Delicatessen, 332
Wong, Dewey, 70
Wo Ping, 333
Writers, Artist and, Restaurant, 19

Xochitl Mexican Restaurant, 334

Yamashiro, 334
Yangtze River, 335
Yano, 336
Yellowfinger's Butcheria, 337
Ye Olde Chop House, 337
Ye Waverly Inn, 338
Ying's, 338
Yvonne l'Escargot, Chez, 55

Z, 338
Zapata Restaurant, 339
Zoe Chase, 339
Zum Zum, 340